Practical

Cost

Benefit

Analysis

For Joanna and Sam

Practical

Cost

Benefit

Analysis

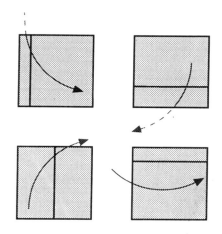

BASIC

CONCEPTS

AND

APPLICATIONS

M

First published 1994 by
MACMILLAN EDUCATION AUSTRALIA PTY LTD
107 Moray Street, South Melbourne 3205

Associated companies and representatives
throughout the world

National Library of Australia
cataloguing in publication data

Perkins, Frances, 1952–
    Practical cost benefit analysis.

    Bibliography.
    Includes index.
    ISBN 0 7329 2784 6.
    ISBN 0 7329 2783 8 (pbk.)

    1. Cost effectiveness.   I. Title

658.1554

Typeset in Goudy and Optima
by Superskill Graphics, Singapore

Printed in Hong Kong

Designed by Sergio Fontana
Cover design by Dimitrios Frangoulis
Index by Bettina Stevenson

Contents

Part Three: The Economic Analysis of Projects

Introduction

This book has grown out of a lecture series given by the author on the financial and economic analysis of projects as part of the National Centre for Development Studies 2 year graduate program in the Economics of Development. It is intended to provide a straightforward guide through the labyrinth of literature that has grown up in this field for the professional practitioner and student of project appraisal. There are a number of texts in this area, some of the more useful being Irvin (1978) and Sugden and Williams (1978), as well as the basic texts by Little and Mirrlees (1974) and the 'UNIDO Guidelines' (1972) and their technical summaries like Squire and van der Tak (1975). However, all of these texts are now somewhat dated and I could not find one single text for my students that coherently explained all the basic concepts underlying cost benefit analysis including recent developments in the subject, as they applied in developing as well as developed countries.

This text is designed to provide a comprehensive and consolidated guide to the essential aspects of cost benefit analysis that it is necessary for the practitioner to master. The text's main objective is to provide a practical and consistent approach to the economic evaluation of projects and policies that is straightforward to apply. It attempts to de-mystify the subject without sacrificing topics or a level of detail necessary for professional practitioners in the area. In some places particular references are made to the many issues that arise in applying cost benefit analysis in developing countries, but in most cases these are equally applicable and relevant to the experiences of developed countries.

The book does not try to cover the issues of project development, planning or implementation. Nevertheless, it would hopefully prove useful as a summary of financial and cost benefit analysis theory, with practical applications, for practitioners in these areas. It could be read in conjunction with the many practical books on project development and implementation produced by national governments and international institutions such as the manuals prepared by the Overseas Development Administration in the United Kingdom (1988), the Australian Department of Finance (1991), the Investment Bureau of the State Planning Commission of China (1990), and Duvingneau and Prasad for the World Bank's Development Finance Commission (1984).

While a sound understanding of the concepts underlying cost benefit analysis is essential, the future practitioner of this very applied economics topic must also be exposed as much as possible to its practical applications. It is therefore important to master a spreadsheet computer program such as Lotus 123 or Excel. Such programs provide an easy and readily available tool for setting out cost benefit analysis problems and employing selection criteria such as a project's internal rate of return and net present value. The exercises at the end of each chapter give readers the opportunity to explore the theoretical concepts and methodologies presented. In addition two complete project analyses exercises are given in the appendices at the end of the book. Intending project analysts should therefore obtain access to such a computer program, and use one of the many teach yourself packages to become familiar with these programs.[1] A booklet and computer disk setting out solutions to the problems at the end of each chapter — F.C. Perkins, 'Exercises in Cost Benefit Analysis' (1994) — is available from the National Centre for Development Studies, Australian National University, Canberra, Australian Capital Territory, Australia, 0200.

In this text, a partial equilibrium approach is generally taken to the shadow pricing of project inputs and outputs. Theoretical analysis and empirical research have indicated that in many situations little if any accuracy will be lost by such a simplification (Squire 1989).[2] This approach is taken in recognition of the fact that the project appraisal units in most developing and many developed countries lack sufficient financial and manpower resources to appraise all potential projects in a general equilibrium framework. They will therefore be unlikely to undertake the exhaustive studies needed to fine tune the shadow prices used, unless this is going to produce significant improvements in the accuracy of their appraisals. It is therefore important to recognise where the largest gains can be made from shadow pricing, in terms of increasing the accuracy of project appraisal and hence promoting community welfare. This text attempts to strike a balance between ease of practical application, accuracy and theoretical correctness.

The shadow pricing approach developed by Harberger is used extensively throughout the book. This is a relatively simple yet flexible and accurate approach to shadow pricing, which can be applied to all project inputs and outputs including traded and non-traded goods, labour, foreign exchange and capital. This approach is introduced in Chapter 7 and employed in Chapters 8, 9, 10, and 13.

The text does not attempt to discuss more than a proportion of the immense literature that has been generated by writers in this field in the past 50 years. Several excellent review articles have accomplished this task in recent years, notably Squire (1989) and Dreze and Stern (1987). Rather, the aim here has been to distil, as accurately as possible, the essential elements of this literature for the intending professional practitioner. In addition, some extension topics such as risk analysis and social cost benefit analysis have been included so that the scope of the analysis can be extended if necessary.

Canberra, Australia

References

Australian Department of Finance, 1991. *Handbook of Cost Benefit Analysis*, Australian Government Publishing Service, Canberra.

China, Investment Bureau of the State Planning Commission of China, 1990. *Operational Manual for the Method and Parameters of Construction Project Economic Evaluation*, Research Institute for Standards and Norms, Ministry of Construction, Beijing.

Dreze, J. and Stern, N., 1987. 'The theory of cost benefit analysis', in Auerbach, A.J. and Feldstein, M.,(eds), *Handbook of Public Economics*, North Holland, Amsterdam.

Duvingneau, J.C. and Prasad, R.N., 1984. *Guidelines for Calculating Financial and Economic Rates of Return for DFC Projects*, World Bank Technical Paper No. 33, Development Finance Corporation, Washington.

Irvin, G., 1978. *Modern Cost-Benefit Methods*, Macmillan, London.

Little, I.M.D. and Mirrlees, J.A., 1974. *Project Appraisal and Planning for Developing Countries*, Heinemann Educational Books, London.

Overseas Development Administration, 1988. *Appraisal of Projects in Developing Countries*, 3rd edn, Her Majesty's Stationary Office, London.

Squire, L., 1989. 'Project evaluation in theory and practice' in H. Chenery and T.N. Srinivasan (eds), *Handbook of Development Economics*, Vol. 2, North Holland, Amsterdam.

Squire, L. and van der Tak, H.G., 1975. *Economic Analysis of Projects*, Johns Hopkins University Press, Baltimore.

Sugden, R. and Williams, A., 1978. *The Principles of Practical Cost Benefit Analysis*, Oxford University Press, Oxford.

UNIDO, 1972. *Guidelines for Project Evaluation*, United Nations, New York.

Endnotes

1   One example of such a tutorial package is ECC Learning Lotus 123, Jerold L. Reed, ECC Learning Systems, PO Box 1575 Bellevue, Washington 98009. There are many others available. A program such as 'Excel' includes a tutorial package.

2   Squire (1989) reviewed the extensive literature on general equilibrium shadow pricing and their relationship to the earlier partial equilibrium shadow prices developed by Little and Mirrlees (1974) and UNIDO (1972), *inter alia*.

Part One
OVERVIEW

CHAPTER 1

An introduction to the cost benefit analysis of projects

1.1 What are financial and economic analyses?

A financial analysis of a project is undertaken to assess whether it will be commercially profitable for the enterprise implementing it. A private firm will undertake a financial analysis of a potential investment in order to determine its impact on the firm's balance sheet. Governments and international agencies will also routinely undertake a financial analysis, as well as an economic analysis, of any project in which the output will be sold and a financial analysis will therefore have some meaning.

An economic analysis, also called a cost benefit analysis, is an extension of a financial analysis. An economic analysis is employed mainly by governments and international agencies to determine whether or not particular projects or policies will improve a community's welfare and should therefore be supported. As cost benefit analysis enables the analyst to determine if a project will make a positive contribution to the welfare of a country, it should routinely be undertaken to evaluate major government-funded projects and policies. The government should also undertake a cost benefit analysis of any private project seeking government subsidies or policy support, such as tariff protection.

Figure 1.1 depicts the scope of concerns addressed by cost benefit and financial analyses. While a financial analysis is concerned only with the interests of the implementing agency or firm, cost benefit analysis is concerned with the welfare of all the firms, consumers and government in a particular country. An economic analysis is not, however, concerned about the welfare of foreigners.

The methodology of cost benefit analysis, or CBA, was first developed in the 1930s in the United States when the Federal government had to decide whether to undertake many large, publicly funded irrigation, hydroelectricity and water supply projects in the dry central and western states of the United States. However, modern cost benefit analysis theory and practice has evolved largely from path-breaking work by Little and Mirrlees (1969, 1974), Dasgupta, Marglin and Sen in their UNIDO Guidelines (1972), Harberger (1972), Corden (1974), Squire and van der Tak (1975) and other work collected in Layard (1972). Many other useful contributions have been made by various authors.

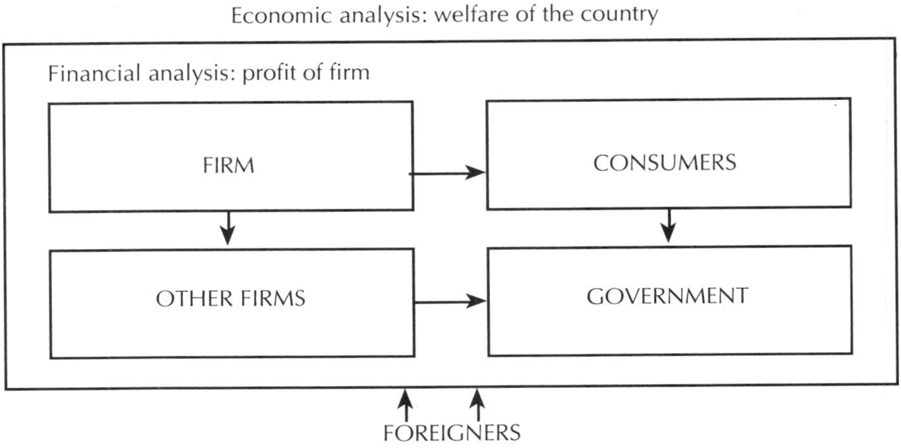

Economic analysis: welfare of the country

Figure 1.1 *Scope of concerns addressed by financial and economic analysis*

The term 'project' is employed throughout this text in the broadest sense to refer to any use or saving of resources. These are not restricted to traditional industrial, infrastructure or agricultural development projects, but may include health, social service provision and environmental control projects. In addition, the welfare impact of a wide range of government policies such as industry deregulation, population decentralisation, training schemes and immigration, to name but a few can be assessed using the methodology of cost benefit analysis.

When a cost benefit analysis is undertaken, microeconomic, macroeconomic and international trade theory is applied to real world situations in order to answer questions such as these:

- Should a new bridge be built, or should the existing ferry service be upgraded?
- Should an export-oriented aluminium refinery be established, or should the unprocessed bauxite and coal be exported?
- Should computers be imported or assembled locally?
- Will this irrigation project be a better use of resources and lead to a greater increase in community welfare than that highway project?
- What fuel should be used to generate electricity?

For the government to answer these questions, it is necessary that it goes beyond a financial appraisal, which determines how commercially profitable these alternative policies and potential investments would be. This is essential for a number of reasons. The first is that governments typically have broader and more complex objectives, which they wish to achieve from public good and social service provision and policy-making generally, than mere profit maximisation. If governments only wished to maximise profits from the operation of state enterprises, they would be well advised to privatise them, as the private sector is likely to be more efficient at pursuing this goal. Government objectives fall broadly under the heading of 'optimisation of community welfare'. The most straightforward economic objective is the optimisation of the level of GNP per capita. Other objectives may include preserving the environment, redistributing income to particular target groups or regions and enhancing national security. Even from this short list it is obvious that there may be conflict between some of these objectives. One of the major reasons that governments use cost benefit analysis is to determine the impact of various competing projects on community welfare, defined in terms of all these different criteria.

The other major reason for the use of cost benefit analysis lies in the many distortions and imperfections that affect prices in factor and goods markets. In many countries market prices, that is, prices quoted in domestic markets, reflect a range of distortions, including taxes, subsidies, controlled prices, tariffs, and monopoly or monopsony rents. These factors distort market prices so that they no longer reflect the true economic value that people place on consuming such goods and services (their demand price), or the true cost to the economy of producing them (their supply price). If a government wishes to determine which projects will make a positive contribution to community welfare, it will not necessarily be able to use the market prices of the projects' inputs and outputs to calculate their true costs and benefits to society.

When undertaking a cost benefit analysis, the project analyst will try to correct for such distortions by calculating **economic**, or **shadow, prices**. The shadow prices of the project's inputs and outputs, like labour and capital, goods that enter international trade, traded goods, and those that do not, non-traded goods, will reflect the true economic value of these inputs and outputs to the economy concerned. In a cost benefit analysis shadow prices for projects' inputs and outputs are substituted for market prices.

1.2 The role of financial and cost benefit analysis in project development, evaluation and implementation

The techniques of financial and cost benefit analysis are employed in three of the six identifiable stages of project formulation and evaluation.[1]

1. **Project identification** At this stage, the initiating agency, such as a government department or utility, defines the initial concept of the project and outlines the objectives that the government wishes it to achieve. These may include the provision of health, transport or education services, for example. The first major issue that must be investigated is the existence of market opportunities. In the case of social services, the analyst must determine the anticipated demand for the project's output and the benefits that the public are expected to derive from these services. An initial assessment of the best technology to employ, given local factor prices, as well as the

appropriate scale and timing of the project is also necessary.[2] Engineers, health specialists, educationalists, environmental scientists, agricultural specialists, market analysts and many other professionals will contribute to this stage of the project's development. Economists may also be involved in a preliminary assessment of the viability of alternative technologies given the relative prices of capital and labour in the country concerned.[3]

This process yields the basic concept of the project and background information, which enables the government to progress to the pre-feasibility study stage.

2. **Pre-feasibility study**   At this stage, the analyst obtains approximate valuations of the major components of the project's costs and benefits: input and output quantities and prices. More precise estimates must be made of the demand for the project's output, the technical capacity and cost of the plant or technology envisaged, and the project's manpower requirements. In many cases this data will be provided by the technical professionals involved in the original project identification stage.

Using this preliminary data, financial and economic analyses of the project will then be undertaken by the economic analyst, to determine whether the project appears to be financially and economically viable. A preliminary financing schedule may also be drawn up to identify the source and costs of funds. If the project appears viable from this preliminary investigation, it will be worthwhile proceeding to the full feasibility study stage.

3. **Feasibility study**   At this stage, more accurate data must be obtained on all project costs and benefits, but particularly those that risk analysis indicates are crucial to the project's viability. The financial and economic viability of the project is then assessed again. If the project is still found to be viable, approval should be sought to proceed to the project design phase.

4. **Project design**   This involves undertaking the detailed engineering design work of the project, based on the technology envisaged at the feasibility stage. Manpower requirements, administration and marketing procedures are all finalised at this point.

5. **Implementation**   At this stage, tenders are let and contracts signed to facilitate the appointment of the project manager, who will oversee the construction and possibly the operation of the project.

6. **Ex-post evaluation**   This final stage of a project is essential, yet frequently overlooked in project appraisal and implementation. This evaluation is designed to determine the actual contribution that the project has made to national welfare, after several years of project operation. Its primary purpose is to help to identify the major sources of project success and failure, so that future project development, analysis and operation procedures can benefit from past experience.

This text will not, in the main, be concerned with the first phase of project identification (stage 1), nor with the later phases of detailed project design and implementation (stages 4 and 5). Rather, the major focus will be on the techniques necessary to rationally assess the financial and economic viability of different projects (stages 2, 3 and 6). In practice, of course, the processes of project identification and evaluation may be closely linked, as the project evaluator may make a considerable input into the earlier stages of project development, such as basic technology choice.

This is likely to result in better project design than if the evaluator is brought in only at a late stage, after the project has been designed in detail.

1.3 Current usage of cost benefit analysis techniques

Two recent overviews of the current state of CBA practice by Little and Mirrlees (1990) and Squire (1989) discussed the extent to which cost benefit analysis has been adopted and applied in international institutions, bilateral aid programs and developing countries. The influence of CBA techniques grew in the World Bank in the 1970s. However, the rapid growth in World Bank lending and pressure to disburse funds in the late 1970s and 1980s eventually weakened the practice of CBA in the Bank in the 1980s. The Asian Development Bank and Inter-American Development Bank use versions of the Little and Mirrlees approach, though the rigour of their analyses is certainly no greater than that of the World Bank. Several bilateral aid agencies, notably the British Overseas Development Administration (ODA, 1988), but also the German, Canadian, Australian and Japanese aid agencies, *inter alia*, claim to use cost benefit analysis, though appraisals developed by some of these countries indicate that less than uniform practices are employed.

Among 27 developing countries surveyed by World Bank staff,[4] all except three reported that they undertook some form of project appraisal (Squire, 1989). However, the rigour of their analysis procedures varied considerably. None included the effects of a project on income distribution, or the general equilibrium effects of projects.[5] More serious omissions included those by one group of countries,[6] which did not even discount net benefits or use international border prices to value goods that could be traded. However, a relatively large group of countries, including Ethiopia, Cote d'Ivoire, Republic of Korea, Malaysia, Pakistan, the Philippines, Sierra Leone, Thailand and Yugoslavia reported using both discounting and shadow prices.[7]

It therefore appears that, while the use of cost benefit analysis for all public sector projects is by no means universal, many developing countries, including some of the most successful economies in Asia, are employing CBA in project appraisal. Despite this, Little and Mirrlees (1990) conclude that the failure of many developing countries to properly evaluate the large number of investment projects that they undertook in the 1970s and 1980s, often with foreign capital, resulted in the debt crisis suffered by many in the 1980s.

The situation in developed countries is not much more encouraging. While major public sector investments are usually subject to a financial appraisal, economic analyses using shadow prices are much less common. Several developed countries have produced project appraisal manuals[8] for use by government authorities, but there is little evidence that they are routinely used. Appraisals of major projects are often undertaken by consultancy firms on behalf of the government agencies proposing a project or the private firms who are seeking government assistance. This is likely to give rise to a conflict of interest. There is often no independent, central project appraisal agency with the authority to judge the quality and credibility of these appraisals.[9]

1.4 The financial profitability objective — financial appraisal of projects

Before a set of alternative projects can be evaluated, the agency (either a firm or government authority) considering them must clearly define the objectives it wishes to achieve from any use of its resources. Once these objectives have been defined, it should be possible for the project analyst to choose the appropriate type of analysis for evaluating the particular projects, to determine which will best meet these objectives.

For a firm in the private sector the question of which objectives it will wish to pursue will be reasonably straightforward; it will wish to maximise profits, or the return to shareholders, or the value of its shares. Hence it will usually evaluate a project solely on the basis of its impact on the firm's financial accounts. That is, it will conduct a financial analysis.

In a financial appraisal, the market prices of inputs and outputs are used to calculate the project's net benefit to the investor (benefits minus costs). No attempt is made to correct these prices for any distortions in the markets for these goods because market prices are actually paid by the firm and it will only be concerned with choosing the project with the largest excess of revenue over receipts, after taxes, and loan and interest repayments. Similarly, no attempt is made to include the costs and benefits of the project felt by other people in the community or imposed on the physical environment if these do not show up on the firm's balance sheet. The second part of this text deals with how to undertake financial analyses of projects.

Some government agencies may also pursue a **financial objective** in limited situations. For example, an electricity generating authority may be instructed by the government to operate on a commercial basis. For any given electricity tariff, it may be expected to maximise its operating surplus by minimising its generation and distribution costs. Hence it could be expected to choose between alternative generation projects on the basis of their generation cost per kilowatt hour.

In the simple example in Table 1.1, a government owned electricity authority is considering two alternative generation projects, one coal fired and one hydroelectric powered. Both will earn revenue measured in market prices with a present day value of $600 million, but the direct financial costs of project A, also in market prices, are expected to be $500 million, while those of project B, the hydroelectric scheme, will be $550 million.

Since the net benefits, or benefits minus costs, of the coal fired project A are higher, on the basis of a financial analysis alone, the electricity authority would select project A.

Table 1.1   Financial appraisal of alternative electricity projects ($ million)

	Project A (coal fired)	Project B (hydroelectric)
Financial costs	500	550
Financial benefits	600	600
Net benefits	100	50

1.5 The economic welfare objective — the economic appraisal of projects

Frequently, governments want their agencies to pursue a broader set of objectives than purely financial ones. The government and the people may well expect such agencies to promote 'the public good', or optimise social welfare, rather than merely minimising operating costs or maximising profits. When assessing a project, an agency may be expected to determine the project's impact on the welfare of all the people in a community or country, whether or not this impact on welfare is reflected in the project's financial balance sheet. In this situation, a cost benefit analysis or economic analysis should be undertaken. The third part of this text (Chapters 6 to 13) is concerned with the methodology of cost benefit analysis.

In contrast to financial analysis, in an economic analysis **all** costs incurred and benefits generated by a project, in the country where it is located, are entered into the **economic cash flow** of the project. A cash flow is merely all the expenditures made and receipts incurred by the project over its life, set out in a spreadsheet format. The concept of a cash flow is discussed in detail in Chapter 2. Economic costs and benefits are entered in the economic cash flow irrespective of whether they are incurred or received by the project's implementors and appear on the project's financial balance sheet, or if they are felt by other groups of consumers and producers.

The objective of optimising economic welfare is much broader than that of maximising profits, the financial objective and its pursuit will usually be more complex. In essence, undertaking an economic analysis involves measuring all project input costs and output benefits in such a way that they reflect the true cost to the economy of using inputs required and the true benefit to the country of the output produced by the project. Then, once costs and benefits are measured in this way, a project that is estimated to have positive net benefits (benefits minus costs) is also a project that will make a positive net contribution to the welfare of a country.

The only, unlikely, circumstances in which a financially profitable project will always make a positive contribution to social welfare will be in an economy where there are no price, tax, trade or quantity-rationing distortions. As well, it would be necessary to have perfect knowledge, no government, no externalities or public goods and an optimal income distribution. In the real world these restrictive conditions can virtually never be met.

1.5.1 Alternative measures of community welfare

The problem for decision-makers is how to define such general concepts as 'the public good' or 'social welfare' so that they can become meaningful objectives on which to base project appraisal. Traditional cost benefit analysis normally assumes that the government's major objective is to:

* maximise aggregate per capita GNP, measured in terms of people's willingness to pay for goods and services.

But there are many other objectives that governments may wish to pursue, including the following:

* More equitable distribution of income among regions or income groups.
* Rapid growth of employment.
* Rapid level of future growth (i.e. preference for future as compared with current income).
* An export oriented economy, to reduce foreign exchange constraints on growth, or to promote internal political objectives (e.g. Eastern Europe).
* Self-reliance in the supply of certain goods or services perceived to be of strategic significance, or in general to reduce exposure to international shocks.
* A clean and healthy environment.
* Other merit wants — power, national security, national prestige, etc.

It is obvious from examining even this short list that there may well be conflicts in the pursuit of several of these objectives, for example rapid growth and economic self-sufficiency, and environmental purity. Once the government has determined its priorities, cost benefit analysis attempts to put monetary values on the impact of projects in terms of the objectives selected.

1.5.2 The Hicks–Kaldor compensation criterion and potential Pareto welfare improvements

Faced with conflicting objectives, it is essential that a government has a basic criterion for determining whether a given use of resources will improve community welfare. The concept of a potential Pareto welfare improvement, or the compensation principle, was developed by Hicks (1939) and Kaldor (1939) to meet this need. This criterion states that a given change in social welfare will be desirable if those who gain from it could completely compensate those who lose, and still be better off themselves. The Hicks–Kaldor compensation principle is central to cost benefit analysis. It is the justification for choosing projects whose benefits outweigh their costs. The excess of benefits over costs is called the project's net benefits.

As will be discussed in the chapter that deals with the social appraisal of projects (Chapter 14), the ethical problem with the Hicks–Kaldor criterion is that it takes no account of who gains from a project and who loses. A project could take land from poor peasants and give it to rich land owners, but as long as the extra output produced exceeded the project's costs, the project would be deemed worthwhile. This concern, and the desire of governments to promote equity as well as efficiency objectives, has led to the development of social project analysis, using distributional weights as is discussed in Section 1.6. However, few governments or multilateral banks undertake social analyses of projects. The usual practice is to apply the Hicks–Kaldor compensation criterion in a straightforward way and to select projects whose benefits exceed their costs, irrespective of who gains and loses.

1.5.3 An example of an economic analysis of a project

In the case of the electricity generating authority discussed above, the government may well decide that it does not necessarily want the authority to merely select the plant with the lowest generation costs, measured in market prices. Rather it may want it to employ the generation technique that will result in the greater net improvement in the community's welfare. The coal fired plant may be expected to produce considerable amounts of air pollution such as soot and acid rain, which may reduce the value of agricultural production in the surrounding countryside. This may also adversely affect the health of local residents and reduce their overall environmental amenity, or the pleasure they receive from their local surroundings.

Because the coal-fired generation of electricity produces these negative external effects, the coal-fired power station project's direct operating and capital costs will underestimate the total costs to the community of generating electricity. Hence, in order to meet the government's objective of maximising total welfare, the electricity authority will be required to take the pollution costs of different plants into account, in addition to the market costs of generation, such as fuel, labour and capital, when choosing between alternative techniques.

For example, let us assume that the coal burning power station being considered is expected to deposit acid rain on the fields of surrounding wheat growers, which will reduce their income by $75 million over the life of the project. A financial analysis would not include this item as a cost of the project, unless the generating authority were actually forced to pay this amount in compensation to the growers, or as a pollution fee. On the other hand, a cost benefit analysis would include the $75 million lost by the wheat growers in the cost stream of the project because it does reduce community welfare.

In this situation, the government would select the hydroelectric power project, project B, as the one that would produce the greater increase in community welfare.

Table 1.2   Economic appraisal of alternative electricity projects — pollution costs ($ million)

	Project A (coal fired)	Project B (hydroelectric)
Economic costs*	500	550
Economic benefits	600	600
Pollution costs	75	0
Net economic benefits	25	50

Economic costs equal financial costs in this example

1.6 The estimation of economic, or shadow, prices

In the economy for which a power station was analysed above, there may be distortions in the local labour market, such as minimum wage legislation, which keep wages above the market clearing level and create high local unemployment. In addition, interest rates in the local capital market may be held abnormally low, making capital, and capital intensive technologies like hydroelectric power, appear cheaper. The community's welfare may therefore be improved if less capital and more labour intensive technologies like coal fired generation were used to raise local employment and save scarce capital. The country may have a serious balance of payments deficit and a shortage of foreign exchange. As a result, the government may wish the authority to use locally available fuels, which in this country include coal.

In assessing alternative power station projects, some of which use local and others imported energy sources, and some employing more labour intensive technologies than others, it is necessary to correct for the distortions in local labour, capital and foreign exchange markets. This is done by determining the true economic cost of labour, capital and foreign exchange to the country, by correcting for distortions in local wage rates, interest rates and the official exchange rate prior to valuing labour, capital and traded inputs into the project. The process of correcting for distortions in local market prices is called **economic, or shadow, pricing**, and is used in all economic analyses. Much of the third part of this text, which deals with cost benefit analysis, will discuss how such shadow prices are estimated.

The approach taken to shadow pricing of project inputs and outputs in this text is a simplified version of the shadow prices determined on the basis of a general equilibrium model of the economy. Theoretical analysis and empirical research have indicated that frequently little accuracy will be lost by such a simplification.[10] This approach recognises the fact that project appraisal units in many countries lack the financial and manpower resources to undertake the exhaustive studies needed to fine tune shadow prices unless this will produce significant improvement in the accuracy of their appraisals.

In Table 1.3, shadow pricing of labour[11] and the exchange rate indicates that the true economic cost of hydroelectric power to the economy is higher than its financial

Table 1.3   Economic appraisal of alternative electricity projects — shadow pricing of inputs and pollution costs ($ million)

	Project A (coal fired)	Project B (hydroelectric)
Economic costs	500	590
Economic benefits	600	600
Pollution costs	75	0
Net economic benefits	25	10

cost. As a result, the government would now select the coal fired station, despite its high pollution costs.

1.7 Social welfare and income redistribution — social appraisal of projects

Recent developments in cost benefit analysis maintain that a potential Pareto welfare improvement based only on people's willingness to pay for the project's output is too narrow a definition of an improvement in social welfare. It is argued that such analysis ignores the fact that, even though poorer people may be less able to pay for particular goods and services, they may well obtain more utility from them. Traditional economic analysis is based on the assumption that the community's welfare will be increased by any net increase in consumption, measured in terms of willingness to pay, irrespective of the income levels of those who benefit from, and pay for, the project. Once the costs and benefits of the project are estimated, they are added without any weighting, with each dollar of costs or benefits valued as a one dollar change in overall welfare (Harberger, 1971).

However, the government may not merely wish to promote income growth but also income redistribution via its public investment program. A project analysis that pursues objectives such as improved welfare for a target group of people is called a **social cost benefit analysis**, or **social analysis**. One of the ways such an analysis can be undertaken involves attaching weights to income gains or losses of different income groups.

Looking at the electricity authority example again, it may be that the wheat growers whose incomes will be reduced by pollution are a particularly disadvantaged group. Maybe many are in debt and may be evicted from their farms if they lose income due to the power station's pollution. This may have the effect of further increasing income inequalities between this region and others. Hence the government may decide that a dollar's worth of lost income to the growers is worth two dollars worth of income gained by the consumers of electricity, who are assumed to be better off. Hence a social cost benefit analysis would value the $75 million the wheat growers are expected to lose at $150 million.

This would be entered in the cost stream of the project, as shown in Table 1.4. Social analysis is an extension of economic analysis and all the shadow prices for

Table 1.4 Social appraisal of alternative electricity projects ($ million)

	Project A (coal fired)	Project B (hydroelectric)
Economic costs	500	590
Economic benefits	600	600
Pollution costs (at social cost)	150	0
Net benefits	−50	10

economic costs estimated for the economic appraisal are also included in a social analysis.

On the basis of a social analysis the government would, in this case, decide to select the hydroelectric power project.

Conclusions

Financial, economic and social analysis are flexible tools for assessing alternative uses of resources in order to achieve welfare objectives determined by the government.

A financial analysis indicates whether a project will be profitable to its implementor, by using market prices for inputs and outputs. An economic analysis, using shadow prices, reveals which projects will make a positive contribution to economic welfare. Finally, a social analysis extends an economic analysis, and includes an examination of the distributional impact of the project.

References

Corden, W.M., 1974. *Trade Policy and Economic Welfare*, Oxford University Press, London.

Harberger, A.C., 1971. 'Three basic postulates of applied welfare economics: An interpretative essay', *Journal of Economic Literature*, Vol. IX, No. 3, Sept, 785–97.

Harberger, A.C., 1972. *Project Evaluation, Collected Papers*, Macmillan, New York.

Hicks, J., 1939. 'Foundations of welfare economics', *Economic Journal*, 49:696–712.

Jenkins G.P. and Harberger, A.C., 1991. *Manual — Cost Benefit Analysis of Investment Decisions*, Program on Investment Appraisal and Management, Harvard Institute for International Development, Cambridge, Mass.

Kaldor, N., 1939. 'Welfare propositions in economics and inter-personal comparisons of utility', *Economic Journal*, 49:522–49.

Layard, R. (ed.), 1972. *Cost-Benefit Analysis*, Penguin, Harmonsworth.

Little, I.M.D. and Mirrlees, J.A., 1969. *Manual for Industrial Analysis in Developing Countries, II, Social Cost Benefit Analysis*, OECD, Paris.

Little, I.M.D. and Mirrlees, J.A., 1974. *Project Appraisal and Planning for Developing Countries*, Heinemann Educational Books, London.

Little, I.M.D and Mirrlees, J.A., 1990. '*Project appraisal and planning twenty years on*', proceedings of the World Bank Annual Conference on Development Economics.

Overseas Development Administration, 1988. *Appraisal of Projects in Developing Countries*, 3rd ed., Her Majesty's Stationary Office, London.

Squire, L., 1989. 'Project evaluation in theory and practice', in H. Chenery, and T.N. Srinivasan (eds), *Handbook of Development Economics, Vol. 2*, North Holland, Amsterdam, Chapter 21.

Squire, L. and van der Tak, H.G., 1975. *Economic Analysis of Projects*, Johns Hopkins University Press, Baltimore.

UNIDO, 1972. *Guidelines for Project Evaluation*, United Nations, New York.

Further reading

Duvingneau, J.C. and Prasad, R.N., 1984. *Guidelines for Calculating Financial and Economic Rates of Return for DFC Projects*, World Bank Technical Paper No. 33, Development Finance Corporation, Washington DC, Chapter 2.

Irvin, G., 1978. *Modern Cost-Benefit Methods*, Macmillan, London, Chapter 4.

Pearce, D.W. and Nash, C.A., 1981. *The Social Appraisal of Projects: A Text in Cost Benefit Analysis*, Macmillan, London, Chapter 2.

Ray, A. 1984, *Cost Benefit Analysis — Issues and Methodologies*, Johns Hopkins University Press, Baltimore, Chapters 1, 3.

Sugden, R. and Williams, A. 1978, *The Principles of Practical Cost Benefit Analysis*, Oxford University Press, Chapters 1, 7.

Endnotes

1 This section draws on Jenkins and Harberger (1991).

2 More precise information on this issue can be obtained at the pre-feasibility stage by carrying out financial and economic analyses of various alternative technologies and scales.

3 Jenkins and Harberger (1991), Chapter 5 gives a good discussion of the method of determining optimal timing and scale of a project.

4 The countries included Brazil, China, Cyprus, Dominican Republic, Ethiopia, Guatemala, Fiji, Indonesia, India, Cote d'Ivoire, Republic of Korea, Malaysia, Malawi, Nigeria, Oman, Pakistan, Papua New Guinea, Peru, the Philippines, Senegal, Sierra Leone, Sri Lanka, Somalia, Thailand, Yugoslavia, Zambia and Zimbabwe.

5 For example, none took account of general equilibrium effects related to project financing (if public projects had to be financed from tax revenue, rather than lump sum transfers) and the impact on tax revenue if projects affected the prices of non-traded intermediate goods and primary factors like labour and capital.

6 Cyprus, Dominican Republic, Guatemala, Nigeria, Senegal, Somalia and Zimbabwe.

7 China has developed a national CBA manual and is starting to employ CBA for some public projects.

8 For example, the Australian Department of Finance released its Handbook of Cost Benefit Analysis in 1991.

9 For example, the author was asked to examine a consultant's report for the Dampier–Perth gas pipeline in Australia in the early 1980s. Although it included many 'heroic' assumptions about the likely rate of growth of real oil prices (10 per cent per annum for ever!), no one in the Federal or Western Australian governments prevented this project from going ahead.

10 Squire (1989) examined the literature on general equilibrium shadow pricing and this methodology's relationship to the earlier partial equilibrium shadow prices developed by Little and Mirrlees and UNIDO, *inter alia*. He showed that the shadow pricing of tradables at border prices was robust in a general equilibrium analysis. Also, the shadow pricing of non-tradables at their border price equivalents, and productive factors at producer prices was justifiable except if the project producing a free, non-tradable output, such as an infrastructure project, caused a net transfer of income to the private sector. If lump sum taxes were not available, the distortionary taxes required to re-establish fiscal equilibrium would effectively reduce the economic value, or shadow price, of such an infrastructure service. This issue is discussed in Chapter 12, which deals with public goods.

11 Shadow pricing of capital is handled by determining the social discount rate, with which future net income flows are discounted to their present value. This topic is addressed in Chapters 4 and 13.

Part Two
FINANCIAL APPRAISAL OF PROJECTS

CHAPTER 2

The valuation of financial costs and benefits

2.1 When to undertake a financial analysis

A financial analysis must be undertaken if it is necessary to determine the financial profitability of a project **to the project implementor**. Normally it will only be worthwhile carrying out a financial analysis if the output of the project can be sold in the market, or otherwise valued in market prices. This will almost always be the case for a privately sponsored project, but will also apply to some government business undertakings. A private firm will primarily be interested in undertaking a financial analysis of any project it is considering, and only in some special circumstances will it wish to undertake an economic analysis.[1]

Commercially oriented government authorities that are selling output, such as railway, electricity, telecommunications, or freeway authorities, will usually undertake a financial as well as an economic analysis of any new project they are considering. They need to assess the project's potential impact on their budget, as well as its impact on the country's welfare. Another situation where a government will be interested in undertaking a financial analysis of a project is when the project's private sponsor has approached the government for some form of subsidy, or tax or tariff relief. In this situation the government will need to know if the project is financially viable without the subsidy or other forms of assistance. In practice, governments and international agencies routinely undertake a financial as well as a cost benefit analysis of any project where a financial analysis will have some meaning — essentially, if the output will be sold. It can then compare the results of the financial and economic evaluation, to determine the project's budgetary impact on the government, as the implementor, as well as its contribution to national welfare.

Even non-commercial government institutions may sometimes wish to choose between alternative facilities on the basis of essentially financial objectives. For example, in the case of a hospital service, the management of the hospital could well be required to select the cheapest method of providing a given standard of accommodation or care. A national defence force will often choose between available alternative methods of achieving a physical goal, such as airborne troop movement capacity, on the basis of the cheapest financial option. This procedure is called **cost**

minimisation or cost effectiveness. It differs from a full financial analysis in that only the **costs** of a project are estimated in market or conceivably in economic prices. The benefits are specified in terms of some quantitative target, such as the number of patient beds to be provided or number of troops that can be moved.

2.1.2 How to value project benefits and costs in a financial analysis

The financial benefits of a project are just the revenues received and the financial costs are the expenditures that are actually incurred by the implementing agency as a result of the project. If a project is producing some good or service for sale, the revenue that the project implementors expect to receive each year from these sales will be the benefits of the project. The costs incurred are the expenditures made to establish and operate the project. These include capital costs; the cost of purchasing land, equipment, factory buildings, vehicles and office machines, and working capital, as well as its on-going operating costs: for labour, raw materials, fuel and utilities.

In a financial analysis, all these receipts and expenditures are valued as they appear in the financial balance sheet of the project, and are therefore measured in **market prices**. Market prices are just the prices in the local economy, and include all applicable taxes, tariffs, trade mark-ups and commissions. Since the project's implementors will have to pay market prices for inputs they use and will receive market prices for the output they produce, the financial costs and benefits of the project are measured in these market prices.

2.2 Valuation of a project's benefits in a financial analysis

The financial benefits from a project are measured by the market value of the project's output, net of any sales taxes. If the project's output is sold in a competitive market, with no rationing or price control for the good concerned, and the project is small and does not change the good's price, its market price will equal its competitive **demand price**. This is a minimum measure of what people are **willing to pay** for a unit of the good or service produced by the project, at each level of output demanded. The theoretical bases for these propositions are discussed in an appendix to this chapter.

If a project is expected to be large enough to change the price of a good produced as an output or used as an input by the project, the expected new demand price can be read off the aggregate demand curve for the product, if this is known. Alternatively, if this information is not available, it may be necessary to undertake market surveys or employ available cross-sectional or time series data on demand for this product at different prices to estimate its demand curve econometrically. In Sections 2.2.1 and 2.2.2, below, the measurement of projects' financial benefits is examined in more detail, in situations where the market price of the project's output is expected to stay constant and situations where the price is expected to vary as a result of the project.

2.2.1 Cases where the project does not change the domestic price of the project's output

In many cases, the establishment of a project will not affect the domestic market price of the good produced. This will be so if the good produced is traded internationally, or if the project makes a relatively small contribution to the total supply of a good that is not traded.

If a new project will increase the production of any product that is, or could be, traded internationally by the country concerned, this increase in domestic supply is unlikely to reduce its domestic price. In the case illustrated in Figure 2.1, for example, the project produces portable radios for export. The enterprise will then face a perfectly elastic international demand curve for portable radios, DD_w, as well as a downward sloping domestic demand curve DD_d. The increased production of radios from this project is not going to force down the international price of radios. As the country's supply curve for radios will move out from SS_0 to SS_p as a result of the project, the quantity of radios exported will increase, from $Q_0 - Q_d$ to $Q_1 - Q_d$. However, there will be no impact on the price the project receives for radios, which in the absence of taxes and subsidies on exports will remain at the world price, P_w. The project's total financial benefits will therefore be the shaded area Q_0Q_1FE.

If there is an export subsidy of s_e per cent paid to exporters by the government, this will be added to the world price of the radios when determining the financial benefits (or receipts) of the radio project, $P_w(1 + s_e)$. If an export tax of t_e per cent is imposed on the project's exported output, this should be deducted from the

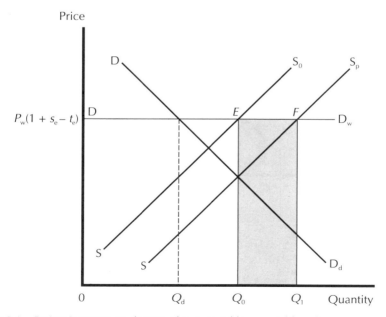

Figure 2.1 *Project increases production of an exportable — portable radios*

world price of this output when the financial benefits of the project are estimated, $P_w(1 - t_e)$. Hence the total financial price received by the project per unit will be $P_w (1 + s_e - t_e)$.

If a country currently imports a commodity (that is, it is an importable) the relevant supply curve will be the perfectly elastic international supply curve, SS_w shown in Figure 2.2. If a new project is established to produce an importable such as computers locally, the domestic supply curve for computers will move out, from SS_0 to SS_p. As a result, the quantity of computers imported will be reduced, from $Q_d - Q_s$ to $Q_d - Q_1$. In the absence of import tariffs or quotas on computers, the domestic price will remain constant at the world price of computers of a similar quality, P_w. P_w will therefore be the appropriate measure of the benefit of producing one computer, and total project benefits will be measured by the shaded area Q_sQ_1CA. If tariffs or quotas with a tariff rate equivalent of t_m per cent are imposed on computers, the financial benefit of producing each computer will be $P_w(1 + t_m)$, as the project will be able to sell its computers for this price in the domestic market.

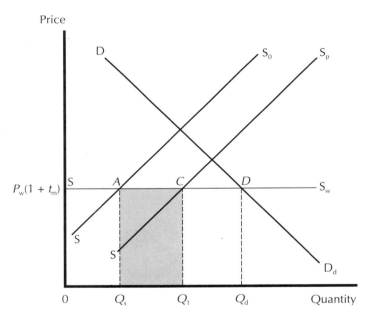

Figure 2.2 *Project increases production of an importable — computers*

If the output to be produced by the project is not traded internationally, for example a new bus service, but the project will produce at a level that is small in relation to total domestic supply, the increase in bus services available from the project would not be expected to reduce domestic bus fares. This situation is illustrated by the horizontal, or elastic, section of the domestic demand curve for bus services confronting the project illustrated by DD_d in Figure 2.3.

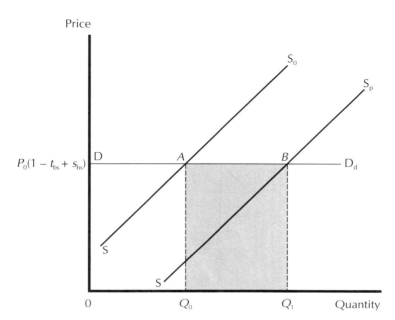

Figure 2.3 *Project output does not affect price of a non-traded service — bus service*

In this situation, the project will have no discernible impact on the level of bus fares prior to the commencement of the project, P_0, which is also the demand price of bus services. If domestic bus fares are not subject to tax and do not attract subsidies, s_{bs}, P_0 will be the appropriate measure of the benefit of producing one passenger bus trip and total project benefits will be measured by Q_0Q_1BA. If a tax, t_{bs}, is included in bus fares, this tax must be subtracted from the market price P_0 if the project is privately operated. In this case the financial benefits from producing one trip will be $P_0(1 - t_{bs})$.[2] Similarly, if a subsidy is paid, this should be included in the financial benefits of the project if it is a privately operated project and the benefit per passenger trip will then be $P_0(1 + s_{bs})$.[3] In the most general case, the financial benefit will be $P_0(1 - t_{bs} + s_{bs})$.

2.2.2 Cases where the project does change the domestic price of the project's output

In some situations, the project may produce a good or service that is not traded internationally, and the project may be large enough to cause such a significant increase in the supply of these services that the equilibrium price for the output falls. For example, if a new domestic satellite project significantly increases the capacity of the local telephone system, it may be possible to reduce connection charges and call tariffs and still cover costs and meet demand. This will imply that the project is sufficiently large that the domestic demand curve for phone services confronting the project is less than perfectly elastic, that is, it is downward sloping.

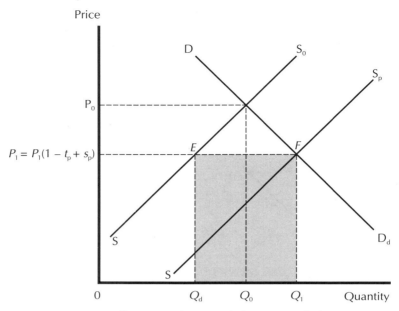

Figure 2.4 *Project output affects price of a non-traded service — telephone service*

In Figure 2.4, an increase in the domestic supply of phone services as a result of the project will cause the supply curve to move out, from SS_0 to SS_P. For equilibrium to be re-achieved the market price of phone services will have to fall from P_0 to P_1. In the absence of taxes or subsidies the financial benefits of the project per unit of output will be P_1 and the total benefits will be the shaded area Q_dQ_1FE. Part of this increase in supply, $Q_1 - Q_0$, will meet increased demand for phone services and part, $Q_0 - Q_d$, will displace marginal producers of telephone services who can no longer afford to supply them at the lower price P_1.

Once again, as long as the project implementor is not the government, any taxes included in the market price, t_p per cent, should be deducted and any subsidies received, s_p per cent, should be added when determining the project's financial benefits, $P_1(1 - t_p + s_p)$. If the project is implemented by the government, these taxes will represent a financial benefit of the project, but any subsidies will only be a transfer within the government sector. The financial price of the project's output will in this case be the new price, P_1, including any sales tax but excluding any subsidy.

2.2.3 Imputed income from non-marketed output

In some cases the project's output may not be sold in the market but may be wholly or partially consumed on the farm or in the household where it was produced. An irrigation scheme to increase the output of subsistence farmers would be an example of such a project. In this situation, the imputed, or estimated, value of the additional output consumed by the household must be added to the value of any output sold.

Market prices of the same product, or close substitutes, will usually provide a good estimate of the imputed value of the home consumed output, but it may be necessary to make adjustments if is believed that the quality of the home consumed item differs from that available in the market. For example, home consumed rice may be of superior, or inferior, quality to marketed rice.

2.2.4 Incremental output

In the case of an incremental project where, for example, capacity is added to an existing factory or an irrigation project is installed on an existing farm, it is important that **incremental** output and costs as a result of the project are measured, rather than the total costs and output of the project. In this case it is necessary to deduct the output (and costs) of the going concern **without** the project from its output and costs **with** the project to construct the **incremental** benefits, costs, and net benefit streams that can be attributed to the project.

2.3 The valuation of project costs

The prices that the project actually pays for inputs are the appropriate prices to use to estimate the project's financial costs. These prices may include taxes, tariffs, monopoly or monopsony (seller monopoly) rents, or be net of subsidies. Actual market prices should be used because it is the cost of the project to the project implementor that is of interest in assessing its financial profitability.

In a freely operating perfectly competitive market, without taxes or subsidies, the market price of an input will equal its competitive **supply price** at each level of production. This is the price at which producers are just willing to supply that good or service. The supply price will reflect the **opportunity cost**, or the value in their next best alternative use, of the resources used to produce that input. In equilibrium, the supply price of an input will equal its demand price at the market clearing price for that input. The theoretical bases of the use of market prices to measure costs are included in the first part of the technical appendix at the end of this chapter.

2.3.1 Cases where the project does not change the domestic price of an input needed by the project

If the project uses an input that is traded internationally, for example plastic pipes used by a water supply project, we would not expect any increase in domestic demand for pipes as a result of the project to be enough to raise their international price. If the pipes used as an input are exportable they will face a perfectly elastic international demand curve, DD_w in Figure 2.5. As the domestic demand curve for pipes moves out as a result of the project, from DD_0 to DD_p, the quantity of plastic pipes exported will decline, from $Q_s - Q_0$ to $Q_s - Q_1$. However, there will be no impact on the domestic price of pipes, which in the absence of export taxes and subsidies will remain at the world price, P_w. The cost of each pipe will therefore be P_w, and the total financial cost of plastic pipes to the project will be the shaded area Q_0Q_1FA. If there are export subsidies, s_e per cent, on the plastic pipes, the domestic price will be the world price plus these subsidies, $P_w(1 + s_e)$, because domestic producers would not be willing to supply pipes for less than the amount they could earn from exporting them. If there are export taxes of t_e per cent on locally produced exportable inputs, the financial costs of the pipes will be the world price minus this export tax, $P_w(1 - t_e)$, because this will be the price for which the exportable will sell domestically. In general, the market price of an exportable input will be $P_w(1 + s_e - t_e)$.

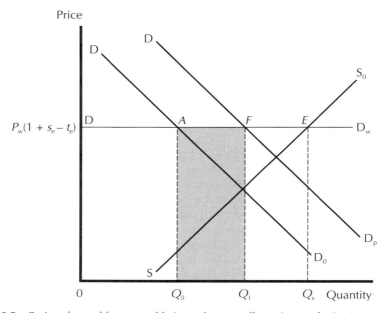

Figure 2.5   *Project demand for exportable input does not affect price — plastic pipes*

If the project needs an input that must be imported, for example electricity generators for a power station, the relevant supply curve facing the project will be the perfectly elastic world supply curve for generators, SS_w in Figure 2.6. The curve is horizontal because the world price of generators will not increase merely because the project buys a small number. If the domestic demand curve for generators moves out, from DD_0 to DD_p, the quantity of generators imported will need to increase, from $Q_d - Q_s$ to $Q_1 - Q_s$, while the price will remain constant at the world price, P_w. In the absence of import tariffs or quotas on generators, P_w will be the appropriate measure of the financial cost of each generator and total financial costs associated with purchasing these generators will be measured by the shaded area Q_dQ_1DC. If a tariff or quota with a tariff equivalent of t_m per cent is applied to generators, then their financial cost to the project will be the world price of generators plus the domestic tariff, $P_w(1 + t_m)$.

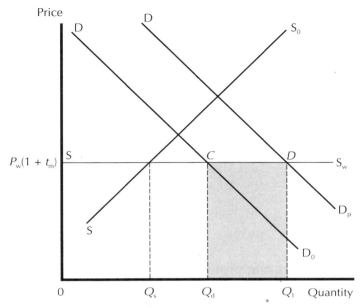

Figure 2.6 *Project demand for importable input does not affect price — electricity generators*

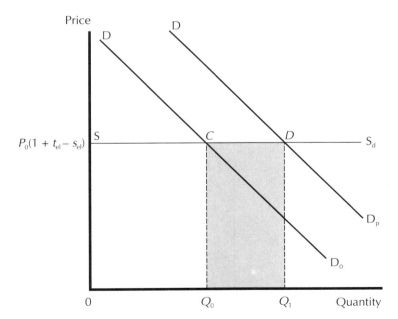

Figure 2.7 *Project demand for non-traded input does not affect price — electricity*

An input needed for the project may not be traded internationally (for example electricity) but the project's use of electricity may be small in relation to total domestic supply. This situation is represented in Figure 2.7, where the relevant section of the domestic supply curve for electricity confronting the project is horizontal or elastic, SS_d. In this case, the project's extra demand for electricity will have no discernible impact on the market price of electricity prior to the commencement of the project, P_0, the supply price of electricity. In a financial analysis of the project, P_0 will therefore be the appropriate measure of the unit cost of electricity for the project, and the total financial cost of electricity will be measured by the shaded area Q_0Q_1DC. Any taxes, such as a value added tax of t_{el} per cent, which must be paid by the project implementor, should be added to the supply price of electricity to determine the financial cost of electricity purchases, $P_0(1 + t_{el})$. Any subsidies received by the electricity producer or user, s_{el} per cent, should be subtracted from the supply price, $P_0(1 - s_{el})$. In general, the market price of a non-traded input whose supply is elastic will be $P_0(1 + t_e - s_e)$.

2.3.2 Cases where the project does change the domestic price of an input needed by the project

If an input needed by the project, for example a specialised type of chemical engineer, is not traded internationally, and the project causes such a significant increase in the demand for this type of labour that their salaries increase, this implies

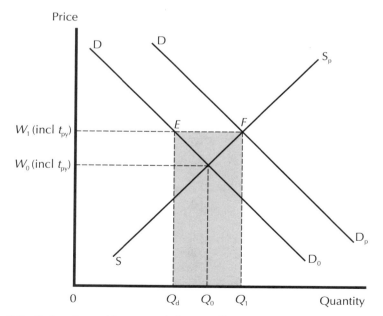

Figure 2.8   *Project demand for non-traded inputs affects price — chemical engineer*

that the domestic supply curve for chemical engineers confronting the project is less than perfectly elastic.

In Figure 2.8, the supply curve for engineers is given by SS_p and an increase in the domestic demand for chemical engineers as a result of the project will cause a right-ward shift of the demand curve for this category of skilled labour, from DD_0 to DD_p. For equilibrium to be re-attained, the market wage for chemical engineers will have to rise from W_0 to W_1. The financial costs to the project from employing one chemical engineer will rise to W_1 and the total costs from employing all engineers needed by the project will be the shaded area Q_dQ_1FE. If personal income tax at a rate of t_{py} per cent, is included in this market salary, this should be included as a financial cost of the project. Part of this increase in supply, $Q_1 - Q_0$, will be met by an increased supply of electrical engineers,[4] and part, $Q_0 - Q_d$, will be met by displacing other employers of chemical engineers (that is, head-hunting these engineers from other employers).

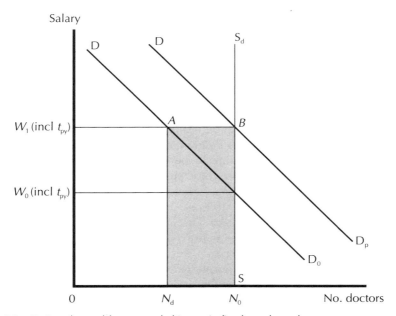

Figure 2.9   *Project demand for non-traded inputs in fixed supply — doctors*

If the production of the input required by the project cannot be expanded in the short to medium term, that is, its supply is inelastic, then all of the input used by the project must be bid away from other consumers. An example of such an input may be doctors needed for a new hospital project, assuming there are no unemployed doctors in the country who could be utilised, and there are strict controls on the immigration of doctors. This situation is shown in Figure 2.9, where the supply of doctors is fixed in the short term at SS_d and the demand curve for doctors shifts from DD_0 to DD_p as a result of the project. In freely operating markets, the cost to the project of employing each doctor will rise from W_0 to W_1, and the total cost of employing doctors in the hospital will be the shaded area N_dN_0BA. Once again, if personal income tax at a rate of t_{py} per cent is included in this market salary, this should be included as a financial cost of the project. All of these doctors will have to be bid away from other employers (or self-employment), and W_1 is the salary that the marginal alternative employer was willing to pay for doctors' services.

Some examples of inputs in fixed supply in the short to medium term include unskilled labour, unless there is migration or unemployment; skilled labour with long training periods; and electricity, if there is full utilisation of existing capacity. Other inputs, the production of which requires long lead times associated with the installation of new capacity, may also be considered in fixed supply in the short to medium term, for the purpose of valuing them in a project appraisal.

2.4 Real or nominal prices?

It is obviously very important to know whether the input and output projections given by the proposing firm or agency are valued in current prices (nominal) or constant prices (real). This is necessary to ensure that all the analysis is carried out in a **consistent set of prices**, so that the total net value of the project ultimately calculated is a **real** figure.

Often, constant (say 1990) prices, rather than current prices, are used in a project's cash flow. A project's cash flow is merely the costs and benefits paid and produced by the project over its lifetime in the years that they occur. The cash flow is usually entered on a spreadsheet like those provided in computer packages such as Lotus 123 or Excel. The use of constant prices simplifies the analysis, as it relieves the analyst of the need to make projections about the anticipated inflation rate in the country over the life of the project. This procedure is quite appropriate if input and output prices in domestic currency are expected to increase at approximately the same rate over the life of the project.

However, there are several situations where the use of constant prices may not be appropriate. The first is when the analyst is drawing up project financing plans. In this situation, the analyst will need to estimate expenditures in nominal terms to ensure that planned sources of finance will be sufficient to cover all project costs. The second is a situation where the investment is privately operated and will pay company tax. The financial analysis will need to be carried out in both nominal and real terms because the rate of inflation will affect the interest payments, depreciation allowances and the cost of holding stocks. All these will influence the firm's tax liability. Working capital requirements will also be affected by the level of inflation. Finally, if input and output prices are expected to rise at different rates over the life of the project, and vary from year to year, it will usually be simpler to include all prices in current terms.

2.5 Internal transport and handling costs

It is important to be clear about **where** inputs and outputs should be priced in a project appraisal. In the case of a project's output, it could be valued at the project gate or in the market for the project's output. In the case of project inputs, they could be valued at the project gate, at the gate of the input supplier's factory or mine or at the port of entry into the country. In order to determine which is the appropriate price, it is necessary to remember that in a financial appraisal it is the net incremental benefit of the project to the implementing agent that is of interest.

In the case of project outputs, they should therefore be valued at the market price received for them at the project gate. Transport costs from the project to market should be subtracted from the wholesale price received in the market. Project inputs should also be valued at their market cost at the project gate. This price will include the transport and handling costs of getting them there.

2.6 Local and foreign costs

Some project appraisals split costs (and sometimes benefits) between locally incurred and foreign exchange costs and benefits. This is useful if policy makers wish to judge the impact of the project on the balance of payments, or if foreign financing agents such as aid agencies or multilateral banks wish to see the distribution of items eligible for aid grants or loans.

Usually, even if local and foreign costs are identified, in a financial analysis all costs and benefits are then expressed in **local currency**, converted at the **official exchange rate**. However, the foreign currency costs may in some instances be expressed in a common international currency like $US, or in terms of the local currency of a bilateral aid donor country.

In order to separate the cash flow into local and foreign prices, and also to predict the future price of a project's tradeable inputs and outputs, it may be necessary to make projections about future exchange rates. To do this it will be necessary to assess, *inter alia*, if local inflation rates are likely to diverge from average international inflation rates, and particularly those of the host country's major trading partners. If local inflation is expected to be **higher** than the average for major trading partners, devaluation of the local currency could be anticipated, increasing both the costs of imported inputs and the local currency value of exported outputs. If local inflation is expected to be **lower** than that of the country's major trading partners, it is likely that the local currency will appreciate over the life of the project. If this is a real appreciation, it will have the effect of lowering imported input prices as well as lowering the local currency receipts from exported outputs and/or reducing the international competitiveness of these exports.

The following chapter discusses how the inputs and outputs of a project that are valued in market prices should be incorporated into a project's cash flow in order to undertake a financial analysis.

APPENDIX 1
Theoretical rationale for the use of market prices to measure economic value

There is theoretical support from neoclassical and price theory for the use of undistorted market prices to measure the **economic** value, value to the economy, of output produced or inputs used by a project. If market prices are undistorted a financially profitable project will also make a positive contribution to a country's economic welfare. This is the concept of the 'invisible hand' of capitalism developed by Adam Smith in his classic text, *The Wealth of Nations.* Many individual firms and consumers responding to uncontrolled market prices and signals could be expected to produce an economically optimal welfare outcome under certain assumptions regarding perfect competition.

The theoretical rationale for the use of market prices can best be explained by examining the valuation of project benefits and costs separately.

1. Rationale in terms of price theory for the use of the demand price of outputs to measure their economic value

Neoclassical utility theory indicates that in a competitive market without distortions the demand price for a good reflects the relative utility that consumers receive from consumption of the marginal unit demanded, and therefore the economic benefit from production of this marginal unit, Harberger (1971). In a two-good model, constrained consumer welfare optimisation occurs where the slopes of the consumer's budget line and indifference curves are equal. At this point, the ratio of the marginal utilities obtained from the consumption of the two goods will be equal to the ratio of their prices:

$$\frac{MU_1}{MU_2} = \frac{P_1}{P_2} \tag{A2.1}$$

If $\frac{P_1}{MU_1}$ is set $= 1$, that is, good 1 is the numeraire, then:

$$P_2 = MU_2 \tag{A2.2}$$

If consumers are not at this point, they will be able to increase their overall welfare by substituting one good for another, thereby raising the marginal utility received from the goods whose consumption has been reduced and lowering the marginal utility from the good whose consumption has been increased. If, for example, the marginal utility received from consuming good 1, MU_1 exceeds the price paid for good 1, P_1, the consumer will have an incentive to increase his or her purchases of good 1 up to the point where $MU_1 = P_1$. With a fixed budget constraint and a two-good model, this process of substitution will continue up to the point where the identity in (A2.1) holds.[5]

That is, the price of a commodity reflects its minimum worth to consumers. This can be easily understood by examining consumers' motives whenever they purchase a good or service. Unless consumers expect to get at least as much extra utility, benefit or well-being from consuming a good as they would obtain from alternative uses of their income they will keep their money and not purchase the good.

Of course they may get **more** utility from the consumption of the good than from any other alternative uses of their income, and may have in fact been willing to pay more than the market price. In this situation the consumer is said to have obtained some **consumer surplus**. This concept is discussed in Chapter 7.

On the other hand, if the value or utility that consumers expect to receive from consuming a good is less than the price being charged, they will have an incentive to reduce their purchases of that good. They will continue to do this up to the point where the utility received from the good's consumption just equals its market price.

In summary, it is obviously appropriate to use the market price of the output produced by a project as a measure of its financial benefit to the project concerned. This is because the price it earns in the market will represent its contribution to the project's receipts and profitability. If the demand price is freely determined in a market with no distortions, it will also represent a (minimum) estimate of what people are willing to pay for the project's output. Hence, in the absence of distortions (and consumer surplus), the demand price will also represent a good measure of the economic benefit of a unit of the project's output.

2. Rationale for the use of the supply price of inputs in terms of price theory

A familiar result of neoclassical price theory is that the perfectly competitive firm facing decreasing returns to scale is at its profit maximising equilibrium production level at the point at which its marginal cost of production equals the price at which it can sell its next unit of output:

$$MC_j = P_j \ (= MR) \tag{A2.3}$$

If the producer is producing an input for the project, for example steel girders for a bridge project, they will keep expanding production so long as the marginal cost of production of steel girders, MC_s, is less than the market price that can be earned from selling steel girders, P_s. The producer will have a financial incentive to continue to expand production of steel girders up to the point where MC_s and P_s are equalised.

From the point of view of the project purchasing the steel girders as an input, it will keep purchasing more of these girders up to the point where their marginal contribution to project revenue, that is, their marginal revenue product, MRP_s (the product of their marginal revenue MR_s and marginal price, MP_s), falls to their marginal contribution to project costs, their price, P_s:

$$MR_s \times MP_s = MRP_s = P_s \tag{A2.4}$$

At each level of the input demanded, the input's market price will equal its marginal revenue product in its most marginal use. This will also be the **demand price** of the marginal input user. Hence, for an input whose output can be expanded, at the market clearing equilibrium, the input's demand price will equal its supply price, which will equal its marginal cost of production. In equilibrium, the market price of the input, P_s, will equal both the amount purchasers are willing to pay for it, its economic value in use, MRP_s, and its economic cost of production, the economic cost of the input, MC_s:

$$MRP_s = MC_s = P_s \tag{A2.5}$$

This provides the rationale for the use of market prices to measure the economic cost of inputs, in a situation where there are freely operating markets without taxes or other controls and distortions. However, the existence of producer and consumer surplus, in some circumstances, will upset these neat assumptions. These issues are discussed in Chapter 7.

As in the case of measuring the value of project outputs, the market prices of project inputs may vary as a result of the project being implemented. The project analyst will have to be alert to this possibility and take this into account in his or her analysis.

Exercises

1. A government owned rail authority wishes to estimate the likely impact of introducing a new rail service on freight prices between two major towns in a remote region of the country. The railway could carry 100 000 tonnes of general freight per annum. Currently, 40 000 tonnes of freight is carried by road at an average price of $20 per tonne. Surveys indicate that there is considerable unmet demand, and that local users would demand a further 30 000 tonnes of services at the price of $20 per tonne. However, further increases in demand would only occur if the price were to drop. A further 10 000 tonnes of services would be demanded if the fee dropped to $18, and 20 000 tonnes more if the rate were only $15 per tonne. What will be the revenue earned by the rail service if:
   a it charges a uniform tariff
   b it discriminates between different types of users so as to fully exploit the willingness to pay of the three identified user groups?

2. A telephone company wishes to provide 200 000 more telephone lines. It can either import exchange equipment worth $20 million to do this or use locally produced equipment. Although at current prices local producers could supply this equipment at $18 million, as a result of such a large order, the costs of local suppliers could be expected to rise to $22 million.
   What will be the cost of this equipment if:
   a there are no import restraints on telephone equipment
   b the government owned telephone authority is required to purchase locally
   c there is a 7 per cent tariff on imported equipment, but no other restraints on imports?

References

Gravelle, H. and Rees, R., 1981. *Microeconomics*, Longman, London, Chapter 5.

Harberger, A.C., 1971. 'Three basic postulates of applied welfare economics: An interpretative essay', *Journal of Economic Literature*, Vol. IX, No 3, Sept, 785–97.

Smith, A., 1982 (reprint). *The Wealth of Nations*, with introduction by Skinner, A., Penguin, Harmondsworth.

Further reading

Dasgupta, A.K. and Pearce, D.W., 1978. *Cost-Benefit Analysis: Theory and Practice*, Macmillan, London, Chapter 1.

Duvigneau, J.C. and Ranga, N.P., 1984. *Guidelines for Calculating Financial and Economic Rates of Return for DFC Projects*, Development Finance Corporation, World Bank, Technical Paper no 33, Chapter 3.

Gittinger, J.P., 1982. *Economic Analysis of Agricultural Projects*, Johns Hopkins University Press, Baltimore, Chapter 2.

Irvin, G., 1978. *Modern Cost Benefit Analysis Methods*, Macmillan, London, Chapter 2.

Sugden, R. and Williams, A., 1978. *The Principles of Practical Cost Benefit Analysis*, Oxford University Press, Oxford, Chapter 3.

Endnotes

1   These may include, for example, a situation where a private firm is seeking a subsidy or other form of concession from the government and needs to show that its project would increase economic welfare.

2   If the project is government owned, it may not be necessary to deduct these tax payments from the project's financial receipts, as the government will still receive the tax revenue. If, however, the analysis is only being undertaken from the point of view of the particular government urban transport agency running the bus service, it may not receive these taxes, and hence may not include them in its financial receipts.

3   Similarly, if the financial analysis is being undertaken from the point of view of the bus service, even if it is government run, as long as it actually receives the subsidy it should be included as a financial benefit of the project. However, if the financial analysis is being undertaken from the point of view of the government as a whole, the subsidy would not be a net benefit to the government, but just a transfer from one department to another.

4   In the short term this could occur, as such engineers are induced to return to this career, possibly from administration, self-employment or domestic duties, while in the long term this increased supply would occur as a result of more people being trained in this area.

5   This result is proven in any basic microeconomics text, such as Gravelle and Rees (1981).

CHAPTER 3

The cash flow in financial analysis

3.1 The financial cash flow

The financial cash flow of a project is the stream of financial costs and benefits, or expenditures and receipts, that will be generated by the project over its economic life, and will not be produced in its absence. Before the cash flow of a project can be estimated, it will be necessary for the project sponsors to undertake detailed market research into product markets and prices. They must find out if there will be a market for the project's output and what it can be sold for. Then the analyst will need to assess the sources, quantities and costs of required capital assets, raw materials and labour, to estimate the likely costs of the project. It may also be necessary to determine anticipated inflation rates and exchange rate movements, as they may affect the valuation of the project's expenditures and receipts.

Once these are known, the expenditures and receipts that form the project's cash flow can be entered into a spreadsheet like that shown in Table 3.1. This will typically be done using a spreadsheet computer program such as Lotus 123 or Excel. Expenditures and receipts are entered under appropriate headings, and entries are made for each of these items in the year (or month or quarter) in which payments will be made or received. A generic currency, local dollars, $L, is used in most examples in this text. Since the cashflow entries for years 5 to 19 are identical to year 4's, they can be omitted in a summary table like Table 3.1, but the cashflow for all years must be entered in the computer spreadsheet analysis of the project.

3.2 Project life

Early in the process of constructing a project's financial cash flow it will be necessary to determine the length of the project's economic life. This will be the optimal period over which the project should be run to maximise its return to the project implementor. The project's life is frequently set equal to the technical life of the equipment used. However, various factors, such as the technological obsolescence of equipment, changing tastes, international competitiveness or the extent of a natural resource or mineral deposit, may result in the economic life of the project being shorter than the technical life of the equipment employed. If the project is expected to have long-term environmental impacts, it may be necessary to extend the length of the cash flow so that these costs (or benefits) can be measured. For example, a project to drain mangrove swamps to grow cotton may have an economic life of 20 years, but the negative impact on fish breeding grounds may be irreversible. An alternative to extending the project life for many years (or to infinity) is to include a capitalised value for these costs (or benefits) at the end of the project's economic life — its environmental 'scrap value' (Dixon et al., 1986). The methodology for determining the optimal scale, timing and length of projects is discussed in Chapter 5 and in Jenkins and Harberger (1991).

Often the project's cash flow is separated into start-up and operational phases. The reason for this is that the cash flow of the project is likely to be negative during the start-up period, and the project's financing should be organised to ensure adequate funds are available to finance this. The implementation phase covers the initial construction of the project as well as the period at the beginning of the project's operation. During this period, operating costs will often be higher and capacity utilisation lower than later in the project's life, as workers and managers learn how to operate the new plant and iron out 'teething' problems. Any materials and labour used during this start-up period that are in excess of the volumes employed during

Table 3.1 Simple financial cash flow of a water supply project ($L million)

Costs	Years				
	1	*2*	*3*	*4 ...*	*20*
Capital costs					
Fixed assets:					
Pipes	400	500	300	0 ...	−70
Pumps	50	100	90	0 ...	−30
Storage tanks	140	230	160	0 ...	−100
Jack hammers	20	10	0	0 ...	−5
Construction	200	250	190	0 ...	0
Total fixed assets	810	1090	740	0 ...	−205
Working capital	20	30	40	0 ...	−90
Total capital costs	830	1120	780	0 ...	−295
Operating costs:					
Project management	80	100	120	90 ...	90
Fuel	5	7	8	10 ...	10
Maintenance	30	40	50	50 ...	50
Total costs	945	1267	958	150 ...	−145
Benefits					
Water sales revenue	0	200	250	500 ...	500
Net benefits					
(Benefits − costs)	−945	−1067	−708	350 ...	645

the operational phase of the project should be included in the capital costs of the project. After this start-up period, the analyst can usually expect that the project will reach a steady state of operation, which will continue until the last year of the project's life. The costs and benefits of the project during these years will be entered into the operational phase of the project's cash flow. In the example given in Table 3.1, years 1 to 3 represent the start-up phase, and years 4 to 19 the steady state operational phase. In year 20 the project will be closed down and the equipment sold for scrap.

3.3 Capital costs

The capital costs of a project can be divided into fixed capital costs, or the cost of acquiring fixed assets like plant and equipment, start-up costs, and working capital, which finances the operating expenses of the enterprise. In a financial analysis, all forms of capital expenditure should be entered in the financial cash flow in the years in which the project actually has to pay for them. For example, if the project receives a soft loan from the supplier of its equipment, which involves a grace period before repaying the loan, the cost of this equipment will not be included in the cash flow until it must be paid for by the project.

3.3.1 Fixed capital

The fixed capital requirements of a project will include the cost of any land, buildings, civil works, capital equipment, vehicles and in-plant infrastructure facilities. As well, if the project needs any specialised infrastructure facilities for the project, such as a purpose-built power station or access roads, these costs should be included in the financial capital costs of the project, so long as these capital costs are borne by the project implementor. If the government is implementing the project and it must also provide the infrastructure, then these infrastructure costs will be included in the financial cash flow.[1] If any of the services produced by such infrastructure are sold to firms or households outside the project, revenue earned from them should be included in the benefits of the project.

Any start-up costs incurred in getting the project operational, such as training costs for a new work-force and wasted materials used to make trial production runs, should also be included in the capital costs. Fixed capital costs will also include any periodic replacement of plant, equipment and vehicles during the project's life.

At the end of the project's economic life, the scrap value of the project's assets and land should be included in the cash flow as a negative capital cost. The assets' scrap value will be the actual amount earned from their sale or their value to the enterprise in their best alternative uses, possibly in other projects. The depreciated value of fixed assets is an accounting concept, estimated using arbitrarily determined rates provided by taxation authorities, to estimate taxation liability. It is quite irrelevant to estimating a project's actual scrap value in a financial appraisal. For example, if a bus company is considering cutting out a particular bus service, the depreciated value of the surplus buses would not be relevant in deciding whether to keep the service running or not. The opportunity cost of using buses in this service is the amount that the bus company could earn from using them on other routes or from selling them. This is the true cost to the bus company of maintaining them in their current service and what it would save if it scrapped the service.

Since all capital costs are entered in the project's cash flow in the year in which they are actually incurred, as shown in Table 3.1, it is not necessary to make any provision for depreciation of fixed assets in a financial or economic appraisal. Depreciation is an accounting device that notionally allocates the capital cost of using an asset over its economic life to determine the taxation liability of an enterprise. Adding an additional cost for 'depreciation' each year after the full capital costs of the project have already been included in the cash flow when these costs were actually incurred would result in double counting.

Allowance for **physical and price contingencies**, equal to perhaps from 5 to 10 per cent of the project's capital costs, is often added to base case estimates of capital costs to reflect the fact that these items are usually subject to cost overruns. The extent of the provision for time and cost overruns will depend on the historical experience of similar projects in the country concerned. Sensitivity analyses[2] are often employed at this point to determine the impact of different assumptions about cost overruns on project viability.

3.3.2 Working capital

Several months may pass between an enterprise having to purchase raw materials and pay wages and salaries, and the receipt of revenue from goods produced. The bank deposits, stocks of raw materials, goods in the process of production, finished goods and equipment spare parts needed to enable the enterprise to keep functioning over this period are called working capital. Working capital can be likened to the oil that is needed to lubricate a machine and keep it running smoothly. It is not used up during production, as is diesel fuel, but circulates in the machine. One component of working capital is cash reserves to meet any temporary shortfall between revenue flowing to the project and expenditures incurred by it. Wholesale buyers of finished goods do not usually pay for their purchases immediately. On the other hand, raw material suppliers are also likely to provide some credit to their customers, workers will be paid only every two weeks and utilities such as electicity suppliers may only need to be paid every two to three months. The balance between credit needed to finance debtors and that obtained from input and factor suppliers will determine the level of net working capital requirements for this purpose.

Other components of working capital are the value of stocks of required raw materials, semi-finished goods, spare parts and finished goods. The actual amount of working capital needed to meet these needs, as a proportion of the enterprise's operating costs, will be determined by the nature and location of the business operation. The more remote the location of an enterprise, and the less reliable its transport links, the more likely it is to experience delays in receiving inputs and spare parts, and hence the larger the stocks of raw materials and equipment spares it will need. Similarly, enterprises like aluminium refineries, which incur huge costs if there is production down-time, must usually hold larger than average stocks of raw materials and spare parts. Firms with longer production processes and those who need to meet orders promptly out of stocks must also hold more stocks of raw materials and semi-finished and finished goods.

Working capital reserves are usually built up to full production requirements during the first few years of the project and then form a capital asset held as cash, deposits and stocks of raw materials and finished products, which will be cashed in at the end of the project. Hence, working capital costs are not normally incurred in each year of the project, but only in the first few years, when the stock of working capital is being established or expanded and the enterprise has reached its full production level. However, if the enterprise is continually growing, or if there is significant price inflation in the country concerned, it will be necessary to continually make additions to working capital.

Table 3.2   Estimation of the working capital requirements of a bicycle factory ($L million)

	Years					
	1	*2*	*3*	*4*	...	*20*
1. Working capital held as stocks						
Raw materials	0	7	14	14	...	−14
Work in progress	0	10	15	15	...	−15
Finished products	0	50	80	80	...	−80
Spares for equipment	0	10	30	30	...	−30
Total stocks held	0	77	139	139	...	0
Accumulated needs (A)	0	77	62	0	...	−139
2. Working capital held as cash						
(1) Annual project operating costs:						
Bicycle parts	0	50	100	100	...	0
Raw materials	0	20	40	40	...	0
Labour	0	60	160	160	...	0
Electricity	0	10	30	30	...	0
(2) Proportion of operating costs required to be held in liquid assets:						
6% bicycle parts	0	3	6	6	...	0
5% raw materials	0	1	2	2	...	0
4% labour costs	0	2.4	6.4	6.4	...	0
2% electricity, water	0	0.2	0.6	0.6	...	0
Total liquid assets	0	6.6	15.0	15.0	...	0
Accumulated needs (B)	0	6.6	8.4	0	...	−15.0
Total accumulated working capital needs (A + B)	0	83.6	70.4	0	...	−154.0

Additions to working capital are shown in the project's cash flow in the years in which they are made. At the end of the project's life, a negative cost (that is, a benefit) will be included in the cash flow when these funds are released. This is comparable to the sale of the project's fixed assets in its final year.

Table 3.2 gives examples of how the working capital requirements of a bicycle producer may be determined, how this working capital is accumulated and how it is finally cashed in. Apart from the stocks of raw materials, work in progress, finished products and equipment spare parts held, the enterprise will need to hold a proportion of its labour, electricity and water costs and other expenses in reserves to meet production expenses as they fall due. Such reserves will be held in highly liquid assets, such as demand deposits.

Only annual additions to working capital represent a new capital cost to the project. The working capital already invested by the project is turned over to be reused continually throughout the project's life. These new additions to working capital are shown as accumulated working capital needs in Table 3.2. In the final year of the project, its total working capital of $L154 million will be cashed in, and hence is available as a negative cost, or benefit, to the project.

3.4 Operating costs

The project's operating costs cover its recurrent outlays on labour services (wages and salaries), raw materials, energy, utilities (water, waste removal, etc.), marketing, transport, insurance, taxes and debt service over the life of the project. Each operating cost is entered in the cash flow in the year (month or quarter) in which it is incurred. Total operating costs may also be expressed in terms of costs per unit of output. As was mentioned previously, unit operating costs are likely to be somewhat higher in the first year or two of a project, so the difference between start-up and steady state operating costs may be included as start-up costs under capital costs, and only steady state operating costs will be included as true operating costs.

Net benefits   The project's net benefit stream is calculated as the difference between the total revenue (or benefit) stream and its expenditure (cost) stream.

3.5 Financing schedules — interest payments and loan receipts

After the financial costs and benefits of the project have been entered into the financial cash flow the analyst can estimate a separate financing schedule. This will identify the sources of funds to finance the initial capital investment and any shortfall in cash flow in the start-up years of the project. It will also show when repayments of interest and capital will fall due. Such a schedule will enable the analyst to determine the impact of different sources of finance, with different grace periods, repayment patterns and interest rates, on the project's financial viability. The need to raise equity finance (or self-financing from a public authority) and the anticipated returns to shareholders (or government revenue) could also be assessed.

These issues are mainly the concern of financial planners and controllers in national finance departments and in financial institutions, who will need to draw up financing schedules once a conclusion has been reached regarding the economic and financial viability of projects. If a financial analysis is carried out in current day, nominal prices, uses nominal interest rates as the discount rate (as will be discussed in Chapter 4) and includes a loan schedule detailing the receipt and repayment of loans, it should represent an accurate picture of the financial cash flow of the project, which can then be used by the financial controller.

Table 3.3   The financing schedule for the water supply project ($L million)

	Years					
	1	*2*	*3*	*4*	*...*	*20*
Total capital costs	830	1120	780	0	...	−295
Operating costs	115	147	178	150	...	150
Total costs	945	1267	958	150	...	−145
Benefits						
Water sales revenue	0	200	250	500	...	500
Net benefits						
(Benefits – costs)	−945	−1067	−708	350	...	645

Financing schedule

	Years					
	1	*2*	*3*	*4*	*...*	*20*
Loan receipts:						
(a) World Bank	500	700	400			
(b) Govt Development Bank	200	200	100			
Self-financing from						
Water supply authority	100	100	150			
Government grant	145	67	58			
Total financing	945	1067	708			
Loan repayments (capital):						
(a) World Bank				94	...	94
(b) Govt Development Bank				29	...	29
Total	0	0	0	123	...	123
Net financing cash flow	0	0	0	227	...	423

The financing schedule may be conveniently located at the bottom of a standard financial analysis, once the capital and start-up costs of the project are known. Loan receipts are included as a positive entry, while repayments of capital show up as expenditures. Both are included in the financing schedule in the year(s) in which they are actually received or paid. This is shown in the financing schedule in Table 3.3, which is associated with the water supply project outlined in Table 3.1. However, it should be noted that interest repayments are not included in either a financial or economic analysis cash flow because the interest cost of the loan is taken into account by the discounting of project costs and benefits. This process is discussed in Chapter 4.

The merits of alternative financing options, with, for example, different interest rates, repayment periods and grace periods, can be compared by estimating the financing schedule for each of these financing methods. The profitability of the project for all these alternative methods of financing can then be compared.

3.6 Treatment of taxes

As an addition to a financial analysis undertaken from the owner's point of view, the company tax paid on project profits can be calculated in order to determine the project's net present value after tax. A government may wish to do this to determine whether a project seeking subsidies or concessions will be financially profitable after tax or not. A private firm may merely wish to know if a proposed investment will be profitable after tax, given the tax regime of the country concerned.

Table 3.4 continues the example from Tables 3.1 and 3.3. It is now assumed that the water supply project is privately operated and pays tax. The taxable income of the project will be determined by subtracting all operating costs, interest payments

Table 3.4 Taxation liability and net benefit after tax for the water supply project ($L million)

	Years					
	1	2	3	4	...	20
Total benefits (sales revenue, assets sales)	0	200	250	500	...	795
Total operating costs	115	147	182	150	...	150
Interest payments	0	0	0	146	...	0
Depreciation (5% assets)	40.5	95	132	132	...	132
Taxable income = (revenue – operating costs – interest – depreciation)	−155.5	−42	−64	72	...	513
Taxation liability (25%)	0	0	0	18	...	128.3
Net benefits before tax (from Table 3.3)	945	−1067	−708	350	...	645
Net benefits after tax	945	−1067	−708	332	...	516.7

and allowable depreciation on the capital assets from the firm's revenue earnings each year. The appropriate company income tax rate is then applied to this taxable income to determine the project's taxation liability.

If the country gives incentives to new investments in the form of tax holidays or accelerated depreciation of assets, these should be taken into account in the determination of the project's taxable income and tax liability. The tax liability is subtracted from taxable income to obtain the project's net of tax income. The project's net benefit stream after financing and tax can then be presented after the financial analysis cash flow given in Table 3.1.

3.7 Changes in accounts payable

If not all operating cost payments are made by the project in the year in which inputs are purchased, these liabilities will show up as an increase in accounts payable by the firm. Changes in accounts payable are defined as accounts payable at the beginning of the year minus accounts payable at the end of the year. Positive changes in accounts payable must be subtracted from expenditures made by the firm to calculate the actual annual expenditure of the project, and hence its financial profitability. If accounts payable rise over a year, the contribution of project costs to cash payments falls. This relationship can be summarised as:

Cash payments = expenditures + accounts payable at the beginning of the year – accounts payable at the end of the year

Accounts payable at the end of one year become accounts payable at the beginning of the next year.

3.8 Project benefits

In a financial analysis, the project's benefits equal the cash receipts actually received by the project from the sale of goods or services it produces, or the market value equivalent of home consumed output in the case of non-marketed output. This can be the revenue from sales, rent or royalties, depending on the nature of the project. Other revenue earned from, for example, bank deposits, the sale of fixed assets or insurance claims, will also be included as separate items under project receipts or benefits.

3.8.1 Project sales

If the project sells its output, the benefit stream of the financial cash flow will include the annual revenue earned by the project from sales of all the different products and services produced by it. This output will be valued in terms of the market prices received for the output, net of sales taxes and other imposts that must be paid over to the government by the project or distributors of its output, but will include any subsidies received by the project. The measurement of the market price of the output of a project was discussed in the previous chapter.

3.8.2 Imputed income from non-marketed output

If the project's output will be wholly or partially consumed on the farm or in the household where it was produced, the imputed, or estimated, value of this output must be added to the value of any output sold. The analyst will need to seek information about the market prices of this output, or close substitutes, to determine its imputed value. Appropriate adjustments to market prices must be made for any quality differences between the marketed and home consumed products.

3.9 Changes in accounts receivable

If not all output sales are paid for by customers in the year in which they are purchased, then these will show up as an increase in accounts receivable by the firm. Since it is the actual cash inflows into the project that are measured in the financial cash flow, changes in accounts receivable must be added to sales made by the firm to calculate the actual annual receipts of the project. Changes in accounts receivable are defined as accounts receivable at the beginning of the year minus accounts receivable at the end of the year. If the accounts receivable by a project rise over the year, then this will reduce the contribution of project sales to cash receipts. That is:

Cash receipts = sales + accounts receivable at the beginning of the year – accounts receivable at the end of the year

Accounts receivable at the end of one year become accounts receivable at the beginning of the next year.

Exercises

1. In a middle-income developing country a private consortium is considering investing in an integrated steel mill project and wishes to undertake a financial analysis of the project. Draw up a cash flow of the expected receipts and expenditures on a spreadsheet program like Lotus 123.

   The project will last 25 years and produce 100 000 tonnes of steel products per annum, starting from year 4. Each tonne of output will sell for $L400 in current-day local dollars, but the sales price is expected to rise with the general rate of inflation, which is projected to be 6 per cent p.a. over the life of the project.

   Total investment will be $L200 million, spread evenly over the first 3 years of the project. There will be no inflation in construction costs once the contract for construction is let.

   In the fourth year of the project, when production starts, annual operating costs are expected to be:

- raw materials $L8 million
- labour $L4 million
- overheads $L1 million.

In each year following, raw material prices are expected to rise by 6 per cent, labour costs by 8 per cent, and overheads by 5 per cent.

Draw up a parameters table, as shown below, which lays out clearly all the basic information, or parameters, provided on the project. All quantitative data should be placed in a separate cell so that it can be referenced by formula in the

Table 1   Parameter table

	(Separate cell entries)
Project life (years)	25
Project output volume (tonnes)	100000
Output price ($L/tonne)	400
Investment cost ($L million)	200
Investment period (years)	3
Raw materials cost p.a. ($L million)	8
Labour cost p.a. ($L million)	4
Overheads cost p.a. ($L million)	1
Inflation (% p.a.):	
Output price (% p.a.)	6
Raw materials (% p.a.)	6
Labour costs (% p.a.)	8
Overheads (% p.a.)	5

Table 2   Financial analysis

Divide the cash flow into headings, and estimate the net benefit cash flow of the proposed project.

	Years				
	1	*2*	*3*	...	*25*
1. Expenditures					
Investment costs					
Operating costs					
Raw materials					
Labour					
Overheads					
2. Receipts					
Net benefits (2 – 1)					

financial analysis table (Table 2). Using cell references to this parameter table, draw up the financial cash flow for the proposed project.

The advantage of laying out the project's cash flow in a parameter table is that the analyst, and decision-makers, can clearly see what assumptions are being made about key variables related to the project, such as output quantities and price, input prices, interest and discount rates, inflation and exchange rates, etc. Also, if it is necessary to change the values of any of these variables as the analyst obtains revised information, this can be quickly done by changing the cell reference in the parameter table. If a spreadsheet program is used, the cash flows will then be instantly recalculated, saving the analyst much time, and avoiding errors that may occur if uncorrected data is left embedded in formulas in the cash flows themselves.

2. Assume 90 per cent of the steel output of this project will be exported, while 50 per cent of the raw material inputs and 70 per cent of the investment costs will be imported. Set up a new parameter table, including this information and incorporate it into a new financial analysis (Tables 3 and 4). Split the cash flow entries into local and foreign costs and benefits. (*Hint*: Copy Tables 1 and 2, the first parameter and financial analysis tables, and amend them to take account of this new information.)

3. Starting from the assumptions made in Exercise 1, assume that the government has decided to cut the country off from international trade. As a result, all of the output will now supply the small protected local market, and none of the raw materials will be traded internationally. As a result of the increase in local steel supply caused by the project, it is expected that steel prices will need to fall to $L300 per tonne to clear the market. The extra demand for raw materials (which must now be sourced locally) will increase their cost from $L8 million to $L10 million per annum. Investment costs will also rise 30 per cent because the project will have to purchase from more expensive local suppliers. Set up another parameter table including this information and incorporate it into a new financial analysis (Tables 5 and 6). Recalculate the cash flow. (*Hint*: Copy Tables 1 and 2, the first parameter and financial analysis tables and amend them to take account of this new information.)

4. A private firm wishes to examine the profitability of a fertiliser project.

The project will produce 10 000 tonnes of fertiliser a year, which will be sold on the domestic market for $400 per tonne. It is expected to have a 20 year life.

Investment in plant and equipment will cost $3 million, spread evenly over 3 years, and land will cost $200 000. At the end of the project, the land could be sold for its purchase cost. The plant will depreciate in value by 4 per cent per annum (straight line) and can be sold for its depreciated value after 20 years.

Working capital requirements will be 10 per cent of labour, material and utilities costs. It will be built up in the first 2 years after production begins and liquidated at the end of the project.

The plant will need 100 workers and 20 office and managerial staff. The average wage for production workers is $100 per month, while that for management staff is $250 per month. Raw material costs will be $20 per tonne, energy and utilities a further $5 per tonne. All input and output prices are expected to rise at approximately the overall projected rate of inflation.

Accounts payable will rise from 5 per cent of total operating costs in the first year of production, year 4, to 7 per cent in year 5, and stay constant at 10 per cent of operating costs for the rest of the project. In the last year, 20, these accounts will have to be paid off. Accounts receivable will rise from 2 per cent of total sales in year 4 to 4 per cent in year 5, fall to 3 per cent in year 6 and stay at that level for the rest of the project's life. Purchasers of the project's output will have to pay this amount in the final year of the project.

Set out the parameter table for the project, including all the information outlined above. Using cell references to the parameter table, construct the financial cash flow for the project.

5. Show the net benefit cash flow of the project if its developers take out a loan in year 1 for 50 per cent of investment costs and repay this over 10 years starting in year 4 at a real interest rate of 10 per cent. (*Hint*: Copy your original parameter and financial analysis tables for the fertiliser project and amend these to add the financing schedule of the financial analysis.)

6. Calculate the project's after-tax net benefit cash flow if it pays 25 per cent company tax on its profits.

Annual profits are calculated as: Annual sales revenue, minus annual operating costs, minus annual interest payments (but not capital repayments), minus an allowance for the depreciation of plant and equipment. In this country, the tax authorities allow 4 per cent straight-line depreciation of the purchase price of plant for taxation purposes. (*Hint*: Copy your parameter and financial analysis tables for the fertiliser project and then amend them to undertake the with-tax version of the financial analysis.)

References

Jenkins G.P. and Harberger, A.C., 1991. *Manual — Cost Benefit Analysis of Investment Decisions*, Program on Investment Appraisal and Management, Harvard Institute for International Development, Cambridge, Mass.

Dixon, J.A., Carpenter, R.A., Fallon, L.A., Sherman, P.B. and Manipomke, S., 1986. *Economic Analysis of the Environmental Impacts of Development Projects*, Earthscan, London.

Further reading

Duvingneau, J.C. and Prasad, R.N., 1984. *Guidelines for Calculating Financial and Economic Rates of Return for DFC Projects*, World Bank Technical Paper No. 33, Chapter 2.

Gittinger, J., 1982. *Economic Analysis of Agricultural Projects*, 2nd ed., Johns Hopkins University Press, Baltimore, Chapter 4.

Henderson, J. W. and Maness, T.S., 1989. *The Financial Analyst's Deskbook — a Cash Flow Approach to Liquidity*, Van Nostrand Reinhold, New York.

Irvin, G., 1978. *Modern Cost-Benefit Methods*, Macmillan, London, Chapter 4.

McDonald, A., Evans, D.B. and Sevele, F.V., 1984. *A Guide to Project Planning and Appraisal in the South Pacific* (revised edition), South Pacific Commission, Noumea, Vols I and II.

Ray, A., 1984. *Cost Benefit Analysis — Issues and Methodologies*, Johns Hopkins University Press, Baltimore, Chapters 1, 3.

Sugden, R. and Williams, A., 1978. *The Principles of Practical Cost Benefit Analysis*, Oxford University Press, Oxford, Chapters 1, 7.

Endnotes

1   In the case of an economic analysis, even the cost of essential infrastructure provided by the government for a private project will be included, because although it is not a cost to the project implementator, it is a cost of the economy.

2   Sensitivity analysis merely entails lowering or raising the costs and revenues of the project by plausible percentages to determine the impact on the project's net benefits. This technique is discussed in more detail in Chapter 15, which deals with risk in project appraisal.

CHAPTER 4

Time preference, discounting and the financial discount rate

4.1 Pareto optimality and the Hicks–Kaldor compensation criterion

Once a project's financial costs and benefits have been identified, valued in market prices and entered in the cash flow, the remaining task is to use this information to determine whether the project will be profitable and should be selected for implementation. The basic selection criterion, which is applicable in both financial and economic analysis, is that a project should not be undertaken unless its benefits outweigh its costs. The theoretical justification for this rule is the Hicks–Kaldor selection criterion.

The standard measure employed in welfare economics to determine whether a change in resource allocation will result in people being better off is the Pareto welfare improvement criterion. A Pareto improvement in welfare is said to occur if at least one person is made better off and no one is made worse off by a given change in economic conditions. When using this criterion it is unnecessary to make any comparisons between the utility (welfare) enjoyed by different people as a result of any change in their income, since everyone must either be unaffected or made better off by the change for it to be considered a Pareto welfare improvement.

However, if projects could only be implemented when they were expected to result in an **actual** Pareto welfare improvement, it is obvious that very few, if any, would be approved. This is because there will always be someone who is made worse off by the implementation of a project, such as a tax-payer who does not receive any benefit.

To overcome the restrictiveness of the Pareto unanimity rule, the concept of a **potential** Pareto improvement, or the compensation principle, was developed by Hicks (1939) and Kaldor (1939). This criterion states that a given change in the allocation of resources will potentially improve welfare if those who gain **could** compensate those who lose, and still be better off themselves. The Hicks–Kaldor compensation principle is central to the theoretical justification for cost benefit analysis in welfare economics. This criterion provides the rationale for choosing projects whose benefits outweigh their costs, even if the people who gain from a project are not the same as those who pay for it. The excess of benefits over costs is called the project's net benefits.

A crucial element of this criterion is that it is not necessary for the gainers from a project to **actually** compensate the losers, only for them to be able to do so if they wished and still remain better off than if the project had not been implemented. Hence, a project that meets the Hicks–Kaldor hypothetical compensation criterion will not necessarily result in an actual Pareto welfare improvement, only a **potential** improvement.

If compensation does not actually take place, the Hicks–Kaldor criterion can be criticised because of its failure to address the distributional impacts of projects. Total welfare will not necessarily be increased even if a project meets the Hicks–Kaldor criterion, unless those who gain receive the same increase in their utility from an extra unit of income as those who lose from the project. However, it is a basic tenet of welfare economics that the poor can be expected to receive a greater increase in their utility or welfare from 1 extra unit of income than the rich. That is, the poor are expected to have a higher marginal utility of income[1] than the rich. Put simply, a project that costs the poor 1 unit of income and increases the income of the rich by 1.5 units will pass the Hicks–Kaldor criterion and be selected, but will not increase total community welfare if the poor value their unit of lost income twice as highly as the rich value each additional unit of income they gain.

Nevertheless, in economic analysis these problems are largely ignored and it is implicitly assumed that everyone has the same marginal utility of income. However, the rationale for the social analysis of projects is largely based on this failure of the Hicks–Kaldor compensation criterion to deal with the distributional issues that will arise if actual compensation does not take place.

Before this selection criterion can be used to decide which projects should proceed, it is necessary to address the problem of the differences in the timing of a project's costs and benefits. If the costs and benefits of a project occur over a number of years, they will not be directly comparable. It is not possible to just add all the benefits of the project and subtract all the costs, irrespective of when they occur. This issue is dealt with in the Sections 4.2–4.9. The concepts of time preference and the discounting of project costs and benefits are explored in Sections 4.2–4.7. The appropriate discount rate to use in financial analysis is discussed in Sections 4.8 and 4.9.

Section 4.10 examines the problems with non-discounted measures of project worth. These measures simply add up all the project's costs and benefits, irrespective of the year in which they occur, and subtract the project's total costs from its benefits.

4.2 Time preference

Very rarely will all of a project's benefits and costs occur in the first year of an investment. Figure 4.1 shows a typical project time profile.

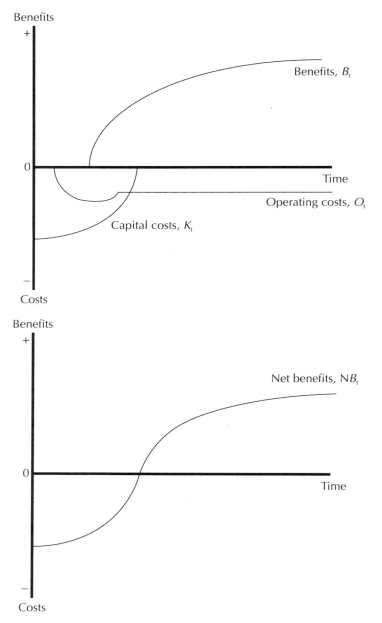

Figure 4.1 *Typical time profile of a project*

The bulk of the project's capital costs will be met in the implementation stage. Its operating costs will be incurred after the project begins and continue throughout the project's life, and its benefits will be realised after operation commences, rising to some plateau when the project reaches full capacity.

For a whole range of reasons, people, enterprises and governments will not be indifferent about whether they receive income (or incur expenditure) now or in some future period. They are said to have time preference in that they will prefer to receive income sooner rather than later, and to pay for expenditures later rather than sooner. Thus, if a person is offered the choice between receiving $10 now or in 10 years time, they will invariably opt to receive $10 now, even if they do not expect there to be any price inflation over the period.

Some of the main reasons people will prefer to have income now rather than in the future include the following.

(i) **Uncertainty about the future**   Life is always uncertain, and people cannot be sure that they will be alive in 10 years time to collect their $10s. They may also be uncertain about whether they really will be paid the $10s in 10 years time, as many factors may change over such a period. Such risks should be reduced if there is a strong legal system, enforcing contracts. This factor could be termed pure risk, or pure time preference.

(ii) **There is an expectation that society and individuals will be better off in the future than they are now**   If this belief is widely held, it will constitute another reason to put a higher value on current rather than future income. It could be expected that people would gain less extra utility or enjoyment from additional dollars of income if they were rich than would the same people if they were poor.[2] An individual would therefore be expected to get less utility from an extra $10 of income received in 10 years time, when he or she expects to be better off, than from $10 of income obtained now.

Governments and private firms and investors will also prefer to receive income now rather than in some future period, as income received now could be invested and, at the margin, receive back the marginal return on capital in the economy. These investors will be willing to pay interest to borrow capital to undertake such investments. If income becomes available from a project in earlier years rather than later ones, these funds can be used to reduce the amount the government or private investors will have to borrow for the project. The value of such funds will therefore be equal to the interest they would otherwise have had to pay to borrow this capital.

For all these reasons, income available from a project today cannot be treated as if it were equally valuable as income that will only be available some period in the future. Currently available income will be more valuable. It is therefore necessary to find some method of standardising the value of the benefits and costs that occur in different periods over the project's life, so that they can be compared and added together.

For the reasons outlined above, income available now is more valuable than future income even if there is no inflation. In the following discussion it is in fact assumed that there is no inflation, but this assumption will be relaxed in Section 4.9.

4.3 The marginal rate of time preference

We need to find out how much more income people will need to receive in the future to make them indifferent to receiving this amount rather than a given amount of income in the present. If a person is indifferent to receiving $10 now rather than $11 in 12 months time, he or she is said to have a marginal rate of time preference, MRTP, of 10 per cent or, more usually, 0.1 per annum. This is calculated from $\frac{(\$11 - \$10)}{\$10}$. This same person would probably also be equally happy to receive $11 1 year from now and $11 \times (1 + 0.1)$, or $12.1, 2 years from now.

In general terms, if an individual is indifferent to receiving 1 unit of income in period 0 rather than $1 \times (1 + r)$ units in period 1, then his or her MRTP is said to be r, where r is a proportion of 1, or a percentage. This person would probably also be indifferent to receiving this $1 \times (1 + r)$ units in period 1 and $1 \times (1 + r)^2$ units in period 2. Hence, the individual would be indifferent to receiving 1 unit of income in period 0 and $1 \times (1 + r)^2$ units of income in period 2. This process could be continued on, and in the most general case we would expect that the person would be equally happy to receive 1 unit of income in period 0 and $1 \times (1 + r)^n$ units of income in period n.

4.4 Discounting of future income flows

It is also possible to consider the value people will put on income in different periods, by working back in time from the future. The person with a MRTP of 0.1 will also be indifferent to receiving $10 1 year from now rather than $\frac{\$10}{(1 + 0.1)}$, or $9.09 now. The relative valuation on income in the two periods is the same as that considered in the previous section, only now future income, $10, is divided by $(1 + 0.1)$ to find its equivalent value in current-day dollars, $9.09, rather than multiplying current income, $9.09, by $(1 + 0.1)$ to find its value in future dollars, $10.

The same individual would probably also consider $10 available in 2 years time and $\frac{\$10}{(1 + 0.1)^2}$, or $8.26, available now as equivalent. As income only becomes available further into the future, its value will fall in terms of current-day dollars. This fits with our intuitive expectation that future income is considered less valuable than current income, for the reasons discussed in Section 4.2.

In general terms, a person with a MRTP = r would be as indifferent to 1 extra unit of consumption in period 1 as to $\frac{1}{(1 + r)}$ of a unit available in period 0. Similarly, 1 extra unit of income in period 2 would be worth the same as $\frac{1}{(1 + r)^2}$ unit of income in period 0, and so on. The unit of income available in period 2 would be worth only $\frac{1}{(1 + r)}$ of a unit in period 1, and this would be worth only $\frac{1}{(1 + r)^2}$ of a unit in period

0. In the most general case, 1 unit of income available in period n will only be worth $\dfrac{1}{(1 + r)^n}$ of a unit of income in period 0.

This process of deflating future income until its value is equivalent to currently available income is called **discounting**. This is the method used to revalue future cost and benefit flows from a project into present-day values so that they are comparable and can be added together. Hence, discounting is very important for project analysis.

4.5 Discounting in project analysis

In project analysis, any costs and benefits of a project that are received in future periods are **discounted**, or deflated by some factor, r, to reflect their lower value to the individual (or society) than currently available income. The factor used to discount future costs and benefits is called the **discount rate** and is usually expressed as a percentage.

For example, suppose the project is expected to yield a stream of benefits equal to $B_0, B_1, B_2, B_3, \ldots B_n$ and to incur a stream of costs equal to $C_0, C_1, C_2, C_3, \ldots C_n$ in years $0, 1, 2, 3, \ldots n$. Then in each period the net benefits (benefits minus costs) of the project will be:

$$(B_0 - C_0), (B_1 - C_1), (B_2 - C_2), (B_3 - C_3), \ldots (B_n - C_n)$$

This is simply the project's net benefit flow.

Assuming that the discount rate, r, is constant,[3] then the **discounted cash flow** of the project can be represented as:

$$(B_0 - C_0), \frac{(B_1 - C_1)}{(1 + r)}, \frac{(B_2 - C_2)}{(1 + r)^2}, \frac{(B_3 - C_3)}{(1 + r)^3} \ldots \frac{(B_n - C_n)}{(1 + r)^n}$$

Once future net income streams have been discounted in this way, expenditures and revenues from all the different time periods will be valued in units of similar value — present-day units of currency. They will then be directly comparable with each other and can be added together. Adding the discounted net benefits from each year of the project's life, its discounted net benefit flow, gives a single monetary value called the project's **net present value, NPV**. From the previous example, the project's NPV is:

$$NPV = (B_0 - C_0) + \frac{(B_1 - C_1)}{(1 + r)} + \frac{(B_2 - C_2)}{(1 + r)^2} + \frac{(B_3 - C_3)}{(1 + r)^3} + \ldots$$
$$+ \frac{(B_n - C_n)}{(1 + r)^n} \tag{4.1}$$
$$= \sum_{t=0}^{n} \left[\frac{(B_t - C_t)}{(1 + r)^t} \right] \tag{4.2}$$

Table 4.1 Manual discounting of a railway project cash flow ($L million)

	Undiscounted				Discounted
	(1)	*(2)*	*(3)* *Net* *benefits*	*(4)* *Discount* *Factor*	*(5)*
Year (t)					*Net benefits*
	Costs	*Benefits*	*(2) – (1)*	$\frac{1}{(1 + 0.08)^t}$	*(3) × (4)*
0	100	0	–100	1	–100
1	400	50	–350	.925	–324.1
2	200	150	–50	.857	–42.9
3	100	200	100	.793	–79.4
4	100	200	100	.735	73.5
5	100	200	100	.681	68.1
6	100	200	100	.63	63.0
7	100	200	100	.583	58.3
8	100	350	250	.54	135.1
Total	**1100**	**1550**	**450**		**NPV = 10.4**

The net present value criterion of a project is the single most important measure of the project's worth. If a project's NPV is positive (i.e. its discounted benefits exceed its discounted costs), then the project should be accepted. If its NPV is negative (its discounted costs exceed its discounted benefits), then the project should be rejected. The NPV assessment criterion will be discussed in more detail in Chapter 5.

In Table 4.1, an 8% discount rate is used to mechanically discount the net benefits of a railway project. The project's NPV can then be estimated by just adding up these discounted net benefits. Columns (1), (2) and (3) show the non-discounted costs, benefits and net benefits (benefits – costs) of the railway project. Column (4) gives the discount factor, $\frac{1}{(1 + .08)^t}$, by which the non-discounted net benefits in column (3) are multiplied, to obtain the discounted value of these net benefits in each year, t, shown in column (5). These discounted net benefits can then be added together to obtain the total discounted net benefits, or net present value, of the project.

Fortunately, this rather tedious manual discounting is not necessary these days. Spreadsheet programs like Lotus 123 and Excel can calculate the NPV of a given stream of costs, benefits or net benefits instantaneously, once a discount rate is specified.

The bottom line of the table shows that the NPV comes to $L10.4 million if an 8% discount rate is used. A NPV greater than zero indicates that the discounted benefits of the project are expected to be greater than its discounted costs and the project will therefore be worth undertaking.

This example illustrates how crucially the estimation of a project's NPV depends on the discount rate employed. A lower discount rate would have deflated future income by less and increased the NPV of the project. A higher discount rate would have deflated future income more heavily and decreased the NPV of the project, possibly changing it from positive to negative. The selection of the appropriate discount rate is therefore a very important issue in project appraisal. The following sections discuss the appropriate discount rate for an individual and for an enterprise if they are discounting a cash flow in a financial analysis. The question of the appropriate discount rate to use in an economic analysis, that is, the level of the **social discount rate**, is left until Chapter 13.

4.6 The individual's discount rate

If an individual is considering making an investment from personal resources (undertaking a project), she is deciding whether to sacrifice some consumption now in the hope of receiving back additional consumption in the future. For the individual, the appropriate discount rate to use when deciding whether such an investment will be worthwhile will be her own marginal rate of time preference, MRTP. This is because the MRTP is the rate of return on current income that individual would have to receive to just make her indifferent to consuming that income now rather than in the future period.

Once a person is sure what his or her personal MRTP is, it can be used to decide whether to undertake personal investments. For example, should the individual with a MRTP of 10 per cent invest $10 now if $12 could be received in 12 months time. This question can be answered by adding the discounted costs and benefits of the potential investment together to obtain its net present value:

$$\text{NPV} = -\$10 + \frac{12}{(1 + 0.1)} = -\$10 + \$10.9 = +\$0.90 > 0 \tag{4.3}$$

The investment of $10 in the present is shown as a drop in current consumption of $10. The $12 earned from the investment in 1 years time, discounted at the individual's MRTP, 0.1, will be worth $10.90 to that individual in current dollars. By adding the –$10 of the initial investment to the $10.90 earned from this investment valued in present dollars, the person will have made a 'profit' of $0.90 in present-day dollar terms from undertaking the investment. From the point of view of her own preferences for current and future income, she would consider herself better off than if she had consumed the $10 now, and so would agree to undertake the investment.[4]

In the general case, an individual with a MRTP of r per cent may be faced with an investment opportunity that would cause his consumption (or net benefits enjoyed) in periods $0,1,2,...n$ to change by the small increments NB_0, NB_1, NB_2,...NB_n. Then the individual would be better off and it would be worth his while making the investment if and only if the present value of the discounted flow of these net benefits, its NPV, were greater than zero where the discount rate used, r, is his own MRTP. That is, if:

$$\text{NPV} = NB_0 + \frac{NB_1}{(1 + r)} + \frac{NB_2}{(1 + r)^2} + \frac{NB_3}{(1 + r)^3} + ... + \frac{NB_n}{(1 + r)^n} > 0 \tag{4.4}$$

In this case, the individual would have more income available, valued in current day dollars, than if he did not make the investment, and should go ahead and undertake the investment.

4.7 Time preference and market interest rates

In the previous section, only an individual's decision on how to allocate his or her income between different time periods was considered. No reference was made to the possible existence of organised financial markets.

Firstly, assume an economy, a desert island, with only two individuals in it, Ms A and Mr B. Suppose the two individuals have different time preferences; A's MRTP = 8 per cent (0.08), and B's = 10 per cent (0.1).

Then A could lend money to B at, for example, a 9 per cent interest rate and both would consider themselves better off. A would lend $10 and receive $10.90 back after 12 months. The present value of this $10.90, payable in 1 year, would be:

$$PV = \frac{\$10.9}{1.08} = \$10.09 \tag{4.5}$$

and the NPV of the whole investment would be:

$$NPV = -\$10 + \$10.09 = \$0.09 \tag{4.6}$$

at A's discount rate, MRTP, of 8 per cent. Hence she would feel better off as a result of lending the $10.

B would borrow $10 now and in 12 months time pay back $10.90. However, using B's MRTP of 10 per cent as the discount rate, this repayment would only have a present value to him of:

$$PV = \frac{\$10.9}{1.10} = \$9.91 \tag{4.7}$$

and the NPV of the whole investment would be:

$$\$10 - \$9.90 = \$0.09 \tag{4.8}$$

Hence B would also feel better off from borrowing the $10.

Theoretically, A could keep lending and B keep borrowing until the point where their MRTPs became equal. This would happen eventually because A's current consumption would decline relative to her future income. She would therefore tend to put more value on her present income and her MRTP would rise. For B, the opposite would occur; his current consumption would increase and his future income would decline as he became more in debt. Hence, B would tend to put more value on future consumption and his MRTP would fall. When eventually A and B reached a point at which their MRTPs were equal, say at 9 per cent, there would be no more opportunity for them to raise their utility by further borrowing and lending.

In a market economy with a freely operating financial market, individuals borrow and lend via financial market intermediaries, but the same principles apply. An individual with a MRTP greater than the market interest rate has an incentive to borrow and to continue doing so up to the point where his MRTP equals that interest rate. The person whose MRTP is less than the market interest rate will wish to lend, and will continue doing so until her MRTP rises to the level of the market interest rate. In the long run, everyone's MRTP should equal the market interest rate. The overall level of interest rates will be determined by the interaction of those supplying and demanding investable funds in the capital market.[5]

If there were freely operating capital markets, with no government intervention in interest rate setting, no taxes, perfect knowledge, perfect competition and no financial market intermediation fees, there would be just one interest rate at which everyone would borrow and lend. This would then be the appropriate discount rate to use in both the financial and economic appraisal of projects. It would equal the MRTP of the whole community, which is called the social rate of time preference, SRTP (as well as the marginal return on invested capital).

However, in the real world there is not one but many interest rates as well as considerable government intervention in the financial market. There are financial intermediation costs so lending rates diverge from borrowing rates. As some borrowers are considered more risky than others and some investments are less secured than others, there will invariably be a spread of borrowing rates. There may not be perfect access to credit. For example, poorer people may not be considered a good risk, so their MRTP may remain above the market interest rate level. This is particularly the case if interest rates are kept artificially low and there is credit rationing.

Finally, since individuals' interest earnings are taxed, people will equate their **post-tax** returns from saving with their MRTP. As people pay different marginal rates of tax, even though they all borrow and lend up to the point where their post-tax returns equal their MRTP, their MRTPs will all be different in the equilibrium situation. For all these reasons the market rate of interest will not represent the MRTP of all members of the community.

4.8 The discount rate in financial analysis — the cost of capital to the project implementor

In a financial analysis market prices are used to value project inputs and outputs, even if these prices are distorted. Market prices are used so that the financial profitability of the project to its implementor can be determined. The market price of capital to the project implementor is the market interest rate, and this represents the cost to the implementor of investing capital in the project. The correct approach to determining the **financial discount rate**, the discount rate used in a financial analysis, is therefore to estimate the actual cost of capital to the project implementor. This will vary depending on whether at the margin the implementor is a borrower or lender of investable funds.

If the project implementor is a **net borrower**, the interest rate at which the enterprise can borrow is the opportunity cost of the funds employed. This market borrowing rate should be used as the financial discount rate for any project appraisal undertaken by the enterprise. If the project implementor intends to draw some funds from its own financial resources and some from market borrowings, the weighted cost of the capital it obtains from these different sources will be the appropriate financial discount rate.

If the firm or government authority considering a project is a **net lender**, in the absence of the project it could invest these funds in the financial market and earn the market lending rate. The opportunity cost of the funds to be used for the project will therefore be the after-tax market lending rate that it could earn on this capital. The project must earn at least this market lending rate for it to be worth doing and the after-tax lending rate should therefore be used as the **financial discount rate** for any project appraisals undertaken by this enterprise. In reality the enterprise will usually want to earn some margin above the market lending rate if the project is considered a riskier use of the firm's funds than available financial investments. The issue of risk premiums is discussed in Chapter 15, Section 15.7.

The following example shows how a financial discount rate will be calculated where the project draws its funds from a variety of sources. Seventy per cent of an infrastructure project in a developing country is to be funded using grant aid from a bilateral donor. Although there will be no direct cost to the recipient government for the donor's component, since such grant aid is limited, and could otherwise be used for alternative projects, it will have a financial **opportunity cost** (the value of the funds in their next best alternative use). At the margin this will be equal to the recipient government's long-term borrowing costs, raised domestically or abroad. The cost of funds to the recipient government is the weighted sum of the long-term government bond rate and the cost of foreign borrowing, where the weights equal the proportions of total government borrowing being raised domestically and abroad. Real government bond rates in this country are on average 12 per cent, and the government draws 20 per cent of its funds from this source. The other 80 per cent of its funds it borrows abroad, where the average real cost of borrowing is 6 per cent. However, since domestic inflation has been approximately 4 per cent above international levels, and the local exchange rate could therefore be expected to devalue by 4 per cent per annum, the principal of these loans will continue to rise by 4 per cent per annum, denominated in local currency. The total real cost of its overseas borrowing will therefore be approximately 10 per cent per annum.

It is planned that the remaining 30 per cent of the project will be funded by local residents. The cost of borrowing to the community will equal the average real commercial lending rate, which is approximately 20 per cent in this country. Then the total weighted real financial cost of funds used in this project will be:

$$0.7[(0.8 \times 10\%) + (0.2 \times 12\%)] + (0.3 \times 20\%) = 13.3\%$$

The weighted cost of capital is also the appropriate financial discount rate for use by public enterprises, which are borrowing or lending in a freely operating capital market. However, it is frequently the case that public enterprises are given grants or subsidised loans by governments and are restricted in the amount they can borrow at these rates. The cost to the government, the ultimate project implementor, is not the subsidised rate but the full market cost to the government of raising capital.[6] In such circumstances, it will not normally be appropriate for the authority to use this subsidised interest rate as its discount rate in a financial analysis. The agency will then require government guidance regarding the discount rate it should employ in financial appraisals.

4.9 Real and nominal discount rates

In the above discussion of discounting and appropriate discount rates the rate of inflation was assumed to be zero, and the effect of inflation on interest and discount rates was ignored. This assumption is now relaxed as most countries experience at least some inflation in prices, and most project appraisals must therefore take account of price inflation.

In Section 2.4 it was indicated that if the analyst expects all input and output prices, domestic and foreign, to experience approximately the same rate of inflation over the life of the project, so that relative prices will remain unchanged, then it will be appropriate to use constant, or real, prices in the cash flow. The use of constant prices in the cash flow is by far the most common way to present financial and economic analyses. If all other inputs and outputs have been valued in real terms, then a **real discount rate** must be used to discount the net cash flow of the project. The real discount rate is calculated by deflating the nominal market interest rate by the expected rate of inflation in the economy. All market interest rates are quoted in nominal, rather than real terms.

For example, in a country in which the long-term inflation rate is projected to be 10 per cent, the **nominal market interest rate** on long-term borrowings made by the project may be 15 per cent per annum. Of this 15 per cent nominal interest rate, approximately 10 percentage points will be needed to compensate lenders for the loss in the real value of their capital due to inflation. Given inflation, the project's capital investment could be expected to increase in value by 10 per cent each year, so the 10 percentage point inflation component of the nominal interest rate is merely a transfer between the borrower and lender of the capital to compensate the lender for the loss of value of his financial holdings. Only the remaining (approximately) 5 percentage points of the nominal interest rate will represent the **real** interest paid by the project, for the use of the capital.

The relationship between the real discount rate, r, the nominal discount rate, R, and the expected inflation rate, f_e is given in (4.9):[7]

$$1 + R = (1 + r)(1 + f_e) \qquad (4.9)$$

$$\therefore \quad r = \frac{(1 + R)}{(1 + f_e)} - 1$$

For the example given above,

$$r = \frac{(1.15)}{(1.1)} - 1 = 0.045, \text{ or } 4.5\%$$

If a project's input and output prices are **not** expected to rise at the same rate over the project's life, it will then be necessary to value inputs and outputs at their expected **nominal** prices for inclusion in the cash flow. They should then be discounted at the nominal market interest rate at which the project has borrowed, in the case of a financial analysis (or a nominal social discount rate in the case of an economic analysis). It will make no difference to the final NPV of a project which method is used — real prices and a real discount rate or nominal prices and a nominal discount rate.

This can be seen from the following general example. If a project's inputs and outputs are expressed in nominal prices and discounted by a nominal discount rate, its NPV can be represented as:

$$\text{NPV} = P_0 Q_0 + \frac{(P_0(1+f).Q_1)}{(1+r)(1+f)} + \frac{(P_0(1+f)^2.Q_2)}{(1+f)^2(1+r)^2} + \frac{(P_0(1+f)^n.Q_n)}{(1+f)^n(1+r)^n} \qquad (4.10)$$

where

> r is the real discount rate
> f is the rate of inflation
> $(1+r)(1+f)$ is 1 plus the nominal discount rate
> P_0 is the weighted sum of the prices of inputs and outputs in the current period, period 0; these will rise only in line with inflation in each period
> Q_x is the quantity of the project's inputs used and outputs produced in the xth period.

The inflation term, $(1+f)$, is used to inflate both input and output prices in the numerator and the real discount rate in the denominator. This term therefore cancels out from the numerator and denominator of (4.10). Hence, this procedure is equivalent to valuing inputs and outputs in real, constant price terms and discounting these real values with a real discount rate. In both cases, the resulting NPV is always a real figure.

Similarly, in the case of an economic analysis, if the cash flow is expressed in constant local dollars then a real social discount rate should be used to discount it. Alternatively, the net benefit flow can be expressed in nominal terms, current value, local dollars and then discounted by the nominal social discount rate, $R = (1+r)(1+f)$. In both financial and economic analyses it is important not to discount a cash flow that is expressed in constant dollars, with a nominal discount rate. Depending on the rate of inflation, the nominal discount rate could be much higher than the correct real discount rate and its use would introduce a serious error into the analysis.

4.10 Non-discounted measures of project worth

Before examining the various discounted measures of a project's worth in the next chapter, this section considers several non-discounted measures of project worth that are commonly used (mainly) in the private sector. Non-discounted measures of project worth are in general based loosely on the Hicks–Kaldor compensation criterion (benefits must exceed costs). However, all fail to distinguish between costs and benefits that occur in different time periods. Figure 4.1 showed a typical time profile of a project, but the net benefits flow of projects will all vary considerably, with some rising to a positive figure much more quickly than others.

For this reason, all non-discounted measures of project worth in common use have major weaknesses and none should be used in any rigorous project appraisal. They are included here to ensure that the reader is aware of their existence and alerted to their deficiencies.

4.10.1 Ranking by inspection

This technique is only applicable in very restrictive circumstances. If two or more projects being compared have the same investment costs and net benefits are received over the same period, but one project has higher net benefits in all or some periods and lower net benefits in none, then this technique can be used. An example of a simple situation where this criterion could be used is given in Table 4.2.

Project B would be selected over project A on the basis of simple inspection. However, the limited applicability of such a technique is obvious.

Table 4.2   Project choice by inspection

	Project A	Project B
Investment cost	1000	1000
Operating costs (p.a.)	200	200
Benefits(p.a.)	300	400

4.10.2 Payback period

This is defined as the number of years it is expected to take from the beginning of the project until the sum of its net earnings (receipts minus operating costs) equals the cost of the project's initial capital investment. The problem with this technique is that it does not tell you anything about the project's net benefit stream after the paying back of the investment. Nor does it take account of differences between projects in the timing of earnings within the payback period.

For example, in Table 4.3 two projects, A and B, have the same payback period, 6 years, but the benefits in A start earlier and are then received evenly over this period, while those of B mainly accrue at the end of the period. Furthermore, the costs of project B occur earlier than those of project A. Finally, after the payback period, project A keeps producing benefits for 12 years, while project B stops production after only 6 years. A discounted analysis would indicate that project A has a much higher net present value, $L797.6 million, than project B, –$275.2 million, but a payback period analysis would be unable to distinguish between the two projects. In fact, since project B has a negative NPV, it should not be selected, while project A has a very high NPV.

Table 4.3 Project choice by the payback period method ($L million)

	Year							
	1	2	3	4	5	6	...	7–18
Investment cost								
Project A	500	500						
Project B	1000							
Operating costs (p.a.)								
Project A	0	50	50	50	50	50	...	50
Project B	0	0	0	50	50	300	...	0
Benefits (p.a.)								
Project A	0	250	250	250	250	250	...	250
Project B	0	0	0	150	250	1000	...	0
Net benefits (p.a.)								
Project A	−500	−300	200	200	200	200	...	200
Project B	−1000	0	0	100	200	700	...	0

Payback period	NPV (@ 8% discount rate)	
Project A	6 years	$L797.6
Project B	6 years	−$L275.2

Another serious problem with this technique is that it does not provide a reliable guide to whether a project should be implemented or not. Is a payback period of 6 years, 10 years or 15 years acceptable or not?

4.10.3 Proceeds per unit of expenditure

This measure is found by dividing total non-discounted net receipts of the project (receipts minus operating costs) by its total investment. On the basis of this criterion a project would be accepted if this ratio exceeded unity by an acceptable amount. In Table 4.4, this technique is used to assess two projects whose time profiles are different.

The proceeds per unit of investment method would rank projects A and B equally, although the benefits of project A are received earlier and the costs paid later. The NPV of project A would be higher than that of project B. At an 8 per cent discount rate, project A has a NPV of $7.5 million but project B has a negative NPV of −$L90 million. Like the payback period technique, this criterion fails to capture significant differences in the timing of the two projects' net benefits and its use could therefore cause serious errors to be made in project selection.

The basic flaw in all of these non-discounted measures of project worth is that they fail to take account of the differences in the time profile, or time stream, of projects' net benefits. In order to compare projects that have cash flows with different net benefit time profiles, it is necessary to use discounted measures of project worth. These are discussed in the following chapter.

Table 4.4 Project choice by the proceeds per unit of investment method ($L million)

	Years					
	1	*2*	*3*	*4*	*5*	*6*
Investment cost						
Project A	400	400				
Project B	800					
Operating costs (p.a.)						
Project A	0	50	50	50	50	50
Project B	0	0	0	50	50	300
Benefits(p.a.)						
Project A	0	250	250	250	250	250
Project B	0	0	0	150	250	1000
Net benefits (p.a.)						
Project A	−400	−200	200	200	200	200
Project B	−800	0	0	100	200	700
Proceeds per unit of investment	NPV @ 8% discount rate					
Project A 1.25	$L26.1					
Project B 1.25	−$L90.0					

Exercises

1–6. Calculate the financial NPV of the six projects in the exercises at the end of Chapter 3. Assume that in each case the real cost of funds to the implementing agency is 10 per cent.

What will the NPV of these projects be if the real cost of funds is only 7 per cent.

References

Hicks, J., 1939. 'Foundations of welfare economics', *Economic Journal*, Vol. 49: 696–712.

Kaldor, N., 1939. 'Welfare propositions in economics and inter-personal comparisons of utility', *Economic Journal*, 49: 522–49.

Sugden, R. and Williams, A., 1978. *The Principles of Practical Cost-Benefit Analysis*, Oxford University Press, Oxford, pp. 25–8.

Further reading

Duvingneau, J.C. and Prasad, R.N., 1984. *Guidelines for Calculating Financial and Economic Rates of Return for DFC Projects*, World Bank Technical Paper No. 33, Chapters 4, 5.

Gittinger, J. Price, 1982. *Economic Analysis of Agricultural Projects*, 2nd edn, Johns Hopkins University Press, Baltimore, Chapter 5.

Irvin, G., 1978. *Modern Cost-Benefit Methods*, Macmillan, London, Chapter 1.

Pearce, D.W. and Nash, C.A., 1981. *The Social Appraisal of Projects: A Text in Cost Benefit Analysis*, Macmillan, London, Chapter 4.

Sugden, R. and Williams, A., 1978. *The Principles of Practical Cost-Benefit Analysis*, Oxford University Press, Oxford, Chapter 2.

UNIDO, 1972. *Guidelines for Project Evaluation*, United Nations, New York, Chapter 13.

Endnotes

1   The marginal utility of income is defined as the change in utility or well-being that an individual gains from a unit change in his or her income, $\dfrac{dU}{dY}$, where U is utility and Y is income.

2   As discussed in Section 4.1.2, the marginal utility of income for a given individual is usually expected to be negative with respect to a rise in income. That is, the rate of interest in utility experienced from a given increase in income is expected to fall as income rises.

3   It is usually assumed that the discount put on the value of future income streams is constant. That is, people prefer income in period 1 over that in period 2, by the same amount by which they prefer income in period 2 over that in period 3. This assumption can be relaxed, however, if there is evidence to the contrary.

4   A formal treatment of time preference using indifference curves, showing an individual's preference between consumption in period 0 and period 1, is given by Sugden and Williams (1978, pp. 15–28).

5   The interaction of borrowers and lenders of investable funds in a competitive capital market is discussed in more detail in Chapter 14. Figure 14.1 shows that a unique market interest rate will emerge if stringent assumptions are made about perfect competition, knowledge and lack of government.

6   Virtually all governments, except those of some oil-rich countries, are net borrowers, so the market cost of borrowing will be the relevant discount rate to use in a financial analysis.

7   When the expected inflation rate and the real discount rate are relatively small, discounting by $R = (1 + r)(1 + f)$ is roughly equivalent to using an approximate nominal discount rate, $R = r + f$. This is acceptable if 'rf' is very small. In this case: $1 + R = (1 + r)(1 + f) \cong 1 + r + f$.

The nominal cash flow then can be discounted at the approximate nominal discount rate, $r + f$, to give the real discounted cash flow of the project.

CHAPTER 5

Discounted project assessment criteria

In the previous chapter we considered the reasons why individuals and governments have time preference, and how time preference is accommodated in project analysis by **discounting** future income flows. The various non-discounted measures of project worth that were examined were found to be inappropriate methods of choosing between different projects in all but a few, very restricted, situations.

The two most commonly used **discounted** measures of a project's net benefit are its **net present value** and **internal rate of return**. The domestic resource cost ratio, benefit cost ratio and net benefit investment ratio will also be discussed in this chapter, as they may also be used in particular circumstances and have their own advantages.

5.1 Project net present value, NPV

As discussed in Chapter 4, the NPV measure of project worth is the most useful and one of the most commonly used criteria for determining whether a project should be accepted.

5.1.1 Definition of NPV

The net present value of a project is simply the present value, PV, of its net benefit stream. It is obtained by discounting the stream of net benefits produced by the project over its lifetime, back to its value in the chosen base period, usually the present. The net present value formula is:

$$\text{NPV} = \sum_{t=0}^{n} \frac{(B_t - C_t)}{(1 + r)^t} \tag{5.1}$$

where
B_t are project benefits in period t
C_t are project costs in period t
r is the appropriate financial or economic discount rate
n is the number of years for which the project will operate.

In Table 4.1, the NPV of a railway project was estimated mechanically. The net benefits of the project each year were deflated by a factor equal to $\frac{1}{(1 + r)^t}$, where r was the discount rate and t the year in which the net benefits of the project were received. These discounted net benefits were then added together for the 'n' years of the project. Fortunately, computer programs such as Lotus 123 and Excel can easily calculate the present value of any cost, benefit or net benefit flow constructed by the analyst.[1]

5.1.2 Decision rule for independent projects

Independent projects are projects that are not in any way substitutes for each other. The analyst is free to choose among such projects, selecting any (or all or none) that will contribute positively to community welfare. In the case of an independent project, the decision rule in relation to its estimated NPV is:

approve any project for which NPV ≥ 0

If the NPV of the project is negative, the funds that would otherwise have been used for this investment should be left in the bank, returned to (or not collected from) tax-payers or used to implement a project whose NPV is positive. If two independent projects, for example a road and a fisheries project in different locations, are being considered, and both have a positive NPV, then **both** should be undertaken. Assuming there is no budget constraint, it will not be necessary to choose between these projects, so it is not important which has the higher NPV. Both will increase community welfare if they are undertaken, and hence both should be undertaken.

5.1.3 Decision rule for mutually exclusive projects

A mutually exclusive project is defined as a project that can only be implemented at the expense of an alternative project as they are in some sense substitutes for each other. Examples of mutually exclusive projects include two versions of the same project (with different technologies, timing or scale), for example two dams on one site, or two factories to supply the one market. By choosing one mutually exclusive project, **the opportunity to do the other will be lost**. If only one of these projects has a positive NPV, the choice is straightforward — the one with the negative NPV should be discarded. But if both projects have a positive NPV, it will be necessary to decide which of them to do on the basis of some other criterion. Both cannot be done by definition, because they are mutually exclusive.

Since the community's chance to undertake the project will not be repeated, it must maximise the net benefits it will receive from the choice it makes. The community will optimise its welfare if it chooses the project with the highest NPV. **The decision rule for mutually exclusive projects is therefore to accept the project with the highest NPV.**

For example, two dams may be proposed for one prime site in a gorge on a fast flowing river, a classic example of mutually exclusive projects. Dam A is small but has a high ratio of discounted benefits to costs (1.37). However, the total benefits it produces, and hence its NPV, are quite small, only $1 million. The alternative dam, B, is much larger and has much larger benefits as well as higher costs. Although its

Table 5.1 Use of NPV to select between mutually exclusive projects ($L million)

					Years					
	1	2	3	4	5	6	7	8	9	10
Dam A										
Costs	3									
Benefits	0	1	1	1	1	1	.5			
Net benefits	−3	1	1	1	1	1	.5			
NPV* $ 1 million										
PV (benefits/costs) = 1.37										
DAM B										
Costs	500									
Benefits	0	100	100	100	100	100	100	100	100	100
Net benefits	−500	100	100	100	100	100	100	100	100	50
NPV* $33 million										
PV (benefits/costs) = 1.07										

* Discount rate 10%

NPV is large, $33 million, its ratio of discounted benefits to costs is much lower than project A's, only 1.07. The two projects' cash flows, NPVs and ratios of benefits to costs are shown in Table 5.1.

If the two dam projects were independent and the country could therefore construct both, then it should do so as they both have positive NPVs. However, since the projects are mutually exclusive, the dam with the higher NPV should be selected, that is, dam B. If dam A were constructed, a gain of only $1 million would be realised, and the community would be prevented for ever from gaining the much greater net benefits of $33 million, which dam B is expected to produce. The opportunity of gaining the other $32 million of benefits from this unique dam site would be lost forever. Consequently, in choosing between mutually exclusive projects, the one with the highest NPV should always be selected.

The choice between two or more projects that have a different life, timing or scale is essentially a choice between mutually exclusive projects, since only one scale, start-up date or project life, can be selected for a given project among the range of alternatives. The basic decision rule is the same in these cases as for other mutually exclusive projects — that the length, timing and scale of the project should be chosen so as to maximise its NPV. It is often useful to map, for example, the range of alternative scales of a project against the project's NPV at these scales, to clearly see at which scale NPV is maximised, as shown in Figure 5.1. This can be done simply by using a computer program such as Costab (Temple, 1993) and Riskmaster (Savvides, 1989) *inter alia*. The issues of the optimal scale, timing and length of projects are discussed in more detail in Jenkins and Harberger (1991, Chapter 5).

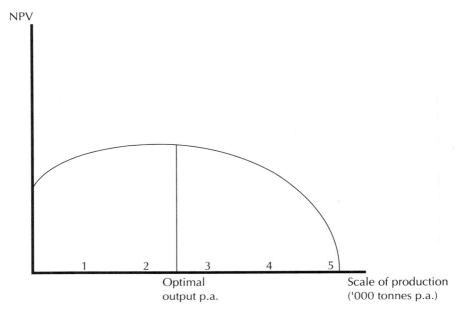

NPV

1   2   3   4   5

Optimal
output p.a.

Scale of production
('000 tonnes p.a.)

Figure 5.1 *Optimal scale of production*

5.1.4 Ranking of alternative projects under a budget constraint

Sometimes a government may have more viable projects with positive NPVs ready to implement than it has available development capital to finance. If this is an unusual occurrence, rather than the norm, the government has a **single period budget constraint**. This may occur because of some unexpected short-fall in revenue (due, for example, to a recession), an unfavourable movement in the country's terms of trade, or an increase in other outlays due, for example, to a natural disaster. In this situation, the government will need to chose which of these alternative viable projects it should select.

The project's NPVs **cannot** be used to rank and choose between these projects without further manipulation. If there is a single period budget constraint, the scarce resource as far as the government is concerned will be the **investment** costs of the project, which will have to be met from government revenue in the next few years, rather than the project's operating costs. These will be drawn from the project's revenue, and presumably will not be a cost for government. The government will want to know which of its alternative viable projects will earn the greatest net receipts (receipts minus operating costs) per unit of investment it outlays.

The ratio of the present value of a project's benefits minus its operating costs, to the present value of its investment cost, is called its **net benefit investment ratio, NBIR**. As is discussed in more detail in Section 5.4, the NBIR is the correct assessment criterion to use when there is a single period budget constraint. It indicates which of the alternative viable projects will earn the greatest net receipts per unit of investment.

A project's NPV, on the other hand, can only show the difference between its discounted benefits and discounted costs, including operating costs, over the project's whole life. The project with the highest NPV is not necessarily the one with the highest net receipts per unit of investment.

Although projects' NPVs cannot be used directly to choose between viable projects if there is a short-term budget constraint, they can be used after some manipulation. However, because this is a more cumbersome technique than ranking projects using their NBIR, this method is shown in the first appendix to this chapter.

If the government's investment budget is always inadequate to fund all the viable projects that have been identified, then the government is said to have a **multi-period**, rather than a single period budget constraint. This may be an indication that the discount rate being used to discount projects' cash flows has been set too low. If a higher discount rate were used then fewer projects would have a positive NPV. Thus the government or analyst may need to raise the discount rate being used sequentially, up to the point that the value of those projects with a positive NPV just exhausts the available government budget.

Alternatively, if the analyst is confident that the discount rate being used has been set equal to the opportunity cost of public funds in the country concerned, and yet the number of viable projects regularly exceeds the funds available, it may be appropriate for the government to raise more funds, from taxation or from domestic or international borrowing, or to allow private enterprises to carry out the projects. If the country already has large outstanding loans, which it is having trouble servicing, and the electorate is unwilling to pay more taxes, options involving increased debt or taxation may not be feasible. In this case, the true opportunity cost of capital is probably higher than the discount rate being used, and the discount rate should be raised.

5.1.5 Summarising the advantages of the NPV approach

The major advantage of the net present value selection criterion is that it is simple to use and does not rely on complex conventions about where costs and benefits are netted out, as do some of the ratio measures examined later in this chapter. In addition, it is the only selection criterion that can correctly be used to choose between mutually exclusive projects, without further manipulation. A project's financial and economic NPV should routinely be estimated by the project analyst, for every project considered.

5.1.6 Disadvantages of the NPV measure

Like all discounted measures except the internal rate of return, the use of the net present value criterion relies on the prior selection of an appropriate discount rate. Furthermore, although it is simple to use, its meaning may not be intuitively obvious to non-economist administrators or politicians. A brief explanation of how an NPV is estimated may therefore be a useful appendix to any report employing it. Furthermore, although it can be used when there is a budget constraint, it is not the simplest method for this situation, especially for a large and complex investment budget. If the budget constraint is long term, it will be necessary to raise the discount rate being used or the size of the budget, so that only projects with a positive NPV will be selected, in which case NPV will again be the most useful criterion for deciding whether to accept or reject projects.

5.2 The internal rate of return of a project, IRR

The internal rate of return, IRR, of a project is probably the most commonly used assessment criterion in project appraisal. This is primarily because the concept of an IRR is in some ways comparable to the profit rate of a project and is therefore easy for non-economists to understand. Furthermore, it does not rely on the selection of a predetermined discount rate. Nevertheless, it does have some limitations as a project selection technique, which are discussed further below.

5.2.1 Definition of the internal rate of return

The internal rate of return is the discount rate that, if used to discount a project's costs and benefits, will just make the project's net present value equal to zero.

Thus the internal rate of return is the discount rate, r^*, at which:

$$NPV = \sum_{t=0}^{n} \frac{(B_t - C_t)}{(1 + r^*)^t} = 0 \tag{5.2}$$

Since the internal rate of return is the discount rate internal to the project, its calculation does not depend on prior selection of a discount rate. A project's internal rate of return can therefore be thought of as the discount rate at which it would be just worthwhile doing the project. For a financial analysis, it would be the maximum interest rate that the project could afford to pay on its funds and still recover all its investment and operating costs.

If the internal rate of return is calculated for a financial appraisal in which all values are measured in market prices, it is called either the financial rate of return, FRR, or the financial internal rate of return, FIRR, of the project. If the internal rate of return is calculated for an economic appraisal, in which values are measured in shadow prices, then it will be called the economic rate of return, ERR, or the economic internal rate of return, EIRR, of the project. The World Bank, for example, employs the terms FRR and ERR in its appraisals.

Table 5.2 illustrates how the internal rate of return for a road project can be calculated mechanically.

At a discount rate of 5 per cent, the NPV of the project is very high, $1130.6 million. At a higher discount rate of 10 per cent, the NPV drops to $241.9 million. At a discount rate of 15 per cent, the NPV becomes negative, –$314.7 million. Trying a somewhat lower rate, 12 per cent, the NPV is only slightly negative, –$12 million, and at 11.89 per cent, the NPV is zero. By iteration it is therefore possible to determine

Table 5.2 Estimation of the internal rate of return of a road project ($L million)

	Year										
	1	*2*	*3*	*4*	*5*	*6*	*7*	*8*	*9*	*10*	*11*
Costs											
Land	1000										
Earthworks	200	600	400								
Equipment	190	200									
Labour	120	120	120								
Total costs	1510	920	520	0	0	0	0	0	0	0	0
Benefits from:											
Time savings	0	0	0	300	300	300	300	300	300	300	300
Maintenance Savings	0	0	0	100	100	100	100	100	100	100	100
Car depreciation Savings	0	0	0	290	290	290	290	290	290	290	290
Total benefits	0	0	0	690	690	690	690	690	690	690	690
Net benefits	−1510	−920	−520	690	690	690	690	690	690	690	690

NPV at:

Discount rate (%)	NPV ($ million)
5	1130.6
10	241.9
15	−314.7
12	−12.0
at IRR = 11.8965%	**0.0**

the discount rate that just makes the project's NPV equal to zero. This rate is the **internal rate of return** of the project.

Fortunately, spreadsheet programs like Lotus 123 and Excel, which can calculate the **IRR** of a project's net benefit flow once a starting value for the iteration is supplied, are now available.[2]

5.2.2 Decision rule for independent projects

In the case of independent projects, all projects with an internal rate of return greater than some **target rate** of return, r', should be accepted. If a project's IRR is less than the appropriate target rate, it should not be accepted.

This target discount rate will be set on the basis of financial or economic criteria, depending on whether a financial or economic analysis is being undertaken. Essentially, the target rate of return will be the same rate as the financial or social discount rate that is employed in the calculation of the project's net present value. Therefore the use of the IRR does not avoid the need to estimate a financial or social discount rate, it merely delays the need to use such a target discount rate until after the IRR has been calculated.

5.2.3 The IRR and mutually exclusive projects

If the government is considering two projects that are mutually exclusive, both having an IRR greater than the target rate, it **cannot** merely choose the project with the highest IRR. The two dams discussed in Table 5.1 are used again in Table 5.3 to show why IRR cannot be used to choose between mutually exclusive projects.

The smaller dam, A, has a higher IRR, 22%, than does dam B, whose IRR is only 13%. However, as was discussed previously, because dam B will provide higher discounted net benefits than dam A, and the two are mutually exclusive projects, dam B should be selected.

Figure 5.2 also illustrates this case.[3] Project A has a higher IRR, IRR_A, than project B, IRR_B. However, at the appropriate social (or financial) discount rate, which we have assumed is R_t'' in this case, project B has a higher NPV. If the two projects are mutually exclusive, project B should be selected as it has a higher NPV at R_t''. The IRR of the projects is irrelevant in choosing between mutually exclusive projects, as long as both projects have IRRs that exceed the target discount rate, R_t''. If the social discount rate were R_t, then project A would have the higher NPV and should be chosen. If the social discount rate were the much higher R_t', only A would have a positive NPV, and obviously only it should be undertaken, even if the projects were independent.

While the IRR cannot be used directly to chose between mutually exclusive projects, it can be employed with further manipulation. This manipulation entails subtracting the cash flow of the smaller project from the cash flow of the larger one and calculating the internal rate of return of the residual cash flow. If the residual cash flow's internal rate of return exceeds the target discount rate, which could only occur if the larger project has a higher NPV, then the larger project should be undertaken.

Table 5.4 illustrates this method in the case of the two dam projects.

Table 5.3 Impossibility of directly using IRR to choose between mutually exclusive projects ($ million)

					Years					
	1	2	3	4	5	6	7	8	9	10
Dam A										
Net benefits	−3	1	1	1	1	1	.5			
NPV*	$1 million									
IRR	22.2%									
Dam B										
Net benefits	−500	100	100	100	100	100	100	100	100	50
NPV*	$33 million									
IRR	13.7%									

Discount rate and target IRR rate = 10%

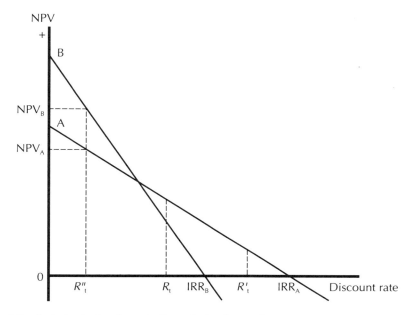

Figure 5.2 *Project selection for mutually exclusive dam projects*

Table 5.4 Use of IRR after manipulation to choose between mutually exclusive projects ($L million)

	Year									
	1	*2*	*3*	*4*	*5*	*6*	*7*	*8*	*9*	*10*
Dam A										
Net benefits	−3	1	1	1	1	1	.5			
Dam B										
Net benefits	−500	100	100	100	100	100	100	100	100	50
Residual cash flow										
= NB for project B − NB for project A										
	−497	99	99	99	99	99	99.5	100	100	50
IRR residual cash flow **13.66%**										
Target rate **10%**										

The IRR of the residual cash flow (project B's cash flow minus project A's) is 13.66 per cent, which is greater than the target discount rate of 10 per cent. As the additional investment involved will yield a rate of return greater than the target rate, it will be worthwhile undertaking the larger dam, B. Since this investment opportunity will be lost for ever if it is not undertaken now, the larger dam should in fact be built.

5.2.4 Ranking of alternative projects under a budget constraint

Another common misconception regarding the IRR is that it can be used to choose between alternative independent projects if the government has a single period budget constraint. However, the internal rate of return of projects **cannot** be used to rank a group of independent projects whose IRR is greater than the target rate. If all of the projects have an IRR greater than the target discount rate, all that can be said in this situation is that all projects should be done.

The problems that would arise if IRR is used in this way can be seen from Figure 5.3. Project D has a higher internal rate of return than project C, but at RT″, the social discount rate, the NPV of project C is greater than the NPV of project D.[4] The use of the two selection criteria will yield contradictory results. **This is because it is incorrect to use either the internal rate of return or the net present value** of the two projects to rank projects if the projects are **independent**. All that the IRR will tell us is that independent projects should be implemented if their IRR is greater than the target rate of return, and not if their IRRs are less than this target rate. IRR cannot be used to rank projects if there is a short-term budget constraint for much the same reason as NPV cannot be used. It does not differentiate between a project's investment costs, which are in short supply in this situation, and operating costs, which will not necessarily be in short supply. As was discussed in Section 5.1.4, if there is a short-term budget constraint, the net benefit investment ratio is the best selection criterion to employ to rank alternative projects.

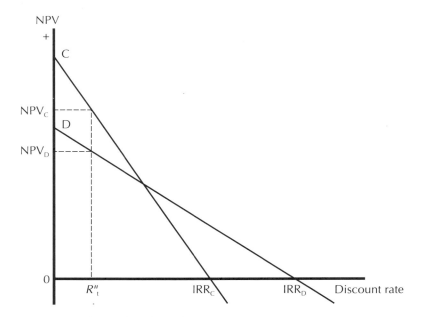

Figure 5.3 *Project selection for independent projects*

If there is a **long-term** budget constraint, the target rate of return should be raised to the point where the value of those projects with an internal rate of return greater than the target discount rate just exhausts the available funds. This occurs at SDR$_2$ in Figure 5.4. At this discount rate, only projects B and C will have a higher IRR than the target rate, and therefore only these two projects should be selected.[5]

This figure also shows why in the situation of a long-term budget constraint it is **incorrect** to merely select those projects with the highest NPV until the budget is exhausted. For example, the total government budget may be $L100 million, but there may be three viable projects under consideration, A, B and C, each with investment costs of $L50 million. The NPVs of the alternative projects A, B and C will fall as the discount rate increases.[6] The internal rates of return of the three projects (IRR$_A$, IRR$_B$, IRR$_C$), are the discount rates at which their NPVs just equal zero.[7] At the first discount rate employed by the analyst, DR$_1$, all three projects have a positive NPV, but projects A and B have the higher NPVs. Since together their investment costs exhaust the budget, the analyst may be tempted to recommend that projects A and B be implemented, and project C be dropped. However, if the budget constraint is a long-term one, this indicates that the opportunity cost of capital for this country is in fact higher than DR$_1$, possibly DR$_2$. At this higher discount rate, project A has a negative NPV and should not be undertaken at all. Projects B and C, which are now the only ones with a positive NPV, should instead be selected. Hence, once the discount rate has been raised to its appropriate long-term level, the NPV of a project will be a reliable method of determining whether to accept it or not. However, NPV

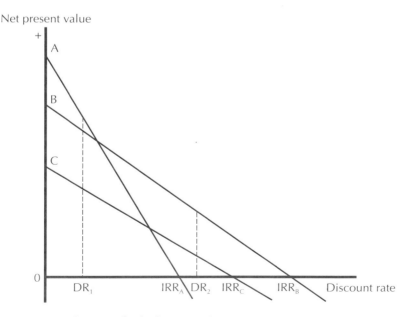

Figure 5.4   *Project selection with a budget constraint*

should not be used as a criterion for selection until the discount rate has been set at a level at which the supply of funds is equal to the cost of the remaining viable projects.

5.2.5 Advantages of the IRR

The major advantage of the internal rate of return is that it is the only measure of project worth that takes account of the time profile of a project but can be calculated without reference to a predetermined discount rate. For international institutions like the World Bank this is a major advantage, as it overcomes the political problems that would arise if they had to select different discount rates in different member countries or use ones chosen by recipient governments. In addition to the technical problems of determining different financial and social discount rates, it would be seen as unfair if some countries received more loan funds because their discount rate was set lower than the discount rate of other countries.[8]

Another major advantage of the internal rate of return is that it is readily understood as a measure of project worth by non-economists. This is because it is closely related to the commercial concept of the return on investment.

5.2.6 Disadvantages of the IRR

Apart from the inappropriateness of using IRR to choose between mutually exclusive projects and independent projects when there is a single period budget constraint, the IRR methodology has several other disadvantages. Firstly, a project must have at least one negative cash flow period before it is possible to calculate its internal rate of return. This is because the net present value of the project will always be positive, no matter how high the discount rate used to discount it, unless the project has at least one negative cash flow period. However, this is not normally a problem as most projects will have at least one negative cash flow period, particularly as the periods in the cash flow can be specified as months or quarters if necessary, rather than years.

A second problem with the IRR is that in some instances it may be possible to compute more than one IRR for a project. This is because the internal rate of return is just the solution of a polynomial, and the net benefit stream of the project will have more than one root, and hence more than one IRR if the project's net benefit cash flow becomes negative again after the initial investment period. This situation is shown in Figure 5.5, which shows the net benefit stream of an oil drilling project. This becomes negative half-way through the project's life because it is necessary to replace rigs after a number of years of use.

If a project does have more than one internal rate of return, then **neither** can be reliably used and another decision rule, such as NPV, must be used rather than IRR. However, in practice this is not a common problem.

Finally, prior to the advent of business calculators and computer software programs like Lotus 123, estimation of the internal rate of return was a tedious process involving interpolation. This is no longer a problem.

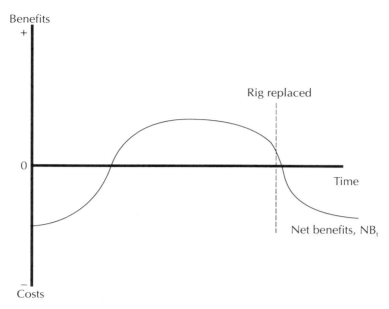

Figure 5.5   *Time profile of an oil drilling project*

5.3 The net benefit investment ratio, NBIR

As has been discussed in several of the previous sections, the NBIR is the most convenient selection criterion to use when there is a single period budget constraint.

5.3.1 Definition of the net benefit investment ratio

The net benefit investment ratio, NBIR, of a project is the ratio of the present value of the project's benefits, net of operating costs, to the present value of its investment costs. Its formula is given by:

$$\text{NBIR} = \frac{\displaystyle\sum_{t=0}^{n} \frac{(B_t - OC_t)}{(1+r)^t}}{\displaystyle\sum_{t=0}^{n} \frac{IC_t}{(1+r)^t}} \tag{5.3}$$

where

   OC_t are the project's operating costs in period t
   IC_t are the project's investment costs in period t
   B_t are the benefits in period t
   r is the appropriate discount rate.

   The NBIR therefore shows the value of the project's discounted benefits, net of operating costs, per unit of investment.

Gittinger (1982) gives an alternative, probably more useful, specification of the formula:

$$\text{NBIR} = \frac{\displaystyle\sum_{t=0}^{n} \frac{N_t}{(1+r)^t}}{\displaystyle\sum_{t=0}^{n} \frac{K_t}{(1+r)^t}} \tag{5.4}$$

where

N_t is the incremental net benefit of the project in later years when the net benefit stream has turned positive

K_t is the incremental net benefit of the project in the early years when the net benefit stream is still negative

In this situation the net benefit investment ratio measures the ratio of the project's benefits, net of operating costs, to its actual budget cost to the government. Any small benefits generated in the early years are used to defray the project's investment costs. Any small investment outlays in later years of the project, which are financed from project benefits, do not show up in the denominator, as they will not be a cost for the government.

5.3.2 Decision rule of net benefit investment ratio

The decision rule for the net benefit investment ratio is that all projects that have a net benefit investment ratio greater than unity should be selected. This selection criterion is completely compatible with those for the net present value and the internal rate of return of a project, as can be seen from the second appendix to this chapter.

5.3.3 The NBIR and ranking of projects with a single period budget constraint

If there is a single period budget constraint and it is necessary to choose between independent projects, all of which pass the above selection criterion, then the net benefit investment ratio is the appropriate criterion to use. The NBIR of all projects under consideration should be estimated, and those with the highest net benefit investment ratio should be selected, up to the point where the budget is exhausted. This is an appropriate approach because, at a given discount rate, the net benefit investment ratio shows which projects have the highest return per unit of investment. If the government has a single period budget constraint, it is precisely these investment funds that are in short supply.[9]

Table 5.5 shows how the use of the NBIR criterion would simplify the ranking of the five viable projects considered in appendix Table A5.1 when the government faced a short-term budget constraint of $L20 million.

Once the NBIR of each project has been calculated, in the last column of Table 5.5, it is a simple matter to rank the projects by their NBIR and determine which

Table 5.5 Use of NBIR to select projects when there is a single period budget constraint ($L million)

Project	Investment cost (IC)	NPV (B – C)	Benefits (B)	Operating cost (OC)	NR (B – OC)	NBIR (B – OC)/IC
A	3	10	14	1	13	4.33
B	5	15	22	2	20	4
C	2	6	8.5	.5	8	4
D	10	22	35	3	32	3.2
E	10	20	32	2	30	3
Total	**30**					

Ranking according to NBIR: Projects A, B, C, D, then E

should be included in the government's investment budget. Project A has the highest NBIR, followed by projects B and C, then D and finally E. Projects A, B, C and D should therefore be given highest priority and since they will exhaust the government's investment budget, project E should be left until some later date. This is the same outcome produced by grouping projects and finding the group with the highest NPV, as is done in the first appendix to this chapter. However, for a large investment program it is a much less cumbersome exercise to rank the alternative projects by their NBIR.

5.3.4 Advantages of the NBIR

The main advantage of the net benefit investment ratio is its capacity to determine the group of priority projects if there is a single period budget, or investment, constraint. However, the issue of ranking may not always be of great practical importance. Some countries may not often have such a large range of potential projects, which are analysed, economically viable and ready to be implemented, that they have to choose between them. Furthermore, once projects meet formal selection criteria, if they do have to be ranked because of a budget constraint, they may more frequently be ranked on the basis of criteria such as administrative feasibility or the promotion of social or political objectives. Nevertheless, if projects have been ranked using their NBIR, the analyst will be able to show the social cost of not selecting projects with the highest returns per unit of investment.

5.3.5 Limitations of the NBIR

The net benefit investment ratio is not suitable for choosing between mutually exclusive projects, for the same reason that the IRR cannot be used for this purpose. This is because in choosing between mutually exclusive projects, a project with a high NBIR but low absolute net present value should not receive priority over a project with a higher net present value, even if it has a lower NBIR. The NBIR is only a relative measure of project worth, while NPV shows the absolute change in welfare from selecting alternative mutually exclusive projects.

The main disadvantage of the net benefit investment ratio is that the conventions used for allocating certain costs (such as maintenance) between investment and operating costs are likely to vary between institutions unless a rigorous control of methodology is maintained. Any difference in conventions would make it impossible to compare net benefit investment ratios for different projects in order to rank them.

5.4 The domestic resource cost ratio, DRCR

The domestic resource cost ratio is a quite commonly used method of determining the net benefit to a country of implementing a particular trade oriented project or trade policy. It can also be used for a range of broader purposes, including determination of a country's comparative advantage.

5.4.1 Definition of the domestic resource cost ratio

In its simplest form, the domestic resource cost ratio or Bruno ratio (Bruno, 1967) is an undiscounted measure of project worth calculated for a single typical year of project operation. For the reasons discussed in the previous chapter, undiscounted measures are excessively crude and almost invariably inaccurate. For this reason, only the discounted version of the domestic resource cost ratio, the modified domestic resource cost ratio or internal exchange rate method, which was developed subsequently, will be discussed.

In the numerator of the discounted domestic resource cost ratio, or DRCR, is the present value of the project's net domestic resource costs. These are the costs of any inputs the project purchases in the local economy minus any domestic sales, all valued in domestic prices and denominated in local currency. In the denominator of the DRCR is the present value of the project's net foreign exchange earnings. These are the value of the project's exports minus its import costs, all valued in foreign exchange. The formula for the domestic resource cost ratio is therefore:

$$\text{DRCR} = \frac{\displaystyle\sum_{t=0}^{n} \frac{(C_{tl} - B_{tl})}{(1 + r)^t}(\$L)}{\displaystyle\sum_{t=0}^{n} \frac{(B_{tf} - C_{tf})}{(1 + r)^t}(\$US)} \tag{5.5}$$

where

B_{tl} are the benefits of the project obtained in local currency
C_{tl} are the costs of the project incurred in local currency
B_{tf} are the benefits of the project obtained in foreign exchange
C_{tf} are the costs of the projects incurred in foreign exchange.

5.4.2 Decision rule for the DRCR

The decision rule when undertaking a financial appraisal is that a project should be accepted if its domestic resource cost ratio is less than or equal to the **official exchange**

rate, OER. That is, the project should proceed if it uses less domestic resources, measured in local prices, to earn 1 unit of foreign exchange than is the norm for the whole economy.[10]

The modified domestic resource cost ratio is also called the internal exchange rate approach. This is because calculation of the DRCR is independent of any predetermined exchange rate, in the same way that the calculation of the internal rate of return is independent of any predetermined discount rate. It produces its own internal 'exchange rate', specific to the project. This can then be compared with the official exchange rate in the case of a financial analysis,[11] to determine whether the project should be accepted. As can be seen from the second appendix to this chapter, which compares the five selection criteria, this decision rule is mathematically equivalent to those for the other four selection criteria considered.

Tables 5.6a and 5.6b give an example of the calculation of the DRCR for an export processing zone project. The sum of the discounted domestic production costs, measured in local dollars, is estimated in Table 5.6a. The sum of the discounted net foreign exchange earnings of the project, measured in US dollars, is calculated in Table 5.6b.

The DRCR is the ratio of the sum of the discounted net local costs to the sum of the discounted net foreign exchange benefits. The project's DRCR is estimated to be $L8.21 per $US.

If the official exchange rate in the country is $\frac{\$L8}{\$US1}$, a financial analysis of the project will indicate that it is not worthwhile doing. This is because the project is expected to use more domestic resources to earn a dollar of foreign exchange than is the norm for the economy.

Table 5.6a Estimation of the domestic resource cost ratio, special economic zone project — local cost component (numerator) ($L million)

	Years								
	1	*2*	*3*	*4*	*5*	*6*	*7*	*...*	*30*
Local costs									
Investment	40	60	30	10					
Production	0	50	75	90	100	100	100	...	100
Total local costs	40	110	105	100	100	100	100	...	100
Local sales	0	0	20	25	25	25	25	...	25
Net local costs									
(total local costs – local sales)	40	110	85	75	75	75	75	...	75
PV of net local costs $L712 million									

Table 5.6b Estimation of the domestic resource cost ratio, special economic zone
project — foreign exchange component (denominator) (million $US)

	Years								
	1	*2*	*3*	*4*	*5*	*6*	*7*	*...*	*30*
Foreign exchange earnings									
Exported output	0	3	20	30	30	30	30	...	30
Foreign exchange costs									
Imported investment goods	20	40	12	2					
Other imported inputs	0	5	7	8	10	10	10	...	10
Net foreign exchange earnings (exports – imports)	–20	–42	1	20	20	20	20	...	20
PV of net foreign exchange earnings	$US 86.7								

$$\text{DRCR} = \frac{\text{PV of net local costs}}{\text{PV of net forex earnings}} = \frac{\$L711.6}{\$US86.7} = 8.21 \ \$L \text{ per } \$US$$

5.4.3 Advantages of the DRCR

The main advantage of this approach is that its decision rule can be readily understood by non-economists. Particularly in economies facing serious balance of payments constraints and where this imbalance is a major preoccupation of policy makers, the domestic resource cost ratio will clearly show the potential of a project to earn foreign exchange, in a form that can be used to win support from non-economist decision-makers.

The other advantage of the DRCR is that it avoids the need to specify a shadow exchange rate in advance. This can be an advantage for an international agency, in the same way that the internal rate of return criterion can be useful, in that the latter avoids having to calculate a social discount rate in advance.[12]

5.4.4 Limitations of the DRCR

Like the IRR and NPV criteria, the DRCR cannot be used to rank projects that pass the selection criterion if the government faces a single period budget constraint. In addition, the DRCR cannot be used to choose between mutually exclusive projects if both use less domestic resources to earn a unit of foreign exchange than the OER. This is because it does not indicate which of two or more mutually exclusive projects will generate the greatest net benefits for the country. The DRCR only identifies which of the alternative projects is the most economical in its use of domestic resources when it generates 1 unit of foreign exchange.

Finally, if an economic analysis is undertaken, the use of the DRCR methodology does not overcome the need to determine the true opportunity cost of foreign exchange to the economy concerned. After undertaking an economic analysis, the shadow exchange rate for the country concerned must be estimated for comparison with the project's estimated DRCR.

5.5 The benefit cost ratio, BCR

The benefit cost ratio was the earliest discounted project assessment criterion to be employed. However, due to problems associated with its applied use, it is rarely used in project appraisal today.

5.5.1 Definition of the benefit cost ratio, BCR

The benefit cost ratio is simply the ratio of the sum of the project's discounted benefits to the sum of its discounted investment and operating costs. This can be expressed mathematically as:

$$\text{BCR} = \frac{\sum_{t=0}^{n} \frac{B_t}{(1+r)^t}}{\sum_{t=0}^{n} \frac{C_t}{(1+r)^t}} \qquad (5.6)$$

5.5.2 The decision rule of the BCR

A project should be accepted if its BCR is greater than or equal to 1, that is, if its discounted benefits exceed its discounted costs. Table 5.7 shows the BCR of the road project examined in Table 5.2, for a range of different discount rates.

Table 5.7   Estimation of the BCR of a road project ($L million)

	Years										
	1	*2*	*3*	*4*	*5*	*6*	*7*	*8*	*9*	*10*	*11*
Costs											
Land	1000										
Earthworks	200	600	400								
Equipment	190	200									
Labour	120	120	120								
Total	1510	920	520	0	0	0	0	0	0	0	0
Benefits											
Time savings	0	0	0	300	300	300	300	300	300	300	300
Maintenance savings	0	0	0	100	100	100	100	100	100	100	100
Car depreciation savings	0	0	0	290	290	290	290	290	290	290	290
Total	0	0	0	690	690	690	690	690	690	690	690
Net benefits	−1510	−920	−520	690	690	690	690	690	690	690	690

Discount rate	*NPV*	*PVB*	*PVC*	*BCR*	*Accept project?*
5%	1130.6	3852.4	2721.8	1.4	Yes
10%	241.9	2765.7	2523.7	1.1	Yes
15%	−314.7	2035.8	2350.6	0.9	No
12 %	−12.0	2439.7	2451.8	0.995	No
11.89% = IRR	0.0	2456.4	2456.4	1.0	Yes

The BCR of the project will therefore be greater than 1 when the rate used to discount the benefit and cost streams is less than 11.89%, the project's IRR. If the BCR is greater than 1 when the appropriate discount rate has been used, then the project should be accepted. However, the BCR will be less than 1 if the discount rate used is greater than 11.89%, and, if the BCR is less than 1, the project should be rejected. The BCR will just equal 1 when the discount rate used is equal to the IRR of the project, 11.89%. The BCR will therefore give exactly the same result as the NPV and IRR selection criteria at each alternative discount rate.

5.5.3 Mutually exclusive projects and budget constraints

In common with the IRR and DRCR, the benefit cost ratio, BCR, cannot be used to choose between mutually exclusive projects. This was shown in the example of two mutually exclusive dam projects in Table 5.1. Dam A has a higher BCR than dam B, but the NPV of dam B is higher than that of dam A and, therefore, dam B should be selected.

Similarly, the BCR cannot be used to rank projects if there is a single period budget constraint. The government will wish to rank and select projects so as to maximise net receipts per unit of **investment** costs, rather than per unit of total costs, as it will be investment funds that will be in short supply if there is a single period budget constraint.

5.5.4 Advantages of the BCR

One major advantage of the benefit cost ratio is that it is readily understood by non-economists. Another advantage is that it is easy to show the impact of a percentage rise in costs or fall in benefits on the project's viability.

5.5.5 Disadvantages of the BCR

The major disadvantage of the BCR is the need to specify and adhere to conventions regarding the designation of expenditures as costs and benefits. For example, if the cost of transporting finished goods to market is included as a cost in one project, sales prices cannot be given as net of transport costs in another if the BCR of the two projects are to be comparable. Clear conventions on such issues would be necessary to ensure that the benefit cost ratios calculated for different projects are comparable.

Appendix 1
Use of the NPV criterion to rank projects if there is a budget constraint

Ranking of projects if there is a budget constraint using their NPV is done by grouping together projects with a positive NPV into all possible combinations that satisfy the government's budget constraint. Then, the projects in the combination with the highest NPV should be undertaken. In this case, the different groups of projects in effect become mutually exclusive projects. The decision rule for mutually exclusive projects can be used, and the group with the highest NPV should be selected.

A simple example of this use of the NPV selection criterion is shown in Table A5.1. The government's investment budget for next year is $L20 million. However, it is considering five projects with a positive NPV, which together have investment costs of $L30 million.

Table A5.1   Use of NPV to select projects when there is a single period budget constraint

Project	Investment cost ($Lm)	NPV
A	3	10
B	5	15
C	2	6
D	10	22
E	10	20
Total	30	73
Considering alternative combinations:		
Projects A + B + C + D	20	53
Projects A + B + C + E	20	51
Projects D + E	20	42

First, it is necessary to determine which of the alternative feasible combinations of the five projects will meet the government's budget constraint. These groups are then considered in the same way as mutually exclusive projects. That is, that group of projects that has the highest NPV should be selected. In Table A5.1, the best combination is of projects A, B, C and D. Together they have a net present value of $L53 million and a total investment cost of $L20 million, which just exhausts the government's investment budget. Hence the government should do projects A, B, C and D if it can only spend $L20 million. This is the same result as was found by ranking the projects by their NBIR, in Table 5.5.

APPENDIX 2
The mathematical relationship between the five discounted selection criteria

All five criteria are in fact mathematically equivalent and collapse to the same decision rule. This can be seen from the following mathematical manipulation of the formulae for the five assessment criteria. The project is just worth doing if:

(i)   **The internal rate of return, r^*, of the project just equals the target rate of return, r. At this discount rate, r, the following relationships will hold:**

(ii)   **Net present value = 0**

i.e., $NPV = \displaystyle\sum_{t=0}^{n} \frac{(B_t - C_t)}{(1 + r)^t} = 0$

$\therefore \quad \displaystyle\sum_{t=0}^{n} \frac{B_t}{(1 + r)^t} = \sum_{t=0}^{n} \frac{C_t}{(1 + r)^t}$

(iii)   **Benefit cost ratio = 1**

i.e., $BCR = \dfrac{\displaystyle\sum_{t=0}^{n} \dfrac{B_t}{(1 + r)^t}}{\displaystyle\sum_{t=0}^{n} \dfrac{C_t}{(1 + r)^t}} = 1$

$\therefore \quad \displaystyle\sum_{t=0}^{n} \frac{B_t}{(1 + r)^t} = \sum_{t=0}^{n} \frac{C_t}{(1 + r)^t}$

(iv)   **Net benefit investment ratio = 1**

i.e., $NBIR = \dfrac{\displaystyle\sum_{t=0}^{n} \dfrac{(B_t - OC_t)}{(1 + r)^t}}{\displaystyle\sum_{t=0}^{n} \dfrac{IC_t}{(1 + r)^t}} = 1$

$\therefore \quad \displaystyle\sum_{t=0}^{n} \frac{B_t}{(1 + r)^t} = \sum_{t=0}^{n} \frac{OC_t + IC_t}{(1 + r)^t}$

$\therefore \quad \displaystyle\sum_{t=0}^{n} \frac{B_t}{(1 + r)^t} = \sum_{t=0}^{n} \frac{C_t}{(1 + r)^t}$

(v)   **Domestic resource cost ratio = official exchange rate, OER, (or shadow exchange rate for economic analysis)**

$$\text{i.e., DRCR} = \frac{\displaystyle\sum_{t=0}^{n} \frac{(C_{tl} - B_{tl})}{(1 + r)^{t}}(\$L)}{\displaystyle\sum_{t=0}^{n} \frac{(B_{tf} - C_{tf})}{(1 + r)^{t}}(\$US)}$$

$$\therefore \quad \sum_{t=0}^{n} \frac{(C_{tl} - B_{tl})}{(1 + r)^{t}} = \sum_{t=0}^{n} \frac{(B_{tf} - C_{tf})}{(1 + r)^{t}} \times OER$$

$$\therefore \quad \sum_{t=0}^{n} \frac{(B_{tl} + B_{tf} \times OER)}{(1 + r)^{t}} = \sum_{t=0}^{n} \frac{(C_{tl} + C_{tf} \times OER)}{(1 + r)^{t}}$$

$$\therefore \quad \sum_{t=0}^{n} \frac{B_{t}}{(1 + r)^{t}} = \sum_{t=0}^{n} \frac{C_{t}}{(1 + r)^{t}}$$

Exercises

1. Calculate the internal rate of return of the cash flows in Exercises 1 and 3 (Chapter 3). If you are using Lotus 123, use the IRR formula, @IRR(guess rate, Range), where the guess rate is the guessed discount rate used to start the iteration process, expressed as a proportion or factor of 1, and Range is the range of cells in which the cash flow is located.

2. Calculate the benefit cost ratios of the cash flows in Exercises 1 and 3, Chapter 3 if the discount rate is 7 per cent.

3. Calculate the net benefit investment ratios of the two cash flows in Exercises 1 and 3, Chapter 3, if the discount rate is 10 per cent.

4. If the discount rate is 9 per cent and the official exchange rate is $L10 = $US1, what is the domestic resource cost ratio of the project described in Exercise 2, Chapter 3? Should the project be undertaken?

5. Looking again at Figure 5.2, which project should be undertaken if the projects are independent and:
   (i)   if the discount rate is R'_T, or
   (ii) if the discount rate is R_T?

References

Bruno, M., 1967. 'The optimal selection of export-promoting and import-substituting projects' in *Planning the External Sector: Techniques, Problems and Policies*, United Nations, New York.

Gittinger, J.P., 1982. *Economic Analysis of Agricultural Projects*, 2nd edn, Johns Hopkins University Press, Baltimore, Chapter 9.

Jenkins G.P. and Harberger, A.C., 1991. *Manual — Cost Benefit Analysis of Investment Decisions*, Program on Investment Appraisal and Management, Harvard Institute for International Development, Cambridge, Mass.

Little, I.M.D. and Mirrlees, J.A., 1974. *Project Appraisal and Planning for Developing Countries*, Heinemann Educational Books, London.

Savvides, S.C., 1989. *Risk Master*, Nicosia.

Squire, L. and van der Tak, H.G., 1975. *Economic Analysis of Projects*, Johns Hopkins University Press, Baltimore.

Temple, G., 1993. Costab Manual: *A Practical Guide to Project Costing*, World Bank.

Further reading

Dasgupta, A.K. and Pearce, D.W., 1972. *Cost-Benefit Analysis — Theory and Practice*, Macmillan, London, Chapter 7.

Duvingneau, J.C. and Prasad, R.N., 1984. *Guidelines for Calculating Financial and Economic Rates of Return for DFC Projects*, World Bank Technical Paper No. 33, Chapter 7.

Gittinger, J.P., 1982. *Economic Analysis of Agricultural Projects*, 2nd edn, Johns Hopkins University Press, Baltimore, Chapter 9.

Helmers, F., 1979. *Project Planning and Income Distribution*, Martinus Nijhoff Publishing, The Hague, Chapter 5.

Irvin, G., 1978. *Modern Cost-Benefit Methods*, Macmillan, London, Chapter 1.

Endnotes

1   In Lotus 123 the formula for calculating the NPV of a net benefit stream would be @ NPV(+A3, +B20 ... +M20), where the discount rate (as a proportion of 1) is located in cell +A3, and the net benefit stream of the project is located in cells +B20 to +M20.

2   In Lotus 123 the formula for calculating the IRR of a net benefit stream would be @ IRR(+A21, +B20 ... +M20), where the guess or starting rate (as a proportion of 1) is located in cell +A21, and the net benefit stream of the project is located in cells +B20 to +M20.

3   The relationship between IRR and NPV is in fact non-linear but Figures 5.1 and 5.2 are drawn as if the relationship were linear to simplify their presentation.

4   If the projects are mutually exclusive, the project with the highest NPV should be selected, for the reasons discussed in 5.1.3. However in this example we are told that they are independent.

5   This is equivalent to using the net present value criterion to choose between projects in a situation of a long-term budget constraint, as was discussed in 5.1.4. It is possible to do this by raising the discount rate to a point where only those projects with total costs less than the budget constraint pass the selection test of a positive or zero net present value.

6   As discussed above, the relationship between NPV and the discount rate used should be represented by curved lines. However, for simplicity of explanation they are shown as straight lines in this and the following figures.

7   The estimation of a project's IRR is discussed in Section 5.2.

8   This is not to say that this politically driven practice is in fact correct, as the appropriate target rate, the social opportunity cost of capital, is likely to differ between countries.

9　It should be noted that it is not correct to use the net benefit investment ratio to rank projects **within** the group of selected projects, because of the cross-over phenomenon noted in Figure 5.1 in relation to the net present value and internal rate of return. The net benefit investment ratio can only be used to determine which group of projects should be selected in these circumstances.

10　The problem with a financial appraisal is that the official exchange rate may not reflect the true cost in local resources of earning 1 dollar of foreign exchange. Hence, when undertaking an **economic** appraisal of a project, the decision rule is that a project should be selected if its DRCR is less than or equal to the shadow exchange rate. That is, if the project uses less domestic resources to earn 1 unit of foreign exchange than is the average for the whole economy, once the effect of trade and other distortions have been taken into account in the valuation of domestic costs, then the project should go ahead. The estimation of a country's shadow exchange rate is discussed in Chapter 9.

11　Or the shadow exchange rate in the case of an economic analysis.

12　The alternative solution to this problem is to use the Little and Mirrlees (1974) and Squire and van der Tak (1975) approach to project appraisal. This approach employs a range of individual conversion factors to revalue the domestic resource cost of the project in broader price equivalents, rather than one shadow exchange rate. This is discussed in Chapter 9.

Part Three

THE ECONOMIC ANALYSIS OF PROJECTS

CHAPTER 6

The rationale for economic cost benefit analysis

6.1 The role of a financial analysis

Governments and individuals can usually only pursue limited objectives when they choose projects on the basis of a financial appraisal. In most circumstances, a financial analysis using market prices to value a project's inputs and outputs will merely tell the analyst whether a project will be financially profitable. These market prices usually contain many distortions such as taxes, tariffs and price controls and do not reflect the true costs and benefits to the economy of a project's use of particular inputs and production of various outputs. Therefore a financial analysis will only rarely measure a project's contribution to the community's welfare.

Only in the very unlikely event of perfect competition in factor and goods markets, perfect knowledge and an absence of externalities, public goods, government intervention, taxes, and other market distortions and changes in consumer surplus, will market prices provide a good measure of the economic value of goods and services.[1] In these restrictive circumstances, the market prices of final goods and services will equal the value (utility) people receive from consuming them. In the case of produced inputs, their market price will also equal their cost of production to society, at the margin. Neoclassical theory implies that individuals operating in their own self interest and reacting to such competitive market prices without controls and intervention by government will allocate resources so as to produce a welfare optimising outcome. However, only under these conditions of perfect competition and an absence of externalities, will a financial analysis of a project indicate whether or not a project will make a positive contribution to welfare in the country in which it is located. In the absence of these conditions, a financial analysis will only tell us whether a project is profitable or not.

6.2 The rationale for economic analysis

Very often governments will be more concerned that their public works programs promote community welfare than that they merely maximise financial profits at distorted local prices.[2] If public projects consistently achieve only financial profitability but not net welfare gains, the country's welfare could be expected to decline in the long run.[3]

Many developing and developed countries have quite serious distortions in market prices and, despite the recent policies of reform and liberalisation, it is unlikely that government will rapidly remove all such distortions and correct all market failures. The failure of markets, the absence of perfect knowledge, and the existence of externalities, consumer and producer surplus, governments and public goods, are universal in both developed and developing countries. In this situation, if a government does wish to promote the community's welfare,[4] it must choose projects on the basis of an economic analysis. Economic analyses try to correct for distortions in market prices by calculating **economic or shadow prices**, which better reflect the true economic value of a project's inputs and outputs.

In many developing countries distortions introduced by government may be even more extreme than in developed countries. Dwight Perkins (1991) attempted to compare the level of price distortions in developed and developing countries. He came to the conclusion that prices in developing countries are from two to three times more distorted than those in developed countries. If this is the case, the need to undertake an economic appraisal of projects will be even more urgent in developing countries than in developed ones. Examples of the consequences of government induced distortions include widespread open unemployment, suppressed interest rates and credit rationing in financial markets, currency over-valuation and the heavy protection of domestic industries and services resulting in an overvalued foreign exchange rate.

It is useful to have a fuller understanding of the areas where government intervention and market failure result in serious distortions in market prices. This will help in understanding the process of correcting for these distortions when shadow pricing project inputs and outputs. The following sections will deal in more detail with the conditions under which it is impossible to use market prices to assess the economic worth of projects. These circumstances can be grouped under four major headings:

- Intervention in and failure of **goods markets**, including the markets for internationally traded goods.
- Intervention in and failure of **factor markets**, including the markets for labour, capital and foreign exchange.
- The existence of **externalities, public goods** and **consumer** and **producer surplus**.
- **Imperfect knowledge.**

6.3 Government intervention in, or failure of, goods markets

6.3.1 Failure of domestic goods markets

The true economic value of a good produced by a project, which can be called its **marginal social benefit**, or how much it will add to community welfare, is in general measured by what people are **willing to pay** for that good. This is not a perfect measure of welfare derived from consumption because of the existence of income inequalities. These mean that people on different incomes may derive the same utility from consuming a particular good, but the poorer person may not be able to pay the going demand price paid by the richer person.[5]

Apart from this problem, the market price of a good will not measure what people are willing to pay for it unless the following three conditions are met:

- There is no rationing of sales or price controls in the market for the good. That is, the quantity of the good that is demanded by consumers must equal the quantity supplied by producers, and the price of the good must be its competitive demand price.
- There is no consumer surplus from the consumption of the good.[6] If some people are willing to pay more than they actually have to pay for a project output, then these market prices will underestimate the true value of the good produced by the project. This issue is dealt with in more detail in Section 6.6.
- There is no monopsony buyer[7] who is large enough to force the project to sell its output below the price that the monopsonist is really willing to pay. This is a reasonably rare situation but, once again, in such circumstances the market price would underestimate the competitive demand price and hence the true economic value of the good concerned.

Unless all these conditions are met the good's market price will not reflect people's true willingness to pay for the good and will not be a good measure of the increase in welfare (or utility) that people will obtain from consuming the project's output. If any of these market imperfections exist, it will be necessary to shadow price project outputs so that their prices better reflect their marginal social benefit.

In many developing countries, particularly centrally planned ones, at least some prices are set by government regulatory agencies. As these prices are usually set below market clearing levels and therefore at less than people are willing to pay, such controlled prices underestimate the true value of these goods to consumers. This situation occurs in China in relation to essential raw materials such as oil, utilities like water and transport services. Public infrastructure such as electricity, water and rail services have also been underpriced in many developed and developing countries, for example Indonesia, India, Thailand and Australia. This situation is illustrated in Figure 6.1, where the price of a controlled commodity is set at P_{mf}, below the market clearing equilibrium price, P_e. This results in excess demand for the good, $Q_d - Q_s$. The existence of controlled prices that are set below the amount that people are willing to pay for a given quantity of output will frequently result in the rationing of limited supplies, either formally or via queuing, as well as corruption and black markets. Alternatively, the government may enforce compulsory deliveries of agricultural or industrial commodities at these artificially low controlled prices. The existence of any of these phenomena will provide evidence that prices are not market clearing and do not reflect people's willingness to pay for the goods in question.

On the other hand, prices may be set above market clearing levels, resulting in a large accumulation of unwanted goods in warehouses. This has also been a common phenomenon in countries like China. Use of government controlled prices in a project appraisal would, in this case, result in an overvaluation of the marginal social benefit that would be gained from production of such goods.

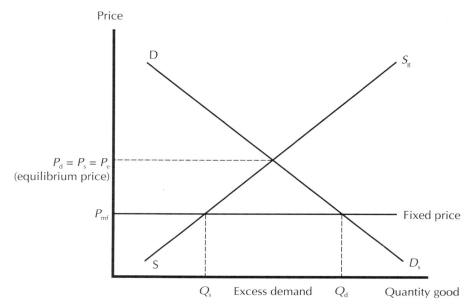

Figure 6.1   *Goods markets distortions — price fixing*

6.3.2 Trade protection and intervention in the markets for internationally traded goods

Governments frequently intervene in import markets by imposing quotas and tariffs to protect infant industries or activities that are not internationally competitive. Many countries such as India, and other South Asian countries, many Latin American countries, the Philippines and Thailand have high levels of protection for their domestic markets, though many successful East Asian and South East Asian countries, as well as Australia, are now reducing their tariff protection. Tariffs and quotas will cause a divergence between local market prices and the world prices of internationally traded goods. The extent of this divergence will vary from industry to industry, depending on their tariff and non-tariff (quota) protection levels.

This situation is shown in Figure 6.2, in which an import quota, Q_f, is imposed on an input required by a project. This will push up the domestic market cost of the input to P_{md}, well above the actual foreign exchange cost to the economy of importing the input, which is the world price, P_w. In these circumstances, a project analysis that uses local market prices, including the value of tariffs and the effects of quotas and other non-tariff barriers, to value internationally traded goods will overvalue the social cost of traded inputs used by the project. Similarly, the benefit of a project output that substitutes for an imported good cannot be measured in terms of the local market price for this output if this price includes a protective tariff. The economic benefit to the country from producing the import substitute will only be the foreign exchange saved by reducing its import bill as a result of increased local production. The local market price of this protected traded good will exceed world prices by the amount of the tariff protection. However, the latter component is not an economic benefit of the production, but just a tax on local consumers.

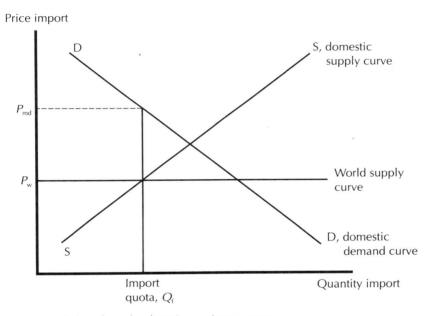

Figure 6.2 *Traded goods market distortions — import quota*

6.4 Failure of, or intervention in, factor markets

The true economic cost to an economy of a project's input, its **marginal social cost**, will be measured by its economic opportunity cost to suppliers. The market price of an input will only equal its social opportunity cost of production if the following three conditions are met:
- There is no rationing, price controls or taxes in factor markets, such as fixed minimum wages, controlled interest rates, price controls on raw materials or taxes on labour, savings and profits, raw materials, equipment or other project inputs.
- There is no producer surplus in the market price of the input.[8] For this to be the case, the supply curve for the input should be perfectly horizontal (elastic), over the range of the project's demand for it. This issue is dealt with in more detail in Section 6.6.

- There are no monopsony buyers who are in a position to force the factors' market price below their marginal revenue product and hence the price they would be willing to pay for it.

If any of these market imperfections exist, it will be necessary to shadow price project inputs so that their prices better reflect their marginal social cost.

6.4.1 Intervention in the market for labour

Labour markets are frequently regulated in both developed and developing countries, with fixed minimum wage rates or centrally fixed wage rates for formal sector jobs, particularly those offered by large and medium-sized businesses and government. If these wage rates are set above market clearing levels, there is likely to be open unemployment or disguised unemployment in the informal sector as more people offer themselves for employment at the regulated wage than there are jobs available. Indonesia, China and Australia are all examples of countries that have minimum wage legislation and other forms of wage fixing.

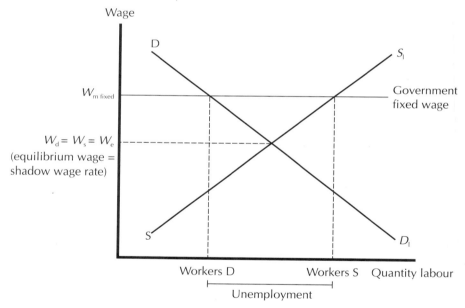

Figure 6.3   *Factor market distortions — wage fixing*

This situation is illustrated in Figure 6.3. The government's fixed wage for unskilled labour, $W_{m\,fixed}$ is set above the market clearing equilibrium wage, W_e. This will result in unemployment of unskilled workers, with the numbers of such workers offering themselves for these formal sector jobs, Workers S, exceeding demand, Workers D. The existence of open unemployment or under-employment will indicate to the project analyst that the market wage for the categories of labour concerned is greater than its marginal social cost. The project analyst will need to adjust these wage rates downwards until they reflect the true social cost of labour in this country, the shadow wage.

In the case of skilled labour, fixed wage rates may actually be set below market clearing levels causing an artificial shortage of skilled labour. If such 'shortages' are apparent the analyst will need to shadow price the wage rates for skilled workers, in this case adjusting them upward to reflect the true social cost of using them in the project.

6.4.2 Intervention in, or failure of, capital markets

Another important factor market in which governments often intervene by fixing prices is the capital market. This is supposedly done to encourage investment by keeping interest rates artificially low. This situation is illustrated in Figure 6.4.

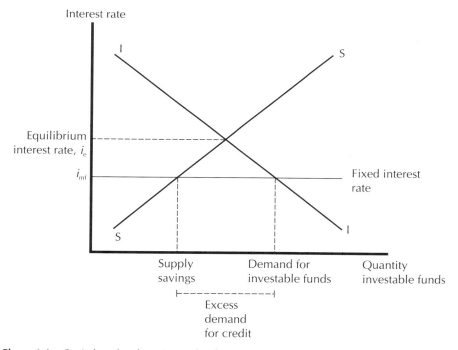

Figure 6.4 *Capital market distortion — fixed interest rates*

In this case the interest rate paid for investable funds is held down to i_{fm}, well below the equilibrium interest rate, i_e. The Republic of Korea and China, for example, have both operated a policy of repressed interest rates for several decades. As more people wish to borrow than to save at this low interest rate there will be an excess demand for capital funds. It will then be necessary to ration available credit to preferred borrowers.[9]

In addition, governments routinely tax both borrowers and lenders, introducing further distortions into capital markets. This is discussed in Chapter 13. For these reasons, market interest rates should not be used to discount future income streams in an economic analysis. The government will need to estimate a social discount rate that better reflects the opportunity cost of using investable funds in a project.[10]

6.4.3 Intervention in foreign exchange markets

Many developing and some developed countries peg or manage their foreign exchange rate. In some cases, the exchange rate is set significantly above its free market level in terms of $US per unit of local currency. For example, China, the Philippines, India and, in the past, Indonesia have all had policies of overvaluing their exchange rate. As in all situations where the price of a commodity, in this case the units of local currency paid per $US, is held down artificially, currency overvaluation creates an apparent 'shortage' of foreign exchange. This shortage occurs because at the overvalued exchange rate imports appear cheap relative to locally produced goods and unless tariffs are imposed, demand for imports will rise. On the other hand, currency overvaluation makes exporting, as compared with supplying the local market, financially unattractive to producers. The price that exporters receive in local currency for a given dollar value of exports is reduced if the exchange rate is overvalued. The pincer effect of these two factors will cause a shortage of foreign exchange.

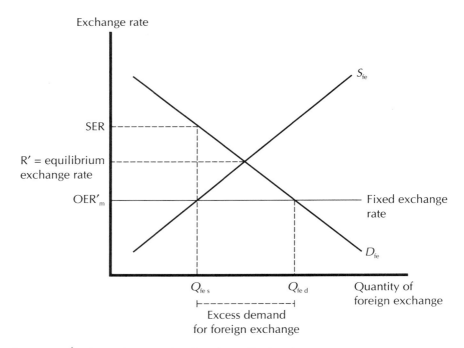

Figure 6.5   *Foreign exchange market distortion — fixed exchange rate*

Figure 6.5 illustrates the situation where the official exchange rate ($L paid per $US) is fixed at OER'_m. This will result in excess demand for foreign exchange, $Q_{fed} - Q_{fes}$. In these circumstances the official exchange rate will understate the true value of foreign exchange to the country concerned. This is given by the shadow exchange rate, SER, the amount residents are willing to pay for the fixed quantity of foreign exchange available, Q_{fes}. Use of the official exchange rate in project appraisal will have the effect of undervaluing projects that produce exportable outputs and overvaluing those that use imported inputs. The overvaluation of the exchange rate, or the **premium** placed on foreign exchange at official rates, must be corrected in an economic analysis. One method of doing this is to employ a shadow exchange rate to convert foreign prices into local currency. This shadow exchange rate attempts to measure the social cost or benefit to the country of using or earning a unit of foreign exchange.[11]

6.5 Externalities and public goods

Another reason why the perfect world of neoclassical theory fails to represent the real world is the existence of public goods and externalities. These goods (or bads) do not usually have a market price that can be used to measure their benefits (or costs) to society and these benefits or costs will not appear in the project's financial cash flow. A financial analysis of a project that uses or produces public goods or externalities therefore will fail to capture the full impact of a project on the community's welfare.

6.5.1 The existence of externalities

Externalities are created in the process of producing, distributing and consuming many goods and services. They are the positive or negative attributes or effects of a good or service, or its production, that are not directly felt by the people who buy it and hence may not be reflected in the price they are willing to pay for it. A major example of a negative externality is the pollution created in production of some goods, such as bleached paper or aluminium. Even if the market price of a good like bleached paper equals the amount that consumers are willing to pay for it, this price will not capture the full impact of the paper's production on community welfare. An economic analysis of a bleached paper factory would subtract the cost of the pollution created, measured *inter alia* in terms of lost fish production in local waters, from the net financial benefits of the paper plant, to determine the project's full impact on community welfare. A financial analysis would not take this additional step.

6.5.2 The existence of public goods

Public goods are goods and services whose use by one person does not reduce their availability to others. Examples of public goods include uncongested urban road networks, TV and radio signals, disease eradication campaigns, defence forces, the legal system, and macroeconomic management. Public goods are usually provided free by governments and in a financial analysis would therefore be priced at zero.

However, they do have a beneficial impact on the welfare of those receiving them, most of whom would be willing to pay for such goods through taxation. It will cost the society significant sums to produce many public goods. This is another case where the market price of a good or service will not reflect its true cost or benefit to society. If the project under consideration uses public goods as an input or, more importantly, produces them as an output, it would be wrong to value them at their market price of zero in any economic analysis of the project. They will have to be valued at the amount that it is estimated people will be willing to pay for them.

6.6 Large projects and consumer and producer surplus

In the perfectly competitive world of neoclassical theory it is assumed that all changes in the supply of output and the demand for inputs are small or marginal in relation to the overall economy and will not affect input or output prices. If this is the case we could expect that projects will not cause changes to occur in the consumer or producer surplus enjoyed by those purchasing project outputs or supplying project inputs. Market prices for project inputs and outputs could then be expected to reflect their full economic cost to and benefit for the economy, in the absence of other distortions. However, some major projects may be very large in relation to the overall economy and their implementation could be expected to alter either the price of the output produced[12] or the price of inputs used, or both. If a project causes such a large increase in the domestic supply of the good it produces that its price falls, those consumers who were previously willing to purchase the good at the higher price will obtain an increase in their consumer surplus. This increase in consumer surplus will represent a real increase in welfare, but will not be reflected in the market price paid for the project's output. In some circumstances these gains in consumer surplus may be very significant. For example, if the output of a project is a social service such as education, or a public good such as a non-toll road, which is provided free of charge, all the benefits of the project will be in the form of an increase in consumer surplus. The failure of market prices, used in a financial analysis, to reflect changes in consumer surplus may therefore result in a serious undervaluation or overvaluation of the project's worth to the economy.

If the project's demand for some input is so great that it increases the input's price, this will cause a gain in producer surplus for the supplier of this input. Although this will be included in the market price, it is not a cost to the economy from the use of this input but just a rent, or transfer to the supplier, from the project.

6.7 Imperfect knowledge

The final assumption made in the perfectly competitive neoclassical model is that consumers and producers have perfect knowledge and information about all aspects of the economy relevant to their choices and operations. This is obviously a rather unrealistic assumption even in a developed country, but is even less realistic in most developing countries, with typically poor transport and communications infrastructure and low education levels. If it is no longer assumed that people have perfect knowledge, there will be institutional charges in the financial market to compensate lenders for bearing the risk of non-repayment. With taxation, this is the main reason why borrowing and lending rates diverge.

If consumers do not have perfect knowledge about all goods and services they purchase, it may not be reasonable to assume consumer sovereignty — that the price consumers pay will always reflect the benefit or utility they get from consuming goods. Advertising may improve consumer knowledge, but if it is misleading, it may further undermine the assumption of consumer sovereignty.[13]

For all these reasons, market prices will frequently not reflect the true economic cost, or marginal social cost of using project inputs or the true economic benefit, marginal social benefit of producing project outputs. It will therefore be necessary to calculate shadow or economic prices that better reflect the economic value of factors used and outputs produced by projects, for use in the economic analyses. Once this is done, the analyst should feel confident that a project showing a positive economic NPV at these economic prices will in fact improve the community's welfare.

6.8 The rationale for social analysis of projects — inequitable distribution of income and wealth

An economic analysis, using shadow prices, will enable the analyst to identify which projects will increase real income per capita. However, the government may consider real income per capita to be an excessively limited definition of community welfare because it ignores the issue of income distribution. If the government considers that existing income inequality is too great, it may wish to approve projects that not only improve economic efficiency but also promote social equity. In this case, a social appraisal of projects, possibly employing distributional weights, will be necessary. A social appraisal tries to provide a coherent framework in which the government may give higher priority to projects that benefit low income groups, over those that benefit high income ones.

6.9 Summary

Market prices often fail to reflect the true economic value of scarce resources to society. The reasons for this include:

*   market failure including monopsony, monopoly, inadequate integration of markets
*   distortions created by government intervention, particularly in the labour, foreign exchange and financial markets and the internationally traded goods sector, but also in the domestic goods market

- the existence of externalities and public goods
- larger than marginal supply and demand changes, producing changes in consumer and producer surplus
- imperfect knowledge and loss of consumer sovereignty
- an inequitable distribution of income.

As a result, the project analyst must make adjustments in the market prices of project inputs and outputs to ensure that they better reflect their true economic value to the economy. Economic analyses using these shadow prices will enable the analyst to determine which projects will make a positive contribution to economic welfare.

Exercise

1. Draw up a financial and an economic analysis of an effluent treatment plant project that processes 1000 tonnes of raw sewage and waste water per day. The market construction cost of the buildings is $2.5 million over 2 years. The labour cost of constructing the building is $0.8 million over 2 years, but these workers must be paid at a minimum wage, which is double the free market wage for this type of labour. Of the remaining $L1.7 million, $L0.5 million represents taxes and tariffs paid on domestic and imported construction materials and a further $L0.2 million is income tax on skilled technicians' and engineers' salaries.

   The imported equipment needed by the plant, landed in the country, costs $L1 million in year 2, but a tariff of 20 per cent, which must be paid by the project, is added to this cost.

   The operating costs of the project are $L0.8 million per annum from year 3 to year 20 and include $0.1 million in income taxes and $0.5 million in taxes on fuel and raw materials.

   The clean water produced by the project can be re-used and is sold to the water supply authority for industrial use at $L2.5 per tonne. However, the environmental benefits of the cleaner water are calculated to be worth another $L3.5 per tonne, in terms of the savings enjoyed by the local fishing and tourist industry, and in the saving in water cleaning costs made by the local water supply authority.

   The real financial cost to the project of borrowing will be 10 per cent but the social opportunity cost of funds to the country, the real social discount rate, is 11 per cent.

   Determine the financial and economic NPV of this project and its financial and economic internal rates of return. Should the project be undertaken:

   - if the operator is private and only concerned with its profitability
   - if the project operator is the government, and is concerned with the welfare of the whole country.

   If the project is privately operated, should the government consider subsidising it?

References

Perkins, D., 1991. 'Economic systems reform in developing countries' in D. Perkins (ed.), *Reforming Economic Systems in Developing Countries*, Harvard Institute for International Development, Cambridge, Chapter 1.

Squire, L., 1989. 'Project evaluation in theory and practice' in H. Chenery and T.N. Srinivasan (eds), *Handbook of Development Economics*, Vol. 2, North Holland, Amsterdam, Chapter 21.

Further reading

Little, I.M.D. and Mirrlees, J.A., 1974. *Project Appraisal and Planning for Developing Countries*, Heinemann Educational Books, London, Chapters 1, 2, 4.

UNIDO, 1972. *Guidelines for Project Evaluation*, United Nations, Chapters 2, 3.

Endnotes

1   The theoretical justification for the use of undistorted market prices to value outputs and inputs was discussed in the appendix to Chapter 2.

2   Nevertheless, if a project makes a financial loss and must be subsidised from government revenue, government should be rightly concerned at the efficiency losses from levying taxes sufficient to meet this revenue shortfall (Squire, 1989).

3   The same of course applies to private sector projects. However, in their case, the best chance of improving private investment decisions to ensure that they promote welfare is to remove as many distortions as possible from the prices faced by firms.

4   The use of cost benefit analysis of course presupposes that the government does wish to select projects that optimise economic welfare, rather than merely the best financial result for the implementing authority (or other even less worthy objectives).

5   This issue is one of the reasons why social analysis of projects was developed — to take account of income distributional issues in project appraisal.

6   The concept of consumer surplus is covered in more detail in Chapter 7. Simply, consumer surplus is the difference between the amount someone would be willing to pay for a good and service and what they actually have to pay. This exists whenever the demand curve for a good is downward sloping as people are able to buy the good at the equilibrium market price, which is less than some consumers would have been willing to pay. It is only when the demand curve for a good is completely flat, such as the world demand curve for a traded good, that increases in supply would probably not result in a drop in price and consumers would not obtain any increase in consumer surplus. Hence, for the market price of a project output to equal the amount people are willing to pay for it, the demand curve for the good must be perfectly flat (elastic) for the increase in supply envisaged by the project. In this situation, an increase in supply will not cause a reduction in the market clearing price, and hence no consumer surplus will be generated for intra-marginal consumers.

7   A monopsonist is a single large buyer in the goods or factor market, who can so dominate the market that it can dictate prices and force them down below the level it would have been willing to pay for this good or factor.

8   The concept of producer surplus is also covered in more detail in Chapter 7. Producer surplus is the difference between the price a producer would be prepared to accept to supply a particular good or factor and the market price of that factor. Producer surplus will exist if the supply curve for an input is upward sloping and the cost of the input rises as more of it is demanded. This implies that some producers can produce this input more cheaply than others. As the project pushes up demand and

raises the market price for the input, the market price will include an element of rent (producers surplus) for those producers who were prepared to supply at the lower price. Since such producer surplus will not represent a real cost to the economy of producing an input, the market value of the input used will exceed its marginal social cost. The only situation where the market value of an input will equal its marginal social cost is if there is no producer surplus element in the price. This will be the case if the supply curve for the good is perfectly horizontal (elastic), or the project's demand for the input is not sufficiently large to raise its price.

9   In many developing countries the severe shortage of credit available to traditional sectors such as agriculture due to segmentation of the financial market may represent a serious case of market failure.

10 Since government taxes on interest earnings and company profits may discourage saving and investment, this will cause a reduction in both the supply of and demand for investable funds. This may reduce the level of investment and growth in the economy below levels that the government considers optimal. In some countries, interest rates may be fixed at artificially low levels by the government, creating a shortage of savings and excess demand for investable funds. Alternatively, low average incomes may result in a low marginal propensity to save in many developing countries — the so-called poverty trap. As a result of these distortions and market failures, the government may wish to raise the current rate of investment to obtain a higher rate of growth than is presently being achieved.

Because of the existence of an anti-investment bias in the economy or a commitment by the government to rapid growth, the government may wish to put a premium on projects that produce output that is freely available for future investment. Such projects may have higher returns to the owners of capital than projects whose output is already committed to consumption because, for example, they have a high wage component. In economic analysis, the use of an investment premium that puts a premium on re-investable output relative to output committed to consumption can enable the government to pursue this objective coherently.

11 Alternatively, 'conversion factors' may be used to revalue inflated local prices down to their border (or international) price equivalents. These alternative approaches are discussed in more detail in Chapters 9 and 10.

12 In the case of goods and services that are not traded internationally.

13 The concept of consumer sovereignty (the consumer is king) maintains that individuals are the best judge of their own welfare, and will allocate their income among goods and services so as to maximise their welfare. Imperfect knowledge may undermine this concept to some extent, but it could be expected that, in most cases, people will learn from experience, and will not buy a good twice that gives them less than expected satisfaction.

CHAPTER 7

Economic valuation in a closed economy — the Harberger approach

7.1 The essential elements of an economic analysis

The economic analysis of a project has many features in common with a financial analysis. Both involve the estimation of a project's costs and benefits over the life of the project for inclusion in the project's cash flow. In both a financial and an economic analysis, this cash flow is then discounted to determine the project's net present value, or other measures of project worth. Both may also use sensitivity or probability analysis to assess the impact of uncertainty on the project's NPV.

However, an economic analysis goes beyond a financial appraisal as it will also involve all or some of the following adjustments:

- The deduction of transfer payments[1] within the economy from the project's cash flow.

- The inclusion of any net changes in consumer surplus in the project's net benefits, and the exclusion of any changes in producer surplus from costs.

- The estimation of economic or shadow prices for project outputs and produced inputs (including internationally traded and non-traded goods), to correct for any distortions in their market prices.

- The estimation of economic prices for non-produced project inputs (including labour, natural resources and land), to correct for any distortions in their market prices.

- The valuation and inclusion of any externalities created by the project.

- The valuation and inclusion of any unpriced outputs or inputs, such as public goods or social services.

- The estimation and use of an appropriate social discount rate to discount the project's cash flow.

This chapter discusses the identification and handling of transfer prices, the concepts of consumer and producer surplus and how to value and include project-induced changes in them in the economic cash flow. It also discusses how to value inputs and outputs in a closed economy, one with no foreign trade. This assumption is made so we can first look at the economic valuation of non-traded goods, but will be dropped in Chapter 8. The valuation of all the other elements of an economic cash flow will be discussed in Chapters 9 to 15.

7.2 Economic or shadow pricing

An economic or shadow price reflects the increase in welfare resulting from one more unit of an output or input being available. The terms shadow, economic and accounting prices are interchangeable. Shadow pricing corrects for any divergence between market and economic prices, due to market failure, government intervention, externalities, public goods, consumer and producer surplus and distributional considerations. These distortions were outlined in Chapter 6.

In practice, economic pricing usually involves making adjustments to market prices to correct for distortions and to take account of consumer and producer surplus. The resulting adjusted price should then reflect the true opportunity cost of an input (its marginal social cost), or people's willingness to pay for an output (its marginal social benefit). Since an economic price indicates the increase in welfare from the availability of one more unit of an output or input, the estimation of economic prices can only be made in the context of a well defined social welfare function. This should specify how the government defines an increase in welfare, such as by an increase in the level of aggregate consumption or by a redistribution of income to low income groups. In the main, cost benefit analyses are undertaken on the assumption that a welfare improvement is defined as an increase in a country's real income per capita, where income is adjusted to measure people's true willingness to pay for the goods and services they consume, at international parity prices.

7.2.1 The Harberger equation approach to shadow pricing

The following chapters on economic analysis have as one of their central themes the extensive use of an approach to economic pricing developed by Harberger (1971) and Jenkins and Harberger (1991). This is a rigorous and yet relatively simple method of measuring economic prices, including consumer surplus but excluding producer surplus, which can be readily adjusted to take account of various distortions such as taxes, tariffs, price controls, subsidies and foreign exchange controls. This methodology can not only be applied to the economic pricing of traded and non-traded goods but also to factors, including labour, capital and foreign exchange. Before introducing this approach in Section 7.6, the concepts of transfer prices and consumer and producer surplus will be explained in Sections 7.3 to 7.5. Understanding of these issues is essential to the estimation of economic prices.

7.3 Transfer payments

Transfer payments are defined as payments that are made without receiving any good or service in return. They involve the transfer of claims over real resources from one person or entity in society to another, rather than payments made for the use of or received from the sale of any good or service. Some examples of items that **in some circumstances** will be transfer payments are:

- **taxes** — personal and company income taxes, value added taxes and other indirect taxes, excises and stamp duties

- **subsidies** including those given via price support schemes

- **tariffs on imports and export subsidies and taxes** *tref w/ foreign entity?*

- **producer surplus** — gains received by an existing supplier of a factor as a result of an increase in the price of that factor *- rent tref'd from consumers to producers*

- **credit transactions** including loans received and repayments of interest and capital when these transactions occur between domestic borrowers and lenders.

7.3.1 Exceptions

It is certainly not always the case that these imposts and credit payments are transfers. For example, if all a project's output meets new demand[2] and there is a sales tax on its market price, the total market price paid including the tax will represent the amount that people are willing to pay for the project's output. This price will therefore measure the gross economic benefit per unit of the project's output. This issue will be discussed further in Section 7.8 which examines the measurement of a project's economic benefits in a market where tax and other distortions are present.

Some special cases also exist. If, for example, a tax is imposed to ensure that the value of an externality is included in the market price of the good generating it, this tax should arguably be included in any assessment of the economic cost of using the particular factor. For example, if a tax were imposed on alcohol so that its market price reflected the health and social costs of drinking alcohol, as well as its manufacturing costs, then arguably a project such as a tourist hotel that used alcohol as an input could include the alcohol tax when estimating the economic costs of the project. Similarly, if a pollution tax were imposed on a manufacturer this could be included in an economic analysis as one of the enterprise's production costs. An alternative, probably more accurate, approach would be to deduct the tax and to make a separate assessment of any negative externalities related to the additional consumption of alcohol, or the pollution created by the manufacturer.

If tariffs are imposed by the government to protect an infant industry and to achieve a specific government objective rather than to merely raise revenue, then one school of thought in project appraisal[3] maintains that such tariffs could be included in the price of any input or output to which it is applied. However, even the supporters of this approach accept that if it is expected that the tariff will be removed within a few years of project commencement, when the 'infant' matures, then the tariff should be excluded from the project's cash flow. The alternative approach[4] to project appraisal does not accept that tariffs should be included in the economic valuation of inputs and outputs, even if they are likely to stay in place over the whole of the project's life.

7.3.2 Credit transactions

Within the broader, economy-wide perspective of an economic analysis, borrowing and lending between local residents merely represent transfers of ownership of resources within the domestic economy. This activity will have no net impact on the project's contribution to the welfare of the overall community. For this reason a cost benefit analysis does not normally include a financing schedule of loan receipts or repayments. The exceptions to this rule include loans that have been financed by foreigners, or if the project operators are foreigners and the loan has been financed by locals.

If the project's financiers are foreigners, then its cost benefit analysis will resemble a financial analysis in the way it includes a financing schedule for these foreign loan receipts and repayments. This is because a cost benefit analysis assesses the net benefits of the project to the local population or the local economy and the interest and repayment terms of any foreign borrowing will affect local residents' welfare.

7.4 Consumer surplus

Even in freely operating markets, prices will not always reflect people's full willingness to pay for goods and services because of the existence of **consumer surplus**. Consumer surplus measures the difference between the amount consumers would be willing to pay for a good or service and what they **actually** have to pay for it. Consumers will obtain additional consumer surplus as a result of a project expanding production of a particular good if this causes a fall in the equilibrium price of this good. This will occur if the demand curve for the project's output is downward sloping, that is, it is less than perfectly elastic. This may happen if the project is a relatively large supplier of the output concerned.

This concept is illustrated in Figure 7.1. A consumer whose demand curve is represented by DD may actually buy quantity Q_1 oranges at price P_1, but would have been willing to buy Q_2 oranges if they had cost P_2 each. Similarly, this consumer would have been willing to buy Q_3 oranges if the price had been P_3 and Q_4 oranges if the price had been P_4. The same situation holds for all quantities of oranges down to zero and prices up to P_{max}. Assuming that the consumers would not be willing to pay these amounts unless they received a commensurate amount of utility, the whole area under the demand curve, $P_{max}AQ_1 0$ represents the utility that the consumer actually obtains from consuming Q_1 oranges.[5]

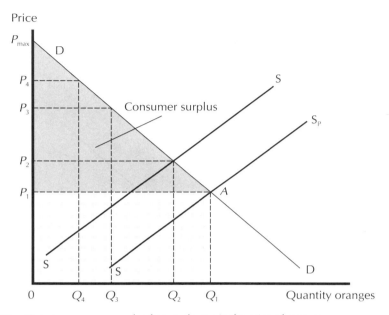

Figure 7.1 *Gain in consumer surplus from a change in the price of oranges*

Since the consumer only actually has to pay the amount represented by rectangle $0Q_1AP_1$ in order to purchase $0Q_1$ oranges and receive all this utility, the remaining triangle, P_1AP_{max} represents what is called **consumer surplus**. This is the difference between what the consumer would have been willing to pay to consume $0Q_1$ oranges, $0Q_1AP_{max}$, and the amount actually paid, $0P_1AQ_1$.

Changes in consumer surplus measure the impact on the welfare of individuals due to changes in the prices of the goods they consume. The utility individuals obtain from consuming a good usually exceeds the price paid. This is because this price only reflects the benefit or utility gained from the last, **marginal**, unit that the consumer is willing to purchase, not that derived from units purchased before this last one, **intra-marginal** units. In an economic analysis of a project any changes in consumer surplus as a result of a project should be included in the project's economic cash flow, because these changes represent real effects on people's welfare.

Figure 7.2 illustrates an example of a person who is willing to buy 2 kg of rice at a price of 15 cents/kg, but will only buy 1 kg if its price is 20 cents/kg. A project may result in a shift in the supply curve for rice from SS to SS$_P$, causing the equilibrium price of rice to fall from 20 to 15 cents/kg. In this case the consumer will gain 5 cents of benefit in the form of consumer surplus on the first kilogram of rice bought, plus *why o.s triangle*

0.5 × 5 cents of consumer surplus from the additional kilogram bought, or a 7.5 cents increase in consumer surplus overall. In addition, the consumer must get 15 cents worth of utility from the extra kilogram of rice supplied by the project otherwise she would not have been willing to pay this for it. So altogether as a result of the project this one consumer will gain:

7.5 cents (consumer surplus) + 15 (actual payment for rice produced)
= 22.5 cents/kg.

inconsistent - isn't gain = 7.5¢?

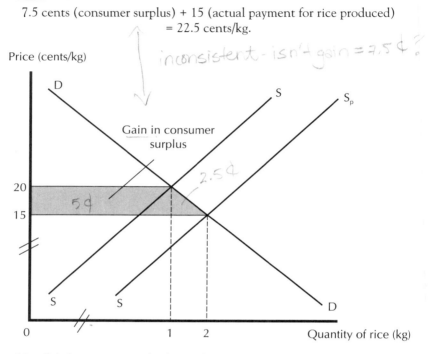

Figure 7.2   *Gain in consumer surplus from reduction in the price of rice*

A second example of when consumer surplus changes will be important and should be included in an economic analysis concerns an electricity supply authority that is deciding whether or not to connect a rural area to the electricity grid. If its electricity supply curve is SS_{el} as is shown in Figure 7.3, it will make a loss of *RUTP* if it carries out the project and supplies Q_e megawatts of electricity. However, if the electricity is connected, the people in the area will gain *RUV* in consumer surplus. If this gain is greater than *RUTP* in revenue lost by the electricity authority, the authority should supply the electricity.[6]

Measurement of consumer surplus changes due to a project will also be important if the project will produce an output that will not be sold at all. For example, if the project is a new hospital that will provide free care to patients, the benefits of the project will be measured by the whole of the area under the hospital services demand curve, DD_h in Figure 7.4. Consumers will pay nothing for the service and will therefore want to use 800 hospital beds per day. It is estimated that if a bed charge of $1000 per

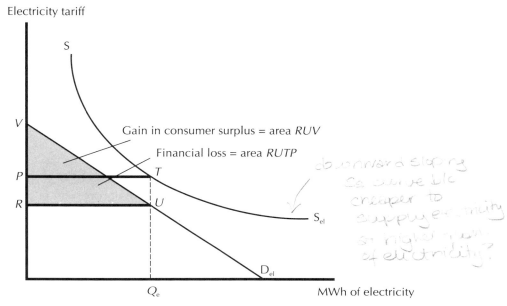

Figure 7.3 *Comparison of an electricity authority's financial loss and gain in consumer surplus*

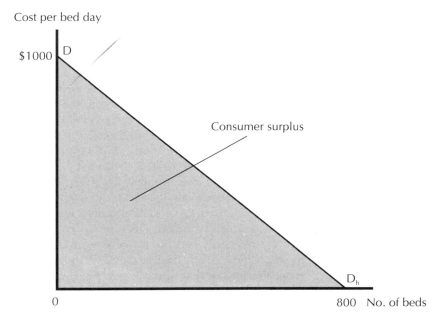

Figure 7.4 *Consumer surplus from the consumption of free hospital services*

day were levied, no one would use the hospital. Assuming the demand curve for hospital services is a straight line, as drawn, the total amount of consumer surplus generated as a result of the provision of the hospital can therefore be estimated as:

$$= 0.5 \times (\$1000 \times 800)$$
$$= \$400\ 000 \text{ per day, or } \$146\ 000\ 000 \text{ p.a.}$$

The gross economic benefits of the hospital project will therefore be $146 million per annum. *but what about the costs to build & operate the hospital?*

7.5 Producer surplus

If the price of a certain input rises as a result of a project's increased demand for it, not all of this increase in price will reflect the real additional resource cost of supplying this input. Some of the producers who were willing to supply this input at the lower price that held prior to the project's commencement will now receive a higher price for these same inputs. The difference between the amount that suppliers of an input would be willing to accept to supply this input and the amount that they actually received for supplying it is called **producer surplus**. It is in many ways analogous to the concept of consumer surplus.

For example, a new aluminium smelter project will use a large amount of electricity, which is not traded internationally and is in relatively fixed supply locally in the short to medium term. The electricity tariff may have to rise in order to encourage an expansion of generation to meet the project's needs.[7] In Figure 7.5, the electricity supply curve in this country is shown by the upward sloping SS_{el}. As the aluminium smelter project will require a total of 800 MWh of electricity, it will push out the local demand curve for electricity from DD to DD_p. As a result, the price of electricity is expected to rise from P_2 to P_3.

However, P_3 represents the real resources used to produce only the **marginal** unit of electricity input (the 1000th MWh).[8] If this marginal cost, P_3, is used to value **all** units of electricity consumed, it will overstate the aggregate cost to the economy of using this electricity. This is because the intra-marginal suppliers of electricity were willing to offer Q_2 (= 800 MWh) of electricity at the lower price P_2, and Q_1 (400 MWh) at price P_1, so on down to Q_0 (= zero MWh) at price P_0. The area, $Q_0Q_3CP_0$ below the electricity supply curve, SS_{el}, and above the horizontal axis therefore represents the actual resources it costs producers to supply Q_3 MWh of electricity. This is the amount that suppliers would be just willing to accept to supply $Q_3 - Q_0$ or 1000 MWh of electricity. In actual fact, when Q_3 units of electricity are purchased, the same price, P_3, must usually be paid for all the electricity supplied, not just for the last unit of electricity.[9] Since the electricity supplier **actually** receives the whole rectangular area $Q_0Q_3CP_3$, for supplying Q_3 MWh, the triangle P_0CP_3 above the supply curve represents a surplus above the amount that suppliers would have been willing to accept. This is the **producer surplus** obtained by the supplier. This producer surplus is not therefore an economic cost of supplying the electricity, just a rent that is transferred from electricity consumers to suppliers.

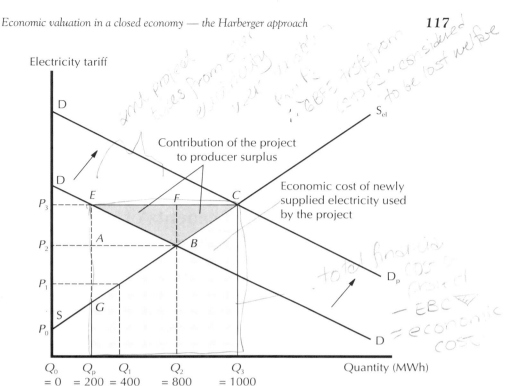

Figure 7.5   *Producer surplus and the economic cost of a project's factor inputs — electricity*

When the tariff rises from P_2 to P_3 the quantity of electricity supplied will increase from Q_2 to Q_3, from 800 to 1000 MWh, and the total amount paid by the aluminium smelter project for this newly supplied electricity will be Q_2Q_3CF. Of this total amount, the shaded area BCF will merely be an increase in the electricity supplier's producer surplus. Only the area Q_2Q_3CB will be the true economic cost of supplying new electricity to the project. In an economic analysis, <u>any change in producer surplus is therefore **subtracted** from market prices paid for inputs to determine</u> the actual cost to the economy of their use by the project.

The project will also take a further $Q_2 - Q_p$ (= 800 – 200 = 600 MWh) of electricity from other electricity users, who are unwilling (or unable) to pay the higher price, P_3. The amount that existing users of electricity are prepared to purchase at the new price, P_3, can be read off the original, pre-project, demand curve for electricity, DD. The project will pay Q_pQ_2FE for this 600 MWh of electricity. The economic **cost of supplying** this electricity is in fact only the area under the supply curve, Q_pQ_2BG, as the amount represented by the area <u>GBFE is a transfer to producer surplus</u>. However, the supply of electricity is not completely elastic, and not all of the project's electricity requirements can be met at the initial, pre-project price of P_2. Hence, the supply price of electricity is not the only relevant price in determining its economic cost. Since the displaced electricity consumers had been willing to pay Q_pQ_2BE for this 600 MWh of electricity, they will have lost this much welfare by being forced out of the market by the project. Hence, the total cost to the economy of this electricity is the area Q_pQ_2BE that these displaced consumers were willing to pay for it.

In total, the cost to the economy of the project's electricity demand is Q_pQ_3CBE. The shaded triangle EBC is deducted from the financial cost of the electricity, Q_pQ_3CE, as it represents a transfer in the form of increased producer surplus. If the price of a factor is expected to rise substantially as a result of a project's demand for it, then changes in producer surplus may be significant and should be deducted from the project's financial cost when undertaking an economic analysis of a project.

7.6 Measuring economic benefits of project outputs in a closed economy with no distortions — the Harberger approach

This section introduces a useful and rigorous approach to the valuation of economic costs and benefits developed by Harberger (1971) and Jenkins and Harberger (1991), which is used extensively throughout this text. This approach measures the economic benefits and costs of project outputs and inputs in terms of their demand and supply prices and elasticities and therefore automatically includes any change in consumer surplus and excludes any change in producer surplus. This approach is used to shadow price non-traded and traded goods (Chapters 7 and 8) as well as foreign exchange (Chapter 9) and capital (Chapter 13).

In order to simplify the general principles applied when valuing project outputs in an economic analysis, it will initially be assumed that there is no international trade between the country where the project is located and the rest of the world; it is a closed economy. Consequently only the economic valuation of non-traded goods, goods that are not traded internationally, will be considered in this chapter. This assumption will be relaxed in Chapter 8 where the valuation of traded goods will be examined.

Furthermore, in Sections 7.6 and 7.7 it will be assumed that there are **no distortions**, such as taxes, subsidies or rationing in the market for this output. This assumption will be dropped in Sections 7.8 and 7.9 of this chapter when the implications for valuing economic costs and benefits in distorted markets are considered in detail.

7.6.1 Economic benefits if project's output meets new demand

The measurement of the economic benefits generated by a project depends on whether the output it produces meets new demand, or merely substitutes for an existing source of supply for that good or service. If a project increases the total supply of a good or service available in a closed economy, its economic benefit will be measured in terms of the extra benefit, or **marginal social benefit,** which people derive from consuming this increased output. The marginal social benefit obtained from consuming a good or service can be reasonably well measured by what people are **willing to pay** for it, assuming that society's income distribution is optimal. In a freely operating market with no externalities or consumer surplus the amount that people are willing to pay for a good will equal its competitive **demand price**, P_d. This situation is shown in Figure 7.6 — a new railway project pushes out the supply curve for rail services from SS to SS_p.

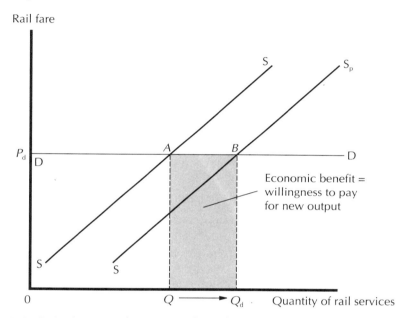

Figure 7.6   *Project's output only meets new demand — railway*

Given that the demand curve for rail services, DD, is completely elastic over this range of increased services, people will be willing to buy all the increased output of a new project at its existing market price, P_d. The shaded area QQ_dBA, representing the amount that people are willing to pay for this newly available rail service, will be the economic benefit of the project.

7.6.2 Economic benefits if project's output substitutes for existing supply

In some cases a project's output may merely be a substitute for some existing local source of supply of goods or services. Since the output was already available, we cannot value it at the amount that consumers are willing to pay for it, its demand price. In this situation, the value of the project's output will be the labour, capital, foreign exchange and raw material resources saved by the displaced suppliers who will be forced out of production as a result of the project, their **supply price**. An example of a project whose output substituted for an existing source of supply was a bakery project

established by Canadian aid in Tanzania. This fully automated bakery produced bread
that replaced the output of 20 small labour-intensive bakeries.

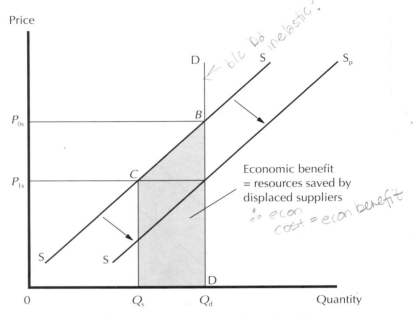

Figure 7.7   *Project's output substitutes for existing source of supply — bakery*

This situation is illustrated in Figure 7.7. The demand for bread is inelastic, DD,
so the increased supply as a result of the project will only drive the price of bread
down, from P_{0s} to P_{1s}, and force some existing producers out of business. The amount
of bread that the existing bakeries will now supply at the lower price, P_{1s}, can be read
off the original supply curve, SS, quantity Q_s. The economic cost of producing this
bread, the supply costs of these displaced suppliers, is the shaded area under the labour-
intensive bakers' supply curve, Q_sQ_dBC. Hence, the benefit of the bakery project is
not the market value, the demand price of the bread produced, as this bread was
available before the project started. Instead, its economic benefit is only the labour,
capital and raw materials released by the displaced small bakeries, the shaded area
Q_sQ_dBC. Obviously, these released resources may have quite a low economic value
compared with the economic costs of a rather capital-intensive automated bakery
project. If the cost benefit analysis were correctly undertaken it would recognise this
and the economic NPV of the project might not be positive.

7.6.3 Economic benefits if project's output partially meets new demand and partially substitutes for existing supply

Often, the project's output will partially increase total available supply and meet new
demand and partially substitute for existing sources of supply.[10] The valuation of the

project's output in this situation can be illustrated by the example of a shoe factory project in Figure 7.8.

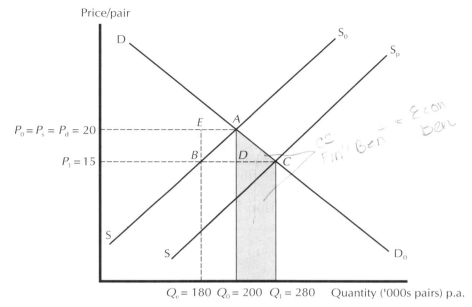

Figure 7.8 *Measurement of economic benefits of outputs in undistorted markets — shoe factory*

Prior to the establishment of the shoe factory the domestic supply of shoes was represented by the supply curve SS_0, and the domestic demand for shoes by DD_0. The equilibrium market price was P_0 ($20 per pair) and the equilibrium quantity traded, Q_0 (200 000 pairs p.a.). Since there were no distortions in the market, the demand price of consumers, P_d, and supply price of producers, P_s, both equalled the market price, P_0.

With the establishment of the new shoe factory, the domestic shoe supply curve will move out to SS_p, the equilibrium price for shoes will fall to P_1 ($15 per pair) and the equilibrium quantity traded will rise to Q_1 (280 000 pairs) p.a. The benefits of the project are derived from two sources. The fall in shoe prices will encourage an increase in people's demand for shoes, from Q_0 to Q_1. Part of the project's output (80 000 pairs) will therefore represent an increase in the availability of shoes in the economy and the economic benefit from this will be measured by the amount people are willing to pay for these shoes. This is represented by the shaded area under the demand curve, Q_0Q_1CA. This includes the amount people actually pay for this increase in supply, which will be the financial benefits the project will earn from this increase in supply, Q_0Q_1CD, plus a gain in consumer surplus that consumers will receive by being able to buy this increased supply at a cheaper price, DCA.

The fall in prices precipitated by the new shoe factory will also force some of the existing shoe producers out of the industry, cutting the amount they supply from Q_0

to Q_e (200 000 to 180 000 pairs). Part of the new factory's output (20 000 pairs) will therefore be a substitute for existing sources of supply. The economic benefit for this part of the project's output will be measured by the supply price of these existing producers, the economic cost of the labour, capital and raw materials used by these displaced producers. These resources can now be released for other purposes in the economy. This second source of benefit is represented by the shaded area under the existing producer's supply curve, Q_eQ_0AB. This represents the loss of sales revenue by existing producers', Q_eQ_0AE, less the producer surplus they enjoyed, AEB, as this was only a transfer and not an economic cost of the displaced producers' production.

The total economic benefits of the project are represented by the shaded area Q_eQ_1CAB. In economic terms, this represents the amount actually paid by consumers for the output produced by the project, Q_eQ_1CB, plus the gain in consumers' surplus, P_1CAP_0 from the lower price of shoes in the economy, minus the loss in existing supplier's producer surplus due to this fall in prices, P_1BAP_0.

7.6.4 The Harberger equation for measuring economic benefits

The project's total economic benefits can therefore be measured by the weighted average of the demand and supply price of its output, where the weights are the quantity of output that meets new demand and substitutes for existing supply, respectively:

$$\text{Benefits} = \text{AvP}_s \times Q_s + \text{AvP}_d \times Q_d \tag{7.1}$$

$$\text{Benefits per unit of output} = \frac{\text{AvP}_s \times Q_s + \text{AvP}_d \times Q_d}{(Q_s + Q_d)} \tag{7.2}$$

where

AvP is the average price of the project's output before and after the project, that is, $\dfrac{(P_1 + P_0)}{2}$

AvP_d is the average demand price (in this case $= \dfrac{P_1 + P_0}{2}$)

AvP_s is the average supply price (in this case $= \dfrac{P_1 + P_0}{2}$)

Q_s is the quantity of output substituting for existing supply, $Q_0 - Q_e$

Q_d is the quantity of output meeting new demand, $Q_1 - Q_0$.

In the example illustrated in Figure 7.8, the average price, AvP will be given by $\dfrac{(20 + 15)}{2} = \$17.50$. The total economic benefits of the shoe factory project are therefore:

$$\begin{aligned}
&= \text{AvP}_s \times Q_s + \text{AvP}_d \times Q_d \\
&= \$17.5 \times 20\,000 + \$17.5 \times 80\,000 \\
&= \$1\,750\,000
\end{aligned}$$

and the economic benefit per pair of shoes is:

$$= \frac{\$1\,750\,000}{100\,000}$$
$$= \$17.50$$

With manipulation, the economic benefits per unit of output, i, can also be expressed in terms of the price elasticities of demand and supply for the project's output, the slopes of its demand and supply curves (Harberger, 1971; Jenkins and Harberger, 1991). This may be useful in a situation where the analyst has estimates of the elasticities of demand and supply for the good to be produced by the planned project, rather than precise data on how much of the planned production will meet new demand and how much will substitute for existing supply. Harberger's equation for the economic benefits of a project per unit of output, i, is just the weighted average of the demand and supply price of the output where the weights are functions of the output's elasticity of supply and demand. The economic benefits of 1 unit of a project's output can therefore be measured by:[11]

$$\text{Benefits per unit of output} = P_{is}W_s + P_{id}W_d \tag{7.3}$$

where

the weight on the supply price,
$$W_s = \frac{\varepsilon_{is}}{\left[\varepsilon_{is} - \eta_{id}\left(\dfrac{Q_{id}}{Q_{is}}\right)\right]} \tag{7.4}$$

the weight on the demand price,
$$W_d = \frac{-\eta_{id}\left(\dfrac{Q_{id}}{Q_{is}}\right)}{\left[\varepsilon_{is} - \eta_{id}\left(\dfrac{Q_{id}}{Q_{is}}\right)\right]} \tag{7.5}$$

ε_{is} is the price elasticity of supply of output i
η_{id} is the price elasticity of demand for output i
P_{id} is the average demand price for project output i
P_{is} is the average supply price for project output i
Q_{is} is the quantity of output i supplied
Q_{id} is the quantity of output i demanded.

Thus the economic benefits per unit of output can be expressed in terms of the elasticities of its demand and supply curves as:

$$\text{Benefits per unit of output} = \frac{\varepsilon_{is}P_{is} - \eta_{id}P_{id}\left(\dfrac{Q_{id}}{Q_{is}}\right)}{\varepsilon_{is} - \eta_{id}\left(\dfrac{Q_{id}}{Q_{is}}\right)} \tag{7.6}$$

If all the project's output will meet new demand, the demand curve facing the project's output must be completely horizontal, as was shown in Figure 7.6 and the elasticity of demand for the output, η_{id} will tend to infinity. In this situation, when measuring the project's benefits, the weight on the demand price, W_d, in equation (7.5) will tend to unity, and the weight on the supply price, W_s, will tend to zero. Hence, the economic benefits measured by equation (7.3) will tend to the demand price of the output, P_d.

If all the project's output substitutes for existing supply, this implies that the demand curve for the project's output is vertical, or completely inelastic, as shown in Figure 7.7. The elasticity of demand for the project's output, η_{id}, is near zero. When measuring the benefit of a unit of the project's output, the weight on the demand price of this output, W_d, in equation (7.5) will tend to zero and the weight on the supply price, W_s, will be unity. Hence, the economic benefits of a unit of output as measured by equation (7.3) will collapse to the supply price of the output, P_s.

Using the example given in Figure 7.8, when the demand curve is downward sloping, the benefits per unit of output are estimated below by employing equation (7.6). Since, in this example the elasticities were not given, the demand and supply elasticities for shoes must be estimated:

$$\varepsilon_{is} = \frac{\delta Q_s}{\delta P} \times \frac{P_s}{Q_s} = \frac{20}{5} \times \frac{20}{200} = 0.4$$

$$\eta_{id} = \frac{\delta Q_d}{\delta P} \times \frac{P_d}{Q_d} = \frac{80}{5} \times \frac{20}{200} = -1.6$$

$$\left(\frac{Q_{id}}{Q_{is}} \right) = 1$$

Substituting the values of ε_{is} and η_{id} into equation (7.6):

$$\text{Economic benefits per unit of output} = \frac{(0.4 \times \$17.50 + 1.6 \times \$17.50)}{(0.4 + 1.6)}$$

$$= \$17.50$$

and total economic benefits $= (17.5 \times \$20\ 000) + (17.5 \times \$80\ 000)$

$$= \$1\ 750\ 000$$

In this example, since the average demand and supply price of the output are equal, the estimation of net benefits is rather trivial. However, if distortions such as taxes are present in the output's market the demand and supply price will no longer be equal and this methodology will be a useful way of measuring the economic benefits of a project. This is illustrated in Section 7.8, below, where price distortions are introduced.

7.7 Measuring the economic costs of project inputs in a closed economy with no distortions — the Harberger approach

In an economic analysis, the cost of a project's inputs are valued in terms of their **opportunity cost**. This is their value in their next best alternative use. In a freely operating market, if the project's requirements for inputs are met from increased production, their opportunity cost will be the marginal social cost of this increased production. In a freely competitive market where producers can meet all the project's demand for inputs without raising their prices because supply is completely elastic,[12] the economic cost of the inputs will equal their **supply price, P_s**. This will usually be the case, as projects will typically not cause the price of their inputs to rise. On the other hand, if the project's demand for inputs must be met by displacing existing users of these inputs, then their economic cost will be the amount that these displaced consumers were willing to pay for the inputs, or their demand price, P_d.

7.7.1 Economic costs if project's input needs are partially supplied from new production and partially met by displacing existing consumers

Sometimes, the project's non-traded inputs will be supplied by a combination of new supply and displaced demand.[13] The economic valuation of a project's input costs in this situation is illustrated in Figure 7.9, which concerns a bridge project's use of steel inputs.

This bridge will require 5000 tonnes of domestic steel products per annum for each of its 4 years of construction. Prior to the commencement of the bridge, the domestic demand for steel products was represented by the demand curve DD_0 and domestic supply by curve SS_0. The equilibrium market price for steel was P_0, \$500 per tonne, and the equilibrium quantity traded, Q_0, was 20 000 tonnes per annum. Since there are assumed to be no distortions such as taxes or subsidies in the market for steel products, the demand price of consumers, P_d, and supply price of producers, P_s, both equalled the market price, P_0, \$500 per tonne.

With the start of the bridge project, the domestic demand for steel products is expected to rise by 5000 tonnes per annum, which is represented by an upward shift of the steel demand curve to DD_p. The equilibrium price for steel products will rise to P_1, \$550 per tonne and the equilibrium quantity traded is also expected to increase to Q_1, or 22 000 tonnes per annum.

The rise in price will force some of the existing consumers of steel products to lower their consumption, reducing their demand from Q_0 to Q_d. On the other hand, the rise in steel product prices will encourage an increase in their supply from Q_0 to Q_1. Hence part of the supply of steel products to the bridge project will be met by existing consumers giving up some of their consumption and part will be met by an increase in the supply of steel products. The total economic cost of the project's inputs will be the combination of these two components.

The first component of the economic cost of steel used by the bridge is the utility lost by the displaced consumers of steel products, measured by the amount they were willing to pay for this steel, WTP. This is represented by the shaded area under the original consumers' demand curve, DD_0, $Q_d Q_0 FE$. The second component of the economic cost of steel is the real resources used by steel producers to increase their steel output by $Q_1 - Q_0$. This is represented by the shaded area under their supply

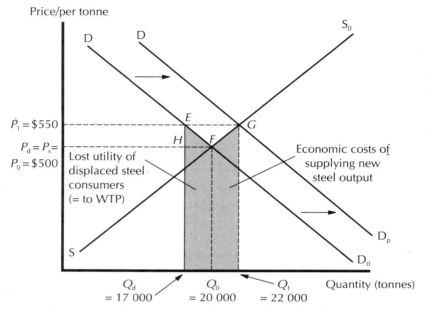

Figure 7.9   *Measurement of economic costs of inputs, undistorted markets — steel products*

curve, SS_0, Q_0Q_1GF. The total economic cost of the project's steel product inputs is therefore represented by the shaded area Q_dQ_1GFE.

This economic cost represents the actual financial cost to the project of the steel products purchased, Q_dQ_1GE, minus the gain in producer's surplus as a result of the project, P_dFGP_1, plus the loss in consumer surplus from increased steel prices, P_dFEP_1. Producer surplus is subtracted because it does not represent a true economic cost to the economy, but is just a transfer from the purchasers to the producers of steel products. The loss in consumer surplus does, however, represent a loss of welfare in the economy, and is included as an economic cost of the project.

The economic costs of the projects inputs can therefore be measured by:

Economic costs $= AvP_s \times Q_s + AvP_d \times Q_d$ (7.7)

Economic costs per unit of input $= \dfrac{AvP_s \times Q_s + AvP_d \times Q_d}{(Q_s + Q_d)}$ (7.8)

where

AvP_d is the average demand price of the input where this is the input's average demand price before and after the project

AvP_s is the average supply price of the input where this is the input's average supply price, before and after the project

Q_s is the quantity of input met by new supply, equal to $(Q_1 - Q_0)$ in this example

Q_d is the quantity of input met by displacing existing consumers, equal to $(Q_0 - Q_d)$ in this example.

With manipulation, the economic costs of a unit of input can also be expressed in terms of the price elasticities of demand and supply for a project input, j, if these elasticities are readily available. This is done using the same Harberger (1971) equation employed in (7.6):[14]

$$\text{Economic costs per unit of input} = P_{js}.W_s + P_{jd}.W_d \tag{7.9}$$

where

the weight on the supply price of input j, $W_s = \dfrac{\varepsilon_{js}}{\left[\varepsilon_{js} - \eta_{jd}\left(\dfrac{Q_{jd}}{Q_{js}}\right)\right]}$ (7.10)

and the weight on the demand price of input j,

$$W_d = \dfrac{-\eta_{jd}\left(\dfrac{Q_{jd}}{Q_{js}}\right)}{\left[\varepsilon_{js} - \eta_{jd}\left(\dfrac{Q_{jd}}{Q_{js}}\right)\right]} \tag{7.11}$$

ε_{js} is the price elasticity of supply of input j
η_{jd} is the price elasticity of demand for input j
Q_{js} is the quantity of input j supplied
Q_{jd} is the quantity of input j demanded

P_{jd} is the average demand price for input j, project output
P_{js} is the average supply price for input j.

The economic costs of a unit of input can also be expressed in terms of the elasticities of the input's demand and supply curves, in the same manner as the project's economic benefits were measured, using the same Harberger equation formulated in equation (7.6):

$$\text{Economic costs per unit of output} = \dfrac{\varepsilon_{js}P_{js} - \eta_{jd}P_{jd}\left(\dfrac{Q_{jd}}{Q_{js}}\right)}{\left[\varepsilon_{js} - \eta_{jd}\left(\dfrac{Q_{jd}}{Q_{js}}\right)\right]} \tag{7.12}$$

Both the economic costs and benefits of the project can be measured using the same expression.

If all the project's input needs will be met by new supply, this means that the supply curve for the project's inputs is completely horizontal and the elasticity of supply for the input, ε_{js}, will tend to infinity. In this situation, when measuring the cost of the project's inputs, the weight on the supply price, W_s, in equation (7.10) will tend to unity, and the weight on the demand price, W_d, will tend to zero. The economic costs of the input, as measured by equation (7.9) will tend to the supply price of the input, P_{js}.

If all the project's input needs are met wholly by displacing other consumers, this implies that the supply curve for the project's input is vertical or completely inelastic. The elasticity of supply for the project's input, ε_{js}, is near zero. When measuring the economic cost of a unit of the project's input, the weight on the supply price of this input, W_s, in equation (7.10) will therefore tend to zero, and the weight on the demand price, W_d, will be unity. Hence, the economic costs of a unit of input, as measured by equation (7.9), will tend to the demand price of the input, P_{jd}.

Using the example given in Figure 7.9, the initial equilibrium price for steel was $500 per tonne, at which 20 000 tonnes of steel was sold per annum. The new equilibrium price after the bridge's requirements for an additional 5000 tonnes of steel per annum have been met will be $550, at which price 22 000 tonnes of steel will be supplied and demanded. The average price for steel products, before and after the project, will be ($500 + 550)/2 = $525/tonne. In Figure 7.9 we saw that existing consumers are expected to cut back their consumption of steel products to 17 000 tonnes per annum at this higher market price.

Using equation (7.7), the economic costs for the project's use of steel inputs will be:

$$= (22\ 000 - 20\ 000) \times \frac{(500\ +\ 550)}{2} + (20\ 000 - 17\ 000) \times \frac{(500\ +\ 550)}{2}$$

$$\therefore \quad \text{Total costs} \qquad = \$2.625 \text{ million}$$
$$\text{Costs per unit of input} = \$525$$

Similarly, the costs per unit of input can be estimated in terms of (7.12) by first estimating the elasticities of supply and demand for steel:

$$\varepsilon_{js} = \frac{\delta Q_s}{\delta P} \times \frac{P_s}{Q_s} = \left(\frac{2000}{50}\right) \times \left(\frac{500}{20\ 000}\right) = 1$$

$$\eta_{jd} = \frac{\delta Q_d}{\delta P} \times \frac{P_d}{Q_d} = \left(\frac{3000}{50}\right) \times \left(\frac{500}{20\ 000}\right) = -1.5$$

$$\left(\frac{Q_{jd}}{Q_{js}}\right) = 1$$

$$\text{Economic costs per unit of input} = \frac{(1 \times \$525\ +\ 1.5 \times \$525)}{(1\ +\ 1.5)}$$

$$= \$525$$
$$\text{Total cost of steel inputs} = \$525 \times 5000$$
$$= \$2.625 \text{ million}$$

7.8 Measuring the economic benefits of non-traded outputs in markets with distortions[15]

The discussion in the previous sections assumes that there are no distortions such as taxes, subsidies, monopolies and quantitative restrictions in goods or factor markets in the economy where the project will be located. This assumption is now relaxed, in order to examine how the economic benefits of projects are measured when distortions exist in goods and factor markets. Section 7.9 considers valuing the economic costs of project inputs if there are distortions in the markets for primary factors and produced inputs used by the project. This is necessary because in the real world it is unusual to find a project in which none of its inputs or outputs are subject to sales taxes, tariffs, price controls or subsidies. If such distortions exist in the markets for the project's inputs and outputs they must be corrected when estimating the project's true economic costs and benefits to the economy.

7.8.1 Sales taxes on the project's output

The method of valuing a project's output in a closed economy where there are distortions in the market for this output is considered in this section. Such distortions may include taxes and subsidies, price controls, rationing and monopoly pricing. To simplify the consideration of these distortions, it will initially be assumed that there is perfect competition in the market for the output, and hence no price control or rationing and the only distortions are government imposed taxes and subsidies.[16]

A common distortion is the imposition of a sales tax on a project's output. For example, a sales tax may be imposed on the producers' supply price of shoes in the factory project considered in Figure 7.8. This situation is shown in Figure 7.10.

Before the imposition of a sales tax, the equilibrium market price for shoes was P_{0m}, and Q_{0m} shoes were traded. If a sales tax, t_{st}, of 15 per cent is imposed on shoes, the **total demand price** per pair of shoes that people are willing to pay at each quantity of shoes available will not change and will still be represented by demand curve DD_0. However, for every quantity of shoes traded the amount that people are willing to pay **to the producers** of shoes could be expected to decline by the proportionate sales tax , t_{st}, 15 per cent, given that they will have to pay the government a sales tax of 15 per cent on every pair they now buy. This new net of tax demand curve will be represented by DD_{st}, which shows the amount consumers are willing to pay **shoe producers** per pair, for each quantity of shoes produced. From the shoe producers' point of view, the imposition of the tax will cause a downward shift in the demand curve for shoes, from DD_0 to DD_{st}. The new equilibrium quantity of shoes traded will occur at Q_{0st}, the intersection of the producers' supply curve, unchanged at SS, and this new net of sales tax demand curve, DD_{st}.

At the lower quantity now supplied, the demand price of shoes including sales tax will rise to P_{1d}, above the initial equilibrium price. The supply price of shoes paid to producers will, however, be lower, at P_{1s}. The wedge that has been driven between the demand price, P_{1d}, which consumers are willing to pay and the supply price, P_{1s}, which is the cost of production of the marginal supplier, is the tax paid to the government, t_{st}. The new market equilibrium price for shoes will rise to P_{1d} if market prices are quoted inclusive of the new sales tax, as is the case in most countries, including Australia, but will fall to the supply price, P_{1s}, if market prices are quoted exclusive of sales tax, as is the case in the United States.

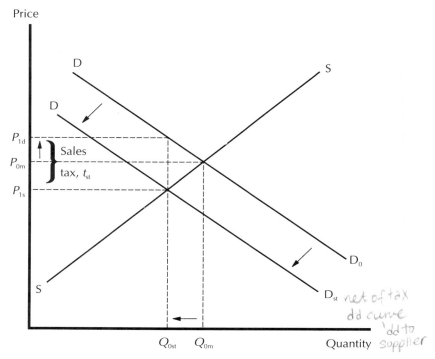

Figure 7.10   *Imposition of a sales tax on a project's output (tax on the supply price) — shoes*

If a project to produce shoes is established in a country that imposes a sales tax on shoes, how should its economic benefits be measured? This situation is illustrated in Figure 7.11.

Establishment of the project will cause a shift in the supply curve for shoes from SS to SS_p, as the total amount supplied by the project will be $Q_{1st} - Q_{1s}$ pairs of shoes. As a result there will be a fall in the supply price (and tax exclusive market price) of shoes from P_{1S} to P_{2S}. The fall in shoe prices will cause an increase in demand, from Q_{0st} to Q_{1st}, and the equilibrium quantity traded will rise to Q_{1st}. The fall in prices will also force some marginal producers out of production, cutting back their production from Q_{0st} to Q_{1s}. Of the project's total output, $Q_{1st} - Q_{1s}$, part will therefore meet this new demand for shoes, $Q_{1st} - Q_{0st}$, and part will substitute for the shoes previously produced by marginal shoe makers, $Q_{0st} - Q_{1s}$.

The economic benefits of the shoes that meet new demand are given by the shaded area $Q_{0st}Q_{1st}CD$, under the total demand curve DD_0. This measures the total amount that consumers are willing to pay for this additional quantity of shoes. Part of this total, $AECD$, is actually paid to the government as sales tax, but it still represents part of the benefits of the project as people are still willing to pay this total amount, including the tax, for this quantity of shoes. The economic benefits of that part of the project's output that substitutes for existing supply are measured by the savings in

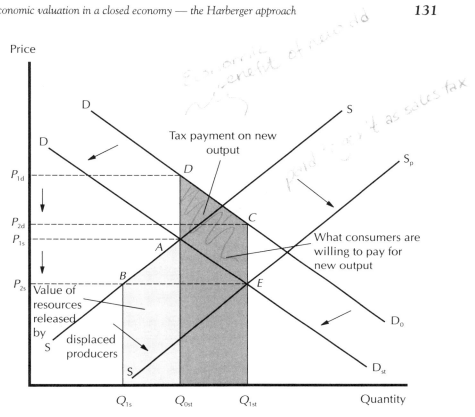

Figure 7.11   *Measuring the economic benefits of a project whose output is subject to sales tax*

the real resources no longer required by these marginal producers. This is given by the area $Q_{1s}Q_{0st}AB$, under the original producers' supply curve, SS.

The total economic benefits of the new project are therefore the shaded areas on Figure 7.11:

Benefits = $Q_{0st}Q_{1st}CD + Q_{1st}Q_{0s}AB$
Algebraically this is equivalent to:

$$\text{Benefits} = \Delta Q_S \times \frac{(P_{2s} + P_{1s})}{2} + \Delta Q_d \times \frac{(P_{2d} + P_{1d})}{2}$$

where

ΔQ_S is the change in the quantity supplied by existing suppliers
ΔQ_d is the change in the quantity demanded by consumers
$\dfrac{(P_{2s} + P_{1s})}{2}$ is the average supply price, after the sales tax is imposed, before and after the project
$\dfrac{(P_{2d} + P_{1d})}{2}$ is the average demand price, including the sales tax, before and after the project.

In terms of equation (7.6), economic benefits per unit can be measured as:

$$\text{Economic benefits per unit of output} = \frac{\varepsilon_{is} P_{is} - \eta_{id} P_{id}\left(\dfrac{Q_{id}}{Q_{is}}\right)}{\varepsilon_{is} - \eta_{id}\left(\dfrac{Q_{id}}{Q_{is}}\right)} \tag{7.13}$$

where

P_{id} is the demand price for shoes $= P_{im}(1 + t_{st})$
P_{im} is the pre-tax market price of output i, shoes
t_{st} is the sales tax on shoes
$P_{is} = P_{im}$ is the supply price of shoes, equal to its pre-tax market price
η_{id} is the elasticity of demand for shoes
ε_{is} is the elasticity of supply of shoes.

Hence, economic benefits per unit in the presence of a sales tax on output are measured as:

$$\text{Economic benefits per unit of output} = \frac{\varepsilon_{is} P_{is} - \eta_{id} P_{im} (1 + t_{st})\left(\dfrac{Q_{id}}{Q_{is}}\right)}{\varepsilon_{is} - \eta_{id}\left(\dfrac{Q_{id}}{Q_{is}}\right)} \tag{7.14}$$

If all the project's output is expected to meet new demand and there is not expected to be any fall in the output's price, this means that at least over the range of output produced by the project the demand curve facing the project will be completely horizontal. This will usually be the case for projects that are small in relation to the total economy. Hence, the elasticity of demand for the project's output, η_{id}, will tend to infinity. In this situation, it can be seen from (7.3) and (7.13) that the project's economic benefits will be measured only by the average demand price of the output before and after the project, which includes the sales tax on that output, $\text{AvP}_{id} = P_{im}(1 + t_{st})$.

If all the project's output is expected to substitute for existing supply, this will imply that the demand curve for the project's output is believed to be vertical, and the elasticity of demand for the project's output, η_{id}, is near zero. In this situation the economic benefits of a unit of output will be measured by the average supply price of existing producers of the project's output before and after the project, AvP_{is}, which will be the pre-tax market price in this case.

7.8.2 Production subsidies on the project's output

Many governments subsidise the production of crops or other goods or services that they think are important to consumers. Measuring the economic benefits of a project's output in the presence of other distortions in its market, such as production subsidies, can be handled using the Harberger equation, in a similar manner to taxes on output.

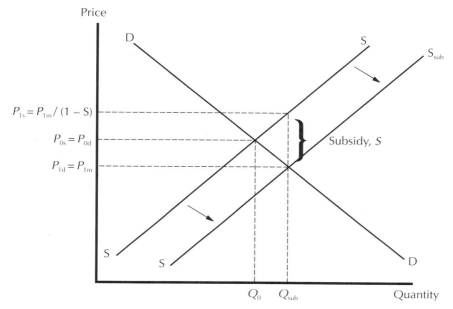

Figure 7.12 *Imposition of a percentge subsidy on rice production costs*

If the government pays a percentage subsidy, S, of the production costs of rice producers, they will be able to supply the same volume of rice for a lower price per kilogram. In Figure 7.12 the provision of a subsidy will cause an outward shift in the supply curve for rice from SS to SS_{sub} and increase the quantity supplied from Q_0 to Q_{sub}. The availability of the subsidy will drive a wedge between the market price for which producers are willing to supply rice after they have received the subsidy, P_{1m}, which will also be the demand price that people are willing to pay for this quantity of rice, P_{1d}, and their higher supply price, P_{1s}, the actual cost of producing this quantity of rice.

Figure 7.13 shows how to measure the economic benefits of producing a good when other producers of that good are receiving a subsidy.

The increased output of rice as a result of a new rice growing project is represented by a shift in the supply curve to $SS_{sub + proj}$. This increase in supply will necessitate a drop in rice prices to P_{1m} to stimulate sufficient additional demand so that the market can be cleared. This price fall will cause some of the higher cost existing rice producers to go out of business, releasing their production resources, $Q_{1s}Q_{0sub}BA$ for other uses in the economy. Some of these production costs were paid for by the subsidy, $ECBA$. The economic benefits of the rice project will equal the amount consumers are willing to pay for new supplies of rice, $Q_{0sub}Q_{1sub}DC$, plus the real resources saved by the displaced marginal rice producers, $Q_{1s}Q_{0sub}BA$.

These economic benefits can also be measured using equation (7.13). In this situation, the market price for rice, P_{im}, will equal the demand price, P_{id}, but not

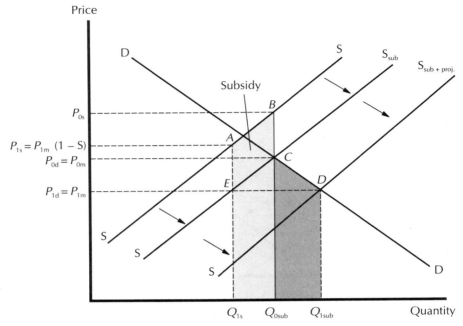

Figure 7.13   *Measurement of benefits from a new rice-growing project if there is a subsidy for the production of rice*

the supply price, P_{is}. The relationship between the supply price and market price is given by:

$$P_{is} \times (1 - S) = P_{im}$$

$$\therefore \quad P_{is} = \frac{P_{im}}{(1 - S)} \tag{7.15}$$

where

S is the percentage rate of subsidy on production costs.

That is, the supply price of rice, P_{1s}, will equal the subsidy inclusive market price divided by one minus the rate of subsidy, $\dfrac{P_{1m}}{(1 - S)}$.

Substituting (7.15) into (7.14) gives an expression for measuring the economic benefits of a project in the presence of a subsidy. If both a subsidy and a tax are imposed, a general formula to measure the economic benefits of a project can be derived as follows:

$$\begin{array}{c}\text{Economic benefits} \\ \text{per unit of output}\end{array} = \frac{\dfrac{\varepsilon_{is} P_{im}}{(1 - S)} - \eta_{id} P_{im} (1 + t_{st})\left(\dfrac{Q_{id}}{Q_{is}}\right)}{\varepsilon_{is} - \eta_{id}\left(\dfrac{Q_{id}}{Q_{is}}\right)} \tag{7.16}$$

This measures the economic benefits of a project's output in terms of observable market prices, tax and subsidy rates, and the elasticities of demand and supply of the project's output.

7.8.3 Price control on the project output

Many government authorities in developed and developing countries, such as railways, water, electricity and telephone, postal and communication supply authorities, cannot freely increase their prices without permission from ministers and hence are subject to a form of price control. In addition, in the remaining centrally planned economies as well as economies like India, Indonesia, the Philippines and Thailand, which still have a significant level of government intervention, many basic commodities and utilities are still subject to some form of price control. How should a project's benefits be measured if its output price is controlled?

Figure 7.14 illustrates a situation where the fares charged on the government owned railway in Indonesia are fixed at a P_f per kilometre, which is below the equilibrium fare, P_e.

Prior to the establishment of a new railway service the supply of rail services was represented by the supply curve, SS. At this artificially low price the demand for seats exceeded supply by the amount $(Q_{0d} - Q_{0s})$.[17] Reading off the demand curve for train seats, DD, some people would have been willing to pay much more, P_d, for this limited number of seats, Q_{0s}, and the total amount that people would have been willing to pay for the Q_{0s} of rail services was $0Q_{0s}AP_{max}$.

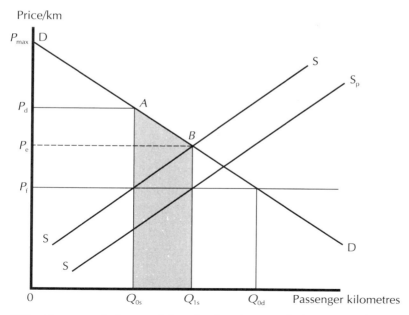

Figure 7.14 *Measurement of economic benefits of a price controlled output — railway services*

In this situation, the Indonesian government intends to expand rail services to meet this excess demand. The new project would push the supply curve out to SS_p, expanding the services delivered at the fixed price to Q_{1s}. However, it would be a mistake to value these services at the fixed price, P_f, as consumers are willing to pay more than this for these train services. The economic benefit of the new rail service will be the total amount that consumers would have been willing to pay for these services. This is the shaded area under the demand curve, $Q_{0s}Q_{1s}BA$. As there will be no drop in rail fares as a result of the project and no displaced alternative producers of rail services, the supply price of the service is irrelevant to measuring its benefit, $(W_s = 0)$.

7.9 The valuation of economic costs of non-traded inputs in markets with distortions

Similar adjustments must be made when measuring the economic costs of project inputs if these are subject to taxes and subsidies. Once again the Harberger approach provides a useful framework for analysing the economic costs of using inputs when there are distortions in their markets.

7.9.1 Sales taxes on the project's input

The example of the steel required by a bridge project can be used to consider how these costs would be measured if there were a sales tax, t_{st}, imposed on steel products.

As illustrated in Figure 7.15, if a sales tax is imposed on steel products the effective demand curve for steel facing suppliers of steel products will fall from DD to DD_{st}. DD_{st} shows how much steel consumers are willing to pay **suppliers** for each tonne of steel. The actual demand curve for steel will remain unchanged at DD, but will include the amount buyers must pay in tax for each tonne of steel they buy. The market clearing supply price will then fall to P_{1s}, which will also equal the tax exclusive market price, P_{1m}.[18] The equilibrium quantity of steel traded will decline from Q_0 to Q_1. The pre-tax market price will be equal to the full supply price of steel products, P_{1s}.

However, the demand price for steel products, which people are willing to pay, will include the sales tax, that is,

$$P_{1d} = P_{1m}(1 + t_{st}) \tag{7.17}$$

If a sales tax is in place when the bridge project increases the demand for steel products, how is the economic cost of the steel measured? In Figure 7.16 the project pushes out the demand curve for steel products to DD_{pst}, raising their price from P_{1m} to P_{2m}. Some of this increased demand for steel as a result of the project will be met by increased production stimulated by the higher price, $(Q_{1st} - Q_{0st})$, and some by displacing existing consumers of steel products who can no longer afford this price $(Q_{0st} - Q_{1d})$. As usual, the economic cost of the new production is its average supply

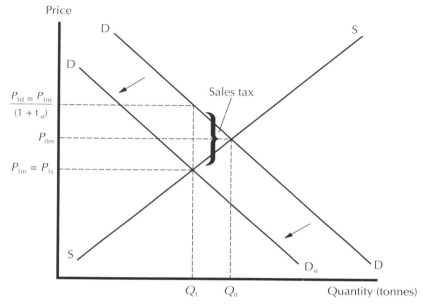

Figure 7.15 *Economic cost of steel inputs if subjected to a sales tax*

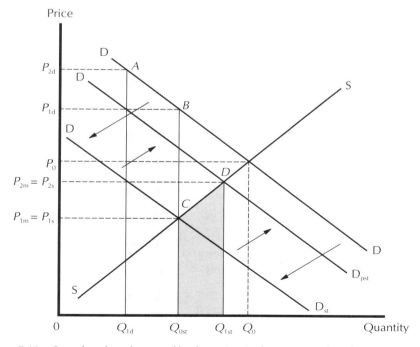

Figure 7.16 *Cost of steel products used by the project in the presence of a sales tax*

price, which is equal to the market price, $\dfrac{(P_{2s} + P_{1s})}{2}$. The total cost of this new production will therefore be $Q_{0st}Q_{1st}DC$. The steel previously used by other consumers, on the other hand, should be valued at the amount these consumers were willing to pay, as this is a measure of the loss of welfare in the economy from these consumers being forced to give up their consumption. This is measured by the average demand price of the input before and after the project, including the sales tax, $\dfrac{(P_{2d} + P_{1d})}{2}$, and the cost to the economy of the project's use of this steel will be the shaded area $Q_{1d}Q_{0st}BA$.

The total economic cost of the steel products in the presence of this sales tax is therefore measured by the resources used to produce the increased production, the shaded area $Q_{0st}Q_{1st}DC$, plus the loss of utility of the displaced steel consumers, the amount they were willing to pay to use it, $Q_{1d}Q_{0st}Q_{1st}BA$.

Substituting (7.17) into equation (7.12), the economic cost per unit of steel used is given by:

$$\text{Economic costs per unit of input} = \frac{\varepsilon_{js}P_{js} - \eta_{jd}P_{jm}(1 + t_{st})\left(\dfrac{Q_{jd}}{Q_{js}}\right)}{\varepsilon_{js} - \eta_{jd}\left(\dfrac{Q_{jd}}{Q_{js}}\right)} \tag{7.18}$$

where

P_{jd} is the demand price for steel $= P_{jm}(1+ t_{st})$
P_{jm} is the pre-tax market price of input j, steel products
t_{st} is the sales tax on steel
η_{jd} is the elasticity of demand for input j
ε_{js} is the elasticity of supply of input j.

7.9.2 Subsidy on the project's input

If a percentage subsidy of S were provided for the production of steel products used by the bridge project, the relationship between the supply price and market price of steel would be given by:

$$P_{js} = \frac{P_{jm}}{(1 - S)} \tag{7.19}$$

That is, the supply price of the steel products, P_{js}, would be greater than its market price, P_{jm}, as a result of the subsidy. Substituting (7.19) into equation (7.12), the economic cost per unit of steel in the presence of a subsidy on steel is given by:[19]

$$\text{Economic costs per unit of input} = \frac{\dfrac{\varepsilon_{js}P_{jm}}{(1 - S)} - \eta_{jd}P_{jd}\left(\dfrac{Q_{jd}}{Q_{js}}\right)}{\varepsilon_{js} - \eta_{jd}\left(\dfrac{Q_{jd}}{Q_{js}}\right)} \tag{7.20}$$

Putting (7.18) and (7.20) together, in the general case, the economic costs of the project inputs in the presence of taxes and subsidies can be measured by:

$$\text{Economic costs per unit of input} = \frac{\dfrac{\varepsilon_{js} P_{jm}}{(1 - S)} - \eta_{jd} P_{jm} (1 + t_{st}) \left(\dfrac{Q_{jd}}{Q_{js}} \right)}{\varepsilon_{js} - \eta_{jd} \left(\dfrac{Q_{jd}}{Q_{js}} \right)} \qquad (7.21)$$

This Harberger equation therefore measures the economic costs of a project's inputs in terms of observable market prices, tax and subsidy rates and elasticities of demand and supply of the project's input. Equations (7.16) and (7.21) are in fact identical. Exactly the same equation can be used to estimate the economic costs of a project and to measure its economic benefits in the presence of tax and subsidy distortions. All that will differ are the actual elasticities of supply and demand of the inputs and outputs of the project and tax and subsidy rates applicable to them, which will of course be specific to the estimations concerned.

7.9.3 Price controls on project inputs

In many countries important inputs into a project, such as rail, water, electricity and communication services, as well as essential raw materials such as oil, coal and labour may be subject to price controls. How should a project's costs be measured in this situation? Once again, the simple framework employed in preceding sections can be used to analyse this issue.

If the controlled price is set above the market clearing price, as is often the case for minimum wages, then the increased demand for labour as a result of a project will cause a reduction in the excess supply of labour. This situation is illustrated in Figure 7.17, where the minimum wage for unskilled labour is fixed at W_f per day, and the initial supply and demand curves for labour are given by SS and DD. At this artificially high wage rate the supply of labour will exceed the demand by the amount $(Q_{sl} - Q_{dl})$. The true cost to workers of supplying Q_{dl} of labour is given by the area under the labour supply curve, $0Q_{dl}AW_s$. If the project increases demand for labour in these circumstances, its economic cost will be measured by the supply cost of this labour, the shaded area, $Q_{dl}Q_{dp}BA$, as there will be no change in the fixed wage and therefore no displaced employers.

If the price of the input is fixed below its market clearing level, as was the case with plan-priced coal in China, these price controls are likely to result in an excess demand for coal. The measurement of the economic cost of this coal is illustrated in Figure 7.18. Before the establishment of a new coal fired power station, there was already excess demand for coal in this country equal to $Q_{0d} - Q_{0s}$ tonnes. With the introduction of the project the demand curve for coal will be pushed out to DD_p and the excess demand for coal will increase by $Q_{1d} - Q_{0d}$ tonnes, say 10 000 tonnes per annum. Since there will be no increase in the fixed price of coal and therefore no supply response, all 10 000 tonnes of the project's annual demand for coal will have to be taken away from other consumers (by some rationing process under the plan).

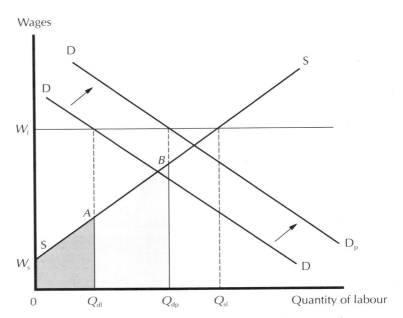

Figure 7.17   *Economic cost of labour in the presence of minimum wage regulations*

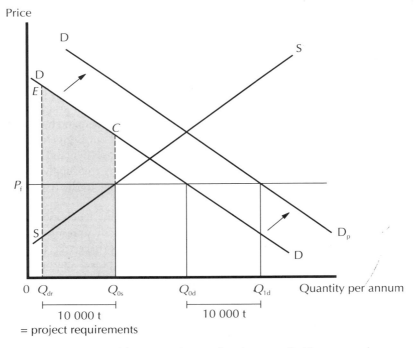

Figure 7.18   *Measurement of the economic cost of a price controlled input — coal*

The economic cost of these 10 000 tonnes of coal is therefore the amount that displaced consumers would have been willing to pay for this coal, the shaded area $Q_{rd}Q_{0s}CE$.

7.10 Summary of economic pricing in the presence of distortions

It is important when undertaking a project appraisal to identify the **major** distortions that will create the most serious divergences between market (financial) and economic prices in the markets for a project's outputs and inputs. This judgement will provide guidance on which goods and factor markets affected by the project should be analysed in more depth. If the project is relatively small and does not intensively use any non-traded good in short supply then, if there is no clear evidence to the contrary, it may be reasonable to assume that all the project's demands for inputs can be met by increased supply without any change in input prices. In this case there will be no displaced consumers of the input as a result of the project and there will be no need to consider changes in producer surplus. The constant supply prices of inputs, net of any sales taxes but gross of any subsidies, should therefore be used to measure the economic cost of inputs.

Similarly, a relatively small project may expect to sell its output without depressing market prices. On-going growth in demand or already suppressed excess demand if there are price controls on this good will often be sufficient to enable the project's output to be absorbed at the current market price. In this case no existing suppliers will be displaced by the project and it will also be unnecessary to consider changes in consumer surplus. The economic value of its output will be measured by its constant demand price, or what consumers are willing to pay for it. This will be the output's constant market price including any sales taxes but excluding any subsidies to consumers.

If, however, any of these simplifying assumptions appear unrealistic and output or input prices are expected to change as a result of the project, it will be necessary to measure its economic benefits and costs using the framework outlined in the preceding

Table 7.1 The relationship between market prices and demand and supply prices, with various types of distortions

Type of tax or subsidy	Supply price, P_{is}	Demand price, P_{id}
Percentage sales tax, t_{st}	$P_s = P_m$ = pre-tax market price	$P_d = P_m(1 + t_{st})$
Unit sales tax, T_{st}	$P_s = P_m$ = pre-tax market price	$P_d = P_m + T_{st}$
Percentage subsidy, S	$P_s = \dfrac{P_m}{(1 - S)}$ = cost of production	$P_d = P_m$ = post-subsidy market price
Unit subsidy, S_u	$P_s = P_m + S_u$ = cost of production	$P_d = P_m$ = post-subsidy market price

P_m = market price; P_s = supply price; P_d = demand price

Source: Jenkins and Harberger (1991), Table 9–1, Chapter 9:14.

sections, 7.6 to 7.9. Table 7.1 summarises how the economic costs and benefits of a project are measured in the presence of taxes and subsidies using the Harberger approach.

Exercises

1. A state owned electricity corporation is considering establishing a new coal fired electricity generation project. It will increase the domestic supply of electricity by 500 000 megawatt hours per annum (MWh p.a.). Currently, 3 million MWh of electricity are supplied and purchased in the country each year.

   The average sales price of electricity prior to the new project was 10 cents per kilowatt hour (kWh). In order to clear the market after the new project comes on stream, it is calculated that electricity prices will need to fall to 9 cents per kWh. At this lower price, some small oil fired generators will become uneconomic. The electricity generating authority is expected to decommission some of these units, reducing supply by 100 000 MWh per annum.

   Calculate the total economic benefits and benefits per unit of output of the new coal fired electricity generation station. Use a diagram and/or the Harberger equation to assist you in these calculations.

   What is the value of the uncompensated gain in consumer surplus as a result of the decline in electricity prices (that is, the gain in consumer surplus that is not offset by the loss in producer surplus)? Show this diagrammatically and calculate the total $ value.

2. The operation of the coal fired electricity generation station will require 100 skilled technicians, a skill category that is in short supply in the country concerned. There are currently only 700 such technicians employed in the country, at an average wage of $500 per month. The additional demands for this type of technician created by the project are expected to result in their wages rising 10 per cent. At this higher wage, it is calculated, from past experience, that approximately 70 workers with these skills, currently working in other occupations, will be induced to return to this employment. In addition, some employers currently employing such workers will no longer be able to afford to employ them at the higher wage rate. It is expected that the additional 30 workers required will be released from employment by such enterprises.

   Calculate the total economic costs and costs per unit of labour employed of the project's requirements for skilled technicians. Use a diagram and/or the Harberger equation to assist you in these calculations.

3. In the same project as described in exercise 1, calculate the total benefits and benefits per unit of the project if electricity consumers were paying a sales tax of 10 per cent on top of the 10 cents per kWh tariff, and will continue to pay sales tax at this rate on the new lower tariff of 9 cents per kWh, after the project begins production. Use a diagram and/or the Harberger equation to assist you in these calculations.

4. What would be the cost to the economy of the project's use of the skilled technicians if their training attracted a government subsidy that, over their working life, reduced the wage they received by 4 per cent. Use a diagram and/or the Harberger equation to assist you in these calculations.

5. Consider a coal mining project that will increase coal supply by 1 million tonnes per annum in a country where the domestic price of coal is fixed at $60 per tonne. Current demand in the country concerned is estimated to be 20 million tonnes, but supply is only 12 million tonnes. The black market (or free market) price for coal is $100 per tonne, and is expected to fall to $95 per tonne as a result of the additional supply from the new mine. Estimate the economic benefits of the new project in these circumstances.

References

Harberger, A.C., 1971. 'Three basic postulates of applied welfare economics: an interpretative essay', *Journal of Economic Literature*, Vol. IX, No 3, Sept , 785–97.

Jenkins G.P. and Harberger, A.C., 1991. *Manual — Cost Benefit Analysis of Investment Decisions*, Program on Investment Appraisal and Management, Harvard Institute for International Development, Cambridge.

Little, I.M.D. and Mirrlees, J.A., 1974. *Project Appraisal and Planning for Developing Countries*, Heinemann Educational Books, London.

Squire, L., 1989. 'Project evaluation in theory and practice', in H. Chenery, and T.N. Srinivasan, (eds), *Handbook of Development Economics*, Vol. 2, North Holland, Amsterdam, Chapter 21.

UNIDO, 1972. *Guidelines for Project Evaluation*, United Nations, New York.

Further reading

Helmers, F., 1979. *Project Planning and Income Distribution*, Martinus Nijhoff Publishing, Amsterdam, Chapters 2, 3.

Jenkins G.P. and Harberger, A.C., 1991. *Manual — Cost Benefit Analysis of Investment Decisions*, Program on Investment Appraisal and Management, Harvard Institute for International Development, Cambridge, Chapters 8, 9.

Sugden, R. and Williams, A., 1978. *The Principles of Practical Cost Benefit Analyses*, Oxford University Press, Oxford, Chapter 9.

UNIDO, 1972. *Guidelines for Project Evaluation*, United Nations, New York, Chapters 4, 5.

Endnotes

1   Transfer payments are defined in Section 7.3.

2   If some of the output substitutes for existing supplies, including imports, the supply price of these displaced suppliers, rather than the demand price for newly available output, will measure the economic benefit of the project's output. This issue is discussed in more detail in Section 7.6.

3   The 'UNIDO Guidelines' (UNIDO, 1972) approach.

4   The Little and Mirrlees (1974) approach. The difference in these two approaches to this question is essentially philosophical. Little and Mirrlees emphasise the need for projects to be judged on the basis of their international competitiveness. Sen, Marglin and Dasgupta in the UNIDO *Guidelines* (1972), on the other hand, maintain that a government has the right to run an independent industrialisation policy, including protection as part of this. However, exhaustive theoretical investigations have supported the Little and Mirrlees approach on this question; traded goods should be valued at their international prices, at the country's border, Squire (1989).

5   Sugden and Williams, Chapter 9, gives a formal proof of this.

6   However, this result assumes that the revenue shortfall could be made up in some non-distorting way by levying lump sum taxes, or, better still, by extracting some of the consumer surplus that will be enjoyed by the new electricity consumers. This could be done, by charging a substantial connection fee, or levying minimum fixed tariffs unrelated to actual electricity consumed each quarter. Otherwise, the welfare losses of levying distortionary taxes to make good the electricity authority's budget shortfall may outweigh the benefits of the electricity consumers' gain in consumer surplus.

7   That is, the supply curve for the factor is upward sloping. An upward sloping long-term supply curve for electricity may occur, for example, if a country had used up all its readily accessible hydroelectric power sites, and was forced to use more expensive thermal power generation to supply any additional power.

8   More realistically, the supply curve for electricity will be a series of steps, as each new power station will have a different average supply cost.

9   Some electricity supply authorities, on the other hand, contract to sell the output from various power stations to different users at the (historical) marginal cost of production. Thus, they discriminate between different consumers and effectively collect revenue only equal to the area under their supply curve. The Tasmanian Hydro Electricity Commission in Australia is one authority that has employed this policy in the past.

10 The discussion in this chapter draws freely from Jenkins and Harberger (*ibid.*), Chapter 8.

11 Harberger, A.C., 1972. *Project Appraisal*. The formal derivation of this expression is given in Jenkins and Harberger (*ibid.*), Chapter 8, p. 6.

12 As the suppliers of project inputs operate on a completely horizontal (elastic) supply curve there will be no producer surplus included in the market price.

13 Jenkins and Harberger, *ibid*, Chapter 8.

14 Harberger, A.C., 1972. *Project Appraisal*. The formal derivation of this expression is given in Jenkins and Harberger (*ibid.*), Chapter 8, p. 10.

15 A detailed analysis of how to measure economic costs and benefits in the presence of these distortions is provided in Jenkins and Harberger (1991), Chapter 9.

16 This section adopts an approach employed in Jenkins and Harberger, *ibid*, Chapter 9.

17 Excessive crowding on trains, and artificially low prices are common for railways in many developing and some developed countries.

18 If it is the convention to include the sales tax in the market price, then the market price will be equal to the demand price, P_{1d}, which will equal $(1 + t_{st})$ multiplied by the supply price, $P_{im} = P_{id} = P_{is} \times (1 + t_{st})$.

19 It is unlikely (but not unheard of) that a government would both impose a sales tax and provide a subsidy on the same product, but this case is given as a general formulation.

CHAPTER 8

The economic valuation of tradeables

8.1 Definition of traded and non-traded goods

The previous chapter examined the economic value of projects in a closed economy with no international trade. We will now relax this simplifying assumption and consider how to value projects in economies that **do** trade with the outside world, that is, virtually all economies. The principles outlined in Chapter 7 are, however, still applicable to the valuation of **non-traded goods, goods that do not enter into international trade**.

In almost all projects many of the inputs will be tradeable goods and a large number of projects will also have tradeable outputs. **Tradeable goods are defined as goods and services whose use or production causes a change in the country's net import or export position**. Tradeable goods produced or used by a project do not actually need to be imported or exported themselves, but must be capable of being imported or exported. Some amount of a tradeable good will usually be traded, as long as the country's trade régime is not excessively restrictive.

If a project uses a tradeable input this will have a negative impact on the country's balance of trade or its exchange rate, either directly or indirectly. The extra demand for the input generated by the project will necessitate an increase in the imports of that input or prevent some domestically produced units of that input from being exported. By similar reasoning, the production of a tradeable output will have a positive impact, either directly or indirectly, on the country's balance of trade or its exchange rate. Examples of traded goods include all kinds of manufactures, agricultural goods, intermediate goods, raw materials and some services such as tourism and consultancy services.

Tradeable goods are either exportable or importable goods (or services). Exportables are goods whose domestic cost of production is below the fob (free on board) export price that local producers can earn for this good on the international market. Figure 8.1 shows the circumstances in which a good or service will be an exportable. The domestic equilibrium price for PNG coffee, P_d, would be below the world price, P_w, which is determined by the world demand curve, DD_w. This makes it profitable for PNG's domestic coffee producers to export and receive the higher world price. Domestic producers will produce Q_s, of which Q_d will be sold locally and $Q_s - Q_d$ will be exported.

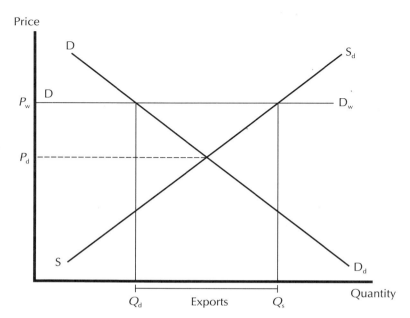

Figure 8.1   *Domestically produced good is an exportable — PNG coffee*

Importables are goods whose landed cif (cost, insurance and freight) import cost is less than the domestic cost of producing these goods. Figure 8.2 illustrates circumstances under which a good will be an importable.

The domestic equilibrium price of cars in China, P_d is above the world price, P_w, which is determined by the world supply curve, SS_w. This will make it worthwhile for domestic consumers to attempt to import cars at the lower world price. In the absence of tariffs and import restrictions, domestic producers would produce Q_s cars and $Q_d - Q_s$ would be the demand for imports.

Figure 8.3 shows a typical case of a non-tradeable good such as cement blocks. **Non-tradeable goods** are goods and services whose marginal domestic production costs, P_d, are less than their cif import cost, P_{wcif}, but greater than their fob export revenue, P_{wfob}. It is not profitable to import or to export such goods or services. Examples of non-tradeables include most services such as domestic transport, utilities and personal services, highly perishable commodities like fresh bread and milk, and commodities like sand, gravel and bricks, whose value is low in relation to their transport costs.

8.2 Measurement of economic values of tradeables in border prices — the Harberger approach

In almost all cases, the economic benefits of producing tradeable outputs and costs of using tradeable inputs are measured by the **border prices** of these outputs and inputs.

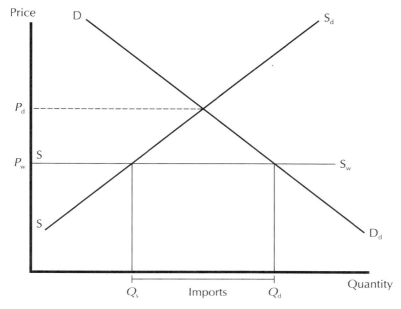

Figure 8.2 *Domestically produced good is an importable — Chinese cars*

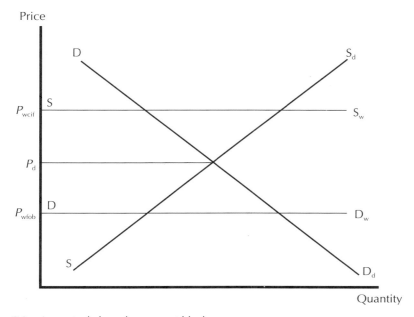

Figure 8.3 *A non-traded good — cement blocks*

An importable's border price is its cif import price — its price landed in the importing country before the effects of any tariffs or quantitative restrictions have been added to its price. An exportable's border price is its fob export price — the price that would be earned by the exporter after paying any costs to get the good to the border, but before any export subsidies or taxes were imposed.

The reason for using border prices to measure the economic value of a project's tradeable outputs and inputs can be understood using the same simple Harberger framework used to value non-traded outputs and inputs in the closed economy scenario.[1]

$$\text{Economic benefits or costs per unit of output} = P_{is}\,W_s + P_{id}.W_d \qquad (8.1)$$

where

$$\text{the weight on the supply price, } W_s = \frac{\varepsilon_{is}}{\left[\varepsilon_{is} - \eta_{id}\left(\dfrac{Q_{id}}{Q_{is}}\right)\right]} \qquad (8.2)$$

$$\text{the weight on the demand price, } W_d = \frac{-\eta_{id}\left(\dfrac{Q_{id}}{Q_{is}}\right)}{\left[\varepsilon_{is} - \eta_{id}\left(\dfrac{Q_{id}}{Q_{is}}\right)\right]} \qquad (8.3)$$

ε_{is} is the price elasticity of supply of good i
η_{id} is the price elasticity of demand for good i
P_{id} is the average demand price for good i
P_{is} is the average supply price for good i
Q_{is} is the quantity of good i supplied
Q_{id} is the quantity of good i demanded.

If a project's output is an exportable, the effective demand curve for the good will usually be a perfectly elastic international demand curve. Substituting an infinitely large elasticity of demand, η_{id}, into (8.2) and (8.3), the weight, W_s, on the domestic supply price, P_{is}, will tend to zero and the weight, W_d, on the demand price, P_{id}, will tend to unity. Hence the demand price for the exportable output, which is its fob border price, will be the appropriate way to measure its economic benefit.

More intuitively, border prices are used to measure the economic benefits of a project's tradeable outputs because they represent the amount of foreign exchange that will be earned, directly or indirectly, as a result of the project. Foreign exchange earnings can be freely converted into goods and services in the international marketplace. These goods and services can then be consumed by the population of the exporting country. Since international markets are comparatively competitive and free of distortions, the international price paid for goods and services will be a good measure of the increase in welfare created from consuming the foreign exchange earnt by producing a particular tradeable good or service. The border price of a tradeable output is therefore a good reflection of the **marginal social benefit** received, or marginal social cost saved by the country from its production.

On the other hand, if an input used by the project is an importable, the effective supply curve for the good will usually be a perfectly elastic international supply curve. Substituting an infinitely large elasticity of supply, ε_{is}, into (8.2) and (8.3), the weight, W_d, on the domestic demand price, P_{id}, will tend to zero and the weight, W_s, on the supply price, P_{is}, will tend to unity. Hence the supply price for the importable input, which is its cif border price, will be the appropriate way to measure its economic cost.

Border prices represent the amount of foreign exchange that must be paid, directly or indirectly, in order to use these inputs in a project. Since such foreign exchange will not then be available to the country to purchase other imports, which will yield utility, the border price of the input will be a good measure of the reduction in welfare that will be caused by using it in a project. The foreign exchange cost of a tradeable input therefore reflects the **marginal social cost** to the country from using such inputs.

After tradeable outputs and inputs of a project are valued in terms of their foreign exchange earnings and costs, they will normally be converted into local currency at the appropriate exchange rate before being inserted in the cash flow of the project. In many countries, the official exchange rate will not reflect the true value placed on foreign exchange because the market for foreign exchange is artificially controlled by the government. This issue is dealt with in Chapter 9. In this chapter it is assumed that the official foreign exchange rate reflects closely the relative valuation placed on domestic and foreign currency.

In order to examine the economic value of traded goods in more detail, it is first useful to group them into three categories:

- Commodities that are **imported or exported** and for which the price **is not** expected to change if more of the goods are demanded or supplied. In such cases, the elasticity of world supply and demand is **infinite**.

- Commodities that are **imported or exported** but for which the price **is** expected to change if more of the goods are demanded or supplied. In such cases the elasticity of world supply and demand is **less than infinite**.

- Commodities that are **not currently traded** but would be if the country adopted optimum trade policies — potentially traded goods.

Non-tradeable goods would not be traded even if the country did have optimum trade policies. Valuation of non-traded goods was discussed in Chapter 7.[2]

8.3 Tradeables whose price will not change as a result of the project

In all but a few rare cases, the price of tradeables will not change as a result of the increase in supply or demand caused by a project. This is because the world demand

for outputs and world supply of inputs is highly elastic, as there are typically a large number of relatively small suppliers producing homogeneous goods or close substitutes.
To value tradeable outputs it is first useful to sub-divide them into:

- exports — project outputs that are actually exported or substitute for other goods that are exported

- or importables — project outputs that substitute for imported goods.

Tradeable inputs can be sub-divided into:

- imports — project inputs that are actually imported or are substitutes for other goods that are imported

- or exportables — project inputs that could have been exported if they had not been used by the project.

8.3.1 Exported output

All of the output from a project such as a PNG copper mine may be exported. The method of valuing exportable output is shown in Figure 8.4. The project will push the domestic supply curve for copper out from SS_0 to SS_p. Since the mine's

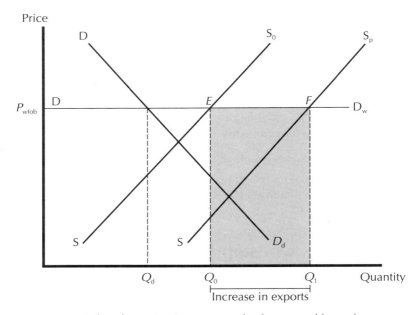

Figure 8.4 *Economic benefits: project increases supply of an exportable good — copper ore*

copper ore output is exported, the relevant demand curve confronting domestic producers is the international demand for copper ore, DD_w. The increase in world output produced by the project will be relatively small compared with world demand, so the world demand curve for copper ore is assumed to be infinitely elastic over this volume change.

As the elasticity of demand for copper ore, η_{id} therefore tends towards infinity, in equation (8.3) the weight on the demand price, W_d, will tend towards unity and W_s, the weight on the supply price, will tend towards zero. Hence the economic benefit from producing this copper ore for export is the world demand price, which is the fob border price that a project can earn for its copper ore output, P_{wfob}. The total economic benefits of the copper mine project will therefore be the extra export earnings of the country from copper ore, the shaded area Q_0Q_1FE.

The fob border price is the free on board price of the export at the border, dock or airport. This is the actual foreign exchange earned from exporting, the export price minus any marketing margins and transport costs to get the copper ore from the project to the border.

8.3.2 Importable output

The case of an import substitution project that produces an importable output, such as motor vehicles in China, is shown in Figure 8.5. The project will push the domestic supply of motor vehicles out to SS_p, and so reduce the quantity of imported cars from $Q_d - Q_s$ to $Q_d - Q_1$. The relevant supply curve for motor vehicles for this country will now be the kinked supply curve, SCS_w. The world price of motor vehicles would not be expected to change as a result of the change in supply caused by the expansion of the local car industry. Consequently, over the range of output of the project, the elasticity of the world motor vehicle supply curve is assumed to be infinite. That is ε_{is}, the price elasticity of supply of motor vehicles, will tend towards infinity.

Substituting ε_{is} in equation (8.3), the weight on the demand price, W_d, will tend towards zero and the weight on the supply price, W_s, will tend towards unity. The economic benefit per vehicle from producing motor vehicles that are import substitutes will therefore be the world supply price or **cif border price**, P_{wcif}, for the imported motor vehicles for which the project's output is a substitute. This is the foreign exchange that the country will save as a result of the project. In Figure 8.5, the total benefits of the motor vehicle plant project will therefore be the shaded area Q_sQ_1CA.

Summarising, if the project's output is an import substitute, it should be valued at the cif border price of the imported good for which it is substituted. This represents the savings in foreign exchange to the country from producing the import substitute and is therefore the economic value of the project to the country. This cif import price will not include any import tariffs or the effects of quantitative restrictions such as quotas. These are merely transfers between consumers of import substitutes and the project, and do not represent an economic benefit of producing motor vehicles locally. The economic cost of any marketing and transport services necessary to get the imported motor vehicles from the port to the local market should be added to

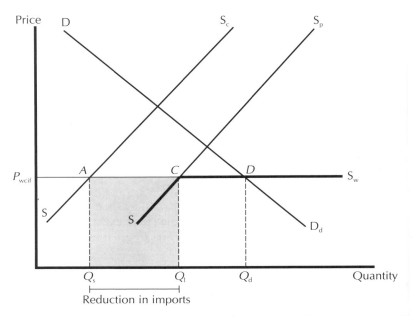

Figure 8.5   *Economic benefits: project increases supply of an importable good — motor vehicles*

this cif value, and the economic cost of any marketing and transport costs incurred in getting the project's locally produced motor vehicles from the project to the domestic market should be subtracted from these economic benefits.

If the project produces import substitutes it is not meeting a new demand but substituting for an existing source of supply. The foreign exchange resources saved by producing these goods and services locally is therefore their marginal social benefit to the country producing them.

8.3.3 Imported inputs

The economic value of imported inputs needed by a project is illustrated by a television assembly plant project in Malaysia, which requires an importable input, TV tubes. In Figure 8.6, the project pushes out the domestic demand curve for TV tubes from DD to DD_p. Since these tubes are imported, the relevant supply curve for any additional supply of TV tubes is the international one, SS_w, which is infinitely elastic. This is because the increased supply of tubes that the project will require will not cause the world price of TV tubes to rise. Since the elasticity of supply of TV tubes ε_{is} is infinite, in equation (8.2), the weight, Ws, on the supply price (in this case the cif import price, P_{wcif}) will be unity and that on the demand price will be zero. Inputs into the project that are imports should therefore be valued at their cif border price. In this case, the total economic cost of the imported TV tubes needed by the project will be the shaded area, Q_0Q_1DC.

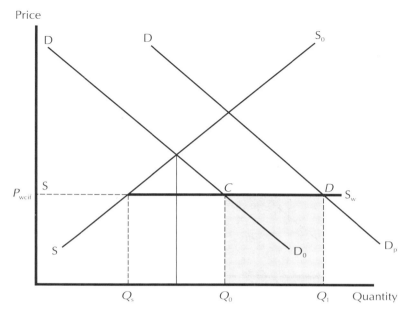

Figure 8.6   *Economic costs: project demands input that is an importable good — TV tubes*

The full economic cost of the TV tubes is therefore their cif import price at the border (landed on the dock or at the airport), including the insurance and freight costs to get them to the country, plus the economic cost of any marketing and transport to get the import to the project. These foreign exchange and domestic costs represent the true cost to the economy of using the imported TV tubes. Any mark-up on the local price of TV tubes due to tariffs or quotas should not be included in the economic cost of using these tubes. These are merely transfers from the project to the government and do not reflect the true economic cost of using the imported tubes.

8.3.4 Exportable inputs

The case of a woollen textile mill project in Australia that requires an exportable input, wool, is shown in Figure 8.7. The textile mill project will push out the domestic demand curve for wool to DD_p, and reduce the supply of wool available to exports from $Q_0 - Q_s$ to $Q_0 - Q_1$. The relevant demand curve facing domestic producers of wool will now be the kinked demand curve DFD_w. The elasticity of the relevant section of this kinked demand curve, the world demand curve for wool, is assumed to be infinite, as a drop in this relatively small quantity of wool supplies will not result in a rise in price. Since the elasticity of demand for wool, η_{id}, is infinite from equation (8.3), the weight on the demand price, P_{wfob}, the fob export price, is unity and the weight on the supply price is zero. The economic cost per bale will therefore be P_{wfob}, the fob world demand price and the total cost of the project's use of wool will be the shaded area Q_sQ_1FE.

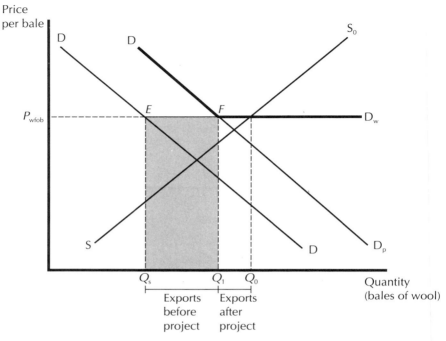

Figure 8.7 *Economic costs: project demands input that is an exportable good — wool*

Exportables that are inputs into the project are therefore valued at their free on board price at the border (dock or airport). This is the foreign exchange that these goods could have earned if they had not been used in the project. This represents their opportunity cost, and hence their true economic cost to the economy. The economic cost of any marketing margins and transport costs to get the input from its source to the border are subtracted from this fob price and the economic cost of any transport and handling in getting the exportable to the project should be added.

8.4 Valuation of traded project inputs and outputs whose price will vary as a result of the project

Most countries are too small for their exports and imports of tradeables to have any impact on the border, or international, prices of these traded goods. This is because their imports and exports only represent a small part of total world supply and demand. . However, some large or specialised countries may supply a significant proportion of the world market for a particular product. This is the case, for example, with silk exports from China, cloves from Zanzibar, oil from Saudi Arabia and wool from

Australia. In these cases, it is conceivable that a project that will significantly increase the supply of such a good may depress its border price. If from past experience this is expected to be the case, the economic valuation of a project's inputs and outputs must take this factor into account.

8.4.1 Exportation of an output lowers the world price

In Figure 8.8, the output from a large group of Chinese silk farm projects is expected to shift the supply curve for silk from SS_0 to SS_p.

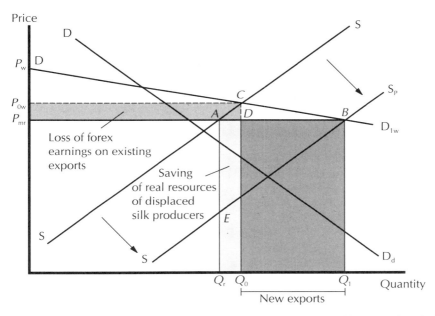

Figure 8.8   *Economic benefits: project increases the supply of an exportable output for which world demand is less than perfectly elastic — silk from China*

The projects are expected to increase the international supply of raw silk to such an extent that they will reduce the fob border price from P_{0w} to P_{mr}. This means that, with respect to the changes in silk export volumes envisaged, the world's demand for raw silk is less than perfectly elastic as is shown by the fact that the world demand curve DD_{1w} is downward sloping. P_{mr} is the **marginal** export revenue expected to be earned by each additional kilogram of silk. The project's total **financial** benefits will therefore be the shaded area Q_rQ_1BA.

The output's **economic** value will, however, diverge from its financial value. The first component of its economic benefits will be the additional foreign exchange earnings from silk exports, Q_0Q_1BD. However, since existing silk exporters in the country will now earn less foreign exchange per kilogram of silk exported, their foreign exchange losses must be subtracted from these extra earnings to obtain the **net** increase in foreign exchange earnings, Q_0Q_1BD **minus** $P_{mr}DCP_{0w}$, the drop in export earnings on existing silk exports. This loss of producer surplus is relevant in this situation, as it is not offset by any increase in domestic consumer surplus. Given that silk exports can now earn lower export prices, some domestic silk producers will cut back their production and in the process save real resources worth Q_rQ_0CA. This represents another economic benefit of the increased production from the project. Although the foreign consumers of raw silk will actually gain the whole amount, Q_0Q_1BC, their net gain in consumer surplus, DBC, does not represent a gain in the welfare of the economy where the project is located. The benefit from the increased silk output from the project is therefore the additional amount of foreign exchange that foreign silk consumers actually pay China, $Q_0Q_1BD - P_{mr}DCP_{0w}$, plus the savings in the real resources of displaced domestic silk producers, ACQ_0Q_r. The potential for welfare losses for countries in a dominant position in the world market, if $P_{mr}DCP_{0w}$ exceeds Q_0Q_1BD plus ACQ_0Q (minus Q_rQ_1BE) for a particular commodity can result in governments imposing export taxes and restraints. Depending on the elasticity of world demand for the good concerned such actions may increase overall welfare.

8.4.2 Importation of inputs raises the world price

In some very unusual cases, a project may be a sufficiently large user of a specialised input to force an increase in the world price for that input. That is, the world supply curve for this imported input may be upward sloping, over the range of additional

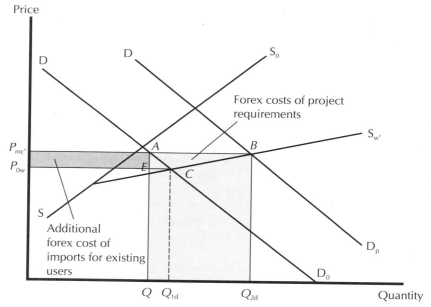

Figure 8.9   *Measurement of the economic costs of an imported input that is less than perfectly elastic in supply — chromium*

input required by the project. For example, the use of imported chromium by a large chromium smelting plant project in the United States may result in the domestic demand curve for chromium being pushed out from DD_0 to DD_p increasing the quantity demanded from Q_{1d} to Q_{2d} and raising the world price, cif border price of chromium, from P_{0w} to $P_{mc'}$ as shown in Figure 8.9. This implies that the international supply curve facing the project is the upward sloping $SS_{w'}$.

The financial cost of a tonne of chromium inputs will be its **marginal import cost**, $P_{mc'}$, and the total financial costs will be shaded area $QQ_{2d}BA$. The economic cost will not only include this financial cost, but also the additional foreign exchange cost born by existing domestic refiners who import chromium, $P_{0w}EAP_{mc'}$. These two components represent the true economic cost of the chromium imports, because the domestic producers must now pay foreign producers this amount of foreign exchange for their chromium inputs. The area $P_{0w}ECBP_{mc'}$ actually represents a gain in the foreign producer's producer surplus. In this case this will not be a transfer within the country, but a true economic cost to the country from using this chromium because the chromium producers are foreigners.

8.5 Valuation of traded goods in distorted markets

Almost all countries in the world employ a range of tariff and non-tariff barriers on imports and many also impose export taxes and subsidies to tax or encourage exports. These do not usually totally prevent trade in these commodities,[3] but merely distort their domestic prices, so that they differ from their border or international price. The domestic market prices of imported inputs will include the tariffs levied on these imports. In a financial analysis, the financial cost of imported inputs will therefore include the effect of any tariff or non-tariff barriers. Similarly, the financial benefits of any exported outputs will exclude any export taxes levied and include any export subsidies. This is because in a financial analysis the prices actually paid and received by the project are entered in the cash flow.

However, the economic valuation of a project must measure the true economic benefits and costs of producing and using these tradeable goods for the economy. The economic valuation of tradeables in the presence of trade distortions is discussed in relation to exportables and importables in the following sections.

8.5.1 Exported outputs subject to export taxes and subsidies

1. Export taxes   If an export tax, t_e, of 10 per cent is imposed on, for example, coffee exports from Ghana, as shown in Figure 8.10, the effective demand curve confronting domestic coffee producers will shift down from the world demand curve DD_w to DD_{w-te}.

The effect of the export tax will be to reduce the supply price received by the grower from \$1000 to \$900 per tonne, P_{fob-t}. This will have the effect of reducing the amount of coffee supplied by the country growers from Q_e to Q_0 tonnes. This adverse effect on export earnings is the main reason that export taxes are now becoming less

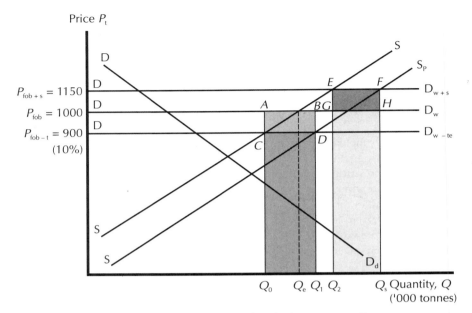

Figure 8.10   *Valuation of an exportable output with trade distortion — coffee exports*

common. If in this situation a large new coffee farm project is begun, it will increase
the supply of coffee for export, pushing out the domestic supply curve from SS to SS_p,
expanding output from Q_0 to Q_1. However, the project will only receive the world
price less the export tax, $P_{w(fob-t)}$, $900 per tonne for the $Q_1 - Q_0$ tonnes of coffee it
produces and the project's total financial benefits will be only Q_0Q_1DC.

The economic benefit to the country from these exports, on the other hand, will
be the world fob export price P_{wfob} of coffee, of $1000 per tonne including the export
tax. The fob export price is the economic benefit per tonne of coffee exported by the
project because it is the amount of foreign exchange actually earned for the country
by these exports. The export tax revenue, $CDBA$, is just a transfer from the domestic
coffee producer to the government and represents one component of the total benefits
that the country derives from producing the extra volume of coffee. Thus the total
economic benefits of the coffee growing project are Q_0Q_1BA. When the elasticity of
demand is infinite, as it is in this situation, the weight on the supply price, W_s is zero,
the weight on the demand price, W_d is unity and the benefits of producing the
additional coffee are just its demand price, the fob export price, which includes the
export tax, P_{wfob}. The domestic supply price of coffee, P_{fob-t}, is not relevant in
determining the coffee's economic value.

2. Export subsides   If instead the government wishes to promote coffee exports
and gives them an export subsidy, S, of 15 per cent, the effective demand curve facing
producers would shift upwards to DD_{w+s} in Figure 8.10. Coffee growers would now

receive P_{fob+s}, $1150 per tonne of coffee produced and would increase their production to Q_2 tonnes. If the coffee growing project is established in this situation, coffee production will increase to Q_s, and the project will receive revenue of Q_2Q_sFE. However, the subsidy, $GHFE$, is only a transfer from the government (the tax-payer) to coffee exporters and is not an economic benefit of the project. The project's economic benefit is still only the foreign exchange earned by the coffee exports, the shaded area Q_2Q_sHG. Since the international demand curve for coffee is infinitely elastic, the benefits of producing the additional coffee are just its demand price, which is its fob export price excluding the subsidy, P_{wfob}.

3. Tariffs on import substitutes   The economic value of import substitutes, such as cars produced by China, is also only the cif import price of the cars for which they are substituted, even though such cars are subject to high tariffs. The economic value to China, the cif import price of their substitutes, may be substantially less than the domestic (financial) price for which such locally produced cars can be sold behind high tariff walls and may not be sufficient to offset the economic costs of resources used to produce the import substitute cars.

Summing up, the economic value of an export is simply its fob border price, irrespective of whether there is any export tax or subsidy imposed on it. The economic value of an import substitute is just the cif import price of the imported good for which it is a substitute, and does not include any tariffs or non-tariff equivalents.

8.5.2 Imported inputs subject to tariffs

If Japan undertakes an oil refining project and its oil imports are subject to a tariff, t, of 10 per cent, the effective supply curve confronting Japan's domestic oil refiners will not be the world supply curve for oil, SS_w but the higher tax inclusive supply curve, SS_{w+t} in Figure 8.11. An increase in demand for imported oil as a result of the oil refining project will push out the domestic demand curve for oil to DD_p. Even though the imported oil is subject to a tariff the economic cost of a barrel of oil to Japan is still its cif import price, the oil's supply price, P_{wcif}. The economic cost of the oil imports will therefore equal their foreign exchange cost, the shaded area Q_0Q_1DC. The tariff revenue, $CDBA$, will merely be a transfer from the refining project to the government.

This conclusion can also be drawn from equation (8.2). Because the elasticity of the international oil supply curve will be infinite the weight on oil's supply price, P_{wcif} will be unity. The weight on the domestic demand price, $P_{w(cif+t)}$, will be zero. Hence only the area Q_0Q_1DC representing the foreign exchange costs of the oil are its true cost to the economy.

8.6 Potentially traded commodities

In some countries, distortions in the trade régime become so great that they can actually prevent the trade of goods that would otherwise be tradeable. Potentially traded goods include all those goods and services currently not traded by a country

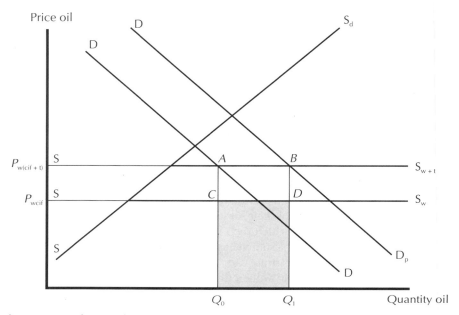

Figure 8.11   *Valuation of imported input with tariff — oil refining project*

but would be traded if it pursued optimum trade policies. Many countries impose rigid import quotas, import embargoes, prohibitive import tariffs or export embargoes on at least some imports and exports. The main reason for imposing prohibitive import quotas, tariffs and embargoes is to protect extremely inefficient local producers. One controversial example of an import embargo is the prohibition of rice imports into Japan to protect Japanese rice farmers, who sell their output domestically for approximately six times the international price for rice. Another is the virtual embargo on the importation of consumer goods into India, to protect local producers. Export embargoes are rarer but are imposed for a range of reasons including the protection of some unnatural comparative advantage. Some examples of this include Australia's export embargo on Merino sheep and the embargo on tea plants from imperial China. Alternatively, export embargoes may be introduced to protect some natural resource believed to be in limited supply. Examples include the export embargo on Australian iron ore in the 1950s and the export embargo on bamboo from the Philippines. National treasures, endangered species and antiques are also often subject to export embargoes.

   If a project uses a potentially traded good as an input or produces one as output, it will be necessary to be clear about how to measure its value to the economy.

8.6.1 Potentially traded inputs

For example, how should a garment factory project's requirement for potentially traded synthetic textile inputs (in Figure 8.12) be valued if they are subject to a rigid quota,

$Q_t - Q_d$, which is already fully taken up. The international price of these textiles is cif price, P_{wcif}, which also equals the domestic price prior to the beginning of the project. The project's demand for synthetic textiles pushes out the domestic demand curve to DD_p. If the project's developers succeed in having the quota expanded to meet this new demand, from $Q_t - Q_d$ to $Q_{nd} - Q_d$ to accommodate their requirements for the synthetic textiles, then these inputs can be imported and should be valued at their cif border price, P_{wcif}. In this case the economic cost of these imported inputs would then be the shaded area $Q_tQ_{nd}EA$.

However, if the quota will not be expanded over the life of the project and at the margin the project will have to purchase the input locally or bid quota allocations away from other users, it will be necessary to value these textile inputs as if they were non-traded goods in the manner discussed in Chapter 7. In this case, while the potential supply curve for the textiles is the kinked domestic and international supply curve SBS_w, the **actual** supply curve is the combined international and domestic supply curve, $SBAHS_d$. If all the project's demand for synthetic textiles can be met from expanded production (the domestic supply curve is infinitely elastic), the input should be valued at its marginal social cost of production. If output cannot be expanded, the domestic supply curve is completely inelastic, and the textile inputs should be valued at their marginal social benefit or at the amount existing consumers were willing to pay for them. In Figure 8.12 the domestic supply curve is upward sloping, SS_d, so if the project cannot secure an expansion of the import quota, from Q_t to Q_{nd}, textile inputs will come from both an expansion of domestic supply and by displacing

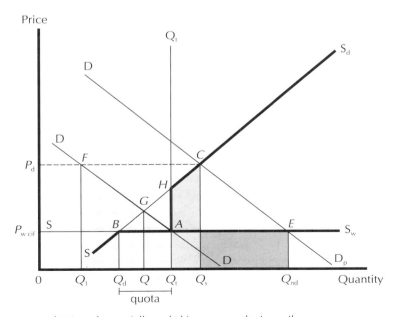

Figure 8.12 *Valuation of potentially traded input — synthetic textiles*

some existing consumers of imported textiles. The domestic market price of textile inputs will rise to P_d as a result of the project increasing demand. The economic cost of these textiles is measured by the economic cost to local producers of supplying the additional textiles, shaded area Q_tQ_sCH, plus the amount displaced textile users were willing to pay for the $Q_t - Q_1$ textiles that were bid away from them when the domestic price rose from P_w to P_d, the shaded area Q_1Q_tAF. In terms of equation (8.1), the economic cost of the textile input will be the weighted average of the marginal social cost, the supply price and marginal social benefit, the demand price.

8.6.2 Potentially traded outputs

Similar problems arise if the good that is potentially traded is a project output. In the example shown in Figure 8.13, a company considering a new ore mining project is in a situation where there was an export embargo[4] in place for iron ore. In this case the domestic price of the iron ore, P_{0d}, is lower than the fob border price, P_w, so the project would have exported if allowed to do so by the government. To value the project's output, it would be necessary to determine whether the export embargo[5] could be lifted or is likely to remain in force over the life of the project. If it **is** expected to be lifted, the output should be treated as a traded good and valued at the fob border price, P_w. This is the shaded area $Q_1Q_{pot}AB$ in Figure 8.13.

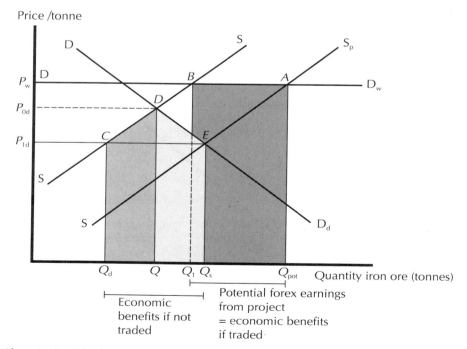

Figure 8.13   *Valuation of potentially traded output — iron ore*

If, on the other hand, the iron ore embargo is not expected to be lifted over the project's life, the demand curve facing producers of iron ore will be the downward sloping domestic demand curve DD_d and the price will have to fall to P_{1d} to clear the market. Production of the iron ore will have no impact on the country's trade position at the margin and the iron ore output should be treated as a non-traded good. The ore produced by the new project should then be valued at the price that domestic consumers are willing to pay for the extra supplies of iron ore from the project, the shaded area QQ_sED, plus the economic value of the resources released by marginal domestic ore producers who can no longer compete at the lower price, P_{1d}. This is the shaded area Q_dQDC. It is obvious that the total level of iron ore produced and associated export earnings will be lower if there is an export embargo in place. The only beneficiaries of such a policy would be domestic steel producers as they would be able to buy iron ore at less than the international price.

8.7 Comparability of traded good data

8.7.1 Locational equivalence

It is important that the prices of inputs and outputs used in a project's cash flow reflect the appropriate location of the goods they are valuing. The preferred option is to value project inputs and outputs at their prices **at the project door**. Project outputs are therefore valued **in the market where they are sold**, or at the border if they are to be exported, less the cost of domestic transport and handling costs from the project to market and prior to the addition of taxes and retailing margins.

Domestic transportation and handling fees are called transfer charges. They are non-traded services, which must themselves be shadow priced to remove the effects of any taxes, monopoly rents, price controls and other distortions. It is necessary to estimate the lowest cost domestic transfer charges available.

8.7.2 Quality equivalence

The quality of imported goods is frequently different from that of locally produced substitutes. If a good is actually exported then its fob border price should be used as its economic value. However, it may not be possible to merely use the cif border price to value an import substitute. If the good is not itself exported and is unlikely to be because of its lower quality, then it could be treated as a non-traded good. Alternatively, the good could be shadow priced at the cif border price of its closest import substitute deflated by the ratio of the domestic price of the project output to the domestic price of its import substitute. This procedure will enable an economic value to be determined that reflects the world price of the substitute and the relative valuation that local consumers place on the domestically produced good and its imported substitute.

$$\text{Economic price} = \frac{\text{fob price of}}{\text{import substitute}} \times \frac{\text{domestic price of good i}}{\text{domestic price of import substitute}}$$

If you are using import price data classified by four digit International Standard Industrial Classification categories, several goods of different quality may be aggregated into one category. It is therefore necessary to ensure that the border price data used relates to the same type or quality of good being considered in the project.

8.8 Sources of traded good data

If the commodity is actually bought or sold on the international market, prices may be obtained directly from the seller or buyer. If the good is produced or sold locally and there is no exact international equivalent available, then the best solution will be to use the adjustment outlined above to correct for any quality differences. The basic approach will be to use the cheapest price at which inputs can be purchased at that time and the most conservative estimate of likely output prices.

Traded good data may also be obtained from international organisations like the World Bank, foreign governments and agencies, trade organisations and journals and consultants. Generally, more data is available for primary commodities than for manufactures because of the enormous diversity of the latter. The project analyst may need to commission more extensive studies of assumptions underlying projections of major input and output prices. This issue is discussed further in Chapter 15, which deals with risk.

Exercises

1. A private enterprise in a low tariff economy is considering establishing an export oriented electronics factory. It would sell 50 000 televisions per annum to the North American market, each for an fob price of $US200. A further 50 000 televisions will be sold in the domestic market, for $L2000 per set as substitutes for imported televisions. The exchange rate is expected to remain at approximately $US1 = $L10 over the life of the project. The cif price of similar televisions imported into the local economy is $US230 per set (due to transport and handling costs).

   The project will import tubes with a cif value of $US35 per television. The fob price of similar tubes exported by this country is $L430 per television. Locally produced exportable inputs used by the project could otherwise earn $US30, fob per television. The cif price of similar imported inputs is $US33 per television.

   Total investment required for plant and equipment will be $L350 million, and $L550 million for land. The plant will take only 1 year to construct and be ready to begin operation in year 2. The land can be sold for the same real price at the end of the 15 years that the project is expected to continue in operation. The plant and equipment will depreciate at 5 per cent per annum, and can be sold for their depreciated value after 15 years.

   The project will require 1000 production workers, each paid $L5000 per month, and will have administrative staff and overhead costs of $L200 000 per month.

Use diagrams to help you to identify the economic costs and benefits of the tradeable inputs and outputs. Construct a parameter table and a financial and economic cash flow for the project. Calculate the project's financial and economic IRR and NPV if:

a the real cost of capital to the enterprise is 12 per cent, and
b the real social discount rate for this country is 8 per cent.

Set out the cash flow in local currency, $L.

2. Businessmen in another, higher tariff, country are considering an electronics project similar to the one being considered in exercise 1. The cif border prices for imported components and televisions and the fob price received for exported components and televisions will be the same as for the project in exercise 1. The local production costs of components are also the same, but domestic prices for traded goods will vary because of the presence of import tariffs and export subsidies in the higher tariff country. A 30 per cent tariff would be incurred on imported tubes and as a result the project would source all its tubes locally. There is a 15 per cent export subsidy on other locally produced exportable components, which pushes up their local price 15 per cent above their fob export price. As a result, the project will import these components, rather than source them locally, as occurred in the country in exercise 1.

A 40 per cent tariff on imported televisions will enable local producers to put their local prices up to $L420 per set. In addition, a 10 per cent export subsidy will be paid to producers on top of the fob price of exported televisions. As a result of the higher profits to be made from producing for the local market, the project will only sell 10 000 televisions per annum to the North American market, each for an fob price of $US200, and a further 90 000 televisions will be sold in the domestic market. Once again, these will substitute for imported televisions, with a cif price of $US230.

Investment of $L52.5 million in plant and $L67.5 million in land is required. As in the case of the project in exercise 1, it is expected that the land could be sold for the same price after the 15 years that the project is expected to last. The plant and equipment will also depreciate at 5 per cent per annum, and can be sold for its depreciated value after 15 years.

The project will still require 1000 production workers, but in the local currency they will each be paid $L300 per month. The project will have staff overheads of $L20 000 per month. The exchange rate is expected to remain at approximately $US1 = $L1.5 over the life of the project.

Use diagrams to help you to identify the economic costs and benefits of the tradeable inputs and outputs.

Construct a parameter table and financial and economic cash flows for the project.

Calculate the project's financial and economic IRR and NPV if:

a the real cost of capital to the project implementors is 9 per cent

    b   the real social discount rate for this country is 11 per cent.

    Set out the cash flow in local currency, $L.

3. A 15 year project to produce 80 000 cars per annum is being considered by a company in a country with extremely high protection. The cars will have production costs (excluding capital) of $US9000 per car, and an investment in plant and equipment of $1 billion in year 1. The cif import price of a similar car is $US7000.

    Determine the financial and economic NPV and IRR of an automobile factory in this country, if automobiles are subject to:

    a   a 150 per cent tariff (assume the project charges the maximum amount that it can for cars and still matches the tariff inclusive price of imports)

    b   an import embargo, which is expected to stay in place over the life of the project. The price of automobiles is twice the cif import price prior to the project, but will fall to 1.8 times the border price after the project expands domestic auto supply. As a result, half of the project's output will supply new demand and the other half will replace output previously supplied by marginal car producers, who will now go out of business.

    The real cost of capital to the entrepreneurs will be 8 per cent, and the social discount rate for this country is 13 per cent per annum. Set out the cash flow in local currency, $L, if the exchange rate is $L20 = $US1.

References

Harberger, A.C., 1971. 'Three basic postulates for applied welfare economies: an interpretive essay', *Journal of Economic Literature*, Vol. 14, No. 3, Sept, 785–97.

Harberger, A.C., 1972. *Project Evaluation, Collected Papers*, Macmillan, New York.

Jenkins G.P. and Harberger, A.C., 1991. *Manual - Cost Benefit Analysis of Investment Decisions*, Program on Investment Appraisal and Management, Harvard Institute for International Development, Cambridge, Mass.

Further reading

Duvingneau, J.C. and Prasad R.N., 1984. *Guidelines for Calculating Financial and Economic Rates of Return for DFC Projects*, World Bank Technical Paper No. 33, Washington, Development Finance Corporation, World Bank, Chapter 6.

Irvin, G., 1978. *Modern Cost-Benefit Methods*, Macmillan, London, Chapters 5–6.

Jenkins G.P. and Harberger, A.C., 1991. *Manual — Cost Benefit Analysis of Investment Decisions*, Program on Investment Appraisal and Management, Harvard Institute for International Development, Cambridge, Mass., Chapters 8–10.

Little, I.M.D. and Mirrlees, J.A., 1974. *Project Appraisal and Planning for Developing Countries*, Heinemann Educational Books, London, Chapters 9, 12.

Ray, A., 1984. *Cost-Benefit Analysis*, Johns Hopkins University Press, Baltimore, Chapter 4.

Squire, L. and van der Tak, H.G., 1975. *Economic Analysis of Projects*, Johns Hopkins University Press, Baltimore, Chapter 9.

Endnotes

1   See Harberger, 1971 and Jenkins and Harberger, 1991.

2   Once again, the valuation of non-traded goods in Chapter 7 does not consider corrections that will have to be made to the relative price of tradeables and non-tradeables if the official exchange rate does not reflect the true economic value placed on foreign exchange. This issue will be considered in Chapter 9.

3   The valuation of economic costs and benefits in such a situation is discussed in the following section, 8.6.

4   If the output of the project were an importable, such as automobiles in China or Australia, the good would become potentially tradeable if the country imposed an exclusive tariff, which was set so high that it effectively prevented any automobile imports.

5   Or exclusive tariff, in the case of the import substituting automobile outputs.

CHAPTER 9

The economic valuation of foreign exchange

9.1 The premium on foreign exchange

Chapter 8 discussed how border prices are used to value the economic benefits and costs of projects' tradeable inputs and outputs. In a project appraisal these foreign exchange earnings and costs are usually converted into local currency so that they can be included in the project's cash flow with its non-traded inputs and outputs. In Chapter 8 we assumed for simplicity that the official price of foreign exchange was a good reflection of its economic benefit to the country concerned. However, this is often not the case and we will now relax this assumption to see what effect this has on the valuation of a project's tradeable inputs and outputs.

In a very few countries in the world there is little or no government intervention and few imperfections in the country's traded goods and foreign exchange markets. For example, the official exchange rate for the Hong Kong dollar would be a good measure of the economic benefit and cost to Hong Kong of earning and using foreign exchange. The official exchange rate, OER, will be equal to the true economic value placed on foreign exchange if it is able to move freely without intervention or control by the government and if there is no rationing of foreign exchange, no tariffs or non-tariff barriers on imports and no taxes or subsidies on exports. In countries where these conditions hold the market price of foreign exchange, the OER, should be a good measure of people's willingness to pay for the foreign exchange needed to buy imported inputs and the economic benefit the local economy receives from any foreign exchange earnings made by a project.

In many developing and developed countries, there are many distortions in the market for foreign exchange and traded goods. The market for foreign exchange may be strictly controlled and it may only be possible to purchase foreign exchange for permitted purposes. These controls will often be imposed because the fixed official exchange rate is overvalued, which results in the demand for foreign exchange greatly exceeding supply. A currency is overvalued if the official exchange rate **understates** the amount of domestic currency that residents of the country would be willing to pay for a unit of foreign currency, such as one dollar US, if they could freely spend it on duty-free goods — goods sold at their border prices. Obviously, in most countries, people would pay more for foreign currency if they could spend it freely on duty-free goods without having to travel internationally to do so. Most currencies in the world are therefore overvalued in this sense, with the exception of those of duty-free economies like Hong Kong and Singapore. Trade distortions such as import tariffs and quotas therefore result in a country's currency being overvalued. This situation is shown in Figure 9.1

In addition, governments still quite commonly fix official exchange rates above equilibrium levels,[1] allowing approved individuals to purchase foreign currency at an artificially low price. In Figure 9.1, DD_{fe} shows the amount of foreign exchange that local residents would demand at each exchange rate if there were no tariffs and import quotas on imports or foreign exchange rationing. SS_{fe} is the hypothetical supply curve for foreign exchange, showing the amount of foreign exchange exporters would be willing to earn at each exchange rate if there were no subsidies or taxes on exports or tariffs on imported inputs. The undistorted equilibrium exchange rate, R', is achieved at the intersection of these hypothetical, distortion-free foreign exchange demand and supply curves. At this exchange rate, the demand for and supply of foreign exchange will be equal at Q_0.

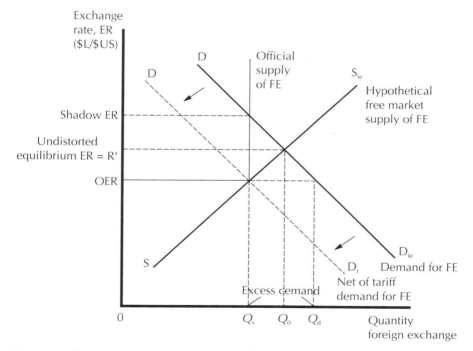

Figure 9.1   *The shadow exchange rate and overvaluation of a currency*

If the official exchange rate, OER, expressed in terms of units of local currency needed to buy one unit of foreign exchange is fixed below this equilibrium level it is said to be overvalued. This means that an unrealistically high value is placed on the local currency in terms of how much foreign exchange can be bought with a unit of currency. At this over-valued exchange rate, exporters will only be willing to export goods and services worth Q_s of foreign exchange because they will receive less in local currency for each dollar of foreign exchange earned than they would have at the equilibrium exchange rate, R'. On the other hand, imports will seem cheap at such a low exchange rate and importers will demand Q_d of foreign exchange to purchase these imports. At this artificially low price for foreign exchange, OER, the economy will therefore experience an excess demand for foreign exchange, $Q_d - Q_s$.

To overcome the resulting balance of trade deficit the government is likely to impose import tariffs. This will shift the net of tariff demand for importables and hence for foreign exchange downwards. In Figure 9.1, tariffs are imposed, causing a downward shift in the demand curve for foreign exchange, to DD_t. This is sufficient to restore an artificial equilibrium in the foreign exchange market so that demand for foreign exchange equals supply at the OER. Alternatively, or additionally, the government may provide export subsidies that expand the supply of foreign exchange available or impose foreign exchange controls to ration access to this supply of cheap foreign exchange, Q_s, to preferred users. Whichever method is used, although these devices will enable an artificial equilibrium to be achieved at the fixed official exchange rate, a country that employs them will have an overvalued exchange rate.

Countries that have an overvalued exchange rate are said to place a premium on foreign exchange, or to have a **foreign exchange premium**. A foreign exchange premium, FEP, measures the extent to which the OER understates the true amount of local currency that residents would be willing to pay for a unit of foreign exchange, or its true opportunity cost to an economy. The FEP can be measured crudely by the ratio of the value of total trade, imports plus exports, valued in domestic prices and therefore including the effect of tariffs and other distortions, to the value of trade in border prices, minus one, as given in equation (9.1).

$$\text{FEP} = \left[\frac{M(1 + t) + X(1 - d + s)}{M + X} \right] - 1 \times 100 \text{ per cent} \tag{9.1}$$

where

> t are the tariffs, or tariff equivalents of non-tariff barriers, imposed on imports
> d are the export tax equivalents of any restraints and taxes imposed on exports
> s are the export subsidy equivalents of any support given to encourage exports
> M is the value of imports in border prices, cif
> X is the value of exports in border prices, fob.

The numerator of this ratio measures the total amount in local currency that residents are **actually paying** to consume imports, including tariffs and taxes, plus the amount they are **actually accepting** for exports, excluding export taxes and including export subsidies. It therefore measures the true value put on traded goods consumed and produced by the country. The denominator of the ratio in (9.1) shows the actual foreign exchange value of these traded goods when they are measured at their border prices, converted into local currency at the OER. The ratio of the domestic value to the border price value of trade therefore shows the true value placed on traded goods, relative to apparent economic value at the official exchange rate. The FEP is usually expressed as a percentage, so the ratio of value of trade in domestic prices to its value in border prices, minus one, is multiplied by 100. The FEP therefore shows the extra percentage local residents would be willing to pay for foreign exchange, above the official exchange rate, if they were able to buy currency freely and spend it on duty-free goods. More sophisticated methods of measuring the foreign exchange premium and the shadow exchange rate are discussed in Sections 9.2.3 and 9.2.4 and the first appendix to this chapter.

When estimating the economic prices of tradeables in countries that have an overvalued exchange rate, it will not be correct to merely value traded goods (which may normally be subject to a tariff) at their border prices and then convert these values to local currency at an artificially low official exchange rate. Such a process would make them appear unrealistically cheap compared with locally produced non-traded goods. This is because the local price of non-traded goods will, over time, have adjusted upwards to equal the **tariff inclusive** price of traded goods, which consumers find equally attractive. Given a choice between a US dollar's worth of imported goods, valued at their **tariff-free** border price and converted to local currency at the official exchange rate, and a US dollar's worth of locally produced non-traded goods, valued at their domestic market price, the average consumer would prefer a dollar's worth of duty-free imported goods. The foreign exchange required to purchase these imported goods will therefore have a higher value to the local consumer than is indicated by the official exchange rate, OER. In this situation, the project analyst must correct for these distortions in the market for foreign exchange and traded goods that result in a premium being placed on foreign exchange.

Almost all projects include a mixture of traded and non-traded inputs and outputs. If no correction is made for this premium on foreign exchange in economic appraisals, projects that produce traded good **outputs** will yield an NPV that is **undervalued**, compared with those producing non-traded goods. This occurs because the traded good outputs would be valued at their fob (or cif) border prices, converted into local currency at the artificially low official exchange rate, in terms of local currency per $US. On the other hand, projects that use imported **inputs** will appear to have low costs when the border prices of these inputs are converted at the OER and will therefore have an NPV that is **overvalued** compared with projects using non-traded good inputs.

If a foreign exchange premium exists, it is therefore necessary to take account of it in all projects where both traded and non-traded goods and services are included among project inputs and outputs, or when comparing projects producing or using traded and non-traded goods and services.[2] If both traded and non-traded commodities are used or produced in a project, they need to be valued in comparable prices before they can be added together in the net cash flow of the project. The reason for this can be seen from the following simple example.

Assume that in a particular economy there are only two homogeneous consumer products produced and consumed. One is a non-traded good, housing, and the other is a traded good, automobiles. The average equilibrium price for both houses and automobiles in the domestic market is $L100 000. At this price, consumers are just as indifferent to purchasing more automobiles as to more housing, since both are equally valuable to them. However, automobiles are subject to a 100 per cent tariff and are sold on the international market for only $US10 000, or $L50 000 (converted at the OER of $5 to $US1). Since automobiles are the only goods traded by this economy, from equation (9.1), the foreign exchange premium will be:

$$\text{FEP} = \left[\left(\frac{100\ 000}{50\ 000} \right) - 1 \right] \times 100 \text{ per cent} = 100 \text{ per cent}$$

In this country, two alternative projects are being considered: one a housing construction program and the other an automobile factory. When an economic appraisal is made of the auto factory, if no account is taken of the foreign exchange premium, automobiles, which are traded goods, would be valued at their border price, $L50 000 per automobile. On the other hand, an economic analysis of the housing construction program would value housing, a non-traded good, at its local free market equilibrium price, $L100 000 per house.[3] If the two projects had the same level of input costs per unit of output and the same project life, the housing construction program would appear to have the higher net present value. It would therefore be selected in preference to the automobile project if only one of two projects could be undertaken.

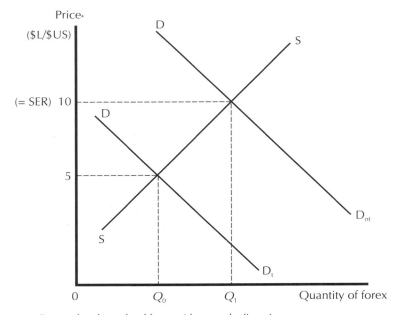

Figure 9.2   *Demand and supply of forex with no trade distortions*

However, if the tariff were removed from automobiles and local residents could buy them for $L50 000 each, domestic demand for cars would increase strongly. As there is only one traded good in this economy, at every exchange rate the demand for foreign exchange would rise, as can be seen from Figure 9.2. The demand curve for foreign exchange, DD_t would move out to DD_{nt}, the tariff-free demand curve for foreign exchange and demand for foreign exchange would expand from Q_0 to Q_1. As a result, if the OER were allowed to float freely it would devalue increasing the units of local currency received for each US dollar of foreign exchange earned. This would encourage producers to export more and earn more foreign exchange, to the point where demand for and supply of foreign exchange would again be equal. In Figure 9.2, this occurs at an exchange rate of $\frac{\$L10}{\$US1}$. At this new distortion-free equilibrium exchange rate, the border price of automobiles would rise to $L100 000 and their economic price would in fact equal the price of the non-traded housing.

Alternatively, if the project were designed to export automobiles, these could be sold for $US10 000 of foreign exchange per automobile. If we continue the assumption that there is only one traded good in the economy, the foreign exchange would be used to import more automobiles for which people would be willing to pay $L100 000. On the other hand, the project might produce automobiles that could be sold locally in competition with imported automobiles, also for $L100 000 per automobile. The $US10 000 of foreign exchange earned for each exported automobile from the project would actually have a value of $L100 000 to the economy at local market prices. Thus, in this one-traded-good economy, the true value of each $US1 of foreign exchange earned would be $L10, not $L5. The results of this simple example can be used to show how the SER of the economy is calculated.

9.2 The shadow exchange rate

9.2.1 Definition of the shadow exchange rate

The **shadow exchange rate**, SER, is the foreign exchange rate that reflects the true economic value placed on foreign exchange in an economy. In an economy with no trade or foreign exchange market distortions the SER would be the equilibrium exchange rate. This is the rate R' in Figure 9.1, found at the intersection of the hypothetical free demand and supply curves for foreign exchange. However, if distortions remain in the market for foreign exchange, the shadow exchange rate will be SER in Figure 9.1. One way of correcting for an overvalued exchange rate in project appraisal is to use a shadow exchange rate, rather than the official exchange rate to value all foreign exchange earned and used by the project.

A simple definition of a country's SER involves addition of the percentage FEP to the OER, or more precisely, multiplication of the OER by one plus the FEP divided by 100:

$$SER = OER \times \left(\frac{FEP}{100} + 1 \right)$$

(9.2)

In our example of the two-good economy, with a FEP of 100 per cent, the shadow exchange rate can be estimated by:

$$\text{SER} = \frac{\$L5}{\$US1} \times \left(\frac{100}{100} + 1 \right) = \frac{\$L10}{\$US1} \qquad (9.3)$$

The **shadow exchange rate** would therefore be $\frac{\$L10}{\$US1}$, so foreign exchange in fact has twice the value indicated by the official exchange rate.

From the definition of the foreign exchange premium, the SER can also be defined as:

$$\text{SER} = \text{OER} \times \frac{\text{value of trade in domestic prices}}{\text{value of trade in border prices}}$$

$$\text{SER} = \text{OER} \times \frac{\left[M(1 + t) + X(1 - d + s) \right]}{M + X} \qquad (9.3)$$

where

X, M, t, d and s are as defined for equation (9.1).

If the country imports 100 cars and its tariff on cars is 100 per cent, its SER will equal:

$$\text{SER} = \frac{\$L5}{\$US} \times \frac{100 \times \$10\ 000 \times (1 + 1)}{100 \times \$10\ 000}$$

$$\text{SER} = \frac{\$L10}{\$US1}$$

In this simple formula for measuring the SER, the OER is inflated by the ratio of the full amount people are actually willing to pay for traded goods in domestic market prices, to the value of these goods in border prices converted at the OER. The SER will always be higher than the OER, in terms of the local currency units people will pay for a unit of foreign exchange, if the value of traded goods in domestic prices, including taxes and tariffs is higher than their value in border prices (assuming export taxes do not outweigh import tariffs).

9.2.2 Estimation of the shadow exchange rate

One common misconception is that an economy's shadow exchange rate is equivalent to its black market foreign exchange rate. Figure 9.3 shows the relationship between the shadow exchange rate, the official exchange rate and the black market exchange rate in a country imposing tariffs.

As only a small residual proportion of the total foreign exchange earnings of a country are traded in the black market and there are risks involved in illegal transactions, the black market rate will typically be above the undistorted equilibrium exchange rate, R', but may be lower than the SER if exchange controls and trade distortions stay in place. The smaller the risks involved and the greater the proportion

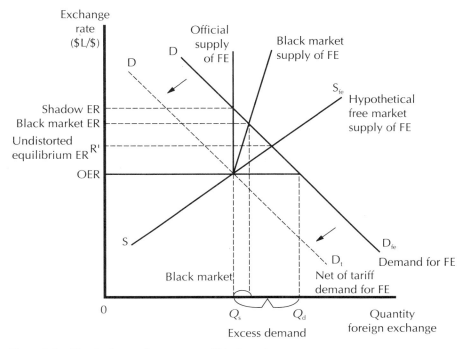

Figure 9.3   *The shadow exchange rate and black market rate*

of foreign exchange traded on the black market the closer will be the black market rate to the distortion-free equilibrium exchange rate of a currency. In these circumstances, the slope of the black market supply curve will converge on that of the hypothetical free market supply curve for foreign exchange.

   Estimation of the precise value of the shadow exchange rate requires a computable general equilibrium, CGE, model of the country concerned. While some attempts have been made in recent years to estimate shadow prices within a CGE framework[4] this is a very data and time intensive approach and will probably not be followed by all countries. There are several alternative partial equilibrium approaches that can be used in these circumstances. All of these attempt to measure the costs or benefits to the economy of one additional unit of foreign exchange spent or earned as a result of the project. The simplest formulation of the SER, which is also the most commonly used in empirical studies, is discussed in the following section. Two other more complex and data demanding SER estimation techniques are discussed in Section 9.2.4 and the first appendix to this chapter.

9.2.3 The UNIDO Guidelines' shadow exchange rate formula

The shadow exchange rate formula developed by Sen, Dasgupta and Marglin in *Guidelines for Project Evaluation* (UNIDO, 1972) attempts to measure, in local domestic prices, the increase in welfare in an economy that will be generated from one additional unit of foreign exchange.[5]

UNIDO's foreign exchange rate formula is the weighted average of the ratios of the domestic prices to border prices (cif or fob) of all goods traded by the country, where the weights reflect how the next dollar of foreign exchange would be spent.

$$\text{SER} = \sum_{a=1}^{n} f_a \left(\frac{P_{ad}}{P_{acif}} \right) + \sum_{b=1}^{h} x_b \left(\frac{P_{bd}}{P_{bfob}} \right) \times \text{OER} \qquad (9.4)$$

where

f_a is the fractional increase in each of the country's n imports as a result of a one local dollar, $L, increase in the availability of foreign exchange

x_b is the fractional fall in each of a country's h exports in response to a $L1 increase in the availability of foreign exchange

P_{ad} and P_{bd} are the domestic market clearing prices of the ath importable good and the bth exportable good, respectively

P_{acif} is the cif price of the ath importable good, measured in $L, converted at the official exchange rate

P_{bfob} is the fob price of the bth exportable good, measured in $L, converted at the official exchange rate.

P_{ad} will diverge from P_{acif} because of the existence of tariff and non-tariff barriers, and P_{bd} will diverge from P_{bfob} because of the existence of export taxes, export subsidies and embargoes.

For example, assume that $L1 of additional foreign exchange becomes available as a result of the project. Of this, 85 per cent is spent on increased imports of wheat (M) and 15 per cent on purchasing rice, which would otherwise have been exported (X). The cif price of the imported wheat at the official exchange rate is $L3/kg and its market clearing domestic price is $L4.5/kg due to tariff and non-tariff barriers with a tariff equivalent of 50 per cent. The fob price of the exportable rice is $L3/kg while its domestic market clearing price is $L2/kg, due to an export tax of 33 per cent. The shadow exchange rate in this simple two-good economy would be:

$$\text{SER} = 0.85 \times \left(\frac{4.5}{3} \right) + 0.15 \times \left(\frac{2}{3} \right) = 1.374 \times \text{OER}$$

Since the official exchange rate in this economy is $\dfrac{\$L10}{\$US1}$, the shadow exchange rate:

$$\text{SER} = \frac{\$L13.74}{\$US1}$$

The problem with this approach is that it does not provide any guidance to the empirical estimation of a shadow exchange rate, as it fails to indicate how the weights f_a and x_b should be calculated. It could be assumed that the **marginal** pattern of expenditure on traded goods will reflect the existing **average** trade pattern, and in practice this is the approach usually taken to estimating a country's SER. The existing trade pattern is used to weight the ratios of the domestic (tariff inclusive) prices to the border prices of all imports and exports.

Estimation of even this rather simple formulation is a major empirical exercise, subject to considerable error. This is compounded by the empirical problems of estimating the tariff equivalents of all the complex non-tariff barriers imposed by countries on imports. If data is available, one method of overcoming this problem is by using the price comparison approach. This entails using the observed domestic market prices of tradeables in the numerator of the price ratios, rather than trying to derive these from the tradeables' border price and the country's tariff schedule. The border prices of the country's tradeables, used in the denominator, can be more readily obtained from international trade data. To assist in dealing with the enormous computational task involved, computer packages have been developed to estimate a country's SER from its import, export and tariff schedule data (see, for example, Fane 1990).

The 'UNIDO Guidelines' approach to the estimation of the SER has been criticised as there is no theoretical justification for using an economy's average trade pattern to proxy its marginal trade pattern, the likely pattern of trade as a result of a marginal change in the availability of foreign exchange due to a project. To overcome this criticism, the supply and demand elasticities of imports and exports could be estimated and used in the calculation of the SER. This is the approach employed by Harberger (1972), Schydlowsky (1968) and Fontaine (1969), who developed more complex SER formulations. These are discussed in the following section. However, in many countries there may be insufficient data on supply and demand elasticities of imports and exports to make these more complex formulations viable empirical alternatives at present.

9.2.4 Harberger, Schydlowsky, Fontaine, HSF, shadow exchange rate formula

The main differences between the UNIDO shadow exchange rate, SER, formula and the shadow exchange rate developed independently by Harberger (1972), Schydlowsky (1969) and Fontaine (1969) and discussed in Jenkins and Harberger (1991) is that the latter is expressed in terms of the elasticity of demand and supply of foreign exchange. It uses an approach that is identical to the general Harberger approach to shadow pricing presented in earlier chapters in relation to non-traded and traded goods (Chapters 7 and 8). The Harberger, Schydlowsky, Fontaine (HSF) shadow exchange rate formula, like the UNIDO formula, attempts to measure, in local currency values, the change in welfare in the economy that occurs as a result of one unit of foreign exchange being used.

Figure 9.4 represents a market for foreign exchange where there are tariffs and quantitative restrictions on imports, which push down the demand curve for foreign exchange from DD_{fe} to DD_t. Export subsidies and taxes on exports have the net effect

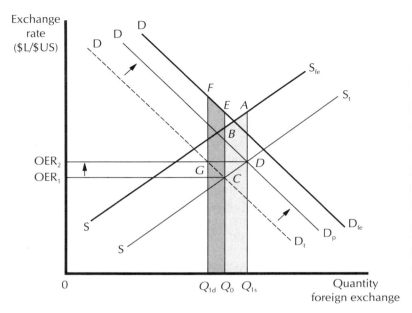

Figure 9.4   *Determination of the shadow exchange rate*

of pushing the domestic supply curve for foreign exchange out from SS_{fe} to SS_t. As a result of the project, the government is expected to increase its demand for foreign exchange, pushing out the demand curve from DD_t to DD_p.

If it is not fixed by the government the exchange rate could be expected to devalue from OER_1 to OER_2 as a consequence of this increase in demand. This devaluation could be expected to stimulate an increase in exports and therefore the supply of foreign exchange from Q_0 to Q_{1s} and a decrease in imports and therefore in the demand for foreign exchange from Q_0 to Q_{1d}. The economic cost of the resources required to earn the additional foreign exchange will be the shaded area $Q_0Q_{1s}AB$ including the net export subsidies of $CDAB$. The welfare loss of consumers who have been forced to reduce their consumption of imports as a result of the devaluation will be the amount they were willing to pay for these imports, $Q_{1d}Q_0EF$, including tariff revenue of $GCEF$. The total economic cost of the foreign exchange required by the project will therefore be the sum of the resources used in earning additional foreign exchange and the amount that displaced consumers were willing to pay for imports bought with foreign exchange that will now be used by the project, $Q_0Q_{1s}AB$ and $Q_{1d}Q_0EF$, respectively.

This can be expressed in terms of the Harberger formula with weights on the market exchange rate, OER, reflecting the extent to which an extra unit of net government demand for foreign exchange will cause an increase in the supply of various categories of exports on the one hand and a decreases in different types of imports on the other.

The HSF shadow exchange rate formula is therefore given as:

$$\text{SER} = \frac{\left[\varepsilon_X(1 + s - d) - \sigma_M(1 + t)\left(\dfrac{X_i}{M_j}\right)\right]}{\varepsilon_X - \sigma_M\left(\dfrac{X_i}{M_j}\right)} \times \text{OER} \qquad (9.5)$$

where

OER is official exchange rate

X_i is the ith export summed over n exports (total exports)

M_j is the jth import summed over m imports (total imports)

ε_x is the elasticity of supply of foreign exchange of the private sector with respect to a change in the exchange rate

σ_m is the elasticity of demand for foreign exchange of the private sector with respect to a change in the exchange rate

t is the uniform *ad valorem* tariff on private sector imports

s is uniform export subsidy on private sector exports

d is uniform export tax on private sector exports.

This formula is conceptually similar to the UNIDO formula, except that it attempts to give a more precise definition of the f_a and x_b terms. Helmers (1979) shows the formal equivalence of the UNIDO and HSF shadow exchange rate formulas if the f_a and x_b terms in the UNIDO formula are the changes in the volume of imports and exports that occur with a unit change in the availability of foreign exchange.

A simple example of the method of estimating the HSF shadow exchange rate formula is given below. As a result of the extra demand for imported inputs into a large project, the currency of a country devalues 5 per cent. As a consequence, there is a 3 per cent reduction in the demand for imports,

that is, the elasticity of domestic demand for imports, $\sigma_m = -0.6$

and a 4 per cent increase in the supply of exports,

that is, the elasticity of domestic supply of exports, $\varepsilon_x = 0.8$.

The tariff rate on imports = 30 per cent

and the tax on exports = 15 per cent.

The value of imports, cif = value of exports, fob = \$L5000.

$$\text{OER} = \frac{\$L10}{\$US1}$$

Hence the HSF SER$'$ =

$$\text{SER}' = \frac{0.8 \times (1 - 0.15) + 0.6 \times (1 + 0.4) \times \left(\dfrac{5000}{5000}\right)}{0.8 + 0.6 \times \left(\dfrac{5000}{5000}\right)} \times \text{OER}$$

$$\text{SER}' = 1.09 \times \text{OER}$$

$$\text{SER} = \frac{\$L10.9}{\$US1}$$

To undertake an actual shadow exchange rate estimation using this formula requires information on the demand and supply elasticities for all traded goods at a highly disaggregated level, as well as the tariff equivalent of tariff and non-tariff barriers and export taxes and subsidies on these tradeables. This heavy demand for data is the major problem with the HSF shadow exchange rate. Short cuts in estimating the shadow exchange rate could be made, including the assumption that $\varepsilon_x = -\sigma_M$, in which case (9.5) collapses to

$$SER' = \frac{M(1 + t) + X(1 - d)}{M + X} \times OER \tag{9.6}$$

9.3 Incorporating the foreign exchange premium into the valuation of traded goods

There are two main approaches to correcting for any premium placed on foreign exchange when valuing traded and non-traded goods in project appraisal. The first is the approach proposed in the *Guidelines for Project Evaluation* (UNIDO, 1972) and the second approach is that developed by Little and Mirrlees in *Project Appraisal and Planning for Developing Countries* (1974) and later elaborated and clarified by Squire and van der Tak (1975). Both of these approaches achieve essentially the same outcome of ensuring that traded and non-traded goods are measured in comparable values even though a country may place a premium on foreign exchange. However, it is important not to confuse these two approaches and use elements of both when undertaking a project appraisal.

9.3.1 'UNIDO Guidelines', or domestic price approach

The traditional method employed in cost benefit analysis to take account of the foreign exchange premium that was used in the 'UNIDO Guidelines' is to value all traded and non-traded goods and services in terms of **domestic price equivalents**. Domestic prices are used as the **numeraire** or common unit of account, in terms of which all project inputs and outputs are valued. For this reason, this approach is called the **domestic price, DP, approach** in this discussion.

The project's traded good inputs and outputs are firstly valued in their fob and cif border prices, as discussed in the previous chapter. They are then converted from foreign currency to local currency using a shadow exchange rate, SER, rather than the official exchange rate, OER. This is done to better reflect the true economic value of foreign exchange to the economy.

In a situation where the local currency is overvalued and the foreign exchange premium is positive, the ratio of the shadow exchange rate to the official exchange rate will be greater than one (when both are expressed in terms of units of local currency per dollar of foreign exchange). Use of a shadow exchange rate to convert the border prices of traded goods into local prices will have the effect of **inflating** these border prices until they equal the amount that people are willing to pay, or receive, for traded goods.[6] These inflated traded goods prices will then reflect the true value placed on traded goods *vis a vis* non-traded goods. As these traded goods will now be valued in domestic price equivalents they will be directly comparable with the project's non-traded inputs and outputs valued in domestic prices.

When using the domestic price approach, a project's **non-traded** inputs and outputs are simply valued in their domestic prices. As was discussed in Chapter 7, adjustments should first be made to the prices of non-traded goods to ensure that they reflect the true marginal social costs and benefits of consuming and producing these goods. This will be done by including consumers' surplus, but excluding producer surplus, and deducting transfers where appropriate. No additional adjustment is made to non-traded goods' prices to reflect their overvaluation in relation to traded goods, the foreign exchange premium, as this would involve double counting. Both traded and non-traded goods will then be valued in comparable, domestic price equivalents and it will therefore be possible to add them together in the project's cash flow.

The domestic price approach therefore corrects for the FEP by inflating the border price values of traded goods, using the economy's estimated SER, until these values correctly reflect the goods' relative worth compared with the domestic prices of non-traded goods.

In summary, the domestic price approach values:

Traded goods	*Non-traded goods*
@ Border price × SER	@ Domestic prices
→ Domestic price equivalent	

Numeraire: domestic prices

9.3.2 Little and Mirrlees, or border price approach

The alternative approach developed by Little and Mirrlees (1974), which is called the **border price**, **BP**, **approach** in this discussion, also values traded goods at their border prices, in the same way as the UNIDO (domestic price) approach. However, these border prices are then converted into local currency at the **official exchange rate** rather than at a shadow exchange rate. The project's traded good inputs and outputs are effectively kept in their border prices. However, if there is a foreign exchange premium in the country concerned the prices of non-traded goods will have risen to match the tariff inclusive prices of tradeables. The price of non-tradeables will therefore overstate the goods' true value to consumers, relative to the border prices of traded goods. The border price approach therefore revalues these non-traded goods in **border price equivalents** using commodity specific **conversion factors**. These conversion factors are the ratio of the border price equivalent of each non-traded good to its domestic price. The derivation of these conversion factors is discussed in more detail in Sections 9.4 and 9.5 and the second appendix to this chapter. Multiplying the domestic price value of a non-traded good by its conversion factor has the effect of converting the good's domestic price into its border price equivalent.

Both traded and non-traded goods are then valued in the same numeraire, border prices, so it will be possible to include them together in the project's cash flow. This is the reason this can be called the border price approach.

The border price approach makes traded and non-traded goods prices comparable by precisely the inverse method to that used by the domestic price approach, which values both traded and non-traded goods in comparable, domestic prices.

In summary, the border price approach values:

Traded goods	*Non-Traded goods*
@ Border price × OER	@ Domestic price i × CF_i
	→ Border price equivalent

Numeraire: border prices

$$CF_i = \text{conversion factor of good i} = \frac{\text{border price equivalent i}}{\text{domestic price i}}$$

The method of estimating conversion factors for project inputs and outputs in elastic and inelastic supply and demand is discussed in the second appendix to this chapter.

9.3.3 Summary of the two alternative methods of incorporating the foreign exchange premium

Summarising, the domestic and border price approaches therefore employ different numeraires in terms of which net benefits are expressed. The domestic price approach uses domestic prices as its numeraire and the border price approach uses border prices.

If the domestic price approach is used, all traded goods are valued at border prices, but are converted into local currency and domestic price equivalents using a shadow exchange rate. Non-traded goods are valued directly in their domestic prices adjusted to take account of market distortions. Both traded and non-traded goods are therefore valued in terms of the domestic price approach numeraire — domestic price equivalents.

If the border price approach is used, traded goods are valued in border prices converted into local currency at the official exchange rate. Non-traded goods prices are converted into border price equivalents by the use of conversion factors. The conversion factor is the ratio of the border price equivalent of the particular good to its domestic price. In this case, both traded and non-traded goods are valued in terms of the border price approach numeraire — border price equivalents.

9.4 Comparing the two approaches to incorporating the foreign exchange premium

In this section, four examples are given to illustrate the differences between the two approaches to valuing traded and non-traded goods.[7]

9.4.1 Example 1: Project produces traded output and traded and non-traded inputs

In the first case, the project, an oil refinery, produces petrol for export, worth X in border prices, and uses imported crude oil, worth M in border prices, and a non-traded input, construction services, worth N in domestic prices. The output of the non-traded input can be expanded to meet the project's requirements.

(i) **Using the domestic price approach, the project's net benefit's will be valued by:**

$$B_1 = (SER) \times X - (SER) \times M - aN \tag{9.7}$$

where

a is the factor that corrects for domestic distortions and converts the market price of construction services, N, to its true economic value measured in domestic prices. It would, for example, correct for taxes, subsidies, price setting and the existence of monopsony or monopoly.

(ii) **Using the border price approach, net benefits will be calculated as:**

$$B_2 = (OER) \times X - (OER) \times M - cN \tag{9.8}$$

where

c is the supply price conversion factor that converts the domestic supply price of construction, N, which is elastic in supply, into its border price equivalent. A **supply price conversion factor** is used because the economic cost of the input whose output can be easily expanded to meet the project's requirements is its **supply price**. This is discussed further in the second appendix at the end of this chapter.

The two approaches lead to an identical result if:

$$c = a \times \left(\frac{OER}{SER} \right) \tag{9.9}$$

Substituting for **c** in (9.8),

$$B_2 = (OER) \times X - (OER) \times M - a \times \left(\frac{OER}{SER} \right) \times N \tag{9.10}$$

Multiplying both sides of (9.8) by $\left(\frac{SER}{OER} \right)$

$$B_2 \times \left(\frac{SER}{OER} \right) = (OER) \times \left(\frac{SER}{OER} \right) \times X - (OER) \times \left(\frac{SER}{OER} \right) \times M - a \times N$$
$$= (SER) \times X - (SER) \times M - aN$$
$$= B_1 \tag{9.11}$$

This means that there is a constant relationship between the net benefits of a project as measured by the two approaches. Consequently, any project with a positive net present value, NPV, using one approach would also have a positive NPV using the other.

The ratio $\frac{OER}{SER}$ in (9.9) is called the 'standard' conversion factor, SCF, and is an average conversion factor for the whole economy. It is discussed in more detail in the second appendix to this chapter. However, the **basic difference** between the two approaches is that, in general, the border price approach conversion factor, **c**, is **not** a standard conversion factor but a commodity-specific conversion factor for the non-traded good concerned, in this case construction services. This individual supply price conversion factor is calculated by the project analyst as the ratio of the border price equivalent of **that particular good or service** (construction) to its domestic price. Each major non-traded good and service should be converted into its border price equivalent using its own conversion factor.

The numerator of the supply price conversion factor, CF_{sp}, for a non-traded input whose supply can be increased, is calculated by breaking down the non-traded good concerned into its traded components and primary factors: labour, land and non-tradeable natural resources. The traded components are valued directly in their border prices. The residual primary factors are valued in their border price equivalents, corrected for price setting, taxes and other relevant distortions and any foreign exchange premium. The denominator of the CF_{sp} is just the domestic price of the non-traded input. A detailed example of the method of estimating supply price conversion factors is given in the second appendix to this chapter.

The method of estimating conversion factors for non-traded inputs in fixed supply, demand price conversion factors, is discussed in Example 4 below.

9.4.2 Example 2: Project produces non-traded output using traded and non-traded inputs

In this second example a highway project produces non-traded road services, with a value of R in domestic prices. As in the previous case, the project uses imported road making equipment, valued at M in border prices, and non-traded gravel, worth N in domestic prices, as inputs. Gravel supplies can be readily expanded.

(i)   **Employing the domestic price approach**   The net benefit of the project in domestic prices is given by:

$$B_1 = R - (SER) \times M - aN$$

where **a** is a factor correcting for any distortions in the domestic price of gravel.

(ii)   **Using the border price approach**   If all of the road services from the new road meets new demand for these services and none substitutes for existing services (railways or boat services, for example) the net benefit of the project in border prices is given by:

$$B_2 = dR - (OER) \times M - \mathbf{sg}N,$$

where

    d is a **demand price conversion factor**, CF_{dp}, relevant to the type of output involved, road services

    sg is the **supply price conversion factor** for gravel, putting it into border price equivalents.

As before, the two approaches will be equivalent if, instead of a specific demand price conversion factor, **d**, a standard conversion factor is used to convert the non-traded output to its border price equivalent and in addition, **sg** = **a** × (SCF).

However, the normal practice of the border price approach is to calculate a commodity specific demand price conversion factor to revalue a project's non-traded output in border price equivalents. In this case the conversion factor will be one specific to road services. If the non-traded output meets new demand, its benefits will be measured by the amount that domestic consumers are willing to pay for this output. The domestic price value of this output should then be converted into border price equivalents using a demand price conversion factor. This is the weighted average of the conversion factors of the major traded goods that are substitutes for the project's output and that consumers will no longer buy because they will instead purchase the project's output. The weights used to estimate this CF_{dp} are the proportions of total expenditure on the project's output that were previously spent on these traded substitutes. The conversion factors of these substitutes are the ratio of their **actual** border price to their domestic price. Hence **d**R is the amount of foreign exchange released when expenditure on tradeable substitutes is reduced by the amount R.

A more detailed discussion of demand price conversion factors and examples of how to calculate them are included in the second appendix to this chapter.

If, instead, the road project has been built to replace an existing river boat service, in this case the net benefit of the project in border prices is given by:

$$B_2 = \mathbf{s}R - (OER) \times M - \mathbf{sg}N$$

where

    s is a **supply price conversion factor** for river boat services

    sg is the **supply price conversion factor** for gravel.

If a project's non-traded output substitutes for existing supply then its economic benefit will be the value of the resources saved by the displaced producers. In this case, this will be the capital, labour and fuel no longer used by the decommissioned ferry boat service. These benefits will be converted from domestic prices into their border price equivalents by the relevant **supply price conversion factor** for river boat services. This supply price conversion factor, CF_{sp}, is estimated by breaking down the non-traded service, river boat services, into its traded inputs and primary factors and valuing these in their border prices and border price equivalents. An example of the estimation of a supply price conversion factor is given in the second appendix to this chapter.

9.4.3 Example 3: Project produces non-traded output whose price falls and increases consumer surplus

In the third case examined, the price of a bridge project's non-traded output, river crossings, is expected to fall as a result of the project. Consequently, the benefits of the project will not only be its bridge toll revenue in domestic prices, R, but also the gain in consumer surplus for people who previously had to use a slow and expensive ferry. Their gain in consumer surplus, valued in domestic prices, is given by B. The net benefits of the project in domestic prices are therefore $R + B$. The project uses traded input, steel girders, M, and non-traded construction inputs, N.

(i) **Using the domestic price approach, net benefits in domestic prices are given by:**

$$B_1 = R + B - (SER) \times M - aN$$

where

> **a** is the factor used to correct the domestic prices of a non-traded input, such as construction services, for any domestic distortions.

(ii) **If the border price approach is used, the net benefits of the bridge project in border prices is given by:**

$$B_2 = mR + bB - (OER) \times M - cN$$

where

> **m** is a composite demand and supply price conversion factor
> **b** is a consumption conversion factor
> **c** is a supply price conversion factor for construction services.

Again, the two expressions for B_1 and B_2 will be equivalent if $\mathbf{b} = \mathbf{m} = SCF$ and $\mathbf{c} = \mathbf{a} \times (SCF)$.

The consumption conversion factor, **b**, is the ratio of the weighted bundle of consumer goods on which consumers will spend their next dollar of income, valued in border prices, to the same bundle's value in domestic prices. As a result of the lower cost of river crossings, bridge users will be able to increase their consumption of other items. A consumption conversion factor shows the cost in border prices of a unit increase in consumption by the typical consumer. It is used to convert the domestic price value of the gain in consumer surplus to its value in border prices.

The data needed to estimate a consumption conversion factor can be obtained from household consumption surveys and the index used to estimate the consumer price index in the economy concerned. An example of how to calculate a consumption conversion factor is given in the second appendix to this chapter.

The composite demand and supply price conversion factor, **m**, is employed to convert the revenue from the bridge services into its border price equivalent. This is used because part of the bridge's economic benefit will come from expanded river crossing services and will therefore be valued at crossings' demand price converted to border prices at the relevant demand price conversion factor. The second source of benefits from the bridge will be the resources saved from the displaced ferry services. The domestic prices of these resources should be revalued in border prices using the appropriate supply price conversion factor. Examples of how to estimate such a composite conversion factor are given in the second appendix to this chapter.

9.4.4 Example 4: Project produces a traded output and uses traded and non-traded inputs, including labour

This example deals with an export oriented textiles factory. It produces textiles worth X in border prices and uses imported yarn worth M in border prices. It also employs local labour worth L in domestic prices, land worth A in domestic prices, and electricity worth E in local prices. Both labour and land are non-traded inputs in fixed supply. The supply of unskilled labour can expand in the long run but this will not normally be in response to labour demand, unless there is an active immigration program. As the elasticity of supply of labour and land is assumed to be close to zero, both factors should be valued at their demand price, the amount that displaced users were willing to pay for them. Part of the electricity requirements of the project can be supplied by expanding production, but part must be bid away from other users.

(i)   **The domestic price approach would value net benefits at:**

$$B_1 = (SER) \times X - (SER) \times M - aA - fL + cE$$

where

   a and **c** are factors correcting for price distortions in the local real estate market and electricity industry
   f is a factor that corrects for distortions in the domestic labour market. These may include minimum wage legislation, the industrial leverage of particular groups of workers, income taxes and other labour market distortions.

(ii) **Employing the border price approach the project's net benefits are given by:**

$$B_2 = (OER) \times X - (OER) \times M - dA - \mu L + mE$$

where

   d is the demand price conversion factor of the non-traded land in fixed supply
   μ is a conversion factor for labour
   m is a composite demand and supply price conversion factor for electricity.

The conversion factor for labour, μ is used here to revalue the wages received by labour in border prices. It will also be necessary to correct for any labour market distortions before converting the economic cost of project labour, measured in domestic prices, into border prices. Consequently, μL measures the impact that employing these workers has on the demand for and supply of foreign exchange. The shadow pricing of labour is discussed in more detail in Chapter 10.[8]

As the supply of land cannot be readily expanded to meet the project's demand, some other users of land will have to be displaced. In this situation, the economic value of the land will be measured by the amount that people are willing to pay for it, its demand price. If there are distortions in the market for the land, such as rationing and price controls, adjustments should be made to the market price as outlined in Chapter 7, so that it reflects the amount that consumers are willing to pay for land in domestic prices. The corrected demand price should then be multiplied by the relevant **demand price conversion factor** for land to show how users value the land in **border prices**. The shadow pricing of land is discussed in more detail in Chapter 10.[9]

The demand price conversion factor of a non-traded input such as land is the weighted average of the conversion factors of the goods into which the displaced consumers are diverted. A more detailed description of the derivation of a demand price conversion factor is given in the second appendix to this chapter. As in the case of the other product-specific conversion factors, since the demand price conversion factor reflects the actual pattern of demand for land, it will indicate the likely impact on the country's balance of trade from the project's use of land.

If some of the project's electricity needs will be met by an increase in local production and some by displacing other consumers, the economic cost of this electricity will be measured by the weighted sum of its supply and demand price. This can possibly be done using the Harberger equation. These components of the input's cost will then be converted from their domestic price to their border price equivalent by the relevant supply and demand price conversion factors, respectively, or the whole cost can be converted using a composite conversion factor. A more detailed description of the method of calculating such a composite demand and supply price conversion factor is given in the second appendix to this chapter.

9.5 Practical examples of the two approaches

This section gives some examples of how the domestic and border price approaches measure economic values if a country places a premium on foreign exchange.

9.5.1 The domestic price approach

(i) Imported input Table 9.1 illustrates how the economic value of a project's imported textile inputs will be measured using the domestic prices approach. It has been estimated that the country has a foreign exchange premium of 30 per cent and the shadow exchange rate is therefore $(1+0.3) \times$ OER.[10] All tariffs and taxes are deducted from the domestic retail price of textiles and their tradeable (foreign exchange) component is inflated by the shadow exchange rate to obtain the domestic price equivalent of the cif import price. The economic cost of domestic transport and handling is then added.

(ii) Exported output Table 9.2 gives an example of the economic valuation of a project's exported garment output, using the domestic price approach. The country

Table 9.1 Valuation of imported textile inputs using the domestic price approach ($L million)

	Financial cost	Economic cost
CIF import price (@ OER)	250	–
(@ SER = 1.3 × OER)		325
Import tariff (40 per cent)	100	0
Internal transport	50	50
Handling and distribution*	50	20
Total	**450**	**395**

Ratio of economic value : financial value = $\frac{395}{450}$ = 0.88

60 per cent of these 'costs' represent rents earned from privileged access to foreign exchange, and are therefore not included in the economic cost of handling and distribution

Table 9.2 Valuation of exported garment output using the domestic price approach ($'000)

	Financial value	Economic value
FOB output value (@ OER)	1200	–
(@ SER = 1.3 × OER)	–	1560
Export tax (10 per cent)	–120	0
Transport to port* (including 25 per cent fuel tax)	–40	–30
Total	**1040**	**1530**

Ratio of the economic value : financial value = $\frac{1530}{1040}$ = 1.47

The market price of transport includes a 50 per cent fuel tax. Since fuel equals half of total transport costs its economic value = 40 – (40 × 0.5 × 0.5) = 30

again has a foreign exchange premium of 30 per cent. The foreign exchange earnings are inflated by the shadow exchange rate and all export subsidies are deducted from the fob export price to obtain the domestic price equivalent of the border price.

(iii) Non-traded input   The domestic prices approach to the valuation of a non-traded input such as electricity is shown in Table 9.3. The financial cost of the electricity is its domestic sales price, $L2 million, plus $L300 000 sales tax. If the non-traded input's supply can be increased, its economic value will be measured by its domestic market supply price, after any adjustments have been made for market imperfections such as taxes, price fixing, subsidies or monopoly pricing. If the project uses electricity that must be bid away from existing consumers, then the electricity should be valued at the price that people are willing to pay for it, its demand price.

Table 9.3   Valuation of 1 gigawatt of electricity input using the domestic prices approach ($L'000)

	Financial cost	Economic cost
Domestic sales price (before tax)	2000	–
Cost of new production	1200	900*
Cost of displaced consumption	800	800
of which monopoly rents are:	(500)	(200)
Sales tax	300	120
Total	**2300**	**1820**

Ratio of the economic value : financial value = $\frac{1820}{2300}$ = 0.79

The economic cost of newly produced electricity is obtained as (2000 × 0.6) – (500 × 0.6) = 1200 – 300 = 900, since that part of monopoly rents that is earned on newly produced electricity is only a transfer

In the example in Table 9.3, electricity is a private monopoly and monopoly rents are found to represent $500 000 of the total $L2 supply price of electricity. If the project uses electricity that must be bid away from existing consumers, then the monopoly rents should be **included** when measuring its economic value, as people are willing to pay this total amount, including these rents for this electricity. Monopoly rents are only treated as a transfer and excluded if the supply of electricity can be expanded to meet the project's needs. In this case only the cost to the economy of producing additional electricity is the relevant economic cost.

Of the project's total electricity input requirements, 40 per cent will be met by displacing existing consumers, and 60 per cent will be met by expanding supply. The economic cost of this displaced consumption is the total amount that people were willing to pay for this electricity, including monopoly rents and sales tax. Approximately $L200 000 (40 per cent of $L500 000) of the monopoly rents should therefore be included in the economic value of the input, but the remaining $L300 000 should not be included. Similarly, approximately 40 per cent of the sales tax ($L120 000) should be included in the economic value of the input, the part that is met by displacing existing consumers, but the remaining $L180 000 of sales tax should not be included in the project's economic costs.[11]

(iv) Non-traded output   If instead the project is producing electricity, a non-traded output, the domestic prices approach to valuing this electricity is as shown in Table 9.4. If all the project's output meets new demand its economic value is simply its domestic market demand price, as long as there is no price fixing or rationing. In this case all new output represents an increment in supply. Consequently, all monopoly rents and sales taxes imposed should be included in measuring the economic benefits of the project as this is the amount people are willing to pay for the electricity. The

Table 9.4 Valuation of 1 gigawatt of electricity output using domestic price approach ($L'000)

	Financial value	*Economic value*
Domestic sales price	2000	2000
of which monopoly rents are:	(500)	(500)
Sales tax*	300	300
Total	**2000**	**2300**

Ratio of the economic value : financial value = $\frac{2300}{2000}$ = 1.15

Sales tax is included as an economic benefit because the country's government will receive the tax revenue even though the electricity authority will not

electricity authority does not receive the sales tax paid on electricity, so it is not a financial benefit to it.

9.5.2 The border price approach

(i) Imported input   If, instead, the analyst decides to use the **border price approach** to incorporating the foreign exchange premium in this country, a project's imported textile inputs would be valued as shown in Table 9.5. All tariffs and taxes are deducted from the domestic retail price but the foreign exchange component of the input is valued at the **official exchange rate**, so that it is expressed in border prices. Non-traded components such as transport and internal handling and distribution, on the other hand, are valued in border price equivalents using individual conversion factors.

Table 9.5 Valuation of imported textile inputs using the border price approach ($L'000)

	Financial value	*Economic value*
CIF import price (@ OER)	250	250
Import tariff (40 per cent)	100	0
Internal transport*	50	40
Handling and distribution**	50	14
Total	**450**	**304**

Ratio economic value : financial value = $\frac{304}{450}$ = 0.68

The conversion factor for transport, CF_t, which puts the domestic price of transport into its border price, = 0.8, hence the transport's economic value = 50 × 0.8 = 40

**60 per cent of this item represent rents earned from privileged access to foreign exchange. In addition, the conversion factor for handling, CF_h, = 0.7. Hence economic value = (financial value × 0.4) × CF_h = 20 × 0.7 = 14*

(ii) Exported output As shown in Table 9.6, to value the exported garment output of a project using the border price approach the foreign exchange component is converted into local currency using the official exchange rate and any export taxes and subsidies are treated as transfers and are deducted. Once again, non-traded

Table 9.6 Valuation of exported garment outputs using border price approach ($L'000)

	Financial value	Economic value
FOB output price (@ OER)	1200	1200
Export tax (10 per cent)	−120	0
Transport to port*	−40	−24
Total	**1040**	**1176**

Ratio of economic value : financial value = $\frac{1176}{1040}$ = 1.13

*The 50 per cent fuel tax is deducted (fuel = half transport costs), and $CF_t = 0.8$, hence the transport's economic value = $[40 − (40 \times 0.5 \times 0.5)] \times 0.8 = 24$

Table 9.7 Valuation of 1 gigawatt of electricity input using the border price approach ($L'000)

	Financial value	Economic value
Domestic market price	2000	
of which monopoly rents are:	(500)	
Sales tax	300	
Cost of new production*	1200	630
Supply price conversion factor for electricity, CF_{sp}		0.7
Sales tax (= 0.6 × 300)	180	0
Cost of displaced consumption (pre-tax)	800	640
Demand price conversion factor for electricity, CF_{dp}		0.8
of which monopoly rents are:	(200)	(160)
Sales tax (= 0.4 × 300)	120	96
Total	**2300**	**1366**

Ratio of economic value : financial value = conversion factor = $\frac{1366}{2300}$ = 0.59

*Economic cost of new production in border prices = economic cost in domestic prices $\times CF_{sp}$ = 900 × 0.7 = 630, see notes at the bottom of Table 9.2 for an explanation of the derivation of the economic cost of new production and displaced consumption in domestic prices

**Economic cost of displaced consumption in border prices = economic cost in domestic prices (including sales taxes) $\times CF_{dp}$ = 920 × 0.8 = 736

components will be valued in their border price equivalents using their own conversion factors.

(iii) Non-traded input The valuation of non-traded electricity inputs using the border price approach is shown in Table 9.7. As in the example in Table 9.3, 60 per cent of the project's electricity requirements will be met by new production and 40 per cent by displacing existing consumers. The electricity is valued at its border price equivalent by multiplying its corrected domestic prices, as calculated in Table 9.3, by its commodity specific demand and supply price conversion factors, CF_{dpi} and CF_{spi}. These conversion factors are the ratio of the economic price (border price equivalent) to the financial (market price) of electricity.

(iv) Non-traded output The method of valuing non-traded electricity output using the border price approach is shown in Table 9.8. If all of the project's electricity output meets new demand, its economic value is its domestic market demand price, including any monopoly rents and sales taxes, multiplied by the demand price conversion factor relevant to electricity output. This CF_{dp} for electricity has already been calculated to be 0.8 for this country.

Table 9.8 Valuation of 1 gigawatt of electricity output using the border price approach ($L'000)

	Financial value	Economic value
Domestic market price (pre-tax)	2000	
of which monopoly rents are:	(500)	
Sales tax	300	
Value of new consumption (pre-tax)	**2000**	1600
Demand price conversion factor for electricity, CF_{dp},		.8
of which monopoly rents are:	(500)	(400)
Sales tax (= 0.8 × 300)	0	240
Total*	**2000**	**1840**

Ratio of economic value : financial value, conversion factor = $\dfrac{1840}{2000}$ = 0.92

*Economic value of new electricity consumption in border prices = economic value in domestic prices (including sales taxes) × CF_{dp} = 2300 × 0.8 = 1840

9.6 Conclusions: usage, advantages and disadvantages of the two approaches

The border price approach is probably the more widely used of the two approaches, according to two recent surveys of cost benefit analysis practice in Squire (1989) and Little (1991). This is because it has been adopted by major international lending institutions like the World Bank and several of the regional development banks like the Asian Development Bank and Inter-American Development Bank. The border price approach is easier to use when analysing projects that use mainly traded good inputs and produce traded good outputs, such as export oriented industries. Tradeables can be readily valued in border prices and converted to local currency at the official exchange rate. The main claim to superiority of the border price approach is that it may enable more precise estimates to be made of the economic value of the project by making use of individual conversion factors for non-traded goods. These show the precise impact of the project on welfare, in border prices. Because the border price approach uses many individual conversion factors and the data requirements for estimating each conversion factor are less, the chance and consequences of making a major error may be reasonably low.

On the other hand, for projects that mainly use non-traded inputs and produce non-traded outputs, such as local infrastructure and social service projects, the domestic price approach may be more appropriate and simpler to use. In this case these non-tradeables can be simply left in their domestic price values once corrections have been made for domestic distortions. It could be claimed that the domestic price approach gives a less precise measure of the project's impact on economic welfare as a result of its use and production of traded goods. This is because the method uses only one parameter, the SER, to revalue traded goods in domestic price values. The SER is an average measure of the value placed on foreign exchange and consequently there are sound theoretical reasons for using it to revalue traded goods in domestic prices. However, there are empirical problems in accurately estimating a country's SER. As this parameter is so central to the domestic price approach, there is scope for making substantial errors in a project appraisal if the analyst has made a mistake in the estimation of the SER. However, if a reliable estimate for the SER is available, this method may be simpler to implement, particularly if the project has many non-traded inputs and outputs.

In summary, because of the difficulty of obtaining accurate data on the ratio of domestic to border prices for all traded goods in an economy, empirical estimates of shadow exchange rates can be subject to considerable uncertainty and may not be very satisfactory. In addition, the use of a shadow exchange rate in project appraisals may be politically unacceptable to a country as it can be seen as an admission of sub-optimal trade and foreign exchange regulation policies. For these reasons, among others, the World Bank and many other international institutions prefer to use the border price approach to correct for the foreign exchange premium in an economic analysis. Nevertheless, both techniques are in common use and the analyst may vary the approach used depending on the nature of the project being appraised.

Appendix 1
The free trade foreign exchange rate

The free trade shadow exchange rate developed by Bacha and Taylor (1971) and Balassa (1974) attempts to estimate the exchange rate that would hold if the economy were in a free trade equilibrium situation. As a country removes tariffs it is expected that it will have to devalue. In a situation where all tariff and non-tariff barriers are removed, the exchange rate will reach the level that will correctly reflect the true value that is placed on foreign exchange, in terms of domestic consumption.

The simplified general expression for the free trade exchange rate is given by:

$$
\text{FTER} = \frac{\left[\varepsilon_X(1 - d) - \sigma_M(1 + t)\left(\dfrac{X_i}{M_i}\right)\right]}{\varepsilon_X - \sigma_M\left(\dfrac{X_i}{M_i}\right)} \times \text{OER} \tag{A1.1}
$$

where

X_i and M_i are the total values of the ith export and the jth import in border prices, summed over n exports and m imports

d is the tax on the ith export (positive if it is a subsidy)

t_i is the tariff or tariff equivalent on the jth import

ε_X is the elasticity of foreign exchange supply with respect to the ith export; as demand for exported output i becomes infinitely elastic, ε_X tends to the price elasticity of domestic supply of export i

σ_M is the elasticity of foreign exchange demand with respect to the jth import; as the supply of the jth import becomes infinitely elastic, σ_M tends to the price elasticity of domestic demand for import j.

The simplifying assumption is usually made that the elasticities of foreign export supply and foreign import demand are infinite, making the empirical estimation of this formula considerably easier. Nevertheless, like the Harberger shadow exchange rate, this formula still suffers from very heavy data requirements. The free trade shadow exchange rate has obvious similarities to the HSF shadow exchange rate, the main difference being the motivation for the change in demand for and supply of foreign exchange.

An example of how the shadow exchange rate is estimated is given below. In a simple two-good economy, six motor vehicles are imported with a border price of $L1000 each, while 10 tonnes of coal are exported at a border price of $L600 per tonne. The official exchange rate is $US1 = $L10 .

A balance of trade equilibrium is assumed; that is, $X = M = \$L6000$.

Currently there is a 30 per cent tariff on motor vehicles and no export tax or subsidy on coal. To estimate the free trade shadow exchange rate, the value of the exchange rate following removal of the tariff on motor vehicles must be ascertained.

The elasticity of export supply is 0.6. The elasticity of export demand is assumed to tend to infinity.

The elasticity of import demand is −1.6. The elasticity of import supply is assumed to tend to infinity.

Then the free trade exchange rate is:

$$FTER = \frac{(0.6)(\$L6000)(1 + 0) + (1.6)(\$L6000)(1 + 0.3)}{(0.6)(\$L6000) + (1.6)(\$L6000)}$$

$$FTER = 1.22 \times OER$$

$$FTER = \frac{\$L12.2}{\$US1}$$

APPENDIX 2
Conversion factors used in the border price approach

1. Supply prices conversion factor for non-traded inputs whose output can be expanded

If the output of a non-traded input required by a project can be readily expanded in the short to medium term, the economic cost of such an input is the **marginal social cost** of the inputs used to produce it, or its **supply price**. As no current users of the input will be displaced by the project the cost of the newly available input is just the economic cost of the resources used to produce it. This situation is shown in Figure A2.1 where the supply curve, SS, for a non-traded input, gravel, is completely elastic.

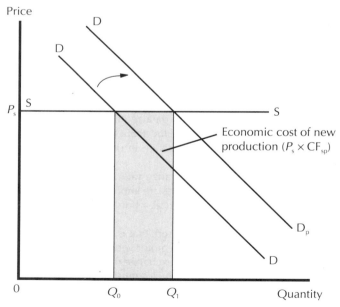

Figure A2.1 *Economic valuation of project non-traded inputs if supply is infinitely elastic — gravel*

If the border price approach is adopted to incorporate the foreign exchange premium, the component inputs required to produce the gravel must be valued in their border prices or border price equivalents, BPE. This is the numeraire of the border price approach. To do this, the non-traded gravel is decomposed into its traded and non-traded components.

The traded components in gravel production, such as excavation equipment and fuel, are valued in their actual border prices. The non-traded components like domestic transport are subjected to a further round of decomposition, into **their** traded and non-traded components, and so on. Eventually the gravel input will be decomposed into traded goods and primary factors: labour, land and non-traded natural resources in fixed supply. Chapter 10 discusses the methods employed to shadow price labour, land and natural resources.

If the industry supplying the input has excess capacity the opportunity cost of the input will be the **marginal variable cost** of supplying it. This is because it will not be necessary to expand the capital equipment of the supplying industry to supply the project with its requirements. To determine the border price equivalent of the input, its marginal variable cost must be decomposed into its traded and non-traded good components and eventually into traded goods and primary factors. The traded components will be valued directly in their border prices and the residual primary factors in their border price equivalents.

If the project input is supplied from an industry that can expand production in the short to medium term but currently has no excess capacity, then the opportunity cost of the input will be the **total marginal cost** of supplying it. In this case it will be necessary to expand the capital equipment of the supplying industry to meet the project's requirements. Hence, the total marginal costs of supplying the input must be decomposed into their traded and non-traded components and measured in their border price equivalents.

Taking another example, consider the valuation of some local construction services required by a project. These are non-traded services whose supply is elastic. The shadow price of these construction services is determined by decomposing the inputs of the construction industry into its:

- **traded components**: construction equipment, cement, timber, glass, steel girders, diesel oil, window sashes, plumbing and electrical supplies, etc., and

- **non-traded components**: gravel, sand, labour, electricity, banking services, domestic transport, etc.

Some of these non-traded components, such as domestic transport, electricity and banking services can be further decomposed into traded and non-traded goods and services.

Eventually, the construction services can be broken down into their traded inputs (direct and indirect) and primary factors: labour, land and non-traded natural resources in fixed supply. The traded inputs, like construction equipment and cement, plus the traded components of non-traded goods and services employed, like the trucks and fuel used in road transport, will be valued in their border prices.

In the case of the residual non-traded goods and services, labour will be valued at the shadow wage rates for the different categories of labour employed, land will be valued at the shadow price of land and natural resources at the shadow price of natural resources, as discussed in Chapter 10. All will then be measured in terms of the impact of using these non-traded inputs on the the demand for and supply of foreign exchange, using the appropriate supply price, demand price or consumption conversion factors.

The economic value of non-traded goods or services, such as construction, can be disaggregated into the following components:

Traded good inputs + **labour** + **natural resources and land**
[valued in border prices]   **[at SWR at BPE]**   **[in BPE]**

Once the economic price of the non-traded good input has been calculated in terms of its border price equivalents, BPE, a **supply price conversion factor**, CF_{sp} for goods and services whose output can be expanded may then be calculated. This is just the ratio of the economic to the domestic price of the particular non-traded good concerned, in this case, construction:

$$CF_{sp} = \frac{\text{economic price of non-traded goods in border price equivalents}}{\text{market price of non-traded good in domestic prices}} \quad (A2.1)$$

Examples of the valuation of non-traded good inputs with elastic supply
(i)   **Example 1: Construction of a factory**   In the case of the non-traded construction services used by the project, their economic cost can be estimated by decomposing the component costs and revaluing them in border prices as shown in Table A2.1.

Table A2.1   Supply price conversion factor of non-traded input — construction services

	Financial cost ($L'000) (1)	Border price ($L'000) (2)	Conversion factor, CF (2) ÷ (1)
Traded items			
Steel girders	400	272	0.68
Cement	100	65	0.65
Non-traded items			
	Financial cost	Border price equivalent	CF
Sand and gravel	75	68	0.9
Skilled labour	90	180	2.0
Unskilled labour	300	210	0.7
Overheads	80	96	1.2
Total building	**1045**	**891**	**0.85**

Hence the supply price conversion factor, CF_{sp}, of construction services is

$$\frac{\text{economic value}}{\text{financial value}} = \frac{\$L891\,000}{\$L1\,045\,000} = 0.85$$

Once this conversion factor has been calculated, it can be used in future appraisals of projects that have a construction component.

(ii)   **Example 2: Railway transport**   Similarly, in the second example below, the analyst has been informed that the non-traded railway services used by the project can be expanded to meet project requirements. Again, the economic cost of these services can be estimated by decomposing the railway's costs into its component parts and revaluing them in border prices as shown in Table A2.2.

Table A2.2 Supply price conversion factor of non-traded input — railway services

	Financial cost ($L'000)	Border price ($L'000)	Conversion factor, CF
Traded items			
Steel tracks	4500	4950	1.1
Engines and rolling stock	7000	4900	0.7
Fuel	1000	800	0.8
Non-traded items			
	Financial cost	Border price equivalent	CF
Engineering costs	5000	18000	3.6
Sand and gravel	800	560	0.7
Land	4000	4800	0.6
Skilled labour	2000	5000	2.5
Unskilled labour	5000	3000	0.6
Total railway costs	**29300**	**42010**	**1.43**

The supply price conversion factor, CF_{sp}, for railway transport is $\dfrac{\text{economic value}}{\text{financial value}}$

$$= \frac{\$L42\ 010\ 000}{\$L29\ 300\ 000} = \textbf{1.43}$$

Once the equilibrium railway tariff revenue has been determined, correcting for price controls or other distortions, it will be necessary to **inflate** this by a conversion factor of 1.43 to give the economic cost of rail transport.[12] In this case the economic cost of the project is higher than its financial cost mainly because of the low salaries paid to engineers and other skilled labour in this country.

Once this conversion factor has been calculated, it can be used in future appraisals of projects that have a railway transport component.

2. Demand price conversion factor for inputs with inelastic supply

Non-traded inputs whose supply is inelastic and cannot be readily expanded include certain produced inputs and primary factors like labour and land. The supply of some produced non-traded inputs such as electricity cannot be readily expanded in the short to medium term. If a new project, for example an aluminium smelter, requires a large block of electricity it will have bid this away from existing consumers. In this situation the economic price of electricity will be its **marginal social benefit** to these displaced users, or the **demand price** for electricity. If the border price approach is used to incorporate the foreign exchange premium, it will be necessary to express this demand price in border prices. This situation is shown in Figure A2.2.

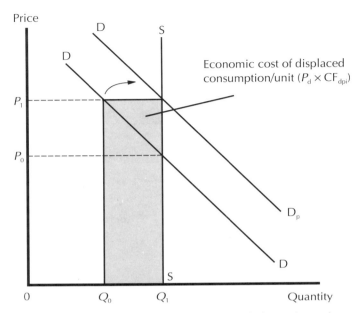

Figure A2.2 *Valuation of non-traded inputs if all requirements bid away from other consumers*

If there are distortions in the market for electricity such as rationing or monopsony buyers or if the project will generate consumer surplus, the market price for electricity will not equal the true amount that consumers are willing to pay for it. In this case it will be necessary to adjust the electricity's market price to correct for these distortions. The economic cost per unit of electricity valued in domestic prices is then multiplied by the relevant **demand price conversion factor** to obtain its economic cost in border price equivalents.

The demand price conversion factor for electricity inputs, CF_{dpi}, is calculated as the weighted average of the conversion factors of the substitute fuels into which the displaced electricity consumers will be diverted. The weights on these conversion factors will equal the proportion of displaced consumption spent on these substitute fuels.

In general, the **demand price conversion factor** for input j, CF_{dpij}, is estimated by:

$$CF_{dpij} = \sum_{k=1}^{n} \alpha_k \times CF_k \qquad (A2.2)$$

where

α_k is the share of displaced consumption diverted into good k, one of *n* close substitutes for input j, as a result of the project's demand for input j

$$CF_k = \frac{\text{border price equivalent of good k}}{\text{domestic price of good k}}$$

In the example considered above, the project's demand for a large bloc of designated electricity whose supply cannot be expanded in the short to medium term is likely to result in an increase in the price of electricity. Some previous consumers of electricity will be forced to substitute into fuels like gas, kerosene, charcoal or solid fuels.

Table A2.3 The demand price conversion factor of electricity

Alternative fuels to which consumption diverted	Proportion diverted, α_k	Conversion factor, CF_k	$\alpha_k \times CF_k$
Gas	0.40	1.5	0.60
Kerosene	0.30	0.8	0.24
Charcoal	0.20	1.2	0.24
Solid fuel	0.10	0.7	0.07
Total	**1.00**		**1.15**

If the displaced electricity consumers are diverted into the four substitute fuels in the proportions given in Table A2.3, which have conversion factors as shown, then the demand price conversion factor, CF_{dpie}, of electricity in this country will be:

$$CF_{dpie} = \sum_{k=1}^{4} \alpha_k \times CF_k = 1.15 \tag{A2.3}$$

Since all the substitute fuels are traded goods the conversions factors of these fuels are the ratios of their actual border prices to their domestic prices. Displaced electricity consumers will be forced to consume more of these substitute fuels, which have border prices. The border price equivalent of the demand price of electricity, calculated as the weighted average of these CFs, will therefore indicate the likely impact on the country's trade balance of the project's use of electricity.[13]

3. Weighted average demand and supply price conversion factors for inputs partially supplied by new production, partially from displaced consumers

If a project's non-traded input is partially supplied from increased production and partially diverted from other consumers, the economic cost of the non-traded input in border price equivalents can be calculated as:

$$\text{Economic cost per unit} = \frac{EP_d \times \alpha + EP_s \times \beta}{\alpha + \beta} \tag{A2.4}$$

where

EP_d is the demand price of the input, $P_d \times$ its demand price conversion factor, CF_{dp}
EP_s is the supply price of the input, $P_s, \times$ its supply price conversion factor, CF_{sp}
α is the number of units drawn away from other users in the economy
β is the number of extra units produced as a result of the project.

In order to provide a more dynamic picture of how the project analyst may estimate the likely source of inputs required by the project and then value them in economic terms, the Harberger formula for economic costs per unit of non-traded input can be adapted for use by the border price approach. This gives an equivalent formula in terms of the weighted elasticities of supply and demand of a project's non-traded input, j:

$$\text{Economic cost per unit} = \frac{\lambda P_s \times CF_{sp} - \phi P_d \times CF_{dpi}\left(\dfrac{D}{S}\right)}{\lambda - \phi\left(\dfrac{D}{S}\right)} \qquad (A2.5)$$

where

P_s is the supply price of input j; if there is a subsidy for the production of j, $P_s = P_m(1 + s)$, where s is the subsidy on input j
P_d is the demand price of input j = $P_m(1 + t)$, where t is the sales tax rate on input j (in the case where taxes are not included in the quoted market price)
CF_{sp} is the supply price conversion factor of input j
CF_{dpi} is the demand price conversion factor of input j
D is total demand for input j
S is total supply of input j
λ and ϕ are the elasticities of supply and demand for input j, respectively.

This situation is shown in Figure A2.3. If the supply elasticity of the input, λ, is very high and tends to infinity, the economic price of the input will tend to its supply price, valued in border price equivalents. This will equal its market supply price multiplied by

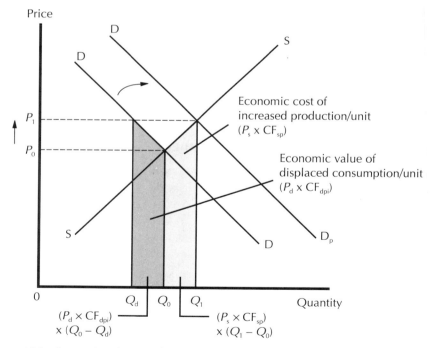

Figure A2.3 *Economic valuation of non-traded input, part of which is supplied from increased production, part from displaced consumption*

its supply price conversion factor. This is the situation examined in Figure A2.1, where supply of an input can be readily expanded.

If the price elasticity of supply of input j, i.e. λ, is very low and tends to zero, then the unit economic price of the non-traded input will tend to its demand price, valued in border price equivalents. This will equal the demand price of input j multiplied by its demand price conversion factor, CF_{dp}. This is the situation examined in Figure A2.2 where the supply of the project's input cannot be expanded at all and other consumers must be displaced to meet the project's requirements.

If λ and ϕ are equal, then the economic price of the non-traded input will equal the arithmetic average of its supply and demand price, in border price equivalents.

4. Supply price conversion factors for project output that replaces existing sources of supply

If demand for a project's non-traded output is completely inelastic the output will merely replace an existing source of supply. The case of the automated bakery, whose output displaced 20 small labour intensive bakeries, is shown in Figure A2.4. In this case, the economic value of the project's bread output will be the opportunity cost of the resources saved by the displaced bakeries, or their adjusted supply price multiplied by their reduced output. Adjustments may be needed to take account of minimum wage legislation, for example, which forces labour costs above their economic cost.

These saved resources will be valued in the same way as a non-traded input whose output can be readily expanded. The economic price of the resources saved by the

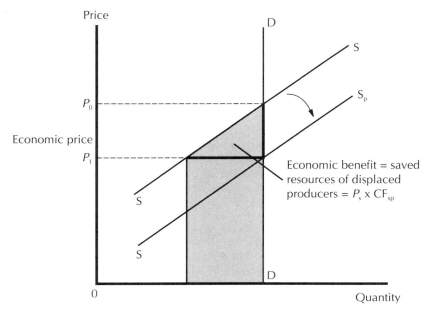

Figure A2.4 *Economic valuation of output if demand elasticity is zero — all output substitutes for existing supplies*

displaced bakers measured in border prices is estimated by decomposing them into their traded components (second-hand equipment, fuel, flour, yeast) and non-traded components (land and labour). They are then valued in their border prices and border price equivalents, respectively.

In these circumstances, the economic benefit per loaf of bread produced, in border prices, will equal:

$$\begin{array}{c}\textbf{(displaced traded inputs}\\\textbf{valued in border prices}\end{array} + \begin{array}{c}\textbf{labour valued}\\\textbf{at SWR)}\end{array} + \begin{array}{c}\textbf{(natural resources}\\\textbf{and land in BPE)}\end{array} \quad \text{(A2.6)}$$

where

SWR is the shadow wage rate
BPE are the border price equivalents.

Once the economic benefit of the non-traded bread is calculated in border price equivalents, a supply price conversion factor, CF_{sp}, can be estimated for use in future projects. Then, economic benefit $= P_s \times CF_{sp}$.

5. Demand price conversion factors for output — non-traded output meets new demand and project is small in relation to total supply

Figure A2.5 illustrates an example of an irrigation scheme project that will increase the production of millet. In the country concerned, this is a non-traded good with a highly

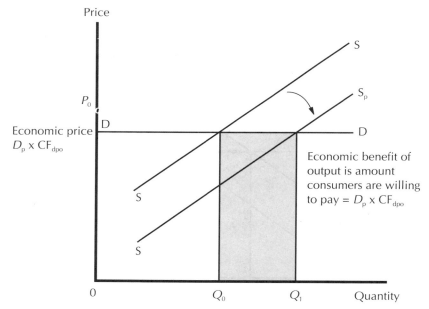

Figure A2.5 *Economic valuation of output if demand elasticity is infinite — all output meets new demand*

elastic demand over the output range planned by the project. As a consequence, there is not expected to be a change in millet prices and all the project's millet output will meet new demand. In this situation, the economic benefit of the millet will equal its adjusted domestic demand price multiplied by the relevant demand price conversion factor for output, CF_{dpo}, for millet. Some adjustments may be needed to the market price of millet to ensure that they accurately reflect consumers' willingness to pay, if there is price setting, etc.

In this case, the demand price conversion factor for millet output, CF_{dpo}, is calculated as the weighted average of the conversion factors of the substitutes **from which expenditure will be diverted** when the project's millet output becomes available. The weights will equal the proportion of total expenditure on project produced millet that was previously spent on the different substitutes.

In these circumstances the economic benefit per unit of the non-traded millet will be:

(Demand price good i in domestic prices) $\times CF_{dpoi}$

$$CF_{dpoi} = \sum_{f=1}^{m} \beta_f \times CF_f \qquad (A2.7)$$

where

β_i is the share of consumption on good i diverted from good f, one of m substitutes for good i, as a result of the project increasing the availability of good i

$$CF_f = \frac{\text{border price equivalent of good f}}{\text{domestic price of good f}}$$

Being a product specific conversion factor, the demand price conversion factor for the millet reflects the actual pattern of demand for the millet. It will therefore indicate the likely impact on the country's trade balance from producing this particular non-traded output. As in the case of the other specific conversion factors, it is more accurate to use such factors rather than a standard conversion factor to value the non-traded good outputs in their border price equivalents.

The method of estimating the demand price conversion factor for millet is shown in Table A2.4. As a result of the project it is expected that the country will be able to import fewer millet substitutes or export more. It has been calculated that 60 per cent of any increase in expenditure on millet will be diverted from maize, which has a 10 per cent export tax and 40 per cent from rice, which has a 60 per cent tariff.

Table A2.4 The demand price conversion factor of millet

Alternative grains, from which consumption diverted	Proportion diverted, β_k	Conversion factor, CF_k	$\beta_k \times CF_k$
Rice	0.60	0.63	0.38
Maize	0.40	1.1	0.44
Total	**1.00**		**0.82**

If the percentage of consumption diverted from these substitutes is as given in Table A2.4 and each of these substitutes has an accounting ratio as shown, then the demand price conversion factor of millet, CF_{dpo}, in this country will be:

$$CF_{dpom} = \sum_{f=1}^{2} \beta_f \times CF_f = 0.82 \tag{A2.8}$$

Once calculated, this conversion factor can be used to revalue millet outputs produced in other projects.

6. Consumption conversion factors for project output that generates a gain in consumer surplus

Often a project will involve production of a public good or social service that will not be sold. In Figure 7.4 in Chapter 7 an example was given of a hospital project whose services were provided free so that all the benefits were in the form of consumer surplus. In the case of a large project that confronts an effective demand curve that is less than perfectly elastic, the price of the project's output will need to fall to re-establish equilibrium after the project commences production. This will create gains in consumer surplus. In this situation it will also be necessary to include an estimate of the net gain in consumer surplus in the economic valuation of the project's output. This situation is shown in Figure A2.6 where the availability of a new product, gas, from a project provides P_1AP_{max} of consumer surplus as well as the revenue from gas sales $0Q_1AP_1$.

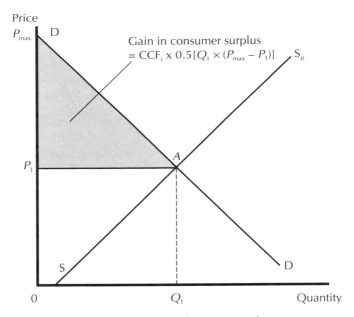

Figure A2.6 *Valuation of gains in consumer surplus — gas supply*

In order to revalue this gain in consumer surplus in border price equivalents it is necessary to multiply its market value by a consumption conversion factor, CCF. This is done to reflect the actual impact of the increase in real income caused by the price fall on the country's trade balance.

A consumption conversion factor, CCF, is the ratio of the weighted bundle of goods on which consumers will spend their marginal consumption dollar, valued in border prices, to the same bundle's value in domestic prices.

$$CCF = \frac{\text{value of marginal consumption in border price equivalents}}{\text{value of marginal consumption in domestic prices}}$$

$$CCF = \sum_{g=1}^{n} \varpi_g \times CF_g \tag{A2.9}$$

where

CF_g is the conversion factor of good g on which the consumer spends part of his or her marginal local dollar

ϖ_g is the fraction of the marginal local dollar received by the average consumer, which is spent on good g.

The economic benefit per unit of the project's non-traded gas output will therefore equal:

$$\begin{array}{c}\text{Economic benefit}\\\text{per unit}\end{array} = \begin{array}{c}(\text{market price}\\\text{gas} \times CF_{dpog})\end{array} + \begin{array}{c}(\text{consumer surplus}\\\times CCF)\end{array} \tag{A2.10}$$

A general consumption conversion factor, or possibly a CCF related to the marginal consumption bundle of specific categories of workers, is also used to convert certain components of the shadow wage of labour into border price equivalents. This is discussed further in Chapter 10. The data needed to estimate such consumption conversion factors can be obtained from household consumption surveys and the indexes used to estimate the consumer price index in a particular country.

An example of the calculation of a simple CCF is given in Table A2.5. Consumer surveys have found that consumers will spend any increase in real income due to their gain in consumer surplus from the gas project on grains, clothing and housing in the proportions outlined in Table A2.5.

Table A2.5 Estimation of a consumption conversion factor

Item on which consumption spent	Proportion of average consumption (1)	Income elasticity demand (2)	Proportion of marginal consumption = (1) × (2) (3)	CF_g (4)	Economic value (3) × (4)
Grains	0.50	0.65	0.33	0.80	0.26
Clothing	0.15	1.40	0.21	0.70	0.15
Housing	0.35	1.30	0.46	1.60	0.74
Total	**1.00**		**1.00**		**1.15**

Hence the consumption conversion factor = 1.15

For example, a study by Scott, MacArthur and Newbery (1976) in Kenya estimated that the consumption conversion factors for:

rural consumers = 0.92
urban consumers = 0.82

7. Weighted average demand and supply price conversion factors — project's non-traded output partially meets new demand, partially substitutes for existing supply

Often, a project's non-traded output may partially meet new demand and partially substitute for existing supply. An example of a new bicycle factory is shown in Figure A2.7. The economic benefit per unit of the non-traded output can be calculated as:

$$\text{Economic benefit per unit} = \frac{EP_d \times \gamma + EP_s \times \tau}{\gamma + \tau} \tag{A2.11}$$

where

EP_d is the demand price of good i in border price equivalents = adjusted market demand price $\times CF_{dp}$, the demand price conversion factor for output i

EP_s is the supply price of good i in border price equivalents = adjusted market supply price $\times CF_{sp}$, the supply price conversion factor for output i

γ is the number of units that meets new demand in the economy

τ is the number of units substituting for existing supply.

In order to estimate the benefits of output produced by a project in terms of the elasticities of its demand and supply curves, the Harberger formula for benefits per unit of output i can be adapted for use by the border price approach.

$$\text{Economic benefit per unit} = \frac{\lambda P_s \times CF_{sp} - \phi P_d \times CF_{dp}\left(\dfrac{D}{S}\right)}{\lambda - \phi\left(\dfrac{D}{S}\right)} \tag{A2.12}$$

where

CF_{sp} is the supply price conversion factor for output i

CF_{dp} is the demand price conversion factor for output i

P_s is the supply price of output i (adjusted for any domestic market distortions)[14]

P_d is the demand price of output i (adjusted for any domestic market distortions)[15]

D is the total demand for output i

S is the total supply of output i

λ and ϕ are price elasticities of supply and demand of output i, respectively.

If the price elasticity of demand for output i, ϕ, is very low and tending to zero (the demand curve is vertical), then the economic value of the non-traded output will tend towards the supply price of the displaced producers, where their resource savings are valued in border prices. The economic benefits of the output will therefore be the market supply price of the displaced producers multiplied by the supply price conversion factor for their saved resources, as was illustrated in Figure A2.4.

If the price elasticity of demand for the project's output, ϕ, is very high and tends to infinity the demand curve is horizontal, then the economic value of the non-traded output will tend towards its demand price, valued in border price equivalents. This will equal the market demand price multiplied by the demand price conversion factor, as was illustrated in Figure A2.5.

If λ and ϕ are equal, then the economic price of the project's non-traded output will equal the arithmetic average of its supply and demand price, in border price equivalents.

8. Aggregate sectoral conversion factors

If individual conversion factors are unavailable it may be acceptable to use aggregate sectoral conversion factors or even a standard conversion factor to convert the domestic prices of less important non-traded inputs or outputs into their border price equivalents. Aggregate conversion factors may also be calculated for groups of commodities such as imports, exports, consumer goods, intermediate goods, capital goods, raw materials and food grains, etc. Such conversion factors are estimated as the weighted average of the conversion factors for the individual commodities making up these aggregates, where the weights equal the pattern of marginal expenditure on commodities in the respective groupings. For example, Scott, MacArthur and Newbery (1976) estimated that in Kenya the medium value of the conversion factors for 28 non-traded goods = 0.77, with a standard deviation = 0.06.

The use of sectoral conversion factors will be more accurate than a standard conversion factor to revalue domestic prices to border price equivalents, but less accurate than individual conversion factors. Individual conversion factors should be used for important variables like the project's output and its major inputs, particularly if the analyst believes that there are specific, atypical distortions influencing the price of these goods and services.

9. Standard conversion factor, SCF

The standard conversion factor, SCF, is an economy wide conversion factor equal to the ratio of the official exchange rate (OER) to the shadow exchange rate (SER):

$$SCF = \frac{OER}{SER} \qquad (A2.13)$$

The various formulas developed to estimate the shadow exchange rate were examined in the first appendix to this chapter. In its simplest formulation, the standard conversion factor is the ratio of the value of trade in border prices to its value in domestic prices:

$$\text{Standard conversion factor} = \frac{M + X}{M(1 + t) + X(1 - d)} \qquad (A2.14)$$

where

X is the value of exports in border prices
M is the value of imports in border prices
t are the rates of tariff and tariff equivalents of non-tariff barriers
d are the rates of export taxes and tax equivalents of export restraints.

The study by Scott, MacArthur and Newbery (1976) estimated that the modal value of conversion factors for 126 goods in Kenya was 0.80, with a standard deviation of 0.21.

The standard conversion factor is therefore a crude conversion factor, aggregated across all tradeables in an economy. The use of a standard conversion factor in place of individual conversion factors is not recommended in project appraisal except when the item being revalued has a small impact on the cash flow or when there is no way of determining precisely the nature of the bundle of goods to be revalued. For example, the use of a standard conversion factor would be justified when obtaining the border price equivalent of the forgone output of urban informal sector workers. The mix of output would be very diverse and while its border price equivalent possibly **could** be determined it would be a very time consuming and costly process. In project appraisals it is often necessary to undertake a *de facto* 'cost benefit' analysis to determine whether the effort and resources involved in calculating a particular conversion factor are in fact justified by the additional accuracy obtained.

For an important project input or output the effort in constructing more precise conversion factors will be justified. In the case of a minor input the effort may not be justified and an aggregated sectoral or, in the last resort, standard conversion factor may be used. The sectoral or aggregated commodity conversion factors are likely to be preferable to the standard conversion factor as they will probably be a better reflection of the individual commodity's conversion factor. The same accuracy problems mentioned in relation to the shadow exchange rate are of course also relevant to the estimation of the standard conversion factor.

10. Simultaneous determination of conversion factors

When calculating the conversion factor for a particular non-traded input, for example electricity, it is often necessary to have available the conversion factor for another non-tradeable such as construction services. However, to estimate the conversion factor for construction it may be necessary to know the conversion factor for electricity. Formally, this circular dependency can be represented as a set of simultaneous equations. There may be a large number of these for an economy in which it is necessary to calculate an entirely new set of conversion factors.

Table A2.6   Simultaneous determination of accounting ratios for electricity and construction services

	Proportionate breakdown of each good's costs		
	Electricity (NT good)	Construction (NT good)	Conversion factor
Import cost (cif border price)	0.60	0.40	1.00
Taxes	0.05	0.10	0
Construction	0.15	–	CF_c
Electricity	0.05	0.30	CF_{el}
Labour	0.15	0.20	0.60*
Total	**1.00**	**1.00**	

The conversion factor for labour, 0.6, is assumed available from a previous study

The conversion factors of electricity and construction services are then calculated as:

$$CF_e = (0.60)(1.00) + (0.05)(0) + (0.05) \times CF_{el} + (0.15) \times CF_c + (0.15)(0.60)$$
$$CF_c = (0.40)(1.00) + (0.10)(0) + (0.30) \times CF_{el} + (0.20)(0.60)$$

Solving the simultaneous equations gives:

$$CF_e = 0.85$$
$$CF_c = 0.78$$

One way to calculate such shadow prices is to construct a general equilibrium model for the economy using input–output table data. However, if the analyst is only estimating conversion factors for a particular project, a partial equilibrium approach should be sufficient. It may then be reasonable to use an iterative approach to calculating the particular conversion factor required for the project. A standard conversion factor, aggregate commodity or sectoral conversion factor may initially be used to revalue the construction input required to produce the electricity needed by the project. Then, the conversion factor for electricity calculated by this means may be used to make a more precise estimate of the conversion factor for construction, which in turn will give a more accurate conversion factor for electricity, the input required by the project. This iterative process could go on for several rounds, but in practice, two rounds should give a sufficiently accurate result.

Alternatively, the solution may be found by solving simultaneous equations. An example of the simultaneous estimation of conversion factors for electricity and construction services is given in Table A2.6.[16]

Exercises

1. An irrigation project located in a country with a 15 per cent premium on foreign exchange is designed to produce 50 000 tonnes of rice for export at an fob price of $US300 per tonne. Rice is subject to an export tax of 15 per cent. The project will require imported pumping and harvesting equipment with a cif price of $US40 million and land worth $L600 million in local dollars. The current and expected future exchange rate is $L5 = $US1. The project will begin production in year 2 and last 30 years. At the end of that period, the land could be sold for 30 per cent more than its current value and the equipment for 10 per cent of its purchase price.

    Imported chemicals and fertilisers required by the project will have a cif cost of $US20 per tonne. These have an import tariff of 40 per cent.

    The project will require 500 farm labourers, each of whom will be paid the government minimum wage of $L600 per month. However, similar labourers in the unprotected sector of this country only receive $L300 per month. The consumption conversion factor is 0.7.

    Other non-traded inputs to the project include electricity, the domestic cost of which is $20 per tonne of rice produced. However, the border price equivalent of this electricity is only $14 per tonne of rice produced due to high tariffs on imported oil used for electricity generation and on imported generating equipment.

    Construct a parameter table for this project and two economic cash flows using:
    a   the domestic price approach to the incorporation of the FEP
    b   the border price approach.

    Show the estimated SER and conversion factors used, your calculations in arriving at these, and the economic values of inputs and outputs.

2. Estimate the IRR and NPV of each of the two cash flows, using a real social discount rate of 10 per cent.

3. In a country with an interventionist trade régime, the average tariff equivalent for the major groups of imports are as outlined below:

Import item	% of imports	Tariff equivalent (%)
Food	30	40
Textiles	20	30
Machinery	40	25
Raw materials	10	5

The export taxes and subsidies on major groups of exports are as outlined below:

Export item	% of imports	Export subsidy (tax) (%)
Electronics	25	10
Coffee	20	(20)
Clothing	35	5
Minerals	20	(30)

For any increase in foreign exchange available, half will be spent on extra imports and half on reduced exports. The official exchange rate is $L10 = $US1. Estimate the shadow exchange rate using the 'UNIDO Guidelines' (UNIDO, 1972) formula and hence calculate the foreign exchange premium and standard conversion factor for this economy.

4. An iron and steel making project is being considered for a country that imposes tariffs and export taxes. The following are the main parameters relating to this country's trade régime.

Market exchange rate ($L/$US1)	3.15
Value exports (fob) ($L million)	35655.00
Value imports (cif) ($L million)	44334.69
Average tariff rate (on cif imports) (%)	22.50
Average export tax on fob exports (%)	1.48
Elasticity of supply of foreign exchange	= 4.8
Elasticity of demand for foreign exchange	= −2.7

Determine the premium on foreign exchange in the country and its shadow exchange rate using the Harberger formula for the economic opportunity cost of foreign exchange.

5. The present value of the financial costs and benefits of the inputs and outputs of a steel plant project are given in the table below. Use the shadow exchange rate calculated in Exercise 4 to revalue the traded inputs and outputs of the project in economic prices, using the domestic price approach to incorporating the foreign exchange premium. Conversion factors are given for two non-traded goods to reflect the extent of domestic price distortions and should be used to convert the financial costs into economic costs, in domestic prices.

Item ($L million)	Financial costs /benefits	Conversion factors	Economic costs and benefits
Traded inputs			
Capital equipment	80		
Iron ore	60		
Steaming coal	70		
Non-traded inputs			
Construction	50	0.7	
Production labour	30		
Overheads	10		
Transport	6	0.8	
Output (traded)			
Steel sheets	500		

Complete the last column of the table and then estimate the financial and economic net present value of the project. Should the project be undertaken? Give reasons.

6. Estimate the supply price conversion factor for electricity in a country if the present value of the financial and border prices of the production costs of a typical electricity generation station and distribution network are as follows:

Item ($L million)	Financial price	Border price (or equivalent)
Costs		
Generation equipment	30	25
Distribution network	5	3.5
Heavy fuel oil	60	80
Skilled labour	3	9
Unskilled labour	4	2

7. Calculate the demand price conversion factor for liquid natural gas, LNG, if the potential consumers of LNG currently consume other fuels in the pattern outlined below and these fuels have conversion factors as given:

Alternative fuels to LNG	Proportion consumed (%)	Conversion factors
Electricity	20	*
Heavy fuel oil	45	1.6
Coal	35	1.3

*Include conversion factor calculated in Exercise 6

8. Estimate the consumption conversion factor for labour in this country if the average pattern of consumption of labour is as shown and the domestic and border prices of these items is as given:

Consumption items	Percentage income spent	Average financial price ($L)	Average border price ($L)
Clothing	20	10	8
Food	50	4	3
Accommodation	10	2	30
Consumer durables	7	50	20
Transport	4	10	15
Other goods	9	20	10

9. Calculate the sectoral conversion factor for capital goods if the average local and border prices of the major items produced in this sector are as follows:

Capital goods	Percentage total production	Average financial price ($L million)	Average border price ($L million)
Electrical equipment	20	1	.5
Transport equipment	15	.3	.15
Mechanical equipment	40	2	3

10. This country is considering undertaking an LNG project. The present values of the domestic value of the project's investment and operating costs and sales revenue are as outlined below:

Item	Financial price ($L million)	Conversion factor
Costs		
Capital equipment	600	*
Construction	200	1.5
Natural gas	1000	1.6
Electricity	100	**
Skilled labour	6	***
Unskilled labour	20	0.5
Benefits		
LNG sales	2300	****

*   Employ the sectoral conversion factor estimated in Exercise 9
**   Employ the supply price conversion factor estimated in Exercise 6
***   Skilled labour's wages on the project exceed their marginal product in their previous employment by 30 per cent. Sixty per cent of skilled workers to be employed in the LNG project will be drawn from the electricity industry and 40 per cent from the capital goods industry. Use the conversion factors of each of these two sectors estimated in previous exercises to estimate the economic cost of the lost production in these sectors. (You may need to refer to the following chapter for the method of calculating the shadow price of labour.) Use the consumption conversion

factor estimated in Exercise 8 to revalue the difference between wages earned and forgone output in other sectors in terms of border prices.
**** Employ the demand price conversion factor estimated in Exercise 7

Convert the financial costs and benefits to border price equivalents. Estimate the financial and economic NPV of the project. Should it be undertaken? Give reasons.

References

Bacha, E. and Taylor, L., 1971. 'Foreign exchange shadow prices: A critical review of current theories', *Quarterly Journal of Economics*, May, 197–224.

Balassa, B., 1974. 'Estimating the shadow price of foreign exchange in project appraisal', *Oxford Economic Papers*, 26, July, 147–68.

Fane, G., 1990. Jakerp, computer package, ANU, Canberra.

Fontaine, E.R., 1969. 'El presio sombra de las divisias en la evaluacion social de proyectos' (translation), Universad Catolica de Chile, Santiago.

Harberger, A.C., 1972. 'Professor Arrow on the social discount rate', *Project Evaluation, Collected Papers*, Macmillan, N.Y., Chapter 5.

Helmers, F., 1979. *Project Planning and Income Distribution*, Martinus Nijhoff Publishing, Amsterdam.

Irvin, G., 1978. *Modern Cost Benefit Analysis Methods*, Macmillan, London, Chapters 1,2,3,4,5,6,14.

Jenkins, G.P. and Harberger, A.C., 1991. *Manual — Cost Benefit Analysis of Investment Decisions*, Program on Investment Appraisal and Management, Harvard Institute for International Development, Cambridge, Mass.

Little, I.M.D. and Mirrlees, J.A., 1974. Project Appraisal and Planning for Developing Countries, Heineman Educational Books, London.

Ray, A., 1984. *Cost-Benefit Analysis*, Johns Hopkins University Press, Baltimore, Chapter 4.

Schydlowsky, D.M., 1968. 'On the choice of a shadow price for foreign exchange', *Economic Development Report*, No. 108, Development Advisory Service, Cambridge, Mass.

Scott, M.F.G., MacArthur, J.D. and Newbery, D.M.G., 1976. *Project Appraisal in Practice*, Heinemann Educational Books, London.

Squire, L., 1989. 'Project evaluation in theory and practice' in H. Chenery and T.N.Srinivasan (eds), *Handbook of Development Economics*, Vol. 2, North Holland, Amsterdam.

Squire, L. and van der Tak, H.G., 1975. *Economic Analysis of Projects*, Johns Hopkins University Press, Baltimore, Chapter 12.

UNIDO, 1972. *Guidelines for Project Evaluation*, United Nations, New York, Chapter 16.

Further reading

Bacha, E. and Taylor, L., 1971. 'Foreign exchange shadow prices: a critical review of current theories', *Quarterly Journal of Economics*, May: 197–224.

Balassa, B., 1974. 'Estimating the shadow price of foreign exchange in project appraisal', *Oxford Economic Papers*, 26, July, 147–68.

Duvingneau, J.C. and Prasad, R.N., 1984. *Guidelines for Calculating Financial and Economic Rates of Return for DFC Projects*, World Bank Technical Paper No. 33, Washington, Chapter 6.

Gittinger, J. Price, 1982. *Economic Analysis of Agricultural Projects*, 2nd edn, Johns Hopkins Press, Baltimore, Chapter 7.

Fane, G., 1991. 'The social opportunity cost of foreign exchange; a partial defence of Harberger et al', *The Economic Record*, Dec, 307–316.

Irvin, G., 1978. *Modern Cost-Benefit Methods*, Macmillan, London, Chapters 5 and 6.

Jenkins, G.P. and Harberger, A.C., 1991. *Manual — Cost Benefit Analysis of Investment Decisions*, Program on Investment Appraisal and Management, Harvard Institute for International Development, Cambridge, Mass, Chapter 10.

Ray, A., 1984, *Cost-Benefit Analysis*, Johns Hopkins University Press, Baltimore, Chapter 4.

Endnotes

1   Where the exchange rate is expressed in terms of the units of foreign currency that can be purchased per unit of local currency.

2   Consequently, except in an economy completely cut off from international trade, or one where there is no premium on foreign exchange, it will be necessary to take account of the FEP in all project evaluations.

3   Assuming there is no change in housing prices as a result of the project and therefore no change in consumer surplus.

4   See Squire (1989) for a discussion of this issue.

5   The formula developed in the 'UNIDO Guidelines' is based on the assumption that the country's future trade policies will reflect existing ones. There is no expectation that optimal trade policies will necessarily be adopted in the future. This is consistent with the approach in the rest of the 'UNIDO Guidelines'. It argues that an optimal trade policy is unlikely in developing countries and therefore is not a useful concept.

6   By multiplying the border price of traded good i, BP_i, by the SER, BP_i, will be converted into its approximate domestic price equivalent, DP_i.

$$BP_i \times SER = DP_i$$

This is because the SER shows the amount that people are on average willing to pay for traded goods, in domestic prices.

$$SER = OER \times \frac{\text{(value trade in domestic prices)}}{\text{(value of trade in border prices)}} = \frac{DP(M + X)}{BP(M + X)}$$

7   This section draws on the approach adopted by Ray (1984) Chapter 14.

8   This example is a simplification of how to revalue the labour costs of a project in border prices. More complicated methods are discussed in Chapter 10.

9   This example is a simplification of how to revalue the land costs of a project in border prices. More complicated methods are discussed in Chapter 10.

10   The method of estimating the FEP and SER was shown in Sections 9.2.2 and 9.2.3 and in the first appendix to this chapter.

11 Only approximately 40 per cent of monopoly rents and sales taxes should be included, because depending on assumptions made about the shape of the average and marginal revenue curves of existing electricity consumers, the economic value of these consumers' lost consumption will be somewhat less than 40 per cent of the financial cost of the electricity.

12 If, as is the case in many countries, the railways are in fact running at a financial loss, this must first be taken into account in determining their financial operating costs from the tariffs charged. For example, if the railways are making a financial loss equal to 25 per cent of their operational expenses each year, the railway's tariffs must be inflated by 25 per cent to determine the financial operating costs. After that, the economic operating costs will be determined by multiplying the financial costs by the railway services conversion factor, 1.43, to, in this case, inflate the domestic cost of railway services to its BPE.

13 It will be more precise to use this product specific conversion factor for electricity than a standard conversion factor, to put non-traded goods into their border price equivalents. Similarly it could be argued that it will be more precise to use individual conversion factors than the UNIDO approach to handling a foreign exchange premium, which uses a single shadow exchange rate, the inverse of the standard conversion factor to convert traded goods into domestic prices.

14 For example, if s = subsidy given for the production of input i, $P_s(1-s) = P_m$ is equivalent to the supply price of output i, where P_m = market price of good i.

15 For example, if t = tax rate on output i, $P_d = P_m(1 + t)$ is equivalent to the demand price of output i, where P_m = market price of good i, pre-tax.

16 See Irvin (1978), Chapter 5 for a discussion of this issue.

CHAPTER 10

The economic cost of primary factors — labour, land and natural resources

10.1 Elements of the shadow wage rate — labour as a non-traded factor in fixed supply

Most people cannot travel freely between countries to sell their labour, so it is not possible to directly establish a border price for most types of labour services. Labour services are therefore a form of non-traded primary factor and can be valued in much the same way as other non-traded goods and services. However, there are of course differences as labour is not just a factor of production. The promotion of the welfare of labour, along with that of other members of the population, is one of the main objectives of governments and the primary rationale for production.

The total numbers of unskilled workers available in an economy cannot normally be expanded in response to market demand unless there is a substantial immigration program in the country concerned. Labour services can therefore be treated as a non-traded primary factor, which is in inelastic supply. Although labour supply can be increased over time by natural increase this will be a result of long run demographic trends such as the age structure of the population and individual decisions about family size and not as a response to a market demand. Unskilled labour cannot therefore be valued at its marginal cost of production.

On the other hand, as the supply of skilled labour can be increased by raising training levels its supply may be more responsive to market demand at least in the medium term. In the short term, however, it will also be in relatively fixed supply, unless the country concerned has an active immigration policy that is oriented to labour market demand. The supply of female labour may be an exception to these general observations, as married women may be more willing to enter the paid work-force if wage levels are raised. Studies have shown that their supply may therefore be considerably more elastic than that of male workers (Filmer and Stilberg, 1977).

10.1.1 Forgone output

Since unskilled labour is generally in fixed supply, when a project uses labour it will have to draw it away from other employment somewhere in the economy. This labour may actually come from another sector, such as agriculture. If a non-traded factor is bid away from other users, its economic cost is what they were willing to pay for it. This can be seen from Figure 10.1, where a highway project will push up demand for labour in a particular region, from DD to DD_p bidding labour away from the local agricultural sector. The economic cost of this labour will be the amount that displaced agricultural sector employers were willing to pay for this labour. This is the shaded area under their labour demand curve, DD.

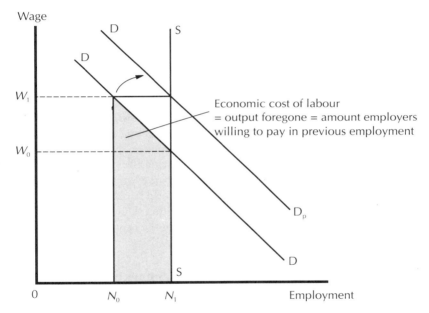

Figure 10.1 *Valuation of unskilled labour — all requirements must be bid away from other employers*

The demand price paid for the last worker hired by an employer will represent the amount that he or she contributes to the total revenue of the employer, or the marginal revenue product of that labour. No private sector employer will pay more in wages than the worker contributes in additional output revenue in the long term.

If labour markets are generally efficient and there is no government intervention in the form of minimum wages, wage fixing, hiring constraints or income taxes, the market wage rate paid for this labour should reflect the contribution the marginal worker makes to the total revenue of the employer. The market wage rate received by the labour in its previous employment will therefore reflect its **forgone output**. In these circumstances, this market wage could be used directly to determine the economic cost of labour. For example, in many developing countries the market price of skilled labour will at least equal its marginal revenue product. Similarly if there is a free and active rural labour market, rural wage rates are likely to reflect the opportunity cost of labour in rural areas.

However, in most countries labour markets are subject to at least some of the controls and distortions mentioned above. If so, it will be necessary to determine the true cost of the project's labour requirements to the economy by calculating the **shadow or economic wage rate**, SWR, or marginal social cost of this labour. The output forgone in the rest of the economy by employing labour on the project will represent the major component of its economic cost. If there is not a freely operating labour market for the actual labour concerned, or for labour with similar skills in similar locations, it may be necessary to directly calculate the economic value of this forgone output.

It is important to note that it is not the marginal contribution of the labour to the revenue **in the project** that is relevant when estimating the shadow wage rate of the labour used. Rather, labour's economic cost is its marginal contribution to the revenue earned in the occupations **from which it has been drawn**. If the labour for the project will be drawn from several sources, its forgone output will equal the weighted average of its marginal revenue product in the sectors from which it will be drawn. An example of how to calculate the forgone output of labour in given in Section 10.2.

If the analyst is undertaking a traditional economic analysis, this forgone output may be the only element considered when estimating the shadow wage rate. This forgone output will be called l in the shadow wage rate formula discussed below. In fact, in most project appraisals carried out by the World Bank and other agencies, the forgone marginal product of labour, measured in either domestic or border prices, is usually the only element considered in determining the economic cost of labour.

10.1.2 Distortions in labour and other markets and market wage rates

Distortions in the market for unskilled and semi-skilled labour may result in the wages of such labour exceeding their marginal revenue product, valued in economic prices. Examples of labour market distortions are minimum wage legislation, centralised wage fixing and restrictive union practices, including the closed shop.[1] These distortions are usually more common in urban labour markets because government control and union activity are stronger there. Australia has a strong system of centralised wage fixing, which has probably contributed to its high level of unemployment. An example of how to value the economic cost of labour in Australia in the presence of minimum wage legislation is illustrated in Figure 10.2. If a project pushes out the demand for labour from DD to DD_p the supply of labour will expand smoothly and there will be no increase in the fixed wage for unskilled labour, just a drop in the level of open (or hidden) unemployment. The economic cost of this labour will therefore be the supply price of labour, the wages that workers were willing

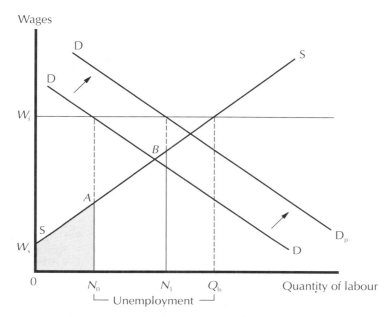

Figure 10.2 *Economic cost of labour in the presence of minimum wage regulations — Australia*

to receive to supply this labour. This is the shaded area N_0N_1BA under the labour supply curve, SS.

In centrally-planned economies like China there are also significant distortions in the markets for skilled labour. Wages for such workers are usually fixed well below their equilibrium level and skilled workers are often allocated to firms for life. This prevents their free movement to employers willing to bid for their scarce skilled labour services. This can result in the market wages for many categories of skilled workers being only a fraction of their marginal revenue product. An economic analysis of a project using skilled labour in a country such as China would therefore need to take this into account. This situation is illustrated in Figure 10.3. If a new computer software firm requires 1000 skilled computer scientists and these are in short supply because of the practice of holding the salaries of such scientists below the equilibrium market salary, then they will have to be bid away from other employers. The economic cost of these skilled scientists will therefore be the amount that their previous employers would have been willing to pay them, had they not been constrained by wage controls. This is the shaded area $N_{rd}N_{0s}CD$ under their labour demand curve. The salaries paid by private firms will give evidence regarding the shape of the demand curve for skilled labour.

Distortions that occur in other factor and goods markets may also result in the market wage of labour used on the project diverging from its true cost to the economy. The suppression of interest rates below their equilibrium level by government intervention may result in excessively capital intensive technologies being chosen.

This may raise the marginal product of labour in favoured sectors above the norm for the economy. In addition, taxes on savings and investments may result in a bias against investment in the economy. This may increase the economic cost of employing workers who will save little or none of their income. Trade distortions, like tariff protection, will inflate the market prices of protected goods and provide the opportunity for workers in protected industries to receive wages in excess of their marginal revenue product, valued in border prices.

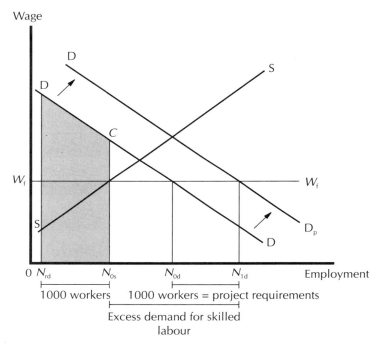

Figure 10.3   *Measurement of the economic cost of skilled labour whose wages are held below their equilibrium level — China*

In the presence of such labour and goods market distortions, the market wage rate that the project is forced to pay may exceed the true economic cost of employing this labour on the project, its shadow wage rate. As mentioned above, in some situations it **may** be necessary to use direct calculations of the market value of the output forgone by employing labour on the project. This is discussed in Section 10.2. However, this approach will normally be time consuming and will not usually be adopted unless there are no parallel free labour markets from which shadow wages may be deduced. This approach is discussed in Section 10.1.3. Other adjustments may also be necessary to ensure the calculated shadow wage rate reflects the true cost to the economy of employing labour, as will be seen in Sections 10.4 to 10.6.

10.1.3 Unprotected labour markets

Often, parallel to the formal urban labour market there will be a labour market that is relatively 'unprotected'. That is, it may not have any significant unionisation and minimum wage legislation and wage fixing in general may not exist or be enforced. If this is the case, an alternative approach to direct calculation of forgone output may be to use wages prevailing in this unprotected sector as a measure of the social opportunity cost of employing labour on the project.

Harberger (1972) is particularly associated with the argument that the wages observed for different categories of labour in unprotected labour markets will be the best guide to the social opportunity cost of labour employed in projects. Harberger advocated a market oriented approach to the estimation of shadow wage rates because in a full employment economy, the supply price of labour in the unorganised, or unprotected, sector will represent a better measure of the marginal social cost of labour than direct estimates of its forgone output. This is because these wage rates should not only reflect the forgone output of this labour in the occupations from which it will be directly or indirectly drawn — they will also include a valuation of the additional presentation costs such as housing, transport, food and the cost of the increased effort involved in the new job. The other advantage is that these unorganised labour markets will provide a large volume of information about the shadow wage rates for a wide range of occupations in different regions, subject to varying demand and supply conditions.

This basic finding holds if the assumption of full employment is relaxed. Modifications to the market wage rate are also necessary in the presence of various types of labour market distortion, such as income taxes and wage fixing.[2]

10.1.4 Impact on migration

In some situations, the creation of a project job may cause output elsewhere in the economy to fall by more than the contribution of the project worker. For example, the provision of one new urban job may encourage more than one rural worker to migrate to the city. This is particularly likely in a situation of labour market disequilibrium discussed above, where the protected urban wage rate is above the equilibrium wage rate. Also, in many cases, a male worker's family will accompany him. There may be fewer opportunities for wives and older children who were previously engaged in agriculture or village crafts and industries to find employment in the city. If these additional migration effects are believed to be widespread it will be necessary to take them into account in the economic evaluation of the project's labour costs.

10.1.5 Rural labour markets and family farm workers

In some cases the labour for the project may come from family farms where family members receive incomes related to their **average**, rather than their marginal, product. This is because the total income generated by the farm is split somewhat evenly among all family members, rather than each member receiving only an amount equal to his or her marginal contribution to the farm's revenue. It has been argued that it may be necessary for the project to pay these labourers a wage in excess of their forgone **marginal product**, to induce them to leave their farms. However, as long as these farms also hire some labourers, the wages of the hired labourers will be a reasonable guide to the marginal revenue product of a family member farmer. This is because hired labour will not be employed unless their wages at least equal their marginal revenue products. Their wages should be approximately equal to, or somewhat lower than, the marginal revenue product of the last family member employed.

In the situation where no hired labourers are employed on the family farms from which labour is drawn for the project, there may be so-called 'disguised unemployment'. This means that it may be possible to withdraw a family member from the farm to work on the project without reducing total farm output because other farm members will merely increase their supply of labour in response to the higher average income they will receive. The extent to which this happens will depend on the marginal disutility of effort of the remaining family members over the range of hours concerned. In such cases, the marginal social cost of forgone output will be between the marginal product of the departing family member and zero. This issue is discussed further in Section 10.3.

10.2 The direct valuation of labour's forgone output in economic prices

If there is not a freely operating unprotected labour market in the rural or urban area where the project will be located, it may be necessary to **directly estimate** the value of the output forgone, *l*, from labour drawn into the project. For example, assume the project is located in a rural area in China where there is no free rural labour market and that the project will draw labourers away from rice farming. In this situation it will be necessary to determine the market value of the rice production that will be lost each year as a result of these labourers being employed by the project, in order to determine the cost to the economy of employing each worker for a year.

Investigation reveals that each farmer produces on average 3 tonnes of rice per annum, which is sold in the local market for $L2000 per tonne. The farmers' other input costs are land, worth $L400 per tonne, and traded good inputs (farm equipment, seeds and fertiliser) costing $L300/tonne. The net revenue earned by each farmer is the value of their labour input. This is the output that will be lost if the project employs these workers. The forgone value of the labour input in market prices is therefore:

Market value of labour per tonne of rice – cost of non-labour inputs
= $L2000 – $L700 = $L1300/tonne.
Market value of one farmer's forgone output per annum, *l* = $L1300 × 3
= $L3900

It will then be necessary to value this forgone output at its economic cost. If the analyst is using the border price approach, the forgone output should be revalued in border prices. If the domestic price approach is employed, the forgone output will be valued in adjusted domestic prices. The labour used in this project is valued in border and domestic prices in the following examples.

10.2.1 Border price approach — valution of forgone output in border prices

In the example of the rice farmers employed by the project discussed above, a 33 per cent tariff has been placed on rice imports, so the border price of this rice will in fact be only $L1500. There is also a 100 per cent tariff on the traded inputs, farm equipment, seed and fertiliser used by rice farmers so the border price of these traded inputs is only $L150. The border price conversion factor for land has been estimated previously and found to be 0.875, so the value of the land used for rice growing in border prices is $L350 per tonne.[3] The border price equivalent of each rice farmer's annual forgone output will therefore be:

$$\$L\ (1500 - 150 - 350) \times 3 \text{ tonnes} = \$L3000 \text{ per annum}$$

The net economic value in border prices of the rice output lost as a result of employing one worker on the project will therefore be $L3000 per annum. This should be used to value the labour inputs into the project, assuming that none of the other adjustments discussed in Section 10.3 are considered relevant. The border price conversion factor for labour's forgone output, which we will term μ, would in this case equal $\frac{3000}{3900}$ = 0.77. This conversion factor can be used again in appraisals of other projects using this type of labour.

If the project's labour was previously employed in producing a mix of different types of output, the relevant border price conversion factor for the forgone output, μ, can be calculated by estimating the weighted average of the conversion factors of the goods that the labour would otherwise have produced. The weights used will equal the proportion that each good represented in the total forgone output, l.

If urban unprotected labour market wage rates are being used to measure the marginal social cost of skilled and semi-skilled labour in an urban project, it may not always be possible to identify the nature of the output forgone by using this labour. Even though it may be reasonable to assume that the market wage paid is a good measure of the market value of the forgone output, it may be impossible to identify the appropriate conversion factor to use to revalue these goods in economic prices. In this case it may be necessary to use a standard conversion factor (= $\frac{\text{official exchange rate}}{\text{shadow exchange rate}}$) to revalue the output in terms of border price equivalents. The second appendix at the end of Chapter 9 discusses the method of estimating a standard conversion factor and the circumstances where it is appropriate to use it.

10.2.2 Domestic price approach — valuation of forgone output in domestic prices

Alternatively, the rice farmers' labour must be valued in domestic prices if the domestic price approach is used. Studies have shown that there is a 20 per cent premium on foreign exchange in the economy concerned, so its shadow exchange rate is 1.2 times the official exchange rate. The domestic price equivalent of the traded rice will therefore be its border price, $L1500 per tonne, converted into local currency at this shadow exchange rate, or $L1800 per tonne. The traded good inputs will also initially be valued at their border prices (excluding tariffs) $L300 per tonne and then converted into domestic price equivalents using the shadow exchange rate. These traded inputs will therefore be worth $L360 per tonne in domestic prices. Land, a non-traded good, will just be valued at its domestic price, $L400 per tonne. The value of each rice farmer's annual forgone output in domestic prices will therefore be:

$$\$L\,(1800 - 360 - 400) \times 3 \text{ tonnes} = \$L3120 \text{ per annum}$$

10.3 Zero marginal productivity of labour?

In many developing countries and quite a number of developed ones there is a significant level of long-term open or disguised unemployment. Frequently this is the result of wage rates in the protected sector exceeding the market clearing wage. In the presence of such involuntary unemployment some analysts like Sen (UNIDO, 1972) have argued that if the project employs some unskilled labour the output forgone in the rest of the economy may be close to zero.

However, it is in fact unlikely that the output forgone elsewhere in the economy from using labour on the project will be zero, at least in developing countries. This is because unemployed people in low income developing countries with no social security system will almost always involve themselves in some productive activities. These may include house repair, fishing, scavenging or marginal informal sector activities, which will have some productive worth. These activities must be forgone if the person gets a formal job on the project. Furthermore, as is discussed in Section 10.6, there may be costs to unemployed persons in having to forego leisure if they take up a job in the project. If people actually suffer a loss of self-esteem when they are unemployed, they may place little or no weight on their loss of leisure.

Another factor to be aware of is that in rural areas, labour surpluses are likely to be seasonal so it will be necessary to value labour inputs according to the season in which they will be required by the project. Also, there are considerable regional variations in labour market conditions, which must be recognised in determining shadow wage rates. If the project is going to employ labour over a long period, it may not be reasonable to assume that current unemployment levels will persist in the long term. In the case of unemployed workers, it may be necessary to determine the minimum wage necessary to draw them into employment — their reserve wage. Squire and van der Tak (1975) indicate that there is evidence that the minimum supply wage of an unemployed man is a bare subsistence wage of 3 kilograms of grain equivalent per day. Hence the supply price of such unemployed persons is not zero.

Finally, several authors including Harberger (1972) dispute the existence of large pools of underemployed or unemployed labour in the rural areas of developing countries. It will be necessary for the analyst to carefully analyse the employment situation in the country concerned before making any judgements on this issue. However, even if there is unemployment, the shadow wage rate is unlikely to be zero, for the reasons discussed above and below.

10.4 The impact of changes in income on consumption and saving

Apart from forgone output by the workers, and possibly their families, there may be other costs to the economy involved in employing labour. By getting jobs in the project, workers are likely to increase their income, and as a result, will probably increase their consumption. This in itself is of course desirable, since one of the major objectives of economic development is an increase in consumption by the country's population. If policy makers believe that investment is at an optimal level then they will be as indifferent to marginal increases in consumption as to investment. However, if there are distortions in the capital market, such as taxes on savings and company profits from investment and regulation of interest rates, the government may believe that the overall level of investment is deficient.[4] In this situation, the government may consider an increase in consumption of one local dollar to be less valuable to the country than a similar increase in investment.

If:
ω is market wage received in the new job
l is the forgone output in the old job, assumed to be equal to the worker's wage in that job

then
$(\omega - l)$ = change in income earned by the worker employed on the project.

If the worker consumes all of the additional income earned on the project, the cost of this increased consumption in border prices will be $(\omega - l)\mathbf{b}$. The consumption conversion factor, $\mathbf{b}$, is the weighted sum of the conversion factors on the basket of commodities on which workers spend their extra income. This whole term $(\omega - l)\mathbf{b}$ will represent the cost in border prices of the increase in employment generated by the project, valued in border prices.

10.5 The distributional gain from increased consumption

Against the cost of additional consumption in an economy with an anti-investment bias must be set the social and distributional benefits of this increase in consumption. The group of workers who are employed on the project may be particularly poor, and the government may believe it is just as useful for them to consume this additional income as it is for it to be available for investment by the government or the private sector.

The social benefit of the increased consumption can then be measured by $(\omega - l)\dfrac{d}{v}$, where:

- $\dfrac{d}{v}$ represents the value of private consumption at the income level of the workers employed, relative to the value of income held by the government and available for investment

- d is the value of private consumption at the consumption level of the group whose income is affected, called group c, (W_c), relative to the value of consumption by average income recipients (W_a); $d = \dfrac{W_c}{W_a}$

- v is the value of income available for investment in the government sector (W_g), relative to the value of private sector consumption at the average level of consumption (W_a); $v = \dfrac{W_g}{W_a}$.[5]

10.6 The disutility of effort and presentation costs

It is generally recognised that there are likely to be other costs involved in employing labour apart from the output forgone. These will generally raise the shadow wage rate of even previously involuntarily unemployed labour above zero. One such cost of employing labour may be the reduction in the worker's welfare due to having to work harder on the project than was necessary previously, particularly if the individual was unemployed. This is a cost associated with the disutility of effort. The new job may require more hours and harder work and have more unpleasant or dangerous surroundings than the previous employment of the worker. As a result the worker will normally require more compensation, a higher wage, than in his or her previous job to be willing to make the move.

In addition workers may incur additional costs just to present themselves to work on the project. In particular, if the workers have moved to the city to take up the job, presentation costs such as housing, food and transport costs are likely to be higher there. These are real costs incurred by the worker and the economy if the project employs this worker and the project must therefore compensate the worker for these costs if they wish to attract staff. Extra presentation costs in urban areas can be valued by comparing household expenditure surveys in rural and urban areas.

Both of these factors may therefore raise the supply price of a worker in a new job above that in his or her previous position and will represent a genuine economic cost of employing the labour on the project. The project may try to defray some of these costs by, for example, providing free or subsidised housing, canteen meals, subsidised transport or improved working conditions. In this case the cost of providing these services will enter under these headings in the financial cost stream of the project and the supply price of labour for the project may apparently be reduced. However, these items will essentially be a cost of employing the labour.

The additional disutility of effort involved in a particular job may be very hard to objectively measure if it is not revealed in free market wage rates. It could be assumed that this additional disutility would be zero if the worker was previously employed in a similar job. In a freely operating competitive labour market, the ratio of the private valuation of the additional effort and presentation costs involved in undertaking the new job to the extra income earned will equal unity. If there is not a free market for the labour required by the project, the disutility of effort involved may be gauged by examining market determined wages in similar occupations, subject to similar working conditions, to determine the premium (or discount) that must be paid to attract workers to these jobs. The ratio of the private valuation of the additional effort to the extra income earned is designated as λ in the shadow wage rate formula in equation (10.2). If λ is unity, the wage paid will be the supply price of labour. If no private cost is put on the additional disutility of effort, this ratio will be zero.

In one well known shadow wage rate formula developed by Squire and van der Tak (SVT) (1975), the social cost of reduced leisure and increased presentation costs, is represented as:

$$(\omega - l)\phi\lambda \times \frac{d}{v} \tag{10.1}$$

The term ϕ represents the government's valuation of the reduction in leisure suffered by workers on the project. The whole term for the additional social and presentation costs of labour, which will be one component of the shadow wage rate, will therefore disappear if either the individual's or the government's valuation of this extra effort is zero. If the individual and the government believe that the extra wage paid is necessary to repay the extra effort ($\phi\lambda = 1$), then the shadow wage rate will equal the market wage (multiplied by $\frac{d}{v}$). The term $\frac{d}{v}$ will equal 1 if the increase in the worker's income (and consumption) is equally valuable as an increase in investment.

10.7 SVT shadow wage rate formula

The true economic cost of employing labour will include all the elements that have been discussed in the previous sections: forgone output, the net social gains of increased consumption, and the social costs of the disutility of effort and presentation costs.

Both the border and domestic price approaches include these same elements in their shadow wage rate formulae. The only differences relate to the numeraires used in the two approaches.[6] The shadow wage rate formula outlined in equation (10.2) was developed by Squire and van der Tak and uses the border price approach formula so the economic cost of labour is measured in border prices equivalents.

Assuming that all the increase in income accruing to workers above their forgone marginal product is consumed, the shadow wage rate will be:

$$\text{SWR} = \mu l + (\omega - l)(\mathbf{b} - \frac{d}{v}) + (\omega - l)\phi\lambda \times \frac{d}{v} \qquad (10.2)$$

where μl is the labour's forgone income in economic prices, the efficiency cost of labour, as μ is the conversion factor for the output forgone, converting it into border prices.

$(\omega - l)(\mathbf{b} - \frac{d}{v})$ is the net social cost of the increase in consumption. This is equal to the cost of the increased consumption in terms of forgone foreign exchange $(\omega - l)\mathbf{b}$, where $\mathbf{b}$ is the relevant consumption conversion factor, minus the social benefits of increased consumption relative to the value of increased investment $(\omega - l)\frac{d}{v}$. The term d is the social value put on an increase in consumption by the workers employed and v is the social value put on an increase in investment.

$(\omega - l)\phi\lambda \times \frac{d}{v}$ is the social cost of reduced leisure and increased presentation costs.

Relaxing the assumption that all extra income is consumed, so that only a fraction, c, is consumed the shadow wage rate formula becomes:

$$\text{SWR} = \mu l + c(\omega - l)(\mathbf{b} - \frac{d}{v}) + c(\omega - l)\phi\lambda \times \frac{d}{v} \qquad (10.3)$$

10.8 Simplifying assumptions

Very often, the project analyst will not have the time or resources to accurately measure all these elements of the economic cost of employing each category of labour on the project. Particularly if labour is a rather minor part of total costs it may be necessary or desirable to make simplifying assumptions. However, it will be necessary for the analyst to look at each case closely to determine whether such approximations are close enough to the actual situation in the country concerned, so that no major bias is introduced into the analysis by taking this approach. Some of the simplifying assumptions often adopted include the following:

- If:
  - the wage labour receives on the project is just equal to its forgone marginal product, that is, $\omega = l$ or
  - the social costs of increased consumption are just offset by the benefits, that is, $\mathbf{b} = \frac{d}{v}$, or

    – income distribution is optimal and the social value of consumption and investment are equal when both are valued in border price equivalents, that is, $d = 1$ and $\mathbf{b} = \frac{l}{v}$, and

    – $\phi\lambda = 0$, government's or individual's valuation of increased effort is zero, then the economic cost of labour equals μl, the forgone output in economic prices, the efficiency shadow wage rate. Output forgone, μl, is in fact commonly used in simple economic analyses to measure the shadow wage rate. However, it is doubtful whether the analysts using this simplification always recognise and have tested the rather stringent assumptions they are making.

- If the government places no value on increased private consumption and only pursues an objective of high economic growth, that is, if v tends to infinity, then the economic cost of labour will equal the economic cost of the forgone output of the labour plus the total border price value of the extra consumption generated by the higher incomes paid by the project. That is,

$$SWR = \mu l + (\omega - l)\mathbf{b} \tag{10.4}$$

If the government places a high value on growth this may raise the economic cost of labour above the output forgone by using it in the project. This may in turn result in somewhat more capital intensive technologies and projects being chosen than would otherwise have been the case. In this case no social value will be placed on the increased consumption generated by employing more workers.

- If the public or private valuation of increased effort is zero, that is, $\phi\lambda = 0$, then the economic cost of labour will be just the economic cost of its forgone output plus the net social cost of the additional consumption:

$$SWR = \mu l + (\omega - 1)(\mathbf{b} - \tfrac{d}{v}) \tag{10.5}$$

The shadow wage rate will be higher the more important the growth objective; the higher the value placed on v. The shadow wage rate will be lower the more important the income distribution objective and the poorer the income recipient, that is, the higher is the value of d.

10.9 Conclusions regarding the shadow price of labour

Summing up, traditional economic analyses carried out by many developed and developing countries and international agencies like the World Bank and Asian Development Bank assume that the shadow wage rate is only the economic value of forgone output of the labour employed. However, this can be seen as a special case of the more general shadow wage rate formula in (10.3). The use of forgone output alone implies that a large number of simplifying assumptions have been made.

    Depending on the assumptions made regarding government policy, parameters d, v and ϕ and the estimated levels of $(\omega - l)$, and $\mathbf{b}$, the shadow wage rate of even previously unemployed labour may in fact represent a large percentage of the market wage or even exceed it.[7]

If unprotected labour markets are present, however, these will provide a more readily accessible source of data on the economic cost of employing labour. Such market wages will not only provide information on the forgone output of labour but also include compensation for additional presentation costs and effort. Nevertheless, it will still be necessary to adjust these market prices to convert them to border price equivalents if the border price approach is being used. Furthermore if there are excess migration effects and negative effects on investment these will also need to be taken into account in deriving the economic cost of labour from these free market wage rates.

10.10 Shadow price of land

Unimproved land, like unskilled labour, is another non-traded primary factor in fixed supply. Only in a few limited situations can the quantity of such land be expanded, by for example the draining of swamps and reclaiming of land from the sea. In general the economic cost of the land used in a project will therefore be given by the demand price that the displaced users of this land were willing to pay for it.

If there is a freely operating market for land, the market price for land should reflect the demand price that people are willing to pay and therefore the utility they obtain from using it. However, if there are distortions present in the markets for land, capital, foreign exchange or goods, it will be necessary to adjust market prices of land to determine its economic cost. If, for example, the displaced users of the land required by the project were manufacturing a good that was protected by a tariff, their capacity to pay for the land might have been inflated by this distortion. Furthermore, if there is a premium placed on foreign exchange in this country, it will be necessary to take this into account. The economic pricing of land using the border and domestic price approaches is outlined below.

10.10.1 The border price approach to the valuing of land

If there is a freely operating market for land near the location of the project, the market price of that land needs only to be converted into border price equivalents before it can be entered in the project's economic cash flow. The conversion factor for land that is used should equal the ratio of the border to the domestic market price of the output that the land produces. If the land required by the project could produce a variety of crops, a sectoral conversion factor for agricultural output should be used to convert the land's value into border prices. Similarly, if the land could be used for a range of industrial projects a sectoral conversion factor for manufactured products, or possibly a standard conversion factor, could be used to convert its value into border prices.

If there is no freely operating market for land in the vicinity of the project or in similar locations in the country concerned it will be necessary to directly estimate the opportunity cost of the land. The opportunity cost of the land will be the value of the net output that it could have produced in its next best alternative use. If agricultural land is to be used, its economic cost will be the sum of the discounted agricultural output value lost over the life of the project, net of the cost of other inputs, all valued in border prices.

$$\text{Economic cost of land} = \sum_{t=0}^{n} \frac{(X_{tb} - N_{tb})}{(1 + r)^t} \tag{10.6}$$

where

X_{tb} is the value of the crop produced on the land in year t, in border prices
N_{tb} is the value of inputs other than land used to produce this crop in year t, in border prices
r is the discount rate and n is the number of years that the project will use the land.

For example, an industrial project will require 20 hectares of land that would otherwise be used to produce cotton. However, there is no freely operating market for this land and therefore no market price. This could occur, for example, if the land were owned by local tribal groupings, as in the case of many Pacific islands and Papua New Guinea, or by the state as is the case in centrally planned economies like China and Vietnam.

The land currently produces 0.5 tonnes of cotton per hectare, which has a market price of $L800 per tonne. However, there is a 25 per cent tariff on imported cotton so the border price is only $L640 per tonne, giving a border price conversion factor of 0.8. The cotton inputs other than land, which include seed, fertiliser, labour and transport, have a border price equivalent of $L600 per tonne. If a 10 per cent discount rate is used the economic cost of withdrawing this land from cotton production over the 20 year life of the project will be:

$$\sum_{t=0}^{20} \frac{[(640 - 600) \times 0.5 \times 20]}{(1 + 0.1)^t}$$

$$= \sum_{t=0}^{20} \frac{(400)}{(1 + 0.1)^t}$$

$$= \$L3805$$

A similar approach is used to value non-agricultural land. If the land is currently being used for industrial production, its value is the forgone industrial production each year minus the annual cost of the all other inputs excluding land, all valued in border prices, discounted and summed over the life of the project.

The supply of improved land, like cleared and productive agricultural land, can of course be expanded. The cost of such land could therefore be estimated as the value of the raw land, which is valued by the method outlined above, plus the border price equivalent of the inputs used to improve the land. These inputs would include earth-moving equipment, fertiliser and labour. If the displaced users are residential, the free market price of residential land will be the best measure of the utility forgone by the project using this land. This can be expressed in border price equivalents by multiplying the market price by a conversion factor for residential land development, on the assumption that displaced users will, at the margin, be diverted into newly developed residential land elsewhere.

Once the conversion factors for unimproved and improved land have been calculated for a particular location they can be used again in other project evaluations in similar locations.

10.10.2 The domestic price approach to the valuing of land

The economic cost of the 20 hectares of cotton-producing land can also be measured in adjusted domestic prices if this approach is being used to incorporate the foreign exchange premium. If there is a premium on foreign exchange of 20 per cent in this economy, the border price of the cotton, $L640 per tonne, will be converted into domestic price equivalents using a shadow exchange rate that is 1.2 times the official exchange rate. The cotton's value in domestic price equivalents will therefore be $L768 per tonne. The traded inputs into cotton production, seed and fertiliser have a border price of $L200 per tonne, so their domestic price equivalent will be $L240 per tonne. The non-traded inputs other than land are labour and transport, which have a domestic price of $L480. The marginal social benefit of the land over a 20 year project will therefore be:

$$\sum_{t=0}^{20} \frac{\left[(768 - 720) \times 0.5 \times 20\right]}{(1 + 0.1)^t}$$

$$= \sum_{t=0}^{20} \frac{(480)}{(1 + 0.1)^t}$$

$$= \$L4567$$

10.11 The shadow price of natural resources

As was discussed in Chapter 8, if the natural resources used in the project are traded they should be valued at their fob or cif border prices, depending on whether they impact on exports or imports at the margin. For example, imported coal for a steel mill should be valued at its cif border price, while bauxite exported by a mining project should be valued at its fob border price. Any tariffs, export subsidies or taxes should be deducted to obtain the economic cost or benefit of the natural resource input or output. If the country places a premium on foreign exchange, the cost of these traded natural resource inputs will then be converted into local currency at the official exchange rate or shadow exchange rate, depending on whether the border price or domestic price approach is being used, respectively.

If the project uses a non-traded natural resource input whose output can be expanded, this input should be valued at its supply price, its marginal cost of production. Its supply price will equal the economic value of the resources that are used to produce it. As was discussed in Chapter 7 any taxes on the input should be deducted and any subsidies provided should be added to obtain the actual cost of supplying the input. Similarly any producer surplus earned by suppliers of the natural resource input should be deducted. If the country has a foreign exchange premium and the border price approach is employed to correct for this, the non-traded input should be decomposed into its tradeable and non-tradeable components to determine its economic cost in border price equivalents. If the domestic price approach is employed, the domestic market price of the resource can be directly entered into the economic analysis cash flow.

If the project uses a non-traded natural resource that is in relatively fixed supply, it should be valued at its demand price. If a natural resource required by the project is in short supply it is likely to earn a scarcity rent. Market prices will be the best reflection of such rents if there is a freely operating market for the resource. If there is a foreign exchange premium and the border price approach is being used to correct for this, the relevant conversion factor to convert the natural resource's value into border prices is its demand price conversion factor. This is the weighted average of the conversion factors of the resources into which displaced producers will be diverted if the project uses up some of this natural resource in fixed supply. If the domestic price approach is being used, the domestic market price of the natural resource can be directly entered into the project's economic cash flow.

If the natural resource is a depletable one, such as oil or a mineral, the analyst may believe that the market price does not fully reflect the long-term scarcity rent of the resource. This failure may be due, for example, to the market interest rate being higher than the social discount rate. In this situation, the project analyst may wish to add a scarcity premium to the shadow price of the input.

If there is not a free market for the natural resource and it is in relatively fixed supply, an effort must be made to estimate its opportunity cost in terms of its forgone uses. This can be done by the same method as was used to estimate the value of land for which there is no free market. The economic cost of the resource will equal the economic value of the best alternative product that could be produced using the natural resource, minus the economic cost of all other inputs.

For example, a road-making project may require large quantities of gravel, which is currently subject to price control and which is in relatively fixed supply. If the gravel were not used for the road, it might be available as fill for a hydroelectricity dam project being considered in the same area. The economic cost of the gravel will then be equal to the present value of the economic value of electricity sales from the dam project minus the present value of the economic value of all other inputs used in the dam project, including capital, labour and land.

Once the economic price of the non-traded natural resource has been estimated, its conversion factor can be calculated as:

$$CF_{nr} = \frac{\text{economic price natural resource}}{\text{market price of the resource}}$$

This conversion factor can be used in subsequent project appraisals in this country that employ this input.

10.12 Conclusions regarding the shadow price of land and natural resources

If relatively free markets are available for land and natural resources, their market prices will provide a readily accessible source of data on the economic cost of using these inputs, or the benefit of producing them in the case of natural resources — employing labour. As in the case of labour, it will still be necessary to adjust these market prices to convert them to border price equivalents if the border price approach is being used. If no domestic market exists for these primary factors it will be necessary to value them in terms of their opportunity cost — the net value of the output they could have been used to produce in their next best alternative use.

Exercises

1. Estimate the shadow wage rate and conversion factor for unskilled labour employed on an irrigation project where these workers will be drawn from the local peasant farming community. There is no rural labour market for agricultural labourers in this country as all farmers work their own land.

   Farmers can produce 2 tonnes of bananas per annum, which have a border price of $L4000 per tonne. All other agricultural inputs, including the rental value of the land have a border price value of $L1000 per tonne. However, the labourers on the road will have to work 20 per cent harder than peasant farmers and may be expected to demand 20 per cent higher wages than their forgone marginal product in agriculture. They will also need to pay $L5000 more each year for food and accommodation than peasants who remain farming their land. The consumption conversion factor for this additional consumption is estimated to be 0.8.

2. Skilled workers are in short supply in the country where a new road project will be located. Most qualified engineers and technicians prefer to live in urban areas where they earn an average net monthly salary of $L4900, after paying personal income tax of 35 per cent. The road project will need to offer a starting salary of $L5600 per month, plus a once-off dislocation allowance of $L3000, to meet these workers' expenses in moving to the site. One benefit for workers in the region where the project is located is that salaries are exempt from tax.

   Despite these attractive conditions, it is expected that there will be an 18 per cent turnover in skilled workers. Workers who leave will need to be replaced.

   Determine the economic cost of employing each skilled worker on a 3 year road-making project in this country. Also calculate the conversion factor for this kind of skilled labour. The economic cost of different categories of labour will be their supply price wage rate in the unregulated labour markets, plus allowance for any externalities such as forgone taxation revenue.

3. Unskilled labour is readily available in the region where the road will be located. Most will be drawn from the pool of agricultural workers. The prevailing monthly minimum wage rate in $L, observed during the different months of the year, is as follows:

January	700	July	300
February	650	August	280
March	550	September	250
April	450	October	200
May	400	November	350
June	350	December	550

The project's proportional requirements for unskilled labour over the year will be as follows:

January	0.00	July	0.12
February	0.03	August	0.13
March	0.05	September	0.14
April	0.08	October	0.16
May	0.10	November	0.07
June	0.11	December	0.02

Being in the public sector, the project is committed to paying the minimum wage of $L800 per month to every unskilled worker.

Determine the economic cost of employing unskilled labour on this road and calculate the conversion factor for this type of labour.

4. Estimate the shadow price of the 10 hectares of land required for a 25 year industrial project if there is no free market for land in the country. The regulated price for land is $L400 per hectare. Most of the surrounding land is used to grow maize. The land can yield 1.5 tonnes of maize to the hectare and maize can be sold locally for $L1250 per tonne. There is a 40 per cent export tax on maize, which is a major export for the country concerned. The border price equivalent of all the other inputs into maize production, with the exception of the land, equals $L400 per tonne. The value of these inputs in domestic prices is $L500. There is a 30 per cent premium on foreign exchange in this economy.

a   Measure the economic value of this land in border prices over the life of the project if the real social discount rate is 8 per cent.

b   Estimate the border price conversion factor for this land.

c   Measure the land's economic value in domestic prices using the same discount rate.

d   Estimate the border price conversion factor for this land.

References

Filmer, R. and Stilberg, R., 1977. *Fertility, Family Formation and Female Labour Source Participation in Australia, 1922–74*, Working Paper BP-08 Impact Project, University of Melbourne, Melbourne.

Harberger, A.C., 1972. 'On measuring the social opportunity cost of labour', reprinted in Harberger, A.C., *Project Evaluation*, Macmillan, New York, Chapter 7.

Harberger, A.C., 1972. *Project Evaluation*, Macmillan, New York.

Jenkins, G.P. and Harberger, A.C., 1991. *Manual — Cost Benefit Analysis of Investment Decisions*, Program on Investment Appraisal and Management, Harvard Institute for International Development, Cambridge, Mass.

Squire, L. and van der Tak, H.G., 1975. *Economic Analysis of Projects*, Johns Hopkins University Press, Baltimore.

UNIDO, 1972. *Guidelines for Project Evaluation*, United Nations, New York.

Further reading

Duvingneau, J.C. and Prasad, R.N., 1984. *Guidelines for Calculating Financial and Economic Rates of Return for DFC Projects*, World Bank Technical Paper No. 33, Washington, Chapter 6.

Harberger, A.C., 1972. 'On measuring the social opportunity cost of labour', reprinted in Harberger, A.C., *Project Evaluation*, Macmillan, New York, Chapter 7.

Irvin, G., 1978. *Modern Cost-Benefit Methods*, Macmillan, London, Chapter 6.

Jenkins, G.P. and Harberger, A.C., 1991. *Manual — Cost Benefit Analysis of Investment Decisions*, Program on Investment Appraisal and Management, Harvard Institute for International Development, Cambridge, Mass.

Little, I.M.D. and Mirrlees, J.A., 1974. *Project Appraisal and Planning for Developing Countries*, Heinemann Educational Books, London, Chapter 14.

Ray, A., 1984. *Cost Benefit Analysis — Issues and Methodologies*, Johns Hopkins University Press for the World Bank, Baltimore, Chapter 4.

Squire, L. and van der Tak, H.G., 1975. *Economic Analysis of Projects*, Johns Hopkins University Press, Baltimore, Chapters 9, 12.

UNIDO, 1972. *Guidelines for Project Evaluation*, United Nations, New York, Chapter 15.

Endnotes

1 This is a form of restrictive union practice, which prevents non-union members from obtaining employment in a particular enterprise.

2 A fuller summary of the Harberger approach is included in Jenkins and Harberger, Chapter 13.

3 The method of estimating the shadow price of land and its border prices conversion factor is discussed later in the chapter.

4 This issue will be discussed in some detail in Chapter 13 dealing with the social discount rate.

5 Squire and van der Tak (1975) hypothesised that the distributional gain from extra consumption is equal to the gain in income weighted by the distributional weight relevant to that income group relative to the numeraire.

6 The reader should compare the formulae given in Squire and van der Tak (1975), Chapter 8, (16) and UNIDO (1972), Chapter 15, (15.17).

7 Additional numerical examples of shadow wage rate estimation can be seen in Squire and van der Tak (1975:85).

CHAPTER 11

Valuing externalities including environmental impacts

11.1 Definition of an externality

Often when a project or policy is implemented people other than its owners, workforce and customers benefit or are disadvantaged by its operation. When the existence or operation of a project results in a net gain or loss to society but not to those who undertake the project, then this category of benefit or cost is defined as an external effect or an **externality**.

Some of the most important examples of negative externalities associated with many industrial, agricultural, mining and infrastructure projects are pollution and environmental degradation. These negative environmental effects are felt by residents and other producers living near these projects or sharing the same river basin, air shed or coastal area. However, they are not necessarily felt by people who directly purchase the project's outputs or pay for its inputs. As these costs are not borne by consumers buying the polluting project's output and will not therefore reduce the amount they are willing to pay for this output, these external costs do not affect the project's financial net benefit stream. Similarly, these negative external effects will not inflate the cost of the project's inputs. The financial net benefits of such a project will therefore overestimate its contribution to economic welfare. Because these external effects have an impact on the overall welfare of the community they should, however, definitely be included in any economic analysis of the project.

There are two main problems associated with externalities in cost benefit analysis:
- Identifying the externality, particularly in advance of the project's operation.
- Quantifying the value of the externality for incorporation into the cost benefit analysis.

The latter involves measuring the impact of the externality on people's welfare in monetary terms and determining its economic value so that it can be included in the economic cash flow of the project.

11.2 Identifying externalities

To assist in identifying externalities, it is useful to break them down into their various categories. Externalities can occur during the production, distribution or consumption of either project inputs or outputs. In addition they can either have a positive, beneficial effect or a negative, harmful impact on the welfare of the community.

11.2.1 Technological externalities

True externalities are technological externalities that impact on the actual production or consumption possibilities of other producers or consumers. For example, the discharge of poisonous waste from a factory into a nearby river may kill all the fish and make it impossible for local fishermen to continue to harvest fish from this river. Such pollution is a negative technological externality.

Similarly, the release of noxious gases by the project may force local residents to breath dirty air, causing a loss of their utility and perhaps creating respiratory disorders. As the possibility of residents consuming clean air will be lost, this pollution is also a form of negative technological externality.

A classic example of a positive technological externality is the case of the apple grower and the apiarist whose properties adjoin. The bees from the apiary pollinate the apple blossoms enabling a larger apple crop, while the nectar from the apple blossoms increases the honey production of the apiarist. A more modern example of positive externalities is the benefit to local hotel owners and the tourist industry generally from a city hosting an Olympic Games. The benefit of a pollution control campaign to the local fishing and tourist industries is another example of a positive technological externality.

11.2.2 Pecuniary externalities

Earlier literature used to differentiate technological from pecuniary externalities, which merely change the price of inputs or outputs to other producers or consumers. Unlike a technological externality, a pecuniary externality does not affect the consumption or production **possibilities** of other producers or consumers, just their **costs** of production or consumption. A negative pecuniary externality may occur as a result of the project pushing up the price of a specialised input that is in inelastic supply, such as some category of skilled labour. This externality will impact on other users of the factor who are forced to pay more for it as a result of the project's increased demand.

However, it is now recognised in the cost benefit analysis literature that pecuniary externalities are not true externalities. Any changes in input or output prices induced by a project should be reflected in accurate projections of these prices and these should be included in the cash flow of the project. They will then be internalised in the overall estimation of the social profitability of the project. Any impact of such price changes on the project's consumers or input producers will be included in the economic analysis of the project via the measurement of consumer or producer surplus.

Gains or losses of producer surplus as a result of the project will in most cases merely represent transfers within the economy.

However, if the project causes a reduction in other producers' input prices or an increase in demand for their output and this enables these producers to achieve economies of scale, consumers and hence the economy may obtain real economic benefits. In order to identify and measure all these general equilibrium effects it would be necessary to develop a general equilibrium model of the economy and determine the full impact of the project by running simulations. However, this would only be justified for a very major project.

A concept related to positive pecuniary externalities is the creation of so-called 'linkages' by a project. Backward linkages may be generated if the project stimulates activity in an industry that produces inputs for the project. For example, if a cement plant were established it might stimulate demand for cement bags, making it viable for a firm producing these to be established. Forward linkages are developed when the project stimulates activity in an industry purchasing its output. For example, the new cement plant project may lower cement prices and encourage a cement block manufacturer to establish a business in the area. If a project will only be viable if a second, related project is carried out, then the general rule is that the two activities should be considered as one project and evaluated as such. Only if their joint net present value is positive should they be implemented. In the absence of such information, there are dangers in advancing 'linkage effects' as the rationale for an otherwise unviable project.

11.2.3 Externalities created during the production process

Another useful way to categorise externalities so that they can be identified more easily is to examine each stage in the product's life to determine when externalities will be created. The water and air pollution created by an industrial project are examples of negative externalities created during the production process and are associated with the use and disposal of project inputs. The example of the apple grower and the apiarist is one of positive technological externalities being created during the production process.

Another example of the positive technological externalities generated during a project's production stage are the services produced by a road built to the site of a hydroelectric dam. Although the road is primarily an input to the electricity project it can also be used by local farmers and residents and may extend the production or consumption possibilities of these groups. Local farmers may be able to grow new, more profitable crops because they can now use the road to supply a previously inaccessible market. Local residents may now be able to visit friends and relatives more easily, or to gain access to new goods and services by being able to shop in the local market, visit health clinics or attend schools. Thus the road will expand their consumption possibilities.

A final common example of positive externalities generated by a project during the production process are the skills created when labour is trained for a project.

While this labour is employed on the project the enterprise may capture the benefits of such training if the employer pays a wage that is less than the labour's marginal revenue product. However, eventually the labour will leave the project and become available to other employers. If workers with this training are in short supply their availability may represent a positive externality for other employers enabling them to expand their production possibilities.

11.2.4 Externalities created in the distribution of project outputs

Positive or negative externalities can also be created when a project's output is being distributed. For example, coal may be transported from a coal mining project to the port on heavy coal trucks, which break up local roads, cause noise, air pollution and road congestion and increase the number of road accidents. Another example of a negative externality associated with the distribution of products are ugly advertisement billboards. Positive externalities may be created by street entertainers or buskers who, while distributing their services, entertain passers who may not reward the entertainer.

11.2.5 Externalities created in the consumption of project outputs

The consumption of a project's output may also create externalities for people other than the direct consumers of the good or service. For example, the consumption of soap and cleaning detergents by one person has positive externalities for others, including a more pleasant, odourless, environment and a reduced risk of disease. Similarly, the use of a vaccine by one person reduces the pool of potential carriers of such diseases and therefore the risk to unvaccinated people. Another example of externalities generated during consumption are the benefits generated by those who own telephones for those who do not, who can then ring subscribers on public phones. Finally, the availability of public education will create externalities for the whole community by improving the range of services and goods available.

Respiratory diseases caused by passive smoking (breathing in smoke from someone else's cigarettes) are an example of a negative externality created by the consumption of a product. A second example are the car accidents caused by people who become intoxicated from consuming too much alcohol. A third example of negative externalities created during consumption are the congestion and accidents caused by road users for other drivers. Other effects include noise pollution and pedestrian accidents imposed on residents living near roads.

11.2.6 Treatment of externalities in economic analysis

The social costs or benefits of all these externalities will not show up as negative or positive entries in the financial cash flow of the projects concerned. Industrial projects that pollute the environment frequently do not compensate those who are harmed by their pollution. The apiarist and the apple grower would not normally charge each other for the useful services each provides. Nor, typically, would an electricity generation project charge local farmers and residents for the right to use its road. Employers who provide training can only capture all the benefits from this training if the employee works for them for life. Nevertheless, since all these externalities do have an impact on community welfare, and sometimes a very significant one, the economic cash flows of projects must include an estimate of their economic costs and benefits.

If the value of socially beneficial externalities is not included in the economic cash flow of the projects that produce them, the project may be designed to produce at a socially sub-optimal level or may not be undertaken at all. On the other hand, since the ex-factory prices of products that generate negative externalities such as paper produced by polluting technologies, cigarettes and alcohol do not reflect their harmful side-effects, more of such products may be produced than is socially optimal. Since these negative externalities reduce community welfare they should be included in any economic evaluation of projects producing such products.

11.3 Incorporating externalities in the cash flow

Once the externalities generated by a project have been identified, it is necessary to put some monetary value on them so that they can be included in the project's cash flow and the final calculation of its NPV. Many of the options available for measuring externalities and including them in the project's economic cash flow are discussed in the following sections.

11.3.1 Internalising the externality via project redesign

In many cases the best solution will be for the project designer to try to internalise the externality so that it becomes a direct cost or benefit of the project. In the case of projects producing negative externalities like environmental degradation, it will often be optimal to redesign the project to reduce such negative impacts or prevent them all together. In the case of a project that generates air or water pollution, the project could be redesigned to include anti-pollution devices to prevent the release of these pollutants into the atmosphere or waterways. If a road-building project in a high rainfall area is expected to increase soil erosion and silt run-off into local fields, expenditure should be included to stabilise soils with fast growing shrubs, trees and grasses. This will have the effect of increasing the project's direct production costs but will reduce or eliminate the costs imposed on local residents and other producers by these pollutants . The rationale for a public project adopting this approach is that the project itself should bear all its economic costs of production, even if its legal responsibility to do so may be unclear. Otherwise, the project's implementors may underestimate its true cost of production and production may exceed socially optimal levels.

In the case of a private project where legal property rights are unclear, the government may intervene to force the project to internalise its negative externalities.

It may for example impose emission controls fixing the legal maximum levels of pollutants that may be released by polluting factories. These will usually be related to international standards regarding levels of emissions that do not threaten health. The private developer will then be forced to design the project so that it meets these pollution standards. However, this is a rather rigid approach and may result in a project becoming unviable, even though its economic NPV is positive. Various other devices, including pollution taxes and transferable pollution rights, have been introduced in some countries to increase the efficiency of decisions regarding pollution control. However, in all these cases the externality would be internalised and the project would produce at a lower, socially optimal level of production.

11.3.2 Internalising the externality via compensation

In some industries the technology to control pollution may not exist or may be so expensive that it far exceeds the economic cost of the pollution prevented. In this case the only possible solutions may be either not to produce at all or to compensate those suffering from the pollution. Those receiving compensation could include local farmers whose crops have been destroyed or local residents who have lost their environmental amenity — the utility they received from living in a clean environment. In countries with a strong legal tradition and educated population, those legally entitled to compensation could pursue their claims through the courts.

It may not be feasible to internalise externalities by such means if the victims of some negative externality have inadequate property rights. This may make it difficult to devise satisfactory compensation schemes. For example, workers in nearby factories, casual visitors to a polluted area or fishermen without riparian fishing rights may have only vague legal claims to compensation. The problem will then be how to directly value positive or negative externalities experienced by such groups so that they can be included in the economic cash flow of the project. In such cases, it may be necessary for the analyst to use contingent valuation methods to determine the extent that they have suffered welfare losses. This methodology is discussed further in Section 11.6.

However, if an appropriate level of compensation can be decided and is actually paid, the externality will be internalised because the compensation will enter directly into the project's cost stream, raising the costs of the project.

11.3.3 Internalisation by taxation and subsidies

Another example of forced internalisation of externalities is the taxing of consumer goods whose consumption causes large negative externalities. For example, high excise taxes on cigarettes and alcohol are designed to discourage consumption and internalise the high public cost of individuals consuming these products. In Hong Kong the government has tried to reduce road congestion by introducing extremely high car registration fees, while in Singapore dual registration fees are employed for full week and weekend-only drivers. On the other hand, governments often subsidise or provide free goods and services such as primary and secondary school education and mass inoculation programs whose consumption creates large positive externalities. This is done to ensure that their production is at a socially optimal level.

Sometimes it is not technically possible or socially desirable to internalise an externality associated with a project. In such cases it will be necessary to value the externality directly for inclusion in the project's economic cash flow, even though it will not enter its financial cash flow. For example, in the case of the dam project, the project could conceivably charge local farmers to use the road built as part of the project and add the tolls collected to the project's direct benefits. However, the project may decide that it would be too expensive to set up a toll road. Alternatively, if the project is a public one the government may decide to provide the road as a public good. In this case it will need to directly value the external benefits created by the road so that these can be entered into the project's economic cash flow. Similarly, if a project will damage some important cultural site, it will be impossible and probably meaningless to try to compensate everyone affected as this may possibly include the whole population. Consequently, the potential loss incurred should be estimated, possibly using contingent valuation methods, and then entered directly into the economic cost cash flow. This should be done even though no actual compensation would be made. If the project then has a negative economic NPV it should not proceed.

11.4 Direct valuation of the externality's impact on welfare using market prices

Probably the most satisfactory and commonly used approach to valuing externalities is to measure the market value of goods and services directly produced, destroyed or required as a result of an externality. Dixon et al. (1986) categorise several of the impacts of environmental externalities that can be measured in market prices. However, this same classification can be applied more broadly to all externalities generated by a project.

11.4.1 Measuring productivity changes

The project may create externalities that affect the productivity of other producers and consumers. This productivity change can be measured in terms of the value of the net output produced. For example, the minimum economic cost of the air or water pollution that destroys local crops will be the market value of these crops over the life-time of the project that produces them, or while the damage continues to occur. If some less sensitive but also less profitable crop can be grown instead, the difference between the value of the preferred crop and less valuable substitute can be calculated and used as a measure of the cost of the pollution. On the other hand, a road installed to serve a port project may raise the productivity of local farmers and this could be measured by the increased revenue they earn from selling their farm produce in newly accessible markets.

11.4.2 Change of earnings or human capital approach

Another related measure of the externalities generated by a project is the change in human productivity they cause. This can be measured by the loss or gain of earnings, or change in the value of the human capital, of those affected. For example, air pollution from a coal mining project may cause some miners to develop lung disease, cutting short their working life or even causing their premature death. Their lost earnings will be a measure of their decreased productivity and a minimal estimate of the cost of the pollution. Alternatively, the miners may be restored to health and full productivity by medical care and the cost of this care will be a measure of the cost of the pollution. The pain and suffering of the miners and their families are not included in either of these measures, which is why it is only a minimum measure of the cost of the externality.[1]

The increased earnings of workers who receive training on a project and then go on to work for other employers is another use of the human capital approach to measure the value of externalities. In this case, such earnings are a measure of the positive externalities generated by a project's training. If a project is designed to reduce air, water or toxic waste pollution the savings in health costs that would otherwise have been incurred to maintain people's productivity would be one of its major external benefits.

11.4.3 Opportunity cost approach

If an externality is very difficult to measure, one method of handling this is to measure the NPV of the project that generates the externality and compare it with the NPV of the next best alternative project, which does not. The difference between the two projects' NPVs is the opportunity cost of the externality. The decision-maker can then decide if the cost or benefit of the externality exceeds the difference in the projects' NPVs. For example, a government may be considering either expanding an inner city airport, thereby increasing noise pollution for a large number of people, and a more expensive option of building a new airport on the outskirts of the city. Assuming that both projects have a positive NPV, but that of the expansion project's NPV is larger, the government must then decide whether the reduction of noise pollution from building the new airport would justify the loss of potential income from foregoing the inner city air terminal expansion. This technique has also been used to measure the opportunity cost of wilderness areas that are threatened by dam projects (Krutilla and Fisher, 1985).

11.4.4 Preventive expenditure approach

Another readily identifiable cost of a negative externality will be the **preventive expenditures** that people incur to reduce or avoid the damage from such an externality. Such expenditures are made in order to maintain the productivity of their economic activities or their level of environmental amenity. The cost of sound insulation installed by people living near airports is an example of such preventive expenditure.

One of the costs of soil erosion from a forestry project are the measures taken by rice farmers to stabilise stream run-off. Similarly, the external benefits from flood control due to a dam project could be measured in terms of savings in expenditure on flood control measures that were previously undertaken by local residents.

11.4.5 Replacement costs approach

The preventive expenditure approach is closely related to the **replacement cost method**, which can also be used to measure many of the costs of water, air or soil pollution. Clean water, air and soil provide a multitude of valuable services to human beings and other forms of life. The replacement cost method measures the cost of environmental degradation in terms of the resources that must be used to replace the environmental services lost as a result of this degradation. For example, if the project would result in air pollution the cost of air filters on houses and buildings would be one measure of the cost of this pollution. Alternatively, if the project involves pollution control many of its benefits can be measured in terms of savings in such replacement costs. For example, the benefits of a project to provide clean river water may be measured in terms of the savings in water treatment costs, bottled water sales or well-digging costs. Relocation costs of industries or households that must be moved because they require unpolluted air or water or to escape newly created flood or subsidence risks are effectively another form of replacement cost.

11.5 Indirect measures of the value of the externality using surrogate prices

In addition to the use of directly observable prices, a range of other approaches have been developed in the past 15 years to measure externalities related to environmental amenity. These measures rely on prices that indirectly measure the externality's impact on welfare. Several of these approaches, like travel time costs, can also be employed to value public goods such as roads, bridges and other transport infrastructure.

11.5.1 Hedonic pricing

In countries where a free market exists for land, the present value of an externality generated by a project may be measured indirectly using hedonic pricing techniques. This method is particularly useful in measuring changes in environmental amenity such as noise or air pollution. Hedonic pricing involves comparing the prices for residential, or agricultural land or properties in areas close to a source of pollution, such as an airport, with those for land in similar suburbs away from such pollution sources. Controls are introduced to eliminate differences due to the intrinsic value of the house or land, such as size, age and proximity to shops or other facilities, using large samples and econometric regressions. The difference in land prices that cannot be explained by any of these other factors will represent the present value of the occupant's expected loss of environmental amenity by living close to the pollution source. Such differences in house prices have been used to measure the cost of pollution created by a project such as a new airport.[2] Studies have found that the amount that people are willing to pay will increase with their income level, since environmental amenity is a normal and probably a superior good.[3] Hedonic pricing can also be used to value positive externalities associated with a project. For example, the consumer surplus gained by those living close to a new railway line may be measured by the higher prices of houses close to existing stations.

Hedonic pricing is a rather data-intensive technique as real estate valuations and precise details must be obtained for several thousand properties to make a reasonable estimate of the value that can be attributed to an environmental externality. It will probably not be applicable to projects in rural areas of developing countries where traditional ownership still dominates or to centrally planned economies where land markets are undeveloped. However, it has been extensively used in developed countries, particularly to measure the loss of environmental amenity from large point sources of pollution. Streeting (1990) includes a summary of major studies that have successfully used hedonic pricing to identify the costs of aircraft and traffic noise, pollution levels and land degradation. Attempts to measure the effect of water quality changes have been less successful (Willis and Foster, 1983).

11.5.2 Travel costs

Measuring changes in travel times and travel costs is another indirect use of market prices to value a project's externalities. This approach can be used to measure both negative externalities like traffic congestion, or positive externalities from environmental amenities like national parks or scenic areas generally. In the case of traffic congestion in the vicinity of a project, for example, the additional travel time costs of road users, valued in economic prices, will provide an estimate of the welfare loss as a result of the unmarketed externality, congestion.[4]

Travel costs that people are willing to incur in travelling to scenic areas and national parks have long been used in developed countries as a minimum measure of the benefits that users receive from recreational facilities.[5] These costs will include the actual vehicle operating costs and any entrance fees of visitors, as well as the opportunity cost of the time they spend to make the visit. The basic rationale of this approach is that people will reveal the utility they gain from a recreational facility by the amount they are willing to pay to visit it each year. This data is obtained by carrying out surveys of park visitors to determine how far they travelled to get to the park, their mode of transport and how long they intend to stay.

The travel cost method can also be used to provide a minimum valuation of other unmarketed items like historical and cultural sites. However, other benefits of such sites include tourist income derived, which is a measure of the increased productivity of local tourism activities, and their existence and option values, which are discussed in the following section. The total benefits from new non-toll road projects are also usually measured using data on the total travel costs that people are willing to pay to use new roads and the consumer surplus they gain in the form of saved travel costs from improved road access. This is discussed further in the following chapter on public goods.

11.6 The contingent valuation method

Sometimes the externalities created by a project cannot be measured either directly or indirectly in market prices because there is no actual or even surrogate market for the good or service concerned. Sites of cultural, historical or spiritual importance and the continued existence of species and unspoiled wilderness areas are good examples of items that could not be readily valued in terms of people's observed willingness to pay in market prices.

Furthermore, people may get utility, or pleasure, from the mere knowledge of the existence of environmental or cultural amenities even if they have never used or seen them and do not intend to. This utility is called non-use or passive-use value. Wilks (1990) distinguishes five kinds of passive-use value: existence value, vicarious value, option value, quasi-option value and bequest value.[6] Market price methods are incapable of measuring the utility derived from passive uses of environmental amenities. Contingent valuation methods have therefore been developed to directly ask people what value they put on environmental and other amenities, including facilities from which they get only passive-use value.

The contingent valuation method may involve undertaking surveys of affected individuals to determine how much those affected by a negative externality, such as the flooding of a beautiful lake by a hydroelectricity dam, would be **willing to pay** to prevent the externality occurring. On the other hand, respondents may be asked how much they would be **willing to accept** to induce them to put up with this negative externality. In the case of a positive externality the survey could seek information on how much beneficiaries would be willing to pay to preserve some environmental amenity, like a wilderness area or other amenities such as the road services provided in the electricity project example.[7]

11.6.1 Alternative contingent valuation survey methods

Several different survey methods have been developed to elicit the most accurate response from those questioned. The **private goods market model** involves interviewers offering respondents the opportunity to 'purchase' amenities at a range of prices. Interviewers may engage in bidding games with interviewees to draw out the maximum that people are willing to pay for a particular resource or facility. For example, in the case of the Exxon oil spill in Alaska, a value was put on this wilderness area by asking a sample of people across the USA how much they would have been willing to pay to prevent the oil spill occurring. Usually such interviews must be conducted on a face-to-face basis or on the telephone, so that an iterative bidding process can be conducted.

An approach that is becoming increasingly popular is the **referendum approach**, which asks the respondents whether or not they would be prepared to pay a specified dollar amount of taxes to preserve or obtain some amenity. Respondents can only answer 'yes' or 'no' to this question. Different groups are asked to respond to a range of different dollar amounts and the median value derived is the tax level of which half the population approves. Similar approaches can be used to assess how much people would be willing to pay for public goods such as roads or public buildings or social services such as schools. One advantage of this approach is that it more closely resembles the type of market situation usually faced by consumers, at least in developed countries, where the price is fixed and the consumer has to decide whether or not to buy. It is also more feasible to carry out such surveys by mail.

11.6.2 Potential sources of bias in the contingent valuation method

There has been considerable debate regarding bias that may be introduced by valuing environmental and other amenities using this approach. This debate about the admissibility of contingent valuation evidence was tested in the US courts and through a government inquiry in 1992, as a result of the Exxon compensation decision for the oil spill in Alaska. The courts and subsequent government inquiry decided that contingent valuation evidence was admissible but sought to establish guidelines for how it should be collected.[8] Bias may originate from a number of sources.

Probably the most serious potential problem with the contingent valuation method is the possible existence of hypothetical bias because of the difficulty of obtaining meaningful responses to hypothetical questions. Unlike the methods outlined in previous sections, which rely on valuing resources actually used or saved as a result of externalities, contingent valuation relies on purely hypothetical valuations based on how people **say** they value a particular item.

This source of bias can be minimised, however, by the careful construction of questions and conduct of interviews. In particular, sufficient information should be given to respondents about the environmental amenity concerned, the proposed change in availability and how the respondent would be expected to pay to prevent, or obtain, this externality. If this is done, studies by Mitchell and Carson (1989) and Freeman (1979) indicate that hypothetical bias may not be a serious problem.

A second problem with contingent valuation relates to whether the respondent is asked to pay for an amenity or to accept a bribe to forgo it. This has been found to affect the valuation of an amenity. Theoretically, there should not be a significant difference between valuations based on these two lines of questioning, but Pearce and Markandya (1989)[9] have found discrepancies of a factor of three or more in valuations made depending on whether people thought they would have to pay or would be bribed. This may be because people are constrained by their budget when they have to consider how much they are willing to pay, but not when they are asked how much they are willing to accept. Also, people may act strategically when asked how much they need to be compensated by overstating the amount, if they believe it will prevent a particular loss of environmental amenity occurring. Consequently, most contingent valuations now ask people what they would be willing to pay to have a positive externality or to prevent a negative one. Furthermore, Randall maintains that respondents should be given the distinct impression that they will actually be charged to preserve environmental amenity, through increased taxes and costs of goods.[10]

A third problem with the contingent valuation method is the free rider problem, which may bias responses. People may understate the amount they may be prepared to pay to retain a positive externality, or social service or public good, if they believe that they will be required to pay this amount. At the same time, they may expect that other people will state their true preferences so that their preferred level of the good will be provided in any case.

Bohm (1972) recommended that the interviewer deal with this problem by concealing from the interviewee whether or not he or she would actually be required to pay for a particular public good, social service or externality. In that way, it was hoped that the free rider problem would be overcome, as the tendency of some to overstate the benefit of a service because they thought that they would not have to pay for it may be neutralised by those who understated their expected benefit because they thought that they would have to pay for it. This is contrary to the approach recommended by Randall. However, a number of studies, including Cummings, et al. (1986) and Rowe et al. (1980) have found that this type of strategic behaviour is not a serious source of bias in face-to-face interviews when people are asked how much they are willing to pay.

A detailed description of the methods of employing the contingent valuation methodology and the studies that have been conducted using it are given by Cummings et al. (1986), Mitchell and Carson (1989) and Wilks (1990).

The following section gives an example of how the externalities generated by a pollution control program can be evaluated.

11.7 Example of the valuation of externalities — net benefits of a pollution control program

As pollution has become of increasing concern to populations, most developed countries and an increasing number of developing countries have implemented pollution control programs, and more could be expected to do so in future. An analysis of the external costs and benefits of a pollution control program developed for East Java in Indonesia provides some useful examples of the types of environmental externalities that may be generated by projects and methods of valuing them. There will be several sources of potential benefit from a pollution reduction program, some of which will be quantifiable by the methods outlined in previous sections, others of which will probably not be. Most of the benefits of such a program fall into the category of externalities in that they will not accrue in the form of receipts to the implementing agency, in this case the regional or national pollution control agency. Instead they will provide benefits to members of the community at large, industries using river or coastal waters, those involved in tourism, agricultural and fishery activities and municipal water supply authorities, among others.

11.7.1 Savings of replacement costs

One of the major sources of economic benefit from pollution abatement is the reduction in the replacement costs borne by members of the public, local authorities and industry from the existing and potential future level of pollution. If industries and townships are forced to clean up their own emissions and liquid and solid waste, households, municipal authorities and other industries will not have to do so before they use water, air or land resources.

A large component of the East Javan pollution control project involved reducing water pollution in the Brantas River, which runs through the provincial capital of Surabaya. A major source of benefits was therefore expected to be the savings in replacement costs such as the water cleaning costs of current and future industrial and household users and savings in the cost of obtaining alternative water supplies. The main savings in replacement costs are outlined below.

One of the major financial costs of the current level of pollution in the Brantas River is the high treatment costs of water distributed by water supply authorities in Surabaya and other towns in the Brantas River basin. If the river is up-graded to drinkable quality as a result of the pollution control program, considerable treatment cost savings may be made.

The Surabaya's water supply authority currently takes 126 million m^3 of water per annum from the river for distribution. It plans to increase its use of river water dramatically over the next 20 years, more than doubling its intake by the year 2000 and increasing it more than threefold by the year 2010. In addition, the water supply authorities in two smaller towns in the river basin are currently drawing 33 and 4 million m^3 each year from the river. In Table 11.4 at the end of the chapter, demand by these two supply authorities is assumed to grow somewhat more slowly than that of Surabaya. In the next 30 years it is expected that other water supply networks will be established in smaller urban areas along the river.

Water treatment costs of the city's water supply authority are currently $L0.40[11] per m^3 for river water but are a negligible amount for clean water piped down from nearby mountain springs. Because of the high silt level in the river water, a reasonably high proportion of the treatment costs for river water would still be incurred after a pollution control program was put in place. However, it has been calculated that a saving of $L0.1 per m^3 of total treatment costs could be made as river water quality targets were achieved. Total projected savings from this source would rise to $L7.6 million in 1999 and increase steadily to $L81.9 million in 2023, as outlined in Table 11.4.

Water purification costs may also be incurred by some industries using polluted river water. This will be particularly important for food and beverage industries. Industries in the river basin used 271 million m^3 of water in 1987. This is expected to rise to 280.7 m^3 by the year 1999. This water is mainly drawn from surface water resources. Most of these industries, including the food and beverage, textile and pulp and paper industries, need to treat the water they draw from the Brantas river. These industries would therefore gain from a reduction in their treatment costs if the quality of river water were raised to the standards set by the government's Clean River program targets. It is estimated that their treatment cost savings would be similar to those estimated for the water supply authorities, $L0.1 per m^3, so their total potential treatment savings could be $L13 million per annum by 1999, as shown in Table 11.4.

Throughout the Brantas River basin, because of the relatively low proportion of households with house tap connections, local people replace the environmental services of the polluted river by digging wells. World Bank studies (World Bank, 1990) show that only 36 per cent of urban households and 2 per cent of rural households in East Java have house connections, while 55 per cent of urban households and 70 per cent of rural ones obtain their drinking water from wells. Only 5 per cent of the rural population, or 300 000 households and a negligible percentage of urban households rely on river water. On the other hand, 19 per cent of rural households and 2 per cent of urban ones use spring water (World Bank, 1990). The cost of obtaining water from wells is measured by their capital and operating costs over their lifetime. This can be used to estimate the replacement cost per litre of the polluted water. Savings in such costs may represent another benefit of a pollution control program.

It could be expected that a much higher proportion of households would use river water for drinking, or at least for washing and other household uses, if it were cleaner. This would probably result in a reduction of the amount of water drawn from wells and ultimately in a reduction in the number of new wells that would be needed. It has been estimated that if the river water were drinkable, the number of rural families able to use river water for the bulk of their water needs would double to 600 000 and the number using wells would drop commensurably, by 300 000. As each well could supply 24 families, this would mean that as many as 12 500 fewer wells could be needed in the province.

This would not actually result in any saving until new wells were required, either to meet new demand or because old ones fell into disrepair. These savings would therefore be made over the next 10 to 15 years. Improved wells cost approximately $L135–200. Traditional wells may be less expensive, between $L68 and 135. Hence up to $L0.113 million per annum could be saved over 30 years of the project from reduced well construction costs, as shown in Table 11.4.

In some areas, where river water is polluted and excessive extraction rates or the seepage of pollution has made well water undrinkable, the population without house connections or access to spring water are forced to purchase water from water vendors. The difference between the cost of these purchases and the cost per litre of river water, which is usually measured by the time spent in collecting it, will be another cost of the river's pollution. After river water pollution is reduced, savings in purchases of drinking water are likely to be a major benefit of pollution control.

World Bank studies have estimated that some poorer families in Jakarta are paying from 20 to 30 per cent of their income on water purchases (World Bank, 1990). In

East Java, up to 3 per cent of rural and 1 per cent of urban households are purchasing their drinking water. Payments per cubic metre range from two to three times the rate charged by the urban water supply authorities. Available data on rates of water use indicates that these water purchases total approximately $8.2 million per annum. A large proportion of these costs could probably be avoided by poorer households if surface and ground water pollution were controlled effectively. In Table 11.4 it is assumed that 60 per cent of these costs could be saved by the 10th year of the pollution control program.

If the water from polluted rivers were raised to drinking water quality, another source of saving would be the water boiling costs of households. Indonesian studies have found that the cost of boiling a litre of water is $L.02 and each person on average needs 2 litres of boiled water per day. As about 3 million people live in close proximity to the Brantas River, their annual savings in water boiling costs would be $L44 million, as shown in Table 11.4. However, people could not stop boiling water until the program had met most of its river water quality goals by the 8th year of the project.

11.7.2 Human capital and health cost benefits

Another source of potential benefits from water and air pollution control is the improved health and productivity of people who would otherwise have become ill by drinking polluted water and breathing polluted air. Many diseases like diarrhoea and gastroenteritis, which are prevalent in developing countries, are caused by drinking polluted water. These are caused by biodegradable pollution but more serious complaints can be caused by hazardous waste. Skin diseases can also be caused by a lack of adequate supplies of clean water for washing. The expected savings in the health-care costs of treating people who now contract these diseases is one of the potential benefits of the pollution control program aimed at providing clean drinking water. Data is often available from national or provincial statistics offices on the incidence of such illnesses and data on the cost of average treatment can be obtained from local health authorities.

In East Java, provincial health statistics indicate that on average 32 out of every 1000 people visit local clinics for diarrhoea and gastroenteritis complaints each year. A further 200 in every 100 000 members of the population are admitted to hospital and spend on average over a week there each year due to diarrhoeal complaints. The average cost of a visit to the clinic is estimated to be $L10 and a one week hospital stay costs on average $L61. These costs could be expected to rise in real terms as the incomes of health care providers rise in line with the expected overall increase in income levels over the next 30 years. The total population of East Java is 14 million people. If the diarrhoea and gastroenteritis cases among the population could be reduced by 80 per cent, the health cost savings would be $L4.9 million in 1993 and rise to $L10.34 million by 2007, as shown in Table 11.4.

In addition to these more readily identifiable potential savings in health costs, many rarer but more serious degenerative illnesses can be caused by drinking polluted water or eating fish, shellfish or other foods exposed to organic toxins in water. Data on the incidence of these diseases is often not available from national health statistics as in many cases toxins build up in individuals over many years and an increase in the number of cases of such diseases may not be identified for a number of years. It would be very difficult to project the costs these diseases could impose on the population if a pollution control program were not implemented, but they might be substantial. The estimated health-care savings will therefore be a lower bound to the potential savings in this area.

Another area of potential health cost savings would flow from a reduction in air pollution in Surabaya. However, due to a lack of data on current levels of air pollution and of morbidity that could be meaningfully linked to this pollution, these potential savings have also been omitted from the analysis in Table 11.4. The indicative figures given in Table 11.4 are therefore likely to be a substantial underestimate of the potential health benefits from the pollution control program.

Another cost that could be avoided by pollution control is the lost production of people who are ill. This could be a very high cost in many poorer developing countries, as gastric and diarrhoea related illnesses are often endemic and the major cause of low level illness. Illnesses caused by toxic waste usually take longer to develop but are also likely to have more serious effects on morbidity and mortality. Savings in lost earnings can be calculated from data on average weekly earnings, incidence of the various illnesses and the average length of illness.

In East Java, provincial health statistics indicate that on average each adult loses four working days per annum due to illnesses caused by drinking polluted water. As average annual earnings are $L600, lost earnings are worth $L60 million per annum. If 80 per cent of these costs are saved by the pollution control program, $L48 million of production will be saved each year, as shown in Table 11.4.

11.7.3 Productivity of other industries

The reduction in costs of industries currently filtering polluted water was discussed in the section on replacement costs, 11.7.1. Other major industries whose productivity will be adversely affected by the pollution of surface and ground water are inland and marine fishing, agriculture and tourism.

Fishing industries

In the case of fishing industries, river, estuary and coastal water have all become increasingly polluted in many developed and developing countries in recent years and seepage from ground water pollution may also cause problems. This is likely to reduce fish populations or increase the incidence of food poisoning from the consumption of polluted fish and shellfish. Income from fish exports may disappear rapidly if there is evidence of biological pollution in these fish.

To a lesser extent, agricultural production may also be threatened in some specific locations as a result of dumping of toxic waste into irrigation canals and rivers. Thorough scientific analyses are required to determine the likely impact of uncontrolled industrial and human pollution on agricultural production. The benefits of pollution control will then be measured in terms of a reduction of fishing and agricultural production losses.

In East Java there has been growing evidence of industrial and human waste causing a threat to marine and inland fisheries production. Inland and marine fishing are important industries. The annual inland fish catch in the province was valued at $L202.6 million in 1990, while the marine fish catch was worth $L83 million. The province is particularly famous for the pond production of milk fish, which are a staple source of protein. Studies have found high levels of organic bacteria and potentially harmful levels of organic toxicants and heavy metals in shellfish and fish caught in rivers, fish ponds, estuaries and bays throughout heavily populated parts of Indonesia.[12]

As long as it is kept within reasonable levels, organic waste can actually increase pond fish production as it promotes food growth in the ponds and reduces the need for fertiliser. Marine fish production can also increase in these circumstances. However, the resulting bacteria in the fish will cause health problems unless the fish are well cooked. Another problem arises from the high concentrations of toxic organic chemicals that have been found on the sea bed and in ponds. These chemicals include pesticides like DDT, PBCs and heavy metals. Consumption of fish with high or even moderate levels of such toxins can cause severe health problems in the long term. In addition, if tests in importing countries reveal the presence of such organic toxins in imported fish, valuable export markets will be rapidly lost for Indonesia.

Finally and potentially most seriously, certain hazardous chemicals such as cyanide can have a devastating effect on fish, particularly in a closed river system. A serious cyanide spill could kill 100 per cent of fish in the rivers and ponds that it entered. Experts believe that continued uncontrolled dumping of hazardous waste from industry could easily result in such a disastrous outcome at any time in Indonesia's river system.

Without a pollution control program, the risk of such fish kills will increase steadily in future years. Experts have estimated that the risk of a 100 per cent inland fish kill will rise from 0 in 1993 by 5 per cent of annual fish production a year until it reaches 100 per cent in 2013. It is believed that this risk will be fully averted when the pollution control program is fully operational in year 11. The savings from a probable loss in inland fishing production are therefore included in the program's benefits in Table 11.4.

Marine fishing would not be as seriously affected by a major spill, though it could definitely kill fish in the vicinity of the mouths of polluted rivers. Consequently, although the risk of lost marine fish production is assumed to rise at the same rate as that to inland fisheries, if no pollution control is introduced it is expected that only a proportion, 20 per cent, of the potential marine catch will be adversely affected.

Tourism
Another major industry likely to be adversely affected by environmental degradation and pollution is tourism. One of the benefits from pollution control may be measured by projections of potential net income from visits to tourist resorts, hotels and recreational facilities, which would be lost if pollution remained uncontrolled. It is

very difficult to make rigorous projections regarding how much tourism income could be lost for this reason. Obviously, it is not possible to survey the people who do not come to a location because they are offended by the water, air and solid waste pollution. However, it would be feasible to survey tourists currently visiting more and less polluted tourist destinations in a region. Surveys could ask if they would consider returning, whether they would recommend that their friends make a visit and whether current pollution levels, and potentially higher levels in the future, would influence them in these decisions.

In East Java the tourism sector generated 23 per cent of provincial income in 1989, ahead of the manufacturing sector, which contributed 19.7 per cent of the province's income. Both of these sectors are very dynamic and are currently growing at 10–12 per cent per annum in real terms. Both sectors are very important to the provincial economy and it is important that pollution control policies are devised in such a way that the future growth of both is fostered.

In the base-case scenario, where completely uncontrolled dumping of effluent and hazardous waste would occur, there would likely be a slow deterioration in the income earning capacity of the tourism industry. Surveys of tourists and hotel owners indicate that if pollution is not controlled, 1 per cent of projected tourism sector earnings in 1994 will be lost in that year and that this will rise slowly by approximately 1 percentage point each year thereafter. It is estimated that in the absence of any impact due to pollution, the underlying real growth in tourism, hotel and restaurant sector income would be 8 per cent per annum over the period of the project, slightly lower than the trend growth levels of the past 10 years.

11.7.4 Difficulties associated with quantifying external benefits and costs — recreation, environmental amenity and reduced pain and suffering

Recreation facilities

One of the external benefits from a pollution control program that will be harder to quantify, even after a thorough investigation, will be the ability to use the cleaner environment for free recreational purposes and the utility people will gain from this. As mentioned previously, such benefits are sometimes measured by the travel time costs of individuals using recreational resources. If users did not expect benefits greater than the travel time costs, they would not have bothered to travel to the facility. Surveys of recreational use made of unpolluted sites in similar areas could be used to estimate the potential level of demand and willingness to pay for such services, so that the potential recreational benefits of the pollution control program could be valued. These travel costs will represent the minimum benefit that the users of these facilities expect to obtain from them.

Utility from environmental amenity

The local population of an unpolluted area are also likely to obtain many psychic and unquantifiable benefits from improvements in the quality of the environment. A cleaner environment provides visual and spiritual benefits and cleaner water for washing clothes and utensils and for personal hygiene will also provide health and psychic benefits, which are hard to measure. As discussed in previous sections, hedonic pricing and contingent valuation methods may be useful for measuring some of these less tangible benefits of improved environmental amenity.

Reduced pain suffering and loss of life

Reduced direct health-care costs are only the minimum measure of the benefits enjoyed from reduced illness. Psychic benefits enjoyed by people who will no longer suffer pain, diarrhoea and gastroenteritis cannot be readily measured, but may be at least as important as their reduced health-care costs.

There is also likely to be a reduction in deaths from such diseases as cleaner drinking water becomes available. In low-income developing countries, a major cause of infant deaths is dehydration caused by diarrhoea. The economic costs of such deaths are very difficult to measure. One method is to measure the net present value of the expected life-time earnings of the deceased people, but this fails to take account of the income that those people would have used to maintain themselves over their life. Another approach is only to measure the expected net savings of the people who have died as the net cost of their death. However, neither of these approaches, can capture the pain and suffering experienced by families from such deaths.[13]

New industries

Finally, another potential benefit from a pollution control program that will be difficult to measure will be the net economic benefits generated by new industries that may become viable if cleaner water becomes available. These industries would be marginal enterprises that would become financially viable if they did not have to treat water before using it, but are not financially viable in a situation where they must incur such costs. Such industries are likely to include small-scale food processing and beverage industries, small restaurants and related hospitality enterprises. If the economic benefits of such industries exceed their economic costs, then the local economy will benefit from the establishment of these new industries. To reliably estimate all such effects it would be necessary to construct a general equilibrium model of the Indonesian economy explicitly including environmental amenity as a factor of production.

11.7.5 The economic costs of a pollution control program

A pollution control program will also impose financial costs on the implementing government agency and indirect costs, negative externalities on other sectors of the economy, notably polluting industries and municipal authorities.

The Administration of the environmental protection agency

The first element of the program's costs are those of the government's environmental protection agency, EPA. The East Javan agency will be built up over a 10 year period. It has been estimated that the EPA will eventually require approximately 250 professionals, each with an average annual salary of $L2570, and 200 support staff,

Table 11.1 Economic costs of the East Javan pollution control program — environmental protection agency administration costs ($L'000)

Recurrent costs	
Economic cost of EPA staff per year	861
Other office expenses (factor 0.4)	344
Total recurrent costs	**1205**
Capital costs	
Office accommodation	2500
Computers (100 @ $2000)	200
Vehicles (20 @ $10 000)	2000
Total capital costs	**4700**

each with an average annual salary of $L1285. These costs are outlined in Table 11.1. A factor of 0.4 of direct salary costs has been used to provide for the cost of office supplies, fuel and maintenance, utilities and communications. The capital cost of providing office accommodation, vehicles and computer equipment has been estimated at $L4.7 million over 10 years.

At least one of the components of these cost estimates will require shadow pricing. The wages of some of the support staff, guards, drivers and other unskilled or semi-skilled workers are set by Indonesian government minimum wage regulations and may not reflect their true cost to the economy. A conversion factor of 0.5 is therefore applied to these wages. However, many of the support staff, including secretaries and laboratory assistants, may well be in short supply, so their wages will not require shadow pricing. Only 30 per cent of the support staff's wages are therefore deflated using the unskilled labour conversion factor of 0.5. The estimated requirements of vehicles, computers and office space have already been valued in international prices, so there is no need to shadow price these items. This gives an annual recurrent cost of $L1205 million.

The Indonesian government intends to request bilateral donor assistance to establish the EPA. Support will be given for training, institutional support, technical assistance for foreign experts in pollution control, EPA establishment and project

Table 11.2 Biodegradable and non-biodegradable pollution of the major river system

Source	*Tonnes per day*	*Per cent*
Domestic pollution		
Urban pollution	43	49
Rural pollution	17	19
Total domestic	60	68
Industrial pollution	28	32
Total	**88**	**100**

management. The disbursement of the donor's $L21.5 million support program is included in the cost benefit analysis spreadsheet in Table 11.4.

Costs incurred by local waste disposal authorities

The major source of pollution in the country's rivers is untreated human waste, especially from urban areas located on the banks of the Brantas River. A government report breaks down the major sources of pollution in the Brantas and its tributaries as given in Table 11.2.

The quality of the rivers in the Brantas River basin cannot be raised to their government targets until domestic waste is treated and disposed of correctly. The same government report estimates the capital cost of controlling this domestic waste will be as shown in Table 11.3.

Table 11.3   Capital costs of the pollution control program — costs incurred by local authorities for human waste disposal ($L'000, p.a.)

Years 1–5	23200
Years 6–10	39600
Years 11–20	30200
Total (over 20 years)	**616000**

In addition, recurrent costs of $L2 million will be incurred from 1994 and these will increase by 10 per cent per annum in real terms over the next 30 years. These costs have been included in Table 11.4. It is assumed that these expenditures are spread evenly over the periods shown.

Costs incurred by industry

The other major groups bearing the cost of the proposed pollution control program will be the province's manufacturing and resource processing industries and major service sector polluters like hotels and hospitals. These sectors of the provincial economy have been growing rapidly in recent years. As discussed above, manufacturing industry has grown by 10–12 per cent per year in real terms and is the second largest sector of the provincial economy after the hotel and restaurant sector, providing almost 20 per cent of national income, or $L3.2 billion. The hotel and restaurant sector has been growing at approximately 10 per cent per year and produces 23 per cent of provincial income, $L3.7 billion.

The World Bank estimates that the investment cost of reducing pollution levels in just three of the province's major industries (pulp and paper, food and tanning) would be approximately $L76 million. However, these investment cost estimates do not provide any indication of the total addition to annual production costs as a result of operating these pollution treatment facilities. Studies of the cost impact of introducing pollution controls have found that the appropriate waste treatment processes would, on average, increase industries' capital and operating costs by 3 per cent a year. This includes the cost of plants properly disposing of hazardous, biodegradable and non-biodegradable waste. In Table 11.4, a figure of 3 per cent of projected industrial input costs is therefore used as an estimate of the total annual costs to industry of the proposed pollution control program. Since waste treatment and solid waste disposal is also a problem for large service sector enterprises such as hotels and hospitals, it is assumed that they will need to pay 2 per cent of their projected input costs to properly dispose of their waste products.

11.7.6 Difficult to quantify external costs

Some existing and potential new, highly polluting but marginal industries may become financially unviable as a result of pollution control requirements that force them to pay for the full cost of their pollution. The loss of such industries would only impose a welfare cost if these activities generated positive net economic benefits, despite their lack of financial viability. This could occur, for example, if formal sector wage rates and the foreign exchange rate were set at uneconomically high levels, or those activities were paying high import duties on imported inputs and had low or zero protection for their output, that is, they had negative effective protection.

It would only be possible to estimate the impact of pollution controls on industries' financial viability if a full computable general equilibrium model was developed and various changes in pollution controls simulated. This could be used to estimate whether the costs of the loss of such industries exceeded the benefits generated by the new industrial opportunities opened by the availability of cleaner water. In addition, it would be necessary to closely analyse the comparative advantage and current and likely future industrial structure of Indonesia to draw more accurate conclusions on this matter.

11.7.7 Total net benefits — base-case scenario

Estimates of the approximate total costs and benefits of the East Javan pollution control program are given in Table 11.4. They indicate that the net present value of the pollution control program could be very high, $L14.24 billion, if the assumptions embodied in the above analysis proved correct. As the estimated impact of pollution control on productivity in industries like fishing and tourism may be subject to revision, the sensitivity analysis also indicates the level of the present value of the benefits the program would have to achieve if it were to be able to justify its estimated costs, $L2.5 billion.

If the assumptions made are realistic, the program will be extremely viable in economic terms. As the bulk of these benefits will be received by low income people in rural and urban areas, the program is also likely to have a very beneficial social impact.

11.7.8 Sensitivity analysis

Because of the uncertainty surrounding much of the data used in an economic analysis of this nature, a sensitivity analysis is very important. The level of benefits that is just sufficient to justify the costs incurred by the program is calculated in Table 11.5.

In this scenario it is assumed that:

- the pollution control costs to manufacturing industry will in fact be 4 per cent of its projected input costs, rather than 3 per cent
- the pollution costs of other industries such as hotels will be 2.5 per cent of input costs, rather than 2 per cent
- the savings in water treatment costs to municipal authorities and industry are reduced by half, to only $L .05 per cubic metre
- there are no savings in water boiling costs by households
- savings in health costs are reduced by only 40 per cent as a result of the program, not by 80 per cent as was assumed in the base scenario
- the savings in lost income of people who are sick are only 40 per cent of income currently estimated lost, rather than 80 per cent as was assumed in the base scenario
- the risk of lost fishing industry output is reduced to only 2 per cent of the catch in year 2 of the program, rising by 2 percentage points each year to a maximum of 60 per cent in 2003 after the pollution control program is fully in place
- the averted loss of tourism income falls to zero in the 1st year, 0.15 per cent in the 2nd and rises by only 0.15 per cent each year, rather than 1 per cent as assumed in the base case. By 2023, losses averted will reach only 4.5 per cent of total tourist income rather than 31 per cent, as assumed in the base scenario.

Under this pessimistic scenario, the resulting NPV of the entire program would fall to $L51.05 million. The economic internal rate of return of the program would be 11.71 per cent, still higher than the target rate of return, 11.3 per cent. It therefore appears that even under a pessimistic scenario of projected costs and benefits, the program would be worthwhile undertaking. Looked at from another perspective, this analysis indicates the level of benefits which the program would have to achieve in order to justify the expenditure that would be incurred. This level of benefits would appear to be achievable.

11.8 Conclusions regarding identifying and measuring externalities

The most obvious externalities likely to have measurable effects in terms of market prices should be examined and measured first. Other secondary impacts should then be investigated and, if necessary, surrogate prices and survey techniques such as contingent valuation may be used to measure any other identifiable externalities. It is important that any assumptions made about external impacts should be clearly stated so that they can be tested by other analysts if necessary. The project analyst may well have to work with other professionals to identify complex externalities, especially those associated with environmental degradation.

Once the techniques outlined above have been used to estimate the aggregate value of the externality over the project's life, this should be added to the cost or benefit stream of the project. Costs incurred and benefits forgone as a result of

Table 11.4 Economic analysis of the East Javan pollution control program ($L'000)

	Year							
	1993	1994	1995	1996	1997	1998	1999	2023
COSTS								
Development assistance project costs								
1 Institutional support	1236	1545	562	562	385			
2 Implementation program	689	869	1384	1167	730			
3 Technology support	720	525	575	525	270			
4 Community awareness	136	302	416	397	183			
5 Training	1044	1630	1630	1320	673			
6 Project management	472	476	376	376	366			
Total project costs	4297	5347	4944	4347	2607			
Other administration costs, outside project								
Capital costs (over 10 years)	470	470	470	470	470	470	470	0
Recurrent costs	0	121	241	362	482	603	723	1205
Total costs	470	591	711	832	952	1073	1193	1205
Costs borne by municipal governments								
Capital costs of sewage disposal	23200	23200	23200	23200	23200	39600	39600	
Recurrent costs	0	2000	2100	2205	2315	2431	2553	8232
Estimated costs borne by local manufacturing industry								
Projected output	4685120	5153632	5668995	6235895	6859484	7545433	8299976	43280912
3% projected input costs	0	10823	23810	39286	57620	79227	104580	908899
Estimated costs borne by other local industry (hotels etc.)								
Projected output	5033809	5335838	5655988	5995347	6355068	6736372	7140554	2891638
2% projected input costs	0	7470	15837	25180	35588	47155	59981	404763
TOTAL COSTS	27967	49430	70601	95050	122282	207906	251980	1323099

		Year							
	1993	1994	1995	1996	1997	1998	1999	... 2023
BENEFITS								
Replacement costs								
Reduced water treatment costs by:								
• Local Water Supply Authority:								
Volume treated (millions m³ p.a.)	163	165	166	168	169	171	173	1001
treatment costs ($L per m³), 0.10								
Total savings	0	1261	2523	3784	5046	6307	7569	81994
• Local industry:								
Volume used (millions m³ p.a.)	241	246	251	256	261	266	271	391
Volume surface water	193	197	201	205	209	213	217	313
Potential saving in treatment cost per m³	0.10							
Total savings, industry	0	1968	4016	6144	8352	10640	13008	31280
Net savings in drinking water costs ($L'000)								
Purchases of drinking water	0	410	820	1230	1640	2050	2460	4920
Savings well construction	0	57	113	113	113	113	113	113
Savings in water boiling costs	0	0	0	0	0	0	0	44000
Reduced health costs from improved drinking water								
Clinic visits for diarrhoea, p.a. (32 per 1000 pop'n)	448000	456960	466099	475421	484930	494628	504521	811490
Average cost per visit ($L)	10	10	11	11	11	12	12	24
Total cost clinic visits p.a. ($L'000)	4,480	4707	4945	5195	5458	5734	6024	19697
Hospitalisations for diarrhoea (200 per 100 000)	28000	28560	29131	29714	30308	30914	31533	50718
Average cost per 8 day stay ($L)	60	62	64	66	68	70	73	236
Total cost hospital visits p.a. ($L'000)	1680	1765	1854	1948	2047	2150	2303	11946
Total potential health cost savings (80%)	0	518	1088	1714	2401	3154	3997	25315
Savings in lost earnings (80%) ($L'000 p.a.)	0	4800	9600	14400	19200	24000	28800	48000

	Year							
	1993	1994	1995	1996	1997	1998	1999	… 2023
Reduced risk of lost fisheries production								
• Inland fisheries:								
Current production volume ('000 tonnes p.a.)	115	124	134	145	156	169	182	1157
Current production value ($L'000)	202607	218815	236320	255226	275644	297696	321511	2038761
• Marine fisheries:								
Current production ('000 tonnes p.a.)	201	217	234	253	273	295	319	2,023
Current production ($L'000)	83333	90000	97200	104976	113374	122444	132240	83555
Risk of fish kill, no EPA (%)	0	5	10	15	20	25	30	100
Risk if EPA program implemented	0	4.5	8.0	10.5	12.0	12.5	12.0	0.0
Potential reduction in lost fishing income ($L'000)	0	1184	5115	12430	23866	40273	62633	2206472
Increased tourism income								
Projected value tourism ($L'000)	5944078	6419604	6933173	7487826	8086852	8733801	9432505	59813217
Potential loss tourist income (%)	1	2.0	3.0	4.0	5.0	6.0	7.0	31.0
Expected loss if EPA program implemented	1	1.8	2.4	2.8	3.0	3.0	0.0	0.0
Potential reduction in lost tourism income ($L'000)	0	12839	41599	89854	161737	262014	396165	18542097
TOTAL BENEFITS	0	23037	64874	129670	222355	348551	514745	20984191
NET CASH FLOW	(27967)	(26393)	(5727)	34620	100073	179066	306839	19661092

Discount rate (% per year) 11.3
PV costs: 2493959
PV benefits: 16729400
NPV net cash flow: 14235441

Table 11.5   Sensitivity analysis of the pollution control program ($L'000)

	Year							
	1993	1994	1995	1996	1997	1998	1999	... 2023
COSTS								
Development assistance project costs								
Institutional support	1236	1545	562	562	385			
Implementation program	689	869	1384	1167	730			
Technology support	720	525	575	525	270			
Community awareness	136	302	416	397	183			
Training	1044	1630	1630	1320	673			
Project management	472	476	376	376	366			
Total project costs	4297	5347	4944	4347	2607			
Other administration costs, outside project								
Capital costs (over 10, years)	470	470	470	470	470	470	470	0
Recurrent costs	0	121	241	362	482	603	723	1205
Total costs	470	591	711	832	952	1073	1193	1205
Costs borne by municipal governments								
Domestic pollution control (sewage disposal)								
Capital costs	23200	23200	23200	23200	23200	39600	39600	0
Recurrent costs	0	2000	2100	2205	2315	2431	2553	8232
Estimated costs borne by manufacturing industry								
Projected output	4685120	5153632	5668995	6235895	6859484	7545433	8299976	43280912
4% projected total input costs	0	14430	31746	52382	76826	105636	139440	1211866
Estimated costs borne by other industry (hotels etc.)								
Projected output	5033809	5335838	5655988	5995347	6355068	6736372	7140554	28911638
2.5% projected input costs	0	9338	19796	31476	44485	58943	74976	505954
TOTAL COSTS	27967	54905	82497	114440	150386	207683	257761	1727256

				Year				
	1993	1994	1995	1996	1997	1998	1999	... 2023
BENEFITS								
Replacement costs								
Reduced water treatment costs by:								
• Local Water Supply Authority								
Total volume (millions m³ p.a.)	163	165	166	168	169	171	173	1001
Difference in treatment costs ($L per m³)	0.05							
Total savings	0	631	1261	1892	2523	3154	3784	40997
• Industry								
Volume used (millions m³ p.a.)	241	246	251	256	261	266	271	391
Volume surface water (80%)	193	197	201	205	209	213	217	313
Potential saving per m³	0.05							
Total potential savings ($L'000)	0	984	2008	3072	4176	5320	6504	15640
Net savings in drinking water costs								
Purchases of drinking water	0	410	820	1230	1640	2050	2460	4920
Savings well construction ($L'000)	0	57	113	113	113	113	113	113
Reduced health costs from improved drinking water								
Clinic visits for diarrhoea, p.a. (32 per 1000 pop'n)	448000	456960	466099	475421	484930	494628	504521	811490
Average cost per visit ($L)	10	10	11	11	11	12	12	24
Total costs clinic visits p.a. ($L'000)	4480	4707	4945	5195	5458	5734	6024	19697
Hospitalisations for diarrhoea (200 per 100 000)	28000	28560	29131	29714	30308	30914	31533	50718
Average cost per 8 day stay ($L)	60	62	64	66	68	70	73	236
Costs hospital visits p.a. ($L'000)	1680	1765	1854	1948	2047	2150	2303	11946
Total potential health savings (40%)	0	259	544	857	1201	1577	3997	12657
Savings in lost earnings (40%)($L'000 p.a.)	0	2400	4800	7200	9600	12000	14400	24000

					Year			
	1993	1994	1995	1996	1997	1998	1999	... 2023
Reduced risk of lost fisheries production								
• Inland fisheries								
Current production								
('000 tonnes p.a.)	115	124	134	145	156	169	182	1,157
Current production ($L'000)	202607	218815	236320	255226	275644	297696	321511	2038761
• Marine fisheries								
Current production volume								
('000 tonnes p.a.)	201	217	234	253	273	295	319	2023
Current production value								
($L'000)	83333	90000	97200	104976	113374	122444	132240	838555
Risk of fish kill (%)	0	2	4	6	8	10	12	60
Risk if EPA program implemented	0	1.8	3.2	4.2	4.8	5.0	4.8	0.0
Potential reduction in lost fishing income ($L'000)	0	474	2046	4972	9546	16109	25053	1323883
Increased tourism income								
Projected value tourism ($L'000)	5944078	6419604	6933173	7487,826	8086852	8733801	9432505	59813217
Potential loss tourist income (%)	0	0.15	0.3	0.5	0.6	0.8	0.9	4.5
Expected loss with EPA program	0	0.1	0.2	0.3	0.4	0.4	0.4	0.0
Potential saving tourism income ($L'000)	0	963	4160	10109	19408	32752	50936	2691595
TOTAL BENEFITS	0	6177	15753	29445	48208	73075	105249	4113806
NET CASH FLOW	(27967)	(48728)	(66744)	(84995)	(102179)	(134608)	(152512)	2486445

Discount rate (% p.a.)   11.3
PV costs: 3149948
PV benefits: 3200999
NPV net cash flow: 51051
[Guess IRR %]   1.0%
Internal rate of return: 11.71%

externalities generated will be economic costs of the project, while benefits generated and costs saved will be economic benefits.

Exercises

1. A major airport program is being proposed for the outskirts of a large city. In similar cities, the land within a 1 km radius of the airport sells for $L20 000 less per quarter hectare block than similar land away from an airport. Land in a 2 km radius is found to sell for $L10 000 less a block. It is estimated that 2000 blocks are a kilometre or less from the proposed airport site and 6000 blocks are located in an area between a 1 and 2 km radius of the proposed site. The market for land operates reasonably freely in this country, but the consumption conversion factor for the average wage earner in this country is estimated to be 0.7.

   What is the economic cost of the negative externality of noise pollution that the new airport is expected to create over the lifetime of the program? Explain how this is calculated and why.

2. Emissions released from a planned aluminium smelter are expected to adversely affect the grapes growing in a nearby wine-making region. Annual wine sales are worth $L5 million at present, but production is expected to be cut by one-third if the aluminium smelter goes ahead. Savings in other factors as a result of the lower yields will amount to only $L200 000 a year. The Ministry of the Environment suggests that the aluminium smelter should be required to install new anti-pollution devices, which will cost $L16 million. If the program is expected to have a life of 25 years and the real discount social rate for the country is 10 per cent, should the aluminium program be required to install the anti-pollution devices, or would it be better if they compensated surrounding vineyards?

References

Bohm, P., 1972. 'Estimating demand for public goods', *European Economic Review*, 3:111–30.

Clawson, M., 1959. *Methods of Measuring Demand for and Value of Outdoor Recreation*, Resources for the Future reprint No. 10, Resources for the Future, Washington.

Clawson, M. and Knetsch, J.L., 1966. *Economics of Outdoor Recreation*, Johns Hopkins University Press, for Resources for the Future, Baltimore.

Cummings, R.G., Brookshire, D.S. and Schultze, W.D., 1986. *Valuing Environmental Goods: a State of the Art Assessment of the Contingent Valuation Method*, Rowman and Allenheld, Totowa, New Jersey.

Dixon, J.A., Carpenter, R.A., Fallon, L.A., Sherman, P.B. and Manopimoke, S., 1986. *Economic Analysis of the Environmental Impact of Development Programs*, Earthscan Publications, London.

Freeman, A.M., 1979. *The Benefits of Environmental Improvement: Theory and Practice*, Johns Hopkins University Press, Baltimore.

Jones-Lee, M.W., 1976. *The Value of Life: an Economic Analysis*, Chicago University Press, Chicago.

Krutilla, J.V. and Fisher, A.C., 1985. *The Economics of Natural Environments* (revised edition), Johns Hopkins University Press for Resources for the Future, Baltimore.

Lave, L.B. and Seskin, E.P., 1977. *Air Pollution and Human Health*, Johns Hopkins University Press for Resources for the Future, Baltimore.

Mishan, E.J., 1982. *Cost Benefit Analysis*, 3rd edn, Allen & Unwin, London.

Mitchell, R.C. and Carson, R.T., 1989. *Using Surveys of Public Goods: the Contingent Valuation Method*, Resources for the Future, Washington, DC.

Pearce, D.W. and Markandya, A., 1989. *The Benefits of Environmental Policy*, OECD, Paris.

Pearce, D.W. and Turner, R.K., 1990. *Economics of Natural Resources and the Environment*, Harvester Wheatsheaf, Hemel Hempstead.

Rowe, R.D., d'Arge, P.B. and Brookshire, D.S., 1980. 'An experiment on the economic value of visibility', *Journal of Environmental Economics and Management*, 7:1–19.

Streeting, M., 1990. *A Survey of the Hedonic Price Technique*, Resource Assessment Commission, Canberra.

UNIDO, 1972. *Guidelines for Project Evaluation*, United Nations, New York.

Wilks, L.C., 1990. *A Survey of the Contingent Valuation Method*, Research Paper No. 2, Resource Assessment Commission, Canberra.

Willis, C.E. and Foster, J.H., 1983. 'Hedonic pricing, no panacea for measuring water quality changes', *Journal of the Northeastern Agricultural Economics Council.*

World Bank, 1990, *Indonesia, Sustainable Development of Forests, Land and Water*, Washington.

Further reading

Cummings, R.G., Brookshire, D.S. and Schultze, W.D., 1986. *Valuing Environmental Goods: a State of the Art Assessment of the Contingent Valuation Method*, Rowman and Allenheld, Totowa, New Jersey.

Dixon, J.A., Carpenter, R.A. Fallon, L.A., Sherman, P.B. and Manopimoke, S., 1986. *Economic Analysis of the Environmental Impact of Development Programs*, Earthscan Publications, London.

Dixon, J.A., James, D.E. and Sherman, P.B., 1987. *The Economics of Dryland Agriculture*, Earthscan Publications, London.

Hufschmidt, M.M., James, D.E., Meister, A.D., Bower, B.T. and Dixon, J.A., 1983. *Environment, Natural Systems and Development: an Economic Evaluation Guide.*

Mitchell, R.C. and Carson, R.T., 1986. *Using Surveys of Public Goods: the Contingent Valuation Method*, Resources for the Future, Washington, DC.

Pearce, D.W. and Turner, R.K., 1990. *Economics of Natural Resources and the Environment*, Harvester Wheatsheaf, Hemel Hempstead.

Streeting, M., 1990. *A Survey of the Hedonic Price Technique*, Resource Assessment Commission, Canberra.

Wilks, L.C., 1990. *A Survey of the Contingent Valuation Method*, Research Paper No 2, Resource Assessment Commission, Canberra.

Endnotes

1 Jones-Lee, M.W. (1976), Mishan (1982), Freeman (1979), Lave and Seskin (1977) and many others have explored the human capital and health costs of pollution and the problems of measuring the value of human life.

2 Streeting, M. (1990) provides a summary of the literature on this topic.

3 If environmental amenity is a normal good, the higher people's income the more they will wish to spend on a clean environment. If the income elasticity of demand for environmental amenity is greater than unity, then it is a superior good (that is, for a 1 per cent increase in income, people will wish to increase their expenditure on securing a clean environment for themselves by more than 2 per cent).

4 The private and social cost of traffic accidents, measured in terms of the health-care costs and lost earnings, may be added as an additional cost if this is considered appropriate. These costs relate to the loss of human capital and health-care cost measures discussed in Section 11.4.2.

5 See Clawson (1959) and Clawson and Knetsch (1966). Discussion of the travel cost method is also included in Pearce and Turner (1990) and Dixon et al. (1986).

6 Existence value is value obtained from the knowledge that a certain environmental amenity or cultural resource (such as whales, or sacred or religious sites) exists and is being protected. Vicarious value can be obtained from such resources by reading about them or seeing pictures. Option value is obtained by knowing these resources are available for use at some future date, and quasi-option value from delaying some decision that may result in an irreversible loss, when future improvements in knowledge and technology may enable value to be obtained from the resource concerned. Finally, bequest value lies in the value the current generation obtains from being able to bequeath environmental amenities to future generations.

7 The contingent valuation method is based on the two neoclassical economic measures of consumer surplus, Hicksian compensating variation and equivalent variation. Equivalent variation is the maximum amount people would be willing to pay to avoid a price increase, or the minimum amount people would need to be bribed to forego a price decrease, and still remain at the same level of utility that they would have achieved after the price change. Compensating variation uses the initial level of utility, before the price change, as the benchmark. The change in utility in the case of the contingent valuation method is not caused by a price change, but the changed availability of an environmental (or other) amenity. Hence the contingent valuation method attempts to measure consumer surplus change as a result of a change in the availability of environmental (or other) amenities.

8 Alan Randall, seminar for the Australian Economic Society, Canberra, 23/9/1993.

9 Quoted in Wilks (1990), p. 23.

10 Alan Randall, seminar for the Australian Economic Society, Canberra, 23/9/1993.

11 For consistency, local dollars are used as the currency in this example. The 'exchange rate' used was $L = 1000 Indonesian rupiahs.

12 Discussion with Dr Robin Harger, UNESCO Office, Jakarta, 1992.

13 Jones-Lee (1976) has attempted to explore this difficult moral issue.

CHAPTER 12

Public goods and social services

12.1 Definition of public goods

Up to this point, we have assumed that all goods produced by a project or inputs used by it are **private** goods. Private goods are goods or services that get used up in the process of consumption. Once private goods are consumed by an individual or a family, they cannot be used by another individual. Examples of private goods include food, clothing, consumer durables and most other consumer and producer goods. **Public** goods differ from private ones in two important respects:

- **Non-rivalry in consumption** The consumption of a public good by one individual does not prevent its consumption by another individual. Public goods can therefore satisfy the needs of many consumers at once. If one extra consumer uses a public good, this will not reduce the quantity that can be used by others. Examples of public goods include street lighting and public footpaths. If one person makes use of street lighting provided in a town it does not stop other people using this service.
- **Non-excludability in consumption** If a public good is provided to one person, it will be provided to all others automatically. It is therefore not possible to easily devise ways of excluding people from the use of true public goods.

Other examples of public goods include national defence systems, police forces and legal systems, macroeconomic management, urban road networks, pest and disease eradication campaigns and television and radio transmissions. Once such public goods or services have been provided to one person in a community, they will simultaneously be provided to many people. Also, it is very difficult to exclude individuals in a society from using true public goods such as urban road networks, TV broadcasts or national defence systems once they have been provided.

Some similar goods or services, like toll roads, are not true public goods. Even though an individual can use an uncongested toll road without in any way preventing others from using it, it is possible to exclude motorists from using a toll road. A toll road is therefore not a pure public good, as it only possesses one of the two main characteristics of public goods.

Many of the externalities created by projects discussed in the previous chapter are also public goods, or rather public 'bads'. These include the pollution generated by a factory, the road provided by a hydroelectric project or recreational facilities provided by a dam. Once such externalities are created by these projects, their use by one person will not prevent others from using them and it may be difficult to exclude people from using them or to protect them from negative impacts in the case of pollution.

Since it is not possible to exclude people from the use of pure public goods, it is not possible to charge for them. As a result, private, profit maximising firms will not be prepared to supply true public goods as they will be unable to charge for their use. The existence of public goods such as armies and city fortifications is in fact the main reason why governments have arisen in human society and remains one of the major, some would argue the only, justification for the existence of governments. Only governments are in a position to provide public goods free of direct user charges and to finance their provision from general taxation collections.

12.2 Pricing of public goods

As long as the output of a good or service can be expanded freely, its supply is infinitely elastic, and it should be priced at the cost of producing the next available unit — its marginal cost of production. At the equilibrium level of output, its supply price will equal its demand price, so the marginal cost of production will also equal the marginal utility that the last consumer gains from consuming this good, which will equal the marginal revenue received from its sale.

By definition, public goods can satisfy the needs of many consumers at once. The addition of one extra consumer does not increase the total cost of providing the public good. Consequently, the cost of supplying the marginal consumer with the public good, its marginal cost of production, is zero. Since the efficient price to charge for a good whose supply can be expanded is its marginal cost, or its supply price, the correct and economically efficient price to charge for a public good is zero.

If there is minimal daily wear and tear on a public good like an existing, uncongested bridge, and therefore its marginal cost of production is almost zero, no tariff should be charged for its use. If people are forced to pay for this public good, there is likely to be a reduction in demand for the bridge's services below the optimal full capacity level. Since this drop in its use will not in any way reduce the cost of providing the public good, the result will be the sub-optimal utilisation of the public good and a reduction in the welfare gains to the community from the provision of the bridge. The economic net present value of the bridge project will be lower than would have been the case if no charge were made for those using it.

The efficient level at which to price true public goods is therefore zero. Assuming non-distorting lump sum taxes can be levied, revenue to finance the bridge should not be raised by a tariff on those using it but from general taxes, and the bridge should be used by all who wish to, as long as it is uncongested. This conclusion is, however, based on only a partial analysis as it assumes that the government can pay for the bridge with a non-distorting lump-sum tax. If, as is usually the case, governments will have to use taxes like income and company tax to raise revenue to pay for public goods, the distortions introduced will reduce output and welfare. These welfare losses **may** outweigh the losses caused by imposing the user pay principle on what is essentially a public good. Since this is an example of second best solutions, each case will have to be examined on its individual merits.

Furthermore, if a publicly provided infrastructure service like a highway is congested, then it is not a true public good. The addition of one extra motorist will reduce other motorists' capacity to use the bridge and hence the marginal cost of allowing one extra motorist on the road will not be zero.[1] If users can also be efficiently excluded from using the service, as is the case with a bridge or a toll road, then it is quite appropriate to charge a toll for crossing the bridge in order to ration its use to its full capacity level.

In the case of uncongested, pure public goods, however, it is not only inefficient to charge for their use, but it is almost impossible to do so. It would not be feasible to charge people each time they drove on an urban road network[2] or walked on the footpath. Similarly, it is virtually impossible to charge someone each time they turn on a television set or radio and use public broadcasting services. If a project produces a public good it will be necessary to directly estimate its economic value for inclusion in the project's economic cash flow.

12.3 The valuation of public goods in cost benefit analysis

In a financial appraisal of a project producing a public good that will be supplied free of charge, the revenue side of the financial cash flow will be zero. Similarly, if public good inputs to the project are provided free, they will not show up in the project's financial cost stream. This is because a financial appraisal is only concerned with assessing the actual financial costs and benefits of the project to those who are implementing it.

Since public goods are invariably provided by the government, it will be concerned to ensure that its public good projects improve the community's welfare. The fact that many public sector investments produce public goods is one of the main reasons why cost benefit analysis was developed. Cost benefit analyses, unlike financial analyses, measure and include all impacts of projects on community welfare, including the estimated economic value of public goods. While the economically efficient and often only feasible price to charge for a true public good is zero, public goods usually provide considerable utility to those who consume them. Their economic value is therefore not zero. In addition, public goods also have positive, often quite substantial, production costs. The costs and benefits to the community of any public goods used or produced by a project must be included in its economic cash flow. The problem is how to value public goods since they are not sold in the market.

In the case of projects that produce public good outputs like urban road networks or street lighting, it is necessary to determine the utility that people obtain from consuming these public goods. It is then possible to determine whether these benefits justify the costs of producing the public good and also to decide the optimal level of provision. It is therefore necessary to put an economic value on these unpriced or unmarketed goods.

In the case of projects that use public goods whose supply can be readily expanded, their economic cost is the marginal social cost of providing these public good inputs. If the project is economically viable, its benefits must be sufficient to offset the cost of providing the public good inputs, as well as any private good inputs used. The public good input should be valued at the long run marginal cost of providing it to the next user. An approximate value of this long run marginal cost of supply may be the average economic cost of the last public good project producing this particular input — the total cost of the project divided by the estimated number of users.

A number of different approaches have been taken to the more difficult problem of valuing public good outputs. Since public goods are typically non-traded, if the public good meets new demand it should be valued at the price that people would be willing to pay for it. Because in most instances public goods are unmarketed, however, normal market demand curves do not exist so some form of alternative method of valuation must be found.

12.4 Converting public goods to private goods

One approach that has been advocated in relation to some impure public goods is to treat them as if they were private goods and try to implement the 'user pays principle'. For example, in the 1970s the Australian government tried to impose a system of annual licences on television-set owners. More recently the Australian Bureau of Statistics has imposed user charges equal to the average collection cost for those wanting access to national economic statistics. Many governments impose tolls on uncongested highways and bridges. If a user charge can be imposed some may claim that the valuation problem has been solved. The user charge could in this case be taken as the minimum economic value of a unit of the public good to consumers. In addition, an attempt should be made to value the consumer surplus enjoyed by these users if an economic analysis is being undertaken. However, there are numerous problems with this approach.

12.4.1 Technical problems

In the case of some pure public goods like national defence, urban roads, footpaths and lighting, it would be quite impossible to impose user charges. In others, as in the case of Australia's television licences, it may be possible to charge but the administrative cost of policing the system may be very high and outweigh the revenue collected. Australia was forced to abandon its system of television licences for this reason. The technology of cable or pay television has been developed largely to overcome the problem of imposing user charges on the receivers of traditional television transmissions.

12.4.2 Economic efficiency losses

Since the economically efficient price to charge for a true public good is zero, charging a positive price will result in efficiency losses. Figure 12.1 illustrates the example of the uncongested bridge discussed in Section 12.2.

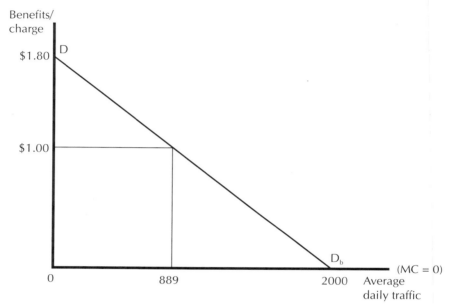

Figure 12.1 *Benefits from a public good — bridge project*

The demand curve for the services of the bridge is represented by the straight line DD_b. The marginal variable cost of supplying bridge services, its supply curve, is zero up to the full capacity level of the bridge, 2100 cars per day. It is estimated that 2000 vehicles cross the bridge each day at present when no toll is being charged and surveys indicate that no vehicles would cross if a toll of $1.80 per car were charged. When no toll is charged, all the bridge's benefits are in the form of consumer surplus. The benefits of the bridge project are then measured by the area under the demand curve and bounded by the vertical and horizontal axes. Thus the total benefits of the project are:

$$0.5 \times \$1.80 \times 2000 = \$1800 \text{ per day}$$

If the local council, who installed the bridge, imposes a tariff of $1 for each trip across the bridge, demand for bridge services is expected to drop to 889 vehicles per day and the total benefits will fall to:

$$\$1 \times 889 + [0.5 \times (\$1.80 - \$1.00) \times 889] = \$1245 \text{ per day}$$

This equals the revenue earned by the project and the consumer surplus received by the people using the bridge.

The bridge will cost \$5.5 million, which at the discount rate appropriate to this country will make its daily capital cost \$1500. The daily economic benefits of the bridge will therefore exceed its daily costs if no toll is levied but will not if a toll is charged. A smaller bridge, able to accommodate only 889 cars per day, could instead be built, for a capital cost of \$1200 per day. However, this bridge would also be able to deliver fewer services and would therefore generate less economic benefits. As the daily net benefits of this smaller bridge would be only \$45, compared with the larger bridge's daily net benefits of \$300, the net value of the smaller bridge project would be less than that of the larger bridge project. Since the two bridges are mutually exclusive projects, building the smaller bridge would result in a loss of welfare for the community.

This analysis therefore indicates that the local council should not charge a toll on the uncongested bridge and should provide a level of service that maximises the economic net present value of the project. Similarly, in the case of television transmissions, where there is no possibility of rivalry in consumption the imposition of television licences will result in a drop in demand for television sets. This will result in a reduction in the number of people receiving transmissions and a drop in people's welfare but will not in any way reduce the costs of television stations. This implies that TV licences should not be imposed. Once again, this conclusion assumes that the revenue to finance the provision of public goods is collected from a non-distorting lump sum tax.

12.4.3 Social welfare objectives for public goods and social services

Many public goods like transport infrastructure in low income regions or community preventive medicine programs are provided without charge even though it may be technically possible to impose user charges. The government may choose not to do so because it wishes to achieve social equity objectives.

Similarly, many social services such as mass education and general health-care services are provided free in order to promote social equity. Charging for such social services, while technically feasible and even economically efficient, may defeat the purpose of their provision — the promotion of social equity. Analysis of projects designed to provide such social services, like those providing public goods, faces the problem of estimating the economic value of this unmarketed output. These valuation problems are similar to those discussed in relation to the externalities generated by a project, as such externalities are also unmarketed.

12.5 Formation of pseudo-demand curves — contingent valuation methods

We have seen that often it will not be feasible, efficient or desirable for the government to treat a public good as if it were a private good and to directly determine in the market how much people are willing to pay for it. If this is the case, one approach may be to indirectly estimate the total utility that people derive from consuming a public good by estimating pseudo-demand curves. This can be achieved by using contingent valuation survey techniques, market simulation exercises or game theory as was discussed in relation to the valuation of externalities. In questionnaires or face-to-face surveys people may be asked how much they are willing to pay for a particular public good. Alternatively they may be engaged in bidding exercises or asked to answer referendum style questions on whether they will pay a certain amount for a particular public good or not. Similar methods may be used to value social service outputs.

As mentioned in Chapter 11, studies have found that there may be a tendency for people to overstate the quantity of a public good that they need if they do not think that they will personally have to pay for it. On the other hand, if asked what they are prepared to pay for a public good or social service, people may understate the amount they are actually willing to pay (Bohm, 1972). It is believed that some people may attempt to 'free ride', in the hope that other people will truthfully declare the value they obtain from various public goods and the amount of the public good they believe is optimal will be provided in any case. However, as was discussed in Chapter 11, careful survey design can help to overcome this and other potential sources of bias in contingent valuation techniques.

12.6 Measurement of prices of closely related private goods

Another frequently used approach to valuing public goods produced by projects is to value them in terms of the changes they cause in the value of closely related private goods or in the productivity of private sector activities. The public good is treated as an intermediate good in the production of a final private good. The value of the 'intermediate' public good is then derived from the value of the private good it ultimately creates, which can be measured in adjusted market prices. This approach is similar to the direct valuation of externalities using market prices, discussed in Section 11.4. It is particularly relevant to valuing infrastructure services such as roads and bridges and social services such as education and health, which are likely to have a measureable effect on private sector productivity. Some of the many private market prices that can be used to value public goods and social services are discussed in the following sections.

12.6.1 Productivity of other activities

The provision of many, if not most, public goods will directly or indirectly increase the productivity of private sector activities. This increased productivity can then be used to measure the benefits of the public good. For example, the provision of an international airport in a scenically attractive region of a country is likely to greatly increase the number of tourists able to visit the area and the productivity and profitability of tourist ventures in the region. In addition, the existence of the airport is likely to increase the economies of scale and profitability of local air services. The value of the airport therefore can be measured in terms of both the direct landing charges levied and the increased profitability of the local air carriers and tourist industry.

12.6.2 Travel time costs

The value of a new urban road or bridge may be measured in terms of the savings in vehicle operating costs and depreciation and drivers' travel time costs. The value of public recreation facilities can also be measured by the amount people are willing to pay to visit such facilities, as was discussed in Chapter 11.

12.6.3 Other time savings

The benefits of other public goods and social services that are provided free can also be measured in terms of savings of users' time and other resources. For example, in the case of rural or urban wells, the time previously used to collect water from traditional water sources as well as time spent collecting newly available water will represent the benefits of such wells. The time collecting the new water will provide a minimum value of how much people are willing to pay for this water, as they would not spend this time collecting it if the water's benefit to them did not exceed this cost. An example of how to value rural well water is given in the first case study in the appendix at the end of the text. Time savings may also represent one of the benefits of decentralised services such as clinics, schools or post offices.

12.6.4 Savings of public and private expenditure

The value of preventive medicine, inoculation, anti-smoking programs or road safety expenditures such as traffic lights may be measured in terms of the estimated savings in medical services that will be achieved. In countries with significant public-health sectors a good proportion of these savings may accrue to public-heath service providers. Similarly, the value of street lighting or police services may be measured by the benefits to the community from avoiding crime and traffic accidents. Some of these savings will accrue to private individuals, some to the public sector and some to institutions like insurance companies but they will all represent gains to the community from the provision of public goods or services.

The benefits of macroeconomic management, another example of a public good, would be very difficult to measure. However, they would include the very substantial value of avoiding output losses and underutilised human and capital resources during depressions and the high costs of hyperinflation to social stability and equity.

12.6.5 Increased human capital measured by increased earnings

Social services like education may be valued in terms of their contribution to human capital formation, which can in turn be measured by the increased earnings of those who are educated.[3] The example in Section 12.9 shows how a tertiary education project may be valued using this method.

Savings in lost earnings from illness or accidents can also be used to value the benefits of public health services, anti-smoking and other public-health campaigns, town-planning and road-safety expenditures.

12.6.6 Willingness to pay for complementary goods

The minimum net present value of television and radio transmissions may be proxied by the total value of television and radio set sales. As television and radio sets are close complementary goods to the broadcast signals, their price will reflect the utility that the marginal consumer gains from receiving television or radio transmissions. People will not pay more for a television set than the enjoyment or utility they expect to receive from watching it. In addition, an estimate should be made of the consumer surplus enjoyed by TV set buyers.

12.6.7 Savings of replacement and restoration costs

One of the benefits of a public good such as a pollution-control program will be the saving in replacement costs for environmental amenities like clean air and water, and the savings in the restoration costs from toxic waste pollution of soil.[4] Similarly, the value of a program to control grazing and erosion on common grazing land will not only be measured by the increased production from the cattle that are permitted access to common land but also the savings from a reduced need to rehabilitate eroded pastures.

There are probably as many prices of closely related private goods that can be used to calculate the approximate value of public goods as there are public good projects. However, these examples are intended to help the analyst to identify the main areas of potential benefits they should consider measuring.

12.6.8 Cost of comparable private services

In the case of social services there may be private sector services such as private schools and hospitals that may be substitutes for social services. Although this is not the case for true public goods, this does apply to impure public goods such as toll roads. In these cases, the cost of equivalent private services may be a good measure of the amount that people would be willing to pay for these social services or public goods. If the services are not considered to be of equivalent standard an adjustment should be made in the value placed on the social services or public goods to reflect this.

12.7 The optimal level of public good provision

Once a public good is provided at a particular level to one person in a community the same quantity of service will be available to all. In estimating the aggregate demand curve for a public good such as street lighting in Figure 12.2, surrogate individual

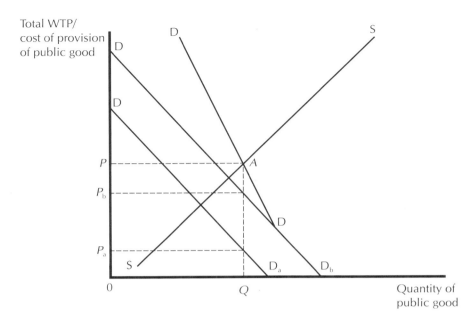

Figure 12.2 *Optimal supply of public goods — street lighting*

demand curves for street lighting, DD_a and DD_b, must first be established. These surrogate demand curves give the prices P_a and P_b, which individuals a and b would be prepared to pay for each additional unit of street lighting provided. They would typically be estimated using data provided by the types of surveys of households and individuals that were discussed previously.

Rather than summing these individual demand curves horizontally, as in the case of private goods, the curves are summed vertically. This is because, once a certain quantity of a public good is supplied, this fixed amount is made available to everyone. The amount that each individual is willing to pay (WTP) per street light for every level of street lighting provided is then aggregated to form the community's demand curve for street lighting, DD. This aggregate demand curve shows the total amount that the community is willing to pay per street light, as the total level of street lighting provided increases. The supply curve of street lighting, SS, indicates the cost per street light as the number of street lights provided increases. The intersection of the aggregate demand curve with this supply curve at **A**, will give the equilibrium level of provision of the public street lighting, Q, at a cost of P per light.[5]

12.8 Cost benefit analysis of projects providing social services

Cost benefit analysis is frequently used to appraise projects designed to produce social services such as health care and public education. As in the case of public goods and externalities, social services are by definition not sold and therefore no market price exists for them. However, such services are highly valued by those receiving them and their provision entails substantial costs. Governments will therefore be concerned to determine whether the benefits generated by providing social services justify these costs and how much of a particular social service should be provided.

As discussed previously, some social services like public education and health services have private sector substitutes — private schools and hospitals. The cost of equivalent private services may be a good measure of the amount that people would be willing to pay for these social services. Alternatively, the value of social services like primary, secondary or tertiary education can be measured in terms of the present value of the increased net income earned by graduates from these different education levels over their lives. Survey data on a large number of people (typically 2000 – 20 000) is required to make econometric estimates of the increase in individuals' earnings that can be attributed to acquiring educational qualifications. This is done by using a whole range of attributes of the survey respondents, including family background, experience, age, sex and intelligence as well as years of education as explanatory variables in an econometric regression to explain variations in income, so that the effect of a tertiary education can be isolated. The coefficient on the years of education will indicate the extent to which education could be expected to increase an individual's annual earnings, with all explanatory variables held constant.

The expected addition to lifetime earnings of the individual due to education, net of income lost during years spent in school, can then be calculated. This benefit is compared with the cost of providing the individual with an education to determine if the investment has a positive NPV in terms of market prices. The economic analysis of the social returns from human resource development would shadow price the value of the educated manpower and the cost of the resources used by the education system to determine whether this investment had a positive economic NPV.

The private returns to education can also be estimated to determine if the investment has a positive NPV for the individual concerned. In this case the analysis will be a financial one and only the costs incurred in undertaking an education and net of tax returns received by the individual will be included in the cash flow. If the education is provided by the government free of charge, the only cost to the individual will be the income lost while undertaking this education.

Finally, the government may wish to undertake a financial analysis of investments that it makes in educational facilities. The financial costs will include the capital and recurrent costs of education at the primary, secondary or tertiary level and the loss of taxation income from individuals while they are undertaking their education. The financial benefits to the government will include the increased income tax paid by individuals who have received education over their lifetimes. An example of how to carry out a financial and economic analysis of an education project is provided in Section 12.9.

Studies in Australia have in fact shown that while the financial return to males from an undergraduate degree is very high, at between 14 and 21 per cent in real terms (Chapman, 1977; Selby-Smith, 1975; Chapman and Chia, 1993) the return to governments is still quite acceptable, from 10 to 16 per cent (Miller, 1977). A study of the returns to Indonesian students who studied at a graduate level in Australia indicated that they achieved a private real rate of return of 17 per cent and that the social rate of return to the Indonesian economy exceeded this (NCDS, 1992).

12.9 Example of an economic analysis of a human resource development project

The government of a rapidly growing developing country is considering establishing a new department of business management at one of the country's better known universities. Surveys of employers in the region where the university is located report a severe shortage of business management graduates. Data was collected on the additional income that locally employed graduates of such courses could expect to earn. Estimates averaged $L190 000 per year. It is planned that after 4 years there will eventually be 400 students in the course. The lost income and the living expenses of each student will average $L25 000 per annum. The average tax rate on income is 33 per cent. The costs and benefits of establishing the business management faculty are shown in Table 12.1.

On the basis of the analysis in Table 12.1, the real economic NPV of the business management course will be a healthy $L916.3 million and its real IRR will be 23.9 per cent. The financial NPV for the government from this investment will be $L177 million and the real financial IRR will be 14.7 per cent. For private individuals, the IRR on their investment is extremely high at 71 per cent. This simple example shows how a government may use cost benefit analysis to make decisions regarding investment in human capital.

12.10 Conclusions

The process of valuing public goods and social services for inclusion in the economic analysis cash flow has many similarities to the valuation of externalities. Wherever possible, their direct effect on private sector activities or human productivity, cost savings of the private or public sector or the value of similar private sector services should be measured in market prices. Such approaches are less liable to subjective judgements by those surveyed or the analyst than some indirect measures of the value of public goods or social services, such as contingent valuation. This approach is particularly applicable to transport and urban infrastructure services and social services such as health care and education. However, in some circumstances it may not be possible to value public goods in terms of market prices and it may be necessary to use contingent valuation techniques. This would be the case if it were found necessary to value public goods that provide less economically measurable services, such as the police force, defence forces and the legal system. Once the value of public goods and social services has been measured they should be entered into the economic cash flow together with directly marketed private goods and services.

Table 12.1   Costs and benefits of business management faculty project ($L'000)

				Year				
	1	2	3	4	5	6	7	40
Costs								
Buildings	100000	30000						
Faculty salaries	0	11200	12400	12400	12400	12400	12400	12400
Administration	0	200	400	400	400	400	400	400
Other costs	0	50	100	100	100	100	100	100
Total government costs	100000	41450	12900	12900	12900	12900	12900	12900
Total private costs (@ $L25 000 per student)	2500	5000	7500	10000	10000	10000	10000	10000
TOTAL ECONOMIC COSTS	102500	46450	20400	22900	22900	22900	22900	22900
Benefits								
Additional income per student, $L190 000 p.a.								
No. students p.a.	100	200	300	400	400	400	400	400
Total graduated	0	0	0	0	100	200	300	3600
Total extra income	0	0	0	0	19000	38000	57000	684000
Income tax rate 33 per cent								
Tax revenue	0	0	0	0	6270	12540	18810	225720
Net economic benefits	-102500	-46450	-20400	-22900	3900	15100	34100	661100
Total net private benefits	-2500	-5000	-7500	-10000	9000	28000	47000	683900
Individual net private benefits	-25	-25	-25	-25	190	190	190	190
Net government financial benefits	-100000	-41450	-12900	-12900	-6630	-360	5910	212820

Economic NPV ($L'000)	916302	IRR	23.91%
Private NPV (total) ($L'000)	1145447	IRR	71.25%
Private NPV (individual) ($L'000)	1176	IRR	71.25%
Govt financial NPV ($L'000)	177036	IRR	14.68%
Economic discount rate 10.00%			

Exercises

1. The government is considering whether the appropriate scale for a new highway project is two or three lanes, and whether or not to impose a toll on the road. Both the two and three lane highways will have a life of 25 years. If a $4 toll is imposed, it is estimated that 40 000 vehicles will use the road each year and a two lane highway will be sufficient. If there is no toll it is believed that 70 000 vehicles will use the road each year, and a three lane highway will be required. If a toll of $10.30 were charged, virtually no vehicles would use the road. Thus the demand curve for the road's services is believed to be approximately a straight line. The consumption conversion factor for this economy is believed to be close to unity because there are few tariff distortions.

   What will be the present value of the total economic benefits of the two alternative projects, including consumer surplus, if the social discount rate is 8 per cent? If the economic cost of a two lane highway is $2.4 million and the economic cost of a three lane highway is $2.8 million, which project should be undertaken? Explain why.

2. The government is considering opening a tract of publicly owned land as a national park. Investment in visitor facilities will cost $1 million, and three rangers, at an annual cost of $100 000, will be needed to provide services to park visitors for the next 25 years. The park is located 80 kilometres from a major city, where most of the visitors are expected to originate from. The average cost of a return trip in terms of petrol and vehicle depreciation is estimated to be $50. If no charge is levied on park visitors, 5000 people are expected to visit each year. If a $5 charge is imposed, visitor numbers are expected to drop to 3000. The real social discount rate for the country is 8 per cent. Should the park be created? Should a visitor charge be levied? Explain your answer.

References

Bohm, P., 1972. 'Estimating demand for public goods', *European Economic Review*, 3:111–30.

Chapman, B., 1977. 'The rate of return to university education for males in the Australian public service', *Journal of Industrial Relations*, 19:2.

Chapman, B. and Chia, T.T., 1993. 'Income contingent charges for higher education: theory, policy and data from the unique Australian experiment', paper to World Bank International Symposium on the Economics of Education, Manchester, 18–21 May.

Miller, P.W., 1977. 'The rate of return to education: evidence from the 1976 census' in B. Chapman and J.E. Isaac (eds), *Australian Labour Economics: Readings*, 3rd edn, Macmillan, Melbourne.

National Centre for Development Studies, 1992. 'Evaluation of Australian educational assistance to South East Asia and the Pacific', report for the Australian International Development Assistance Bureau, Australian National University, Canberra.

Pearce, D.W. and Nash, C.A., 1981. *The Social Appraisal of Projects: a Text in Cost Benefit Analysis*. Macmillan, London, Chapter 8.

Selby-Smith, C., 1975. 'Rates of return to post-secondary education in Australia', *Economic Record*, 51:136.

Further reading

Dasgupta, A.K. and Pearce, D.W., 1972. *Cost-Benefit Analysis — Theory and Practice*, Macmillan, London, Chapter 5.

Little, I.M.D. and Mirrlees, J.A., 1974. *Project Appraisal and Planning for Developing Countries*, Heinemann Educational Books, London, Chapter 16.

Mishan, E.J., 1965. 'The relationship between joint products, collective goods and external effects', *Journal of Political Economy*, May–June.

Sugden, R. and Williams, A., 1978. *The Principles of Practical Cost Benefit Analysis*, Oxford University Press, Oxford, Chapters 10 and 11.

Endnotes

1   In this case, the marginal economic cost of the extra motorist using the road will be the extra travel time costs of other motorists.

2   Recent technological developments may change this situation, however. Several US cities are trying an invention installed under a car, which logs the kilometres travelled by the car over special strips embedded in urban roads. The mini computer can also tell at what hours (peak or off-peak) the car travelled, and relays the information to a central billing area. In this way, motorists could be charged for using urban roads, and in particular, by differential charges for peak and off-peak times, discouraged from making unnecessary trips during peak periods. (Report in *The Economist*, Dec. 1992.)

3   The increased wage or salary received by the educated person should reflect the change in his or her marginal contribution to the total value of production, the change in marginal revenue product.

4   As was discussed in Chapter 11, other benefits will include savings in production from industries like fishing, agriculture and tourism.

5   In a further example, the case of a national defence network, it would be possible to determine how much utility, on average, individuals gain from the provision of the current level of defence preparedness, and how much they would be willing to pay for each additional amount of defence service. Individual demand curves would then be summed vertically to determine the aggregate demand for national defence services. These would show the total amount the community is willing to pay for each level of defence service. The intersection of this aggregate demand curve with the supply curve for defence services, showing the cost of providing each level of defence preparedness, would indicate the optimum level of defence provision.

CHAPTER 13

The social discount rate

13.1 Function of the social discount rate

The social discount rate is the rate used to discount a project's economic cash flow to its present value. It is a crucial parameter in cost benefit analysis. All other things being equal, the higher the social discount rate employed, the fewer projects will be approved. Furthermore, the higher the social discount rate the more project selection will be biased in favour of projects with a short gestation period or pay back period, as future benefits will be heavily discounted.[1]

Chapter 4 discussed why people and governments generally prefer goods and services that are available today rather than ones that will not be available until future years. Discounting the value of costs and benefits received in future periods is the method used in project analysis to take this time preference into account. Discounting involves deflating the value of costs and benefits accruing in a future year, t, by dividing them by a term that is greater than one, $(1 + r)^t$. In this term, r is the discount rate expressed as a proportion of 1.

Once the economic value of all project inputs and outputs is consistently estimated, the social discount rate forms the link between net economic benefits received in different time periods. It enables them to be expressed in terms of net benefits received in the present and they can then be aggregated. In the net present value formula:

$$NPV = \sum_{t=0}^{n} \frac{(B_t - C_t)}{(1 + r)^t} \qquad (13.1)$$

where

r is the appropriate social discount rate for use in an economic appraisal of a project

n is the life of the project

B_t is the benefit obtained in year t, measured in economic prices

C_t is the cost incurred in year t, measured in economic prices.

13.2 Determination of the social discount rate — the neoclassical approach

The crucial question is how to determine the appropriate level of the social discount rate. In a financial analysis of a project, the opportunity cost of capital to the implementing firm is the rate at which the project implementor could borrow or lend, depending on whether he or she is a net borrower or lender in the market. In an economic analysis of a project the social discount rate should reflect the social opportunity cost of the capital funds used **to the country as a whole**. The market interest rate often cannot be employed as the social discount rate because of imperfections in the capital market . These will drive a wedge between the market cost of capital and its demand and supply price. In some situations, however, if distortions in the capital market are not great and are difficult to measure, the market interest rate may be the best approximation of the social discount rate.

There are two distinct approaches to determining the appropriate social discount rate. The first is that adopted by what is known as the neoclassical approach to cost benefit analysis. One of the main tenets of this approach is that the individual is the best judge of her or his own welfare. In determining the appropriate social discount rate, neoclassical theory therefore uses the preferences of individuals regarding saving and investment, as expressed in the capital market, as its starting point.

The second approach, known as the decision-maker interpretation of cost benefit analysis, maintains that a government decision-maker may quite legitimately replace individuals' valuation of investable funds with a value selected by the decision-maker. This approach may be more appropriate to centrally planned or at least heavily regulated economies with high levels of government intervention. The decision-maker approach to the determination of the social discount rate is discussed later in the chapter.

The approach to determining the social discount rate that has received the most attention in the literature, the neoclassical approach, will be examined first. To simplify this analysis it will be initially assumed that there are no distortions in the capital market, such as taxes on savers and investors or interest rate controls. Later, this restrictive assumption will be relaxed in order to assess how the discount rate would be determined in the presence of such distortions.

13.3 The social discount rate in the absence of capital market distortions

In a perfectly competitive neoclassical world, with no public goods, no government taxes or subsidies, perfect knowledge and hence no risk or need for capital market intermediaries, it would in fact be a relatively uncomplicated matter to determine the level of the social discount rate. As can be seen from Figure 13.1, equilibrium in the capital market would occur at the intersection of the demand and supply curves for investable funds, DD and SS. The demand curve for investable funds, DD will be downward sloping because as the market interest rate rises, fewer people will wish to borrow, as fewer potential investments will be viable. On the other hand, the supply curve for savings, SS, will be upward sloping because people will be willing to save more if they receive a higher return on their savings. The market interest rate is just the equilibrium price of investable funds, the price that the marginal investor is willing to pay to borrow investable funds and the price at which the marginal saver is willing to supply investable funds.

At the equilibrium investment level Q_0, there will be one unique equilibrium market interest rate, r_0, which in this undistorted market will be the social discount rate. This equilibrium social discount rate will reflect the true opportunity cost of investable funds to the economy as it will equal both the supply price of savings, P_s, and the demand price of capital, P_d, for the equilibrium quantity of investable funds, Q_0. As was discussed in Chapter 4, the supply price of savings is the social (marginal) rate of time preference, SRTP — the annual return that on average people will require to compensate them for giving up a given level of consumption in the current period. The demand price for investable funds will be determined by the marginal productivity of capital in the economy. This is the rate of return that could be earned on the last unit of funds invested, assuming that the least profitable investments will be made last. The social discount rate, r_0, will therefore equal the opportunity cost of the marginal unit of investable funds to both savers and investors. In an undistorted market of this nature, savers and investors interacting freely would ensure that the economy's resources would be optimally distributed between investment and consumption, and there would therefore be no premium placed on investment.

Assuming that all other economic costs and benefits have been accurately measured, the use of this equilibrium rate, r_0, as the social discount rate would ensure that only projects that raised economic welfare were selected. Projects with a positive NPV[2] using this SDR would not only be able to compensate savers for forgoing current

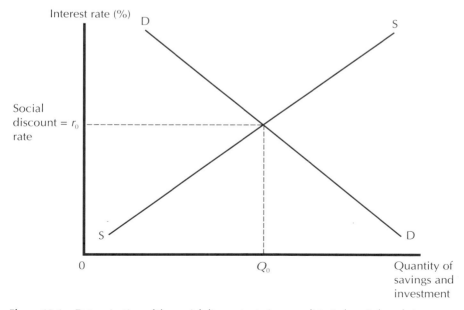

Figure 13.1 *Determination of the social discount rate in an undistorted capital market*

consumption to finance the project, but would also achieve a return on their capital investment (have a marginal productivity of capital) that is at least as high as alternative investments available in the private sector.

13.4 Impact of capital market distortions on the determination of the SDR

In no country in the world is there a completely undistorted capital market with no taxes on savers or investors and no controlled interest rates. In Figure 13.2, once income tax is imposed on the interest earnings of savers, the supply curve for savings shifts inwards to SS_1.

At every real interest rate people will be willing to save less, as their post-tax returns will be lower than their pre-tax return on saving. Similarly, the imposition of company tax on business earnings will shift the demand for investable funds curve inwards to DD_1. Because investors will have to pay company income tax on their profits their post-tax return on investment will be reduced, so that at every real interest rate investors will be willing to borrow less. The resulting equilibrium market interest rate, r_1, will occur at the intersection of these post-tax demand and supply curves for investable funds, DD_1 and SS_1. This market rate, r_1, could be either higher or lower than the social discount rate in the undistorted capital market, r_0, depending on the elasticity of the demand and supply curves for investable funds and the magnitude of

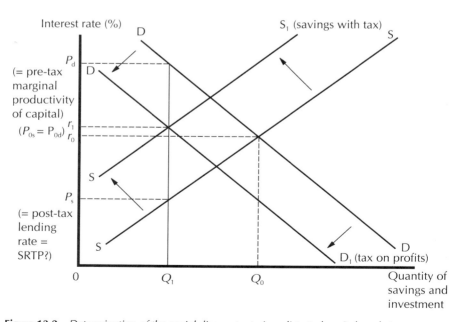

Figure 13.2   *Determination of the social discount rate in a distorted capital market*

the taxes imposed. What is clear, however, is that the equilibrium level of private investment in this distorted capital market will be less than the equilibrium level in an undistorted market.[3]

Whereas in an undistorted capital market, the demand price of capital, P_d, will equal the supply price of capital, P_s, this will not be the case in a distorted capital market. Taxation and other distortions will drive a large wedge between the demand and supply price of capital. Typically, the supply price of savings, the real, post-tax rate earned by savers, may be as low as 1–2 per cent per annum and may even be negative, as was the case in some high inflation countries in the 1970s and 1980s. On the other hand, the real pre-tax earnings of the marginal company borrowing funds, the marginal productivity of capital, may be as high as 15–20 per cent per annum.

It is obvious from Figure 13.2 that, in the presence of tax distortions, neither the pre-tax demand price of capital, P_d, the pre-tax marginal productivity of capital, MPC, in the private sector nor the post-tax supply price of capital, P_s, the post-tax social rate of time preference, SRTP, will equal the social discount rate. The social discount rate would only equal either the demand or supply price of investable funds if there were no taxes on investors and savers and these demand and supply prices, the MPC and SRTP, respectively, were equal to each other. If the analyst adopts the weighted cost of capital approach, which is discussed in the following section, the SRTP and the MPC form the outer bounds of the social discount rate. The true social discount rate will lie somewhere between these two rates.

However, it took many years for this apparently simple point to be first grasped by Marglin (1963a, 1963b) and Feldstein (1964). This misunderstanding generated a long running debate regarding which of these two rates, the SRTP or the MPC, was the appropriate social discount rate. The essential elements of this historical debate are summarised in the first appendix to this chapter. This is done mainly because some cost benefit analysis practitioners may not be aware that this debate has been resolved and may erroneously try to employ a social discount rate based on one of these two prices of capital.

Within the neoclassical framework, there are currently two alternative, but essentially equivalent, methods of determining a country's social discount rate, which are accepted in neoclassical economic literature. These are the weighted cost of capital approach developed by Harberger (1972a, 1972b) and Sandmo and Dreze (1971) and the shadow price of investment approach developed by Marglin (1963a, 1963b) and Feldstein (1964). In addition, there is the decision-maker or interventionist approach. The two neoclassical approaches are examined in more detail in Sections 13.5 and 13.6, while the decision-maker approach is discussed in Section 13.8.

13.5 The SDR as the weighted cost of capital — the Harberger, Sandmo and Dreze approach

The simpler and more applicable of the two neoclassical approaches is that developed by Sandmo and Dreze (1971), Harberger (1972a, 1972b) and Dreze (1974) in the early 1970s. These economists argued that for a small project the correct approach to determining the social discount rate in distorted capital markets was simply to calculate the weighted average of the supply and demand price of investable funds (the SRTP and the MPC). The appropriate weights equal the proportion of the project's investable funds drawn from consumption and investment, respectively. They maintained that this approach would provide a social discount rate equal to the true economic opportunity cost of investable funds used for projects in the public sector.[4]

In the UNIDO Guidelines' (UNIDO, 1972), Marglin claimed that the weighted cost of a capital approach was only correct in a restrictive two-period investment model. However, Sjaastad and Wisecarver (1977) effectively vindicated the weighted cost of capital approach of Harberger, Sandmo and Dreze and showed that under several reasonable conditions it was equivalent to the Marglin shadow price of capital approach. These conditions were that (i) the public investment project generates a perpetuity and (ii) a capital market was grafted on to the Marglin model to provide some guidance regarding, for example, the level of reinvestment from the project. If the project does not produce a perpetuity, Sjaastad and Wisecarver showed that any differences between the two approaches rely on divergent assumptions about the rate at which output from public sector projects would be reinvested. Their analysis indicated that introduction of the option to reinvest some or all of the output from public projects would produce a qualitatively but not quantitatively important adjustment in the discount rate used by Harberger and Sandmo and Dreze and therefore would not produce any significant divergence between the discount rates developed by the two approaches.

13.5.1 Derivation of the weighted cost of capital in a closed economy

The weighted cost of capital approach basically applies to capital services the same analytical framework that was developed by Harberger to measure the net costs and benefits of non-traded and traded goods and services (discussed in Chapters 7 and 8) and foreign exchange (discussed in Chapter 9). The rationale for this approach can be understood by considering the distorted capital market shown in Figure 13.3.[5] In an undistorted capital market, the demand for and supply of investable funds are again represented by the demand and supply curves, DD and SS respectively. In the absence of distortions, the equilibrium market interest rate, r_0, would also be the social discount rate. However, in this country investors must pay company tax at a rate of c_t on their profits, and savers must pay personal income taxes at a rate of p_t, on their interest earnings. The gross of tax savings curve, SS_1 indicates the market returns that savers will require before this tax rate is paid to persuade them to supply each level of savings. Investors' new after tax demand curve for funds DD_1 indicates the interest rate that they will be prepared to pay for each level of investable funds given that they are required to pay this level of company taxes on their profits. The intersection of the post-tax demand curve for funds, DD_1, and the pre-tax supply curve, SS_1, will give the equilibrium market interest rate in the distorted capital market, MIR_0 at r_1 or 4.5 per cent in this example. At this level of saving and investment, Q_1, the MPC will be q_0, or 6 per cent and the SRTP, i_0, will be 2.6 per cent.

If a very large new project is being considered in this country, requiring $Q_2 - Q_d$ local dollars of investment, the demand curve for investable funds will shift from DD_1 to DD_p. If investors in this country cannot draw freely on international capital markets, capital will be essentially a non-traded good. This situation may arise either because of domestic restrictions on overseas borrowing by residents or problems in obtaining access to foreign capital due to the heavy indebtedness of the country concerned and resulting debt service problems. This may be the case in the Philippines, some poorer Indo-Chinese countries and many African and South American countries. In this case the relevant supply curve for investable funds may be the domestic supply curve SS_1, which will be less than completely elastic as is shown in Figure 13.3.

In this case domestic market interest rates will rise from r_1 to r_2 due to the project's demand for funds. As a result of this rise some more marginal investors will be squeezed out of the market, reducing their demand for capital from Q_1 to Q_d. In addition, there will be a supply response from savers to the higher net of tax interest rates offered and the total value of investable funds available in the economy will rise from Q_1 to Q_2.

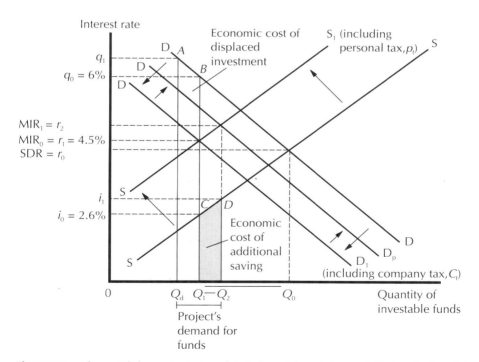

Figure 13.3   *The social discount rate in a distorted capital market — weighted cost of capital approach*

The cost to the economy of the capital required by the project will therefore be the economic cost of the displaced investment, Q_dQ_1BA, plus the economic cost of the additional savings generated, Q_1Q_2DC. The displaced investment will be valued at the demand price of capital, the pre-tax marginal productivity of capital in the economy, q, or its average before and after the project $\frac{(q_0 + q_1)}{2}$. The newly generated saving will be valued at the social rate of time preference, i, or its average before or after the project, $\frac{(i_0 + i_1)}{2}$. When the project is small enough that no perceptible change could be expected in the MPC or SRTP, the weighted cost of capital will just be the weighted average of the MPC and SRTP, where weights are the proportion of new investment funds expected to be drawn from alternative investments and new savings.

We can use the same Harberger formula to measure the economic cost per unit of capital required as was employed to measure the economic cost of other project inputs.

$$\text{SDR} = w_s\, P_s + w_d\, P_d \tag{13.2}$$

where

P_s is the supply price of capital, or the post-tax social rate of time preference, i

P_d is the demand price for capital or the pre-tax marginal productivity of capital in the economy, q

w_s, the weight applied to P_s, is the proportion of project investment drawn from new savings, which in terms of the Harberger approach can be measured by:

$$w_s = \frac{\lambda}{\left[\lambda - \eta\left(\dfrac{Q_d}{Q_s}\right)\right]} \tag{13.3}$$

where

λ is the elasticity of supply of savings (slope of the supply curve)

η is the elasticity of demand for investable funds (slope of the demand curve)

w_d is the weight applied to P_d, or the proportion of project investment drawn from displacing other investments:

$$w_d = \frac{-\eta\left(\dfrac{Q_d}{Q_s}\right)}{\left[\lambda - \eta\left(\dfrac{Q_d}{Q_s}\right)\right]} \tag{13.4}$$

where

$\dfrac{Q_d}{Q_s} = \dfrac{I_t}{S_t}$ is the ratio of total investment to total savings — the ratio of the quantity of investable funds demanded to the quantity supplied.

Substituting (13.2) and (13.3) into (13.1) and reorganising it, the weighted cost of capital social discount rate can be expressed in terms of the elasticity of supply and demand of investable funds:

$$SDR = \frac{\lambda i - \eta q \left(\dfrac{I_t}{S_t}\right)}{\lambda - \eta \left(\dfrac{I_t}{S_t}\right)} \qquad (13.5)$$

where

i is the SRTP

q is the MPC

λ is the elasticity of supply of savings

η is the elasticity of demand for investment

$\dfrac{I_t}{S_t}$ is the ratio of total investment to total savings.

If there are imperfections in the capital market, the demand and supply price of capital funds will not equal each other or the market interest rate. Distortions affecting the demand for funds, such as company income tax, property taxes and investment subsidies like accelerated depreciation, drive a wedge between the market borrowing rate and the demand price for investable funds, the pre-tax marginal productivity of capital, q. Personal income tax, levied at different rates on domestic savers, and withholding tax on foreign lenders similarly cause the market lending rate to diverge from the supply price of savings, i, the post-tax social rate of time preference.

In a situation where there are many investors and savers, each with their own elasticities of demand for and supply of investable funds and each subject to different rates of tax, the weighted cost of capital formula can be disaggregated and expressed in terms of the marginal rate of time preference and MPC of different groups of lenders and borrowers, their different demand and supply elasticities and their rates of tax (Jenkins and Harberger 1991):

$$SDR = \frac{\lambda i' - \eta q' \left(\dfrac{I_t}{S_t}\right)}{\lambda - \eta \left(\dfrac{I_t}{S_t}\right)} \qquad (13.6)$$

where

$$\lambda i' = \sum \left[\lambda_i \times i_i' \left(\frac{S_i}{S_{total}}\right) \right]$$

Summed over all lenders, this is the weighted sum of the product of the elasticities of supply of different groups of lenders and their individual SRTP, where the weights applied are the savings share of each group in total savings:

$$\eta q' = \sum \left[\eta_j \times q'_j \left(\frac{I_j}{I_{total}} \right) \right]$$

Summed over all borrowers, this is the weighted sum of the elasticities of demand of different groups of borrowers, and their demand price of investable funds, MPC, where the weights applied are the share of each group in total borrowings:

$$\lambda = \sum \left[\lambda_i \times \left(\frac{S_i}{S_{total}} \right) \right]$$

$$\eta = \sum \left[\eta_j \times \left(\frac{I_j}{I_{total}} \right) \right]$$

where

i'_i is the rate of time preference of lender i, net of personal income and withholding taxes

q'_j is the return on investment of borrower j, gross of company taxes, subsidies, etc.

λ_i is the elasticity of supply of capital of lender i

η_j is the elasticity of demand for capital of borrower j

$\dfrac{S_i}{S_{total}}$ is the share of savings by lender i in the total amount of savings

$\dfrac{I_i}{I_{total}}$ is the share of capital invested by borrower j in total investment.

The weighted cost of capital approach therefore assumes that the project is funded in exactly the same way as the average for all other investments in the economy.

13.5.2 The social discount rate in an open economy

If the country is not heavily indebted and can draw freely on borrowings from the foreign capital market, the relevant supply curve for its investable funds will be the elastic international supply curve, SS_{int} in Figure 13.4. In this case capital will be a traded good for the country and the social opportunity cost of investable funds or social discount rate will be the international supply price of capital. This will be the interest rate at which the country can borrow on the international capital market, typically the London Inter-bank Borrowing Rate, LIBOR, plus some premium specific to the country concerned. This will vary at different times but averages about 4–5 per cent in real terms in the long term. As countries have increasingly liberalised their capital markets in recent years, most developed and the more successful developing countries are likely to have free access to international capital markets. This would be the case with most OECD countries including Australia, as well as Indonesia, Malaysia, Thailand and all the Asian NIEs (newly industrialising economies). As liberalisation continues in South Asia and Latin America, this will also soon be the case with many of these economies, if it is not already so. This will make the calculation of the SDR quite simple for such countries.

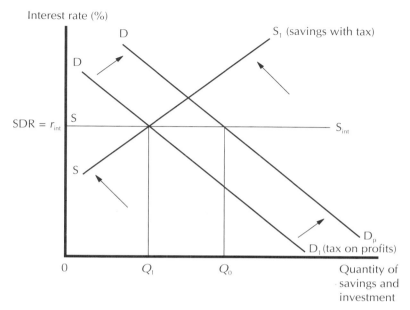

Figure 13.4 *Determination of the social discount rate in an open economy*

This can be seen in Figure 13.4 where the relevant supply curve for investable funds is the perfectly elastic international supply curve, SS_{int}. Although the project will cause an outward shift in the post tax domestic demand for capital from DD_1 to DD_p this will have no effect on the domestic interest rate, which will remain at the international interest rate, r_{int}. This will also be the SDR for this country.

If the country can borrow as much as it wishes on the international capital market at the going international borrowing rate, this will imply that the elasticity of supply of foreign lenders is infinitely large. In equation (13.6), the weight on foreign lenders supply cost of capital, the international interest rate, would therefore become unity and the weight on other lenders and borrowers supply and demand price would tend to zero. The social discount rate would simply be the real international borrowing rate, after account was taken of expected exchange rate movements. The open economy situation is therefore just a special case of the more general Harberger, Sandmo and Dreze formula. However, as capital market liberalisation progresses around the world, it is likely to become the norm that a country's SDR will be the rate at which it can borrow internationally.

13.5.3 Expressing the SDR in market interest rates

If equation (13.6) is to be empirically useful, the unobservable demand and supply prices of capital must be expressed in terms of the observable market interest rate, MIR, with adjustments for taxes and subsidies applying to different groups of lenders and borrowers. If investors are taxed at a rate of t_c on corporate profits net of other taxes and are charged property taxes at a rate of R, expressed as a percentage of their total investment, the market interest rate that investors are willing to pay will equal:

$$\text{MIR} = q' - (q' - R)t_c - R \tag{13.7}$$
$$\therefore \quad \text{MIR} = (q' - R)(1 - t_c)$$
$$\therefore \quad q' = \frac{\text{MIR}}{(1 - t_c)} + R \tag{13.8}$$

If there were also a subsidy of s on the gross of property and company tax rate of return on the total investment, the market interest rate will be:

$$\text{MIR} = (q' - R)(1 - t_c + s) \tag{13.9}$$
$$\therefore \quad q' = \frac{\text{MIR}}{(1 - t_c + s)} + R \tag{13.10}$$

If a personal tax rate of t_p is levied on the personal income of lenders, the social rate of time preference will equal the net of tax market interest rate paid to savers:

$$i' = \text{MIR}(1 - t_p) \tag{13.11}$$

Substituting (13.9) and (13.10) into (13.5), the weighted social discount rate can be expressed in terms of measurable market interest rates, and tax and subsidy rates levied on different categories of lenders and savers, gives:

$$\text{SDR} = \frac{\text{MIR}(1 - t_p)\lambda - \left[\dfrac{\text{MIR}}{1 - t_c + s} + R\right]\eta \times \left(\dfrac{I_t}{S_t}\right)}{\lambda - \eta\left(\dfrac{I_t}{S_t}\right)} \tag{13.12}$$

Other taxes such as withholding taxes on foreign lenders, t_w, can be introduced in the same manner. The shares of each borrower and lender in total investment and savings in the economy are used to weight the demand price and supply price of investable funds.

13.5.4 Expressing the SDR in real terms

Market interest rates are always expressed in nominal terms, while it is usually more convenient to express the social discount rate in real terms. If f_e is the expected rate of inflation, and FIR is the international interest rate, rearranging equation (4.9) in Chapter 4, the real social rate of time preference (i_r) and real marginal product of capital, or gross return from investment, q_r can be expressed as:

$$i_r = \frac{\left[\text{MIR}(1 - t_p) - f_e\right]}{(1 + f_e)} \quad \text{for domestic lenders} \tag{13.13}$$

$$i_{fr} = \frac{\left[\text{FIR}(1 - t_w) - f_e\right]}{(1 + f_e)} \quad \text{for foreign lenders} \tag{13.14}$$

$$q_r = \frac{\dfrac{\text{MIR}}{1 + t_c + s} + R - f_e}{(1 + f_e)} \quad \text{for subsidised and taxed investors} \tag{13.15}$$

An example of how to estimate the social discount rate in a distorted capital market using the weighted source of capital approach is given in the following section.

13.6 Example of the estimation of the weighted cost of capital SDR in a distorted capital market

In the example below, capital is supplied by domestic lenders subject to different levels of marginal tax and foreign lenders who are subject to withholding tax, as outlined in Table 13.1.[6] In this country the market interest rate is 18 per cent, and the inflation rate is 8 per cent.

Borrowers are in the manufacturing, agricultural, mining and housing sectors. Each sector is subjected to different tax and subsidy policies, as shown in Table 13.2.

Hence, using the SDH formula for the real economic opportunity cost of public funds, the social discount rate, is:

$$SDR = \frac{\lambda i - \eta q' \left(\frac{I_t}{S_t} \right)}{\lambda - \eta \left(\frac{I_t}{S_t} \right)} \tag{13.16}$$

where

$$\lambda i' = \sum \left[\lambda_i \times i'_i \left(\frac{S_i}{S_{total}} \right) \right]$$

$$\eta q' = \sum \left[\eta_j \times q'_j \left(\frac{I_j}{I_{total}} \right) \right]$$

i'_i is the rate of time preference of lender i, net of personal income and withholding taxes

q'_j is the return on investment of borrower j, gross of taxes and net of subsidies

$\left(\frac{I_t}{S_t} \right)$ is $\frac{\text{total investment}}{\text{total savings}}$ = 1, that is there is equilibrium in the financial market.

$$\therefore \quad SDR = \frac{0.012 + 0.167}{0.547 + 0.674}$$
$$= 14.65 \text{ per cent}$$

13.7 Marglin's shadow price of investment approach

Marglin (1963a, 1963b, 1967 and in the UNIDO Guidelines, 1972) and Feldstein (1964) were the first economists to develop a method for determining the value of

Table 13.1   Suppliers of capital

Group	Type of tax	Marginal rate, $t\%$	Elasticity of savings supply, λ_i	Savings supplied, S_i ($L billion)	Real net of tax SRTP i'_i (formula)	i'_i	Share $\dfrac{S_i}{S_{total}}$	$i'_i\lambda_i \times \dfrac{S_i}{S_{total}}$	$\dfrac{\lambda_i S_i}{S_{total}}$
High income	Personal income	50.00	0.75	3000	$\dfrac{[MIR(1-t_p)-f_e]}{(1+f_e)}$	0.0093	0.37	0.0026	0.28
Middle income	Personal income	35.00	0.40	1500	$\dfrac{[MIR(1-t_p)-f_e]}{(1+f_e)}$	0.0343	0.19	0.0026	0.08
Low income	Personal income	15.00	0.10	500	$\dfrac{[MIR(1-t_p)-f_e]}{(1+f_e)}$	0.0676	0.06	0.0004	0.01
Foreign lenders	Withholding tax	35.00	0.75	2000	$\dfrac{\left[FIR(1-t_w)\left(1+\dfrac{1}{\lambda_{if}}\right)-f_e\right]}{(1+f_e)}$	0.0343	0.25	0.0064	0.19
Net govt. saving	n.a.	0.00	0.00	1000	n.a.	n.a.	0.13	0.0000	0.00
Total				8000			1.00	0.01202	0.547

Notes:

MIR is market interest rate = 18%

FIR is foreign interest rate = 24%

λ_i is elasticity of savings supply of lender i

t_p is personal tax

t_w is withholding tax

f_e is the rate of inflation = 8%

i' is the real net of tax SRTP

S_{total} = total savings

S_i is savings of lender i

For foreign borrowings, the marginal cost of funds is:

$$MC = AC \times \left(1 + \frac{1}{\lambda_{if}}\right),\ \text{where:}$$

MC is marginal cost

AC is average cost

λ_{if} is elasticity of supply of foreign borrowings.

Table 13.2. Demanders of capital

Sector	Type of tax or subsidy	Marginal tax or subsidy rate (%)	Elasticity of demand, η_j	Investment demanded, I_j ($L billion)	Real before tax return, on investment, q'_j (formula)	q'_j	Share $\dfrac{I_j}{I_{total}}$	$\eta_j q'_j \times \dfrac{I_j}{I_{total}}$	$\dfrac{\eta_j I_j}{I_{total}}$
Manufacturing	Corporate tax	40.00	−0.70	3500	$\left[\dfrac{\dfrac{MIR}{(1-t_c)}-f_e}{(1+f_e)}\right]$	0.204	0.44	−0.0628	−0.31
Mining	Business tax	40.00	−0.60	1500	$\left[\dfrac{\dfrac{MIR}{(1-t_c)}-f_e}{(1+f_e)}\right]$	0.204	0.19	−0.0233	−0.11
Housing	Property tax	35.00	−0.80	2000	$\left[\dfrac{\dfrac{MIR}{(1+s)}+R-f_e}{(1+f_e)}\right]$	0.395	0.25	−0.079	−0.23
	Subsidy on net of tax return	15.00							
Fisheries	Subsidy on interest rate	35.00	−0.40	1000	$\left[\dfrac{\dfrac{MIR}{(1-s)}-f_e}{(1+f_e)}\right]$	0.034	0.13	−0.0018	−0.05
Total				8000			1.00	−0.16685	−0.674

Notes:

MIR is the market interest rate = 18%

η_j is elasticity of demand for investable funds of investor j

q' is the real marginal gross of tax return on investment

t_c is company tax

f_e is the rate of inflation = 8 per cent over the next 20–30 years

I_j is investment demand of the jth borrower

I_{total} is total investment

s is rate of subsidy

R is property tax

The country's financial market is in equilibrium.

the social discount rate in a distorted capital market. Their approach to estimating the SDR involves a more complex two step procedure. The first step involves measuring the effect of distortions in the capital market on savings and investment behaviour by calculating what Marglin called the **shadow price of investment**. This has also subsequently become known as the **premium on investment**. The second step involved shadow pricing all changes in investment caused by the project using this shadow price of investment, so that all flows were expressed in terms of Marglin's chosen numeraire — consumption flows. These were then discounted with the social discount rate appropriate to consumption flows, the SRTP. We will firstly look at how to estimate the shadow price of investment or the investment premium.

13.7.1 The premium on investment in a distorted capital market

In almost all countries as a result of the taxes imposed on savers and borrowers the level of private investment is reduced. This was shown in Figure 13.2, where savings were reduced from their equilibrium level, Q_0 to Q_1. This reduction in private investment may cause the government to believe that there is insufficient investment in the economy and to place a premium on increases in investment compared with increases in consumption. If there are distortions in the capital market causing a premium to be placed on investment, the two types of flows, consumption and investment, will not have an equal economic value to society.

For example, let it be assumed that in the situation shown in Figure 13.2 the real, pre-tax marginal productivity of capital in this country is 18 per cent. The post-tax real SRTP, on the other hand, may be only 3 per cent. This means that at the margin, people in this country only value extra consumption in the current period at 3 per cent more than they value extra consumption available one year from now. On the other hand, the least profitable or most marginal investment that investors are willing to undertake given the limited quantity of investable funds available will earn a real return of 18 per cent per annum. So a $1 addition to investment in the current period will yield six times more utility, or is six times more valuable to the society, than $1 of extra consumption. If this is the case, the country is said to exhibit an **investment premium**. When such a premium exists, the society should not be indifferent as to whether it finances a project by reducing other investment or finances a project by reducing consumption. A project financed by reduced investment will in effect cost the economy six times more than one financed by reduced consumption. Similarly, the government could well prefer to implement a project whose output can be allocated to increased investment, rather than one whose output will be committed to increased consumption. A project will typically cause changes in both the level of consumption and investment in different time periods.

13.7.2 The shadow price of investment, SPI

It was shown in Figure 13.2 that where there were institutional and political distortions in the capital and goods markets such as personal and company taxation, interest rate fixing and other forms of capital market intervention, investment levels and therefore the overall growth rate might be sub-optimal. This implies that the social value of the marginal private sector investment, the marginal productivity of capital, will exceed the social value placed on consumption, the social rate of time preference.

The ratio of the social value of investment to the social value of consumption (MPC/SRTP) is called the **shadow price of investment, SPI**. The SPI is in fact a conversion factor rather than a shadow price. Its function is to convert the unequally valuable changes in consumption and investment caused by the project into a common numeraire. The numeraire chosen by this approach is the project's impact on consumption flows. So changes in investment flows caused by the project are revalued in terms of changes in consumption flows. This is done by multiplying the change in investment flows generated by the project by the shadow price of investment, SPI.[7]

Several closely related concepts have been developed and employed by Little and Mirrlees (1974), UNIDO (1972) and Squire and van der Tak (1975) to define this conversion factor. These include the shadow price of capital, the shadow price of investment and the shadow price of public income, respectively. These concepts differ somewhat and also vary in complexity regarding the assumptions they make about the nature of reinvestment and the divergence of the marginal productivity of capital in the public and private sectors, *inter alia*. However, at the simplest level of assumptions on these issues these conversion factors essentially capture the same set of relationships between the key variables.

Marglin, Sen and Dasgupta, the authors of the 'UNIDO Guidelines' (UNIDO, 1972) define their shadow price of investment, SPI, as follows. Assume the government or a private firm invests in a marginal perpetuity producing a rate of return q, equal to the pre-tax marginal productivity of capital in this economy. Since it is assumed that all of the output of this perpetuity will be consumed the social rate of time preference, i, is the appropriate rate to discount the stream of consumption earned to its present value. In the most straightforward case, where all of these earnings are consumed, the stream of consumption generated by the perpetuity will have a net present value equal to:

$$\text{NPV} = \sum_{t=0}^{\infty} \frac{q}{(1+i)^t} \tag{13.17}$$

where i is the post-tax social rate of time preference, also called the consumption rate of interest. The NPV of this investment, summed to infinity is then:

$$\text{NPV} = \frac{q}{i} = \text{SPI} \tag{13.18}$$

The present value of this marginal perpetuity, q/i, will equal the shadow price of investment, SPI, as it indicates the ratio of the marginal yield on investment in the economy, q, to the social rate of time preference, i. As such it shows the extent to which investment flows are more valuable than consumption flows in an economy with a distorted capital market and a premium on investment. If there are no distortions in the capital market and consumption and investment flows are equally valuable, the MPC will equal SRTP, q will equal i, and the SPI will equal unity.

If we drop the simplifying assumption that all of the project's net benefits will be consumed and it is expected that a proportion, s, will be reinvested, then the marginal perpetuity's income flow will be split between:

- the direct contribution of the marginal investment to consumption, $q(1 - s)$
- the contribution of the marginal investment to investment, sq.

If consumption and investment are not equally valuable in this economy, it will be necessary to revalue the two types of flows in terms of a common numeraire. Using the numeraire used by this approach, that is, changes in consumption flows, changes in investment flows caused by the project must be converted into consumption-flow equivalents. This is done by multiplying the proportion of the perpetuity reinvested, sq, by the shadow price of investment, SPI. As the SPI shows the relative economic value of investment flows to consumption flows, this has the effect of revaluing these investment flows in consumption flow equivalents.

The contribution of the marginal investment to investment flows, expressed in terms of consumption flows, is therefore:

$$sq \times \text{SPI}$$

Taking the net present value of the total income stream generated by the perpetuity, using the social rate of time preference, i, as the discount rate, the shadow price of investment, SPI, is:

$$\text{SPI} = \frac{sq \times \text{SPI}}{i} + \frac{q(1 - s)}{i} \tag{13.19}$$

Solving for SPI gives

$$\text{SPI} = \frac{\left[(1 - s)q\right]}{(i - s)q} \tag{13.20}$$

This term will be defined so long as $i > sq$.

The shadow price of investment is typically greater than unity, reflecting the fact that the value of investment exceeds that of consumption in distorted capital markets. In the example given in the previous section, where the MPC was 18 per cent and the SRTP was 3 per cent, the **SPI** ($= \frac{\text{MPC}}{\text{SRTP}}$) was equal to 6. This shadow price of investment is then used to inflate the value of changes in investment streams caused by the project. This procedure ensures that the changes in investment streams caused by the project reflect the true cost or benefit to the economy of using or producing investment funds in a distorted capital market. They are then comparable with project-induced changes in less highly valued consumption streams.

13.7.3 Marglin's social discount rate, the SRTP or consumption rate of interest

Once changes in investment and consumption flows as a result of the project have been revalued in terms of the Marglin numeraire, that is, changes in the level of consumption, the appropriate discount rate to use is the rate of fall in the value of future streams of consumption to the community. This is the social rate of time preference — the rate of return that, on average, individuals require in order to be persuaded to sacrifice current for future consumption. The social rate of time preference is called by Squire and van der Tak (1975) the consumption rate of interest, CRI. This is the social discount rate used to discount changes in future levels of consumption by Marglin and the 'UNIDO Guidelines'.

Squire and van der Tak (1975:139–40) summarise the determinants of Marglin's SDR, the CRI. If it is assumed that all of the output of a project is consumed, the consumption rate of interest is the same as the social rate of time preference, i, which is given by:

$$i = ng + \rho \qquad\qquad (13.21)$$

where

ρ is the rate of pure time preference, determined by the risk that the future income streams will not eventuate, and the loss of utility from forgone consumption opportunities

g is the expected future growth of real per capita consumption

n is a parameter of the utility function, such that:

$$\frac{\partial MU}{\partial C} = C^{-n} \qquad\qquad (13.22)$$

where C is consumption at level C and MU is marginal changes in utility. The parameter n indicates the rate at which marginal utility from consumption diminishes with respect to rises in per capita consumption. It shows by how much welfare or utility will change with a unit increase in consumption at different levels of consumption. Therefore, if $n = 0$, society (or the individual) will not put any discount on future income flows merely because they expect to be better off in the future. If $n = 1$, and if society (or the individual) expects to be 5 per cent better off in future, they will discount future income flows by 5 per cent for this reason.

The empirical estimation of the CRI is discussed in more detail in the second appendix to this chapter.

13.7.4 Problems with the shadow price of investment approach

A major problem with the shadow price of investment approach to determining the SDR in a distorted capital market is the empirical difficulty of reliably identifying the source of capital funds used to finance a project. The approach depends on having accurate data on the proportions of capital funds that will be drawn from consumption, increased savings, and investment, displaced potential public and private sector projects. However, in practice there is likely to be very little information on these issues available for the analyst of an individual project. If the project is funded from consolidated revenue, some of these funds would otherwise have been consumed by taxpayers and others would have been saved or invested. If the project's funds are raised from borrowing in the domestic capital market they will similarly come from a mix of reduced consumption and displaced investment. The proportion of funds coming from displaced investment would probably be higher in the case of capital raised in the capital market than in the case of capital supplied from consolidated tax revenue, at least that from personal income tax. However, to determine the exact proportions of project funds that will be drawn from savings and investment, the analyst would probably have to carry out an analysis similar to the Harberger, Sandmo and Dreze weighted cost of capital approach for each project undertaken.

While the weighted cost of capital approach assumes that the project is funded in the same way as other investments in the economy it does provide a rigorous method of calculating the sources of investment funds and their economic opportunity cost. The shadow price of investment approach leaves this for the project analyst to do on a case by case basis for each individual project, and without any specific guidance on how to undertake this task. This may be an unrealistically complex task in all but the simplest projects. As a consequence, analysts may be tempted to take short cuts that introduce significant biases. For example, all fixed capital costs of the project may be inflated by the SPI, on the assumption that such funds could otherwise have been used to finance another investment, even though they may have been paid for by new taxes on consumption. Labour costs on the other hand may be treated as though they will affect only consumption flows, even though the cost of such labour may be borne by the public sector investment budget, and could otherwise have been used on an alternative investment. There is really no justification for the analyst to make such assumptions.

The shadow price of investment approach also requires data regarding whether the project's output over its lifetime will result in increased consumption or increased investment. This may be very difficult for the analyst to determine, especially as such decisions will be made several years in the future. In fact, for any but the simplest project it may be a completely impossible task. For these reasons, the shadow price of investment approach, while theoretically correct, may be empirically difficult or even impossible to apply accurately. In seeking to make simplifying assumptions to make the approach useable, the analyst may make serious errors. Consequently, the Harberger approach, which provides a single weighted average cost of funds, is likely to be less open to incorrect application than the shadow price of investment approach and should be used in preference to it in most cases.

13.8 A comparison of the Marglin and LMST approaches to incorporating the investment premium

Little and Mirrlees (1974) and Squire and van der Tak (1975), abbreviated to LMST, used a variant of the Marglin approach to determine the SDR in a distorted capital market. However, the numeraire chosen by Little and Mirrlees and Squire and van der Tak was investable funds, or changes in investment flows, valued in border prices.[8] This approach employs the inverse of a comparable parameter to the SPI, the shadow price of public sector investment, v,[9] (where $\frac{1}{v} < 1$), to **deflate** less highly valued changes in streams of consumption caused by the project, so that they are comparable in value to changes in the more highly valued investment flows. This procedure has the same effect as that employed by Marglin. It makes changes in consumption streams caused by the project comparable to changes in the more highly valued investable funds by converting them both to a common numeraire, in this case investment flows.

Once converted into this numeraire, the project's cash flow can be discounted with the discount rate appropriate for future investment flows, which Squire and van der Tak called the accounting rate of interest (ARI). This SDR is essentially the adjusted MPC in the public sector. This is the appropriate discount rate at which to discount future investment flows, as it is the rate of return that can be made by the marginal investment in the economy. A more detailed discussion of the derivation and empirical estimation of the ARI and the LMST shadow price of public funds, v, is given in the second appendix to this chapter.

Table 13.3 The Marglin and LMST approaches to incorporating the investment premium ($ million)

		Approach	
	Unweighted	*Marglin (Numeraire — consumption)*	*LMST (Numeraire — investment)*
Undiscounted value of project's investment costs (yrs 1–3) drawn from:			
Investment	200	200 × SPI* = 400	200
Consumption	150	150	$\frac{150}{v} = 75$
Total	350	550	275
Undiscounted value of project's net benefits (years 4–20), distributed to:			
Investment	350	350 × SPI* = 700	350
Consumption	100	100	$\frac{100}{v} = 50$
Total	450	800	400
Undiscounted net benefits	100	+250	+125
Discount rate	–	CRI (SRTP)	ARI (MPC)

* *Shadow price of investment, SPI = v = 2*

The following simple example illustrates the differences in the Marglin and LMST approaches to incorporating the investment premium. Suppose that in its establishment phase, from years 1 to 3, a project costing a total of $350 million secures $200 million of these funds by displacing other potential investments and the other $150 million by extracting new savings from the community, and therefore reducing consumption. This example is shown in Table 13.3. Over the rest of its life, from years 4 to 20, $100 million of the discounted net benefits produced by the project will go to increased consumption, and $350 million to increased investment. The premium on investment is such that changes in investment are valued twice as highly as changes in consumption. That is, the shadow price of investment, SPI = v = 2.

Once the SPI (or v) has been used to convert the net benefit stream to the appropriate numeraire, consumption flows for the Marglin approach and investment flows for LMST, the cash flows are then discounted by the appropriate SDRs, the CRI and ARI, respectively.

13.9 The decision-maker approach to the social discount rate

A second and completely different way of resolving the dilemma of selecting an appropriate SDR is the decision-maker approach. The proponents of this approach maintain that individuals do not possess sufficient information to collectively make the choice regarding the level of the SDR through the capital market. They argue that value judgements are therefore unavoidable and that the SDR should simply be selected by governments. In doing so the government should chose a SDR that will optimally allocate output between consumption and investment and therefore optimise the long-run welfare of the community.

The first appendix to this chapter examines the problems of deducing individuals' preferences regarding the social marginal rate of time preference from their observable personal borrowing and lending behaviour — their individual marginal rates of time preference. There is also the ethical argument that the interests of future generations should be taken into account when determining the level of the social discount rate. Finally, there are the empirical problems of measuring the normative elements of the social discount rate, such as the term, n, the commitment of the government to egalitarianism and ρ the rate of pure time preference. However, this would not be a problem if the weighted cost of capital approach was used to determine the SDR.

The proponents of the decision-maker approach argue that someone has to determine what discount rate to use in project analysis and reliance cannot be placed on individual preferences regarding the social discount rate, as these are not known. Furthermore, the government may believe that individuals are too short-sighted and it is therefore their responsibility to represent the interests of future generations or to determine the overall growth rate, in line with their mandate.

If cost benefit analysis is consistently applied by governments to all potential investment projects, the choice of the social discount rate will have direct implications for the total size of the public investment program. The choice of a social discount rate will then have direct policy implications for the growth strategy of the country. The government may, for example, decide to opt for a high growth strategy and set the discount rate very low, as is the case in China. This may result in a large public investment program and the need to make significant sacrifices in current consumption. If the SDR selected is lower than the SRTP, the sacrifices demanded may prove politically unacceptable and a democratic government may be forced to raise the level of the SDR used. Using such an iterative approach, the government should ultimately settle on an optimal social discount rate, which is consistent with a politically acceptable level of public investment.

The decision-maker model believes that it provides pragmatic advice on the appropriate level of the social discount rate. Little and Mirrlees, for example, argue that the best guide to the social discount rate to use is experience. They point out that if the value of projects that have a positive net present value is greater than the investment funds available, this is indicative that the social discount rate should be raised. If the reverse is the case, the social discount rate should be lowered. According to this approach, the aim is to achieve long-term balance between the level of funds available and the level of public investment.

13.10 Conclusions

The decision-maker approach is, however, not really an economic solution to the determination of the SDR, but merely a bureaucratic and possibly a political one. The economic analyst should first attempt to determine the real social opportunity cost of public funds to the country concerned by objective means. If the country is able to borrow abroad freely, then the real cost of foreign borrowing, after adjusting for expected exchange rate movements, is the correct social discount rate to use. If the economy is less open and funds for the project must be drawn primarily from domestic sources, the SDR should preferably be estimated using the Harberger, Sandmo and Dreze weighted cost of capital approach. The Marglin (or LMST) shadow price of capital approach may be used for simple projects where the source of project funds and destination of project outputs (either investment or consumption flows) can be reliably identified. However, the Harberger approach, by providing a single weighted average cost of funds is likely to be less open to erroneous application than the Marglin (or LMST) approach and should therefore be used in preference to it in most instances.

If an objective measure of the SDR is available from such estimations but the value of acceptable public sector projects evaluated using this SDR is persistently greater than the government budget, the correct solution will usually be to raise more finance to implement these projects, rather than to raise the discount rate used, as the decision-maker approach would suggest. If, after applying this objective discount rate, the size of the resulting public sector investment program is too large or too small to be politically acceptable, the government may at this point decide to modify the SDR used to reflect popular preferences on the overall level of public investment and the rate of growth pursued. Alternatively, it may try to change public opinion by pointing out what it believes will be the optimal level of public investment for the economy.

The social discount rate and the shadow wage rate, SWR, are what Little and Mirrlees call the controlling shadow prices. Together they reflect basic government policy with regard to the relative size of the public sector, the distribution of GNP between consumption and investment, technology choice, employment levels and the preference for long or short gestating projects. It is therefore likely that it will be necessary to seek governmental guidance, or at least final approval, regarding the selected level of the SDR and SWR.

The complex nature of the estimation of the appropriate social discount rate indicates that there is a need for caution regarding the use of the rate that is eventually selected. One solution if there is great uncertainty regarding the appropriate discount rate to use is to calculate the project's internal rate of return, the discount rate that will just make the net present value of the project equal to zero. However, once the analyst has calculated the internal rate of return of the project the government decision-maker still has to determine whether this return is high enough or not, that is, what is the level of the target rate of return.

An alternative approach is to undertake a sensitivity analysis using a range of feasible real discount rates, possibly from 7 to 13 per cent, to calculate the project's NPV. If the project concerned has a positive net present value regardless of the social discount rate chosen within this range then it can safely be recommended for implementation. If the sign of the project's net present value is sensitive to the choice of social discount rate within this range, then further analysis of the correct social discount rate for the society should be undertaken. The use of sensitivity and probability analysis is discussed in Chapter 15.

Appendix 1
Review of the social discount rate debate — the social opportunity cost of capital versus the marginal rate of time preference

The debate that occurred in cost benefit analysis literature in the 1960s and 1970s was a result of a misunderstanding of the economic valuation of a good or service, in this case capital services, in a distorted market. As a consequence, two camps formed advocating two alternative candidates for the social discount rate. These proposed alternatives were nothing more than the demand and supply price of capital funds, respectively:

- The marginal productivity of capital in the private sector, MPC.
- The social marginal rate of time preference, SRTP, or the aggregated individual marginal rates of time preference, which reveal the average rate of return for which the community is willing to forgo current consumption.

1. The marginal productivity of capital approach

The proponents of this approach, sometimes called the consistency approach, argued that the appropriate rate at which to discount the cash flow from potential public sector projects was the rate of return that could be earned by the marginal private sector project. This is, they argued that the appropriate SDR was the rate of return at which private sector entrepreneurs considered a project to be just worthwhile doing. Writers like Mishan (1971), Hirschleifer, DeHaven and Milliman (1960) and Stockfisch (1969), and early work by Harberger (1972a) argued that if funds are being drawn away from the private sector to undertake public sector projects, the rate of return earned on the public projects should at least equal that on the marginal private sector project, which must now be forgone. Otherwise, they argued that it was easy to demonstrate that there would be welfare losses to the community and a squeezing out of private sector investments. Authors such as Mishan argued that even if some of the funds employed on the project were actually being drawn away from consumption, the government could always invest them in the private sector at the going marginal rate of return. It was argued therefore that the marginal productivity of capital in the private sector was the true opportunity cost of the investment resources available to the public sector.

For example, it was argued, that in the case of a country where the marginal productivity of capital in the private sector is 10 per cent, the government should not use a discount rate of only 7 per cent for its public sector projects. If it did so, then a project returning 9 per cent would be rejected by private entrepreneurs while one giving a lower return of 8 per cent would be accepted by the government. By taxing the private sector to fund public sector projects the country would, at the margin, be allocating resources to lower return activities and would thereby incur welfare losses.

Even if the return on capital in the private sector were the appropriate discount rate to use in public sector projects, two adjustments would have to be made before the marginal productivity of capital in the private sector could represent the demand price of capital:

(i) Taxation As a rule, public corporations do not pay tax. However, to achieve consistency in the allocation of resources between the private and public sector, the consistency approach would argue that the discount rate employed in the public sector should be the **pre-tax** rate of return of the marginal private sector project. Thus, if the marginal return after tax is 6 per cent and the company tax rate is 50 per cent, then the marginal return before tax will be 12 per cent. It was therefore argued that the public sector should proceed with a project only if it would allow them to pay company income tax and earn the same post-tax rate of return as the marginal private sector project.

(ii) Risk The second adjustment that should be made is to take account of the differences in the riskiness of private and public sector projects. If a private firm undertakes a project with some risk involved, its risk-averse shareholders will typically require a higher rate of return than if there were no risk involved in their investment (for example, if they invested in government bonds). Since virtually all project investments involve some risks, the existence of risk will tend to raise the level of the minimum acceptable return in the private sector above the government bond rate.

Arrow and Lind (1970) argued that public sector projects are not exposed to such risk. This is because there are so many public sector projects that the risk of failure by one particular project would be offset by other projects that were unexpectedly successful. In addition, they argued that there are so many tax-payers over which risks may be spread, that the expected value of losses from undertaking a large number of projects will be zero. The model they developed showed that the risk-free discount rate was the one that should be used to evaluate public sector projects. They therefore argued that the social discount rate should be lower than the risk-inclusive discount rates used in the private sector.

Hirschleifer (1965) disagreed with this view and argued that public sector discount rates should include a risk premium, otherwise, public sector investments would receive preference over private sector ones, and 'crowd them out'. This debate was obviously highly controversial because if the Arrow and Lind argument were accepted, it implied that the public sector would grow relative to the private sector. An alternative view put by Hirschleifer was that given the existence of risk, the government should subsidise private firms to undertake private investment.

Arrow and Lind accepted that their conclusion only held if returns to public sector projects were independent of swings in the business cycle, as these may adversely affect a large number of government projects making it impossible to offset losses incurred. Lind (1982) recognised that if this was not the case, the Hirschleifer results would be consistent with Arrow and Lind's theorems.

Problems with the consistency approach

(i) Lack of theoretical basis The major problem with the consistency approach is that while it is correct as far as it goes in recognising a relationship between the opportunity cost of capital and the demand price of capital in the private sector, it makes no reference to the social rate of time preference, or the supply price of capital. The government employing such a discount rate would merely try to make its investment decisions consistent with the private sector's, whether or not the combined investment of the public and private sector would then be at the optimum level.

In the 'UNIDO Guidelines' (UNIDO, 1972), Sen and Marglin show that it is only valid to use the marginal productivity of capital in the private sector as the social discount rate under the unrealistically restrictive assumption that private sector investment is at an optimal level. That is, the government must believe that growth levels are ideal. Certainly, this is rarely the case in either developed or developing countries.

Investment and growth will only be optimal when the marginal productivity of capital and the social rate of time preference are equal. This therefore implies that the marginal productivity of capital will only be the appropriate social discount rate when it equals the marginal rate of time preference, that is, when there are no distortions in the economy's capital market.

(ii) Invalid assumptions regarding the source of public sector funds It has also been pointed out that it is untrue that all funds used in public sector projects will be drawn away from private sector investment. Krutilla and Eckstein (1958) undertook empirical studies of the uses to which private individuals and firms would put reductions they received in their personal direct and indirect, and company, taxation. They found that in fact, only a small proportion (3.5 per cent) of the tax refunds received by corporations and high income earners' personal tax were spent on private sector investment. An even lower proportion of indirect tax and low income earner personal tax refunds were spent in this way.

The other fallacy in the consistency approach argument is the implicit assumption that all public sector investment program funds could be reinvested in the private sector without reducing the marginal return on private sector investment. The marginal productivity of private sector investment would obviously fall in these circumstances. This can be seen from Figure 13.2 where the reinvestment of all taxation revenue collected in the private sector would push the marginal productivity of capital in the private sector down from P_d to r_0. Hence, it would be incorrect to treat the existing marginal productivity of capital in the private sector as the opportunity cost of public sector investment.

2. The social rate of time preference approach

The major 'alternative candidate' for the social discount rate proposed in the historical literature on this topic was the social rate of time preference, or the supply price of capital. This approach is associated with Marglin (1963a, 1963b), Sen (1961, 1967), Arrow (1966) and Kay (1972), among others. Just as individuals have clear preferences about how they wish to allocate their consumption over time, so, it was argued, do whole societies. It was therefore maintained that it should be possible to estimate a social rate of time preference, as an aggregation of individual rates of marginal time preference, possibly after some adjustments reflecting imperfect knowledge by savers.

An individual's rate of time preference is the rate of return on future income for which he or she is just prepared to sacrifice current income. The social marginal rate of time preference is therefore the rate of return on future income for which the whole of society on average is just prepared to sacrifice current income. It was therefore argued that it was the logical choice for the discount rate to use in evaluating public sector projects.

Arrow (1966) and Kay (1972), for example, argued that the SDR should be merely the social rate of time preference. They developed a model based on the assumptions that public investment was financed only from taxation and that consumers' savings decisions were only responsive to income levels, not to interest rates.

As discussed in Chapter 4, which dealt with time preference, it is possible to observe individual marginal rates of time preference from people's borrowing and lending behaviour. If individuals have a marginal rate of time preference lower than the lending rate offered in the market, they will have an incentive to lend to the bank. The lenders will receive back more than they lend in present day dollars, discounted at their own personal discount rates. They will therefore have the opportunity to increase their welfare. Such individuals will keep lending until their marginal rate of time preference just equals the going rate paid on deposits.

Similarly, people who have a marginal rate of time preference higher than the current borrowing rate will have an incentive to borrow money up to the point where their personal marginal rates of time preference just equal the lending rate charged by the banks. It would be very convenient for cost benefit analysis if these observed net of tax market borrowing and lending rates could be used to calculate the social discount rate.

There are two different kinds of problems with this approach:

- Is the social marginal rate of time preference the appropriate social discount rate to use?
- Is it possible to derive the social marginal rate of time preference from individual's revealed marginal rate of time preference?

The social rate of time preference as the SDR

Just as was the case with the consistency approach, the major problem with the social rate of time preference approach is that while it is correct as far as it goes in recognising a relationship between the social discount rate and the supply price of capital in the private sector, it makes no reference to the opportunity cost of capital, or the demand price of capital. In a distorted capital market, the demand and supply price of capital funds will not be equal and hence the social discount rate will not be either one of these rates.

Derivation of the social rate of time preference from individual marginal time preference rates

Another problem with the social rate of time preference approach, which attracted much discussion in the literature, was whether it was correct to assume that private marginal time preference rates, as revealed in the market behaviour of private individuals, in fact truly reflect the relative valuation that society as a whole puts on the future flows of income from public projects. This potential divergence may have several sources.

(i)   Short-sightedness or irrationality of inter-temporal consumption decisions   Some writers, like Pigou (1932) and Eckstein (1961), believed that individuals are too shortsighted for their marginal rates of time preference, as revealed in market interest rates, to be used as the appropriate discount rate for public projects. Marglin (1963a, 1963b) and Sen (1961) also agreed that empirical studies of individuals' inter-temporal consumption choices showed irrationality. Too much is consumed in the present and too little saved for the future. This is because consumers at the age of 60 have no chance to learn from their life-time savings experience and return to their situation at 20 to reallocate their inter-temporal consumption. It was therefore argued that the market-revealed social rate of time preference is likely to be too high.

However, this argument, valid as it may be, does not fit with the neoclassical approach to the determination of the social discount rate. On the other hand, it may provide support for the legitimacy of the decision-maker approach.

(ii) Inter-generational transfers Public investment programs, which typically include long gestating physical and social infrastructure projects like dams, highways and educational institutions, involve the transfer of resources between generations. Some of the people who pay the taxes for projects may die and not receive the benefits, while others who may have been too young to pay taxes or not even have been born when the project was implemented, may receive its benefits.

The ethical problem is whether the preferences of the current generation should be the only determinant of the social discount rate used to evaluate these projects. The claim that it is the responsibility of the government to represent the interests of future generations has also been used to support the decision-maker approach to cost benefit analysis.

In any case, it is a matter for debate whether an individual's marginal rate of time preference, as revealed in the market, may not already reflect that individual's views about the desirability of saving for future generations. Individuals not only save to provide for themselves over their lifetime, but also for their heirs. To the extent that this is the case, their revealed marginal rate of time preference may take account of the interests of future generations.

(iii) The 'prisoner's dilemma' argument for a lower social discount rate This argument rests on the assertion that individuals might be prepared to save even more for future generations if they thought that other people would do the same. They may get utility from providing for future generations, quite apart from their own children, in the same way that people get utility from their government giving foreign aid or welfare assistance to the under-privileged in their own societies. They may in fact vote for a government committed to large-scale, long-gestating public investment programs, which they know that they and other tax-payers will be called on to finance. At the same time they may borrow at high interest rates to finance their own current consumption, for example with house mortgages or hire purchase agreements.

This apparent contradiction can be explained in terms of the so-called prisoner's dilemma or isolation paradox (Sen, 1967). An individual may in fact have a low marginal rate of time preference and prefer that the overall saving rate in the community is high and that a low social discount rate is used to assess public sector projects. However, the individual may not be prepared to make a sacrifice in her or his current consumption levels unless other consumers do likewise. Otherwise, their net effect on the saving rate would be insignificant in generating future growth. Acting in isolation from knowledge about other consumers' true inter-temporal preferences, the individual may seek to minimise his or her losses. Then, acting on the assumption that other consumers will not increase their savings, the individual may also decide not to increase her or his own saving. If all individuals behave in this way, savings may not in fact increase, even though a majority of individuals may have wanted them to rise.

To overcome this dilemma, people may vote for a government committed to a large public investment program. If this happens, it is argued, it would be wrong to use individuals' marginal rates of time preference, as revealed in the market, as a measure of the community's preferred social marginal rate of time preference. Once again, this argument has been used to support the decision-maker's approach to cost benefit analysis.

(iv) Divergence of individual's pre-tax and post-tax rates of marginal time preference
In order to estimate individuals' true marginal rate of time preference it is necessary that

these be measured net of taxes paid on interest earnings and tax deductions received on interest payments. However, this introduces serious empirical problems because in countries with progressive tax régimes the marginal tax rates paid by individuals will vary. Determining the weighted average of individuals' post-tax borrowing and lending rates is extremely complex and hence broad simplifying assumptions must be made.

APPENDIX 2
Empirical estimates of the consumption rate of interest, shadow price of investment, and accounting rate of interest

1. Empirical estimates of the consumption rate of interest, CRI

One approach to the estimation of the social rate of time preference and hence the CRI is that employed by Krutilla and Eckstein (1958). They estimated the weighted average of actual post-tax borrowing and lending rates in the USA in this study. This approach is compatible with the neoclassical approach to the determination of the social discount rate as it relies on the preferences of individuals as revealed by their borrowing and lending behaviour in the capital market, rather than the preferences of governments. Empirical estimates of the CRI are discussed further in Scott (1977) and also Squire and van der Tak (1975).

An alternative approach is to directly measure elements in the identity for the CRI given in (13.21):

$$i = ng + \rho q$$

The only element that can be objectively projected is g, the expected rate of growth of future per capita consumption. This may be determined using projections of GNP, population growth and savings determined by national statistical offices. These variables can also be projected using econometric techniques or various computable general equilibrium models.

Neither of the other two terms, n or ρ, can be measured with complete objectivity and subjective assessments must be made about these by the government. The rate of pure time preference, ρ, reflects the risk that future income streams will not eventuate and also the loss of utility from forgone consumption opportunities. It is usually set at a low level by governments who wish to promote a rapid rate of economic growth — somewhere between 0 and 5 per cent. The higher the government sets this term, the less it is willing to sacrifice current consumption for future growth.

One suggestion is that ρ should be set at the estimated number of annual deaths per 100 in the population, as some proxy of the risk that existing members of society will not be able to enjoy the benefits of a project. However, a society may well believe that the interests of future generations are just as important as those of the current generation. In this case there may be no justification for a positive rate of pure time preference for this reason. Even individuals may place little emphasis on this risk if they are interested in leaving an inheritance for their heirs.

The level of n, the elasticity of the parameter of the utility function (13.21), is characterised by Squire and van der Tak (1975) as the bias of the government towards egalitarianism. It represents the amount by which the government believes that the individual's marginal utility falls as her or his per capita income rises. Attempts have been made to empirically estimate the extent to which people's marginal utility declines as their income increases. This work has been done mainly in the context of estimating distributional weights, discussed in Chapter 14, in cross-sectional comparisons of people in different income groups.

The estimates may have less credibility when applied to inter-generational comparisons throughout a whole country over a period of 20–40 years. For example, a government like that of China may indicate that it has a strong commitment to the more equitable distribution of income within a given generation. On the other hand it may also wish to encourage high levels of saving and investment to promote more rapid growth. It may pursue this policy even though it may mean increased hardship for the current generation, which it could expect to be poorer than future generations.

Reference can be made to the progressiveness of the tax schedule in the host country as an indication of the commitment of the population and government to intra-generational (if not inter-generational) egalitarianism. Plausible values of n probably lie between 0.5 and 1.5. If n is believed to equal 0.5 and per capita consumption is expected to rise by 3 per cent per annum, then income accruing one year in the future will be perceived as 1.5 per cent less valuable than income accruing in the current period and the social rate of time preference will be 1.5 per cent plus the pure rate of time preference, ρ.

The authors of the 'UNIDO Guidelines' therefore claim that determining the level of the consumption rate of interest ultimately involves a value judgement. The only, unlikely, situation in which this will not be the case is if growth and investment levels are considered optimal and the consumption rate of interest equals the accounting rate of interest, or the marginal productivity of capital, which can be more objectively measured. This would only occur if there were no distortions in the capital market.

However, it should be possible to use data on market lending rates and personal tax rates to determine the weighted sum of individual MRTPs, if this is thought to be a reasonable guide to the SRTP. Such data could then be used to calculate a weighted cost of capital, as shown in the example in Section 13.6.

2. Empirical estimates of the shadow price of investment, SPI

The formula for the shadow price of investment was outlined in (13.20):

$$SPI = \frac{[(1 - s)q]}{(i - sq)}$$

Methods of estimating i, the marginal social rate of time preference, were discussed in Section 1. of this appendix. The derivation of q, the MPC, and, s, the rate of reinvestment, are discussed below.

The marginal productivity of capital, q
One approach to estimating q is to use microeconomic estimates of the average rate of return on private sector investment — the average pre-tax returns to the owners of capital. If this approach is used a number of factors need to be taken into account. It is necessary

to ensure that if several sources of capital are used by firms, the return on the investment is the weighted return on each of these. If nominal returns are estimated these must be deflated by the rate of inflation, to put them into real terms. Returns will need to be revalued in border price equivalents using the appropriate conversion factors, if the LMST numeraire of border prices is used, and in domestic prices if the UNIDO numeraire of domestic prices is used. Furthermore, microeconomic estimates of private sector rates of return on capital are average not marginal returns and will therefore exceed the latter by an unknown amount.

Finally, these micro-level estimates measure the return on private, not public, sector investment. It is the latter that is required in the case of the LMST formula for the shadow price of public funds. Little and Mirrlees (1974) suggest obtaining information about the level of the marginal productivity of capital in the public sector from the marginal return on projects already accepted by the government and expected returns on prospective projects being considered for the investment program. Ex-poste returns to recent World Bank or other multilateral banking institution projects in the country concerned, for example, may provide a measure of the return on public sector investments. However, governments are likely to choose the highest return projects for funding from such sources and such measures may be biased upward. In all cases, net benefits should be revalued in terms of economic prices. All of these microeconomic approaches are likely to lack rigour since, on average, existing public sector projects may have a return below the opportunity cost of public funds.

A preferable method of estimating the marginal productivity of capital, q, is to run econometric regressions to estimate the coefficients of an aggregate production function for the country involved, over a period of at least 20 years. Data on aggregate GNP can be regressed on labour, capital and material inputs data. Typically either time-series data on gross output is regressed on data on capital, labour, materials and energy inputs or, alternatively, net value added data is regressed on labour and capital input data. Estimation of the aggregate production function will enable the marginal productivity of capital to be accurately estimated separately from the marginal productivity of labour (and in the case of the gross output formulation, materials and energy) and the influence of technical progress. Either Cobb-Douglas or more flexible translog production functions can be estimated. For example, recent studies by Chen et al. (1988) and Perkins (1993) estimate that the marginal productivity of capital in Chinese industry is in the range of $0.42 - 0.45$.[10]

A quick, alternative method of determining a rough proxy for the marginal productivity of capital, which is used in some studies, is the inverse of the incremental capital output ratio of a country $\left(\dfrac{\Delta Q}{\Delta K} \right)$. If this approach is used, the increment in the national wage bill, $\Delta(wL)$, is usually deducted from output growth as some rough measure of the contribution of labour to increased output. The problem with this very approximate measure of marginal capital productivity is that it tends to subsume the contribution that other factors of production make to output growth into the contribution of capital. These include the contributions made by technical progress, human capital formation and even increases in the quality and quantity of material inputs. Furthermore, the adjusted inverse of the average incremental capital output ratio is in fact an annual incremental measure rather than a truly marginal measure of q. Such estimates should provide the upper limit of the true value of the marginal productivity of capital, q.

The rate of re-investment, s

Data on the marginal propensity to save, s, and consume, $1 - s$, from a unit increase in national income can be obtained from estimating the country's national consumption function. This can be done using long-term time-series data on national income and consumption provided by either national statistical offices or the IMF and World Bank.[11] The average savings rate varies from about 15 to 30 per cent for most countries, but could be expected to be lower than the marginal propensity to save from additional income, particularly in high growth countries.

3. The Little and Mirrlees, Squire and van der Tak (LMST) shadow price of public funds, *v*

The Squire and van der Tak shadow price of public funds, v, is basically equivalent to the 'UNIDO Guidelines' (UNIDO, 1972) shadow price of investment, SPI, except that v is given in terms of the Little and Mirrlees and Squire and van der Tak (LMST) numeraire — investment flows measured in terms of border prices. Squire and van der Tak (SVT) define their shadow price of public income, v, as follows. A unit of foreign exchange is allocated to a marginal investment in the public sector with the characteristics of a perpetuity. This produces a stream of future income at rate of return, q, equal to the marginal productivity of capital. If it is assumed that this income will accrue to individuals with an average level of consumption, this stream of consumption will have a value of $\frac{q}{b}$ valued in border prices, where **b** is the appropriate consumption conversion factor for this economy. Initially it is assumed that all of this increased income is consumed. The present value of the consumption stream generated by the unit of public investment is found by summing the discounted net benefit stream to infinity. Since all of this stream of earnings will be consumed, the appropriate rate used to discount it will be the social rate of time preference or consumption rate of interest, i, and its net present value will be:

$$v = \frac{q}{i\mathbf{b}} \tag{A2.1}$$

The shadow price of public investment, v, is defined by SVT as the marginal social value of uncommitted foreign exchange in the hands of the government, which could be freely invested in the public sector, W_g, relative to the marginal social value of private consumption accruing to the average income recipient, W_c, (that is, $\frac{W_g}{W_c}$). Similar adjustments can be made to v if the assumption that all output is consumed is relaxed, as were made to the Marglin SPI (Squire and van der Tak, 1975, Appendix, pp140–41).

4. Empirical estimates of the shadow price of public funds, *v*

Under the simplest assumptions (no reinvestment from the typical perpetuity) it was seen from equation (A2.1) that $v = \frac{q}{i\mathbf{b}}$. The empirical estimation of i and q is discussed in Sections 1 and 2 of this appendix, while the empirical valuation of **b** is discussed in the second appendix to Chapter 9.

5. The SDR used by the LMST approach, the accounting rate of interest, ARI

The LMST approach to determining the SDR in a distorted capital market is to convert all changes in the streams of consumption brought about by the project into their numeraire, investment streams, by dividing them by the shadow price of public investment, v. Once this has been done, a SDR called the accounting rate of interest, ARI, is used by LMST to discount this cash flow. In its simplest formulation, the ARI is the marginal productivity of capital in the economy, q.[12] This is the case when it is assumed that all the output from public sector projects is consumed. The marginal investment in an economy will produce a return in each period equal to the marginal productivity of capital in that economy. Investable funds available one period in the future are therefore less valuable than ones available in the present by an amount equal to this marginal productivity of capital. Since investable funds are the LMST numeraire, in terms of which all consumption and investment flows are revalued, the social discount rate appropriate for this approach is the accounting rate of interest. The accounting rate of interest is just the rate of fall over time of the LMST numeraire, the social value of investable funds.

Relaxing the assumption that all the net output of the project is consumed, the accounting rate of interest is the social rate of return on the marginal project in the public sector, after adjustments have been made to take account of the social impact of this investment. Squire and van der Tak (1975) define the accounting rate of interest as:

$$\text{ARI} = q - h \tag{A2.2}$$

where q is the return on the marginal public sector investment, the marginal productivity of capital in the public sector, and h is the distributional impact of public sector investment on the private sector. The latter term corrects for the institutional distortions in the trade régime and inequalities of income distribution.

The term h can be further defined as:

$$h = (1 - s)q\left(1 - \frac{d}{v\mathbf{b}}\right) \tag{A2.3}$$

where

   s is the rate of re-investment from public sector projects
   v is the shadow price of public sector investment
   q is the marginal productivity of capital at border prices
   d is the distributional weight attaching to the income group to which benefits are distributed
   $\mathbf{b}$ is the consumption conversion factor for the economy, which is employed to convert increases in consumption into border price equivalents.

Therefore, h is the value of the increase in private sector consumption generated as a result of the project, denominated in terms of the numeraire, and the ARI is:

$$\text{ARI} = sq + (1 - s)q\left(\frac{d}{v\mathbf{b}}\right) \tag{A2.4}$$

The first term represents the proportion of net output of the marginal project that is reinvested, s, at the marginal productivity of capital in the public sector, q. Squire and van der Tak anticipated that this would be the same as the marginal productivity of capital in the private sector. This term is already expressed in terms of the numeraire. The second term refers to the rate of consumption generated by the project and is derived by valuing the part of net output from the project that is consumed, $q(1 - s)$, in terms of the numeraire. This is done by deflating the rate of consumption generated, $q(1 - s)$, by the consumption conversion factor, **b**, and the shadow price of investment, v, and inflating it by the distributional weight, d, attributable to the group who benefit from this consumption.[13]

6. Empirical estimates of the ARI

Squire, Little and Durdag (1979) attempted to measure the ARI as the marginal return on public sector projects. Scott, MacArthur and Newbery (1976) use the cost of foreign borrowing as their approximate estimate of the ARI.

Using the Squire and van der Tak definition of the ARI given in equation (A2.4) necessitates estimating all the individual elements of the identity, q, s, v, **b** and d.

(i) The marginal productivity of capital, q The derivation of q, the marginal productivity of capital in the economy, is discussed in Section 2 of this appendix.

(ii) The rate of re-investment, s Data on the average incremental propensity to save, s, and consume $(1 - s)$ can be readily obtained from national statistical offices, as well as published IMF and World Bank statistics. Its derivation is also discussed in Section 2 of this appendix.

(iii) The consumption conversion factor, b The sources of empirical data for the consumption conversion factor are discussed in the second appendix to Chapter 9. They include household consumption surveys and the consumer price index formula as well as the tariff schedule and estimates of effective protection for various sectors.

(iv) Distributional weights, d The derivation of distributional weights, d, are discussed in Chapter 14, on the social analysis of projects.

(v) The shadow price of public funds, v The empirical estimation of v is discussed in Section 4 above.

7. Deviation of ARI from the marginal productivity of capital, q

The ARI will be lower than the MPC in the public (and private) sectors, q, and more public than private sector projects will be approved, if 'h', the social value of public sector investment, is positive. The term 'h' will be positive if $\frac{d}{v\mathbf{b}}$ is greater than unity, or $\frac{d}{\mathbf{b}} > v$. This is the extent to which the social value of consumption generated as a result of the public project, valued in terms of the LMST numeraire, $\frac{d}{\mathbf{b}}$, exceeds the social value of the lost public sector investment, v. If $\frac{d}{b} = v$, then additional consumption and investment have equal values, and the accounting rate of interest will equal q, the marginal productivity of capital in the public sector. If $\frac{d}{b} < v$, then the ARI will be greater than q, the marginal productivity of capital in the public sector. If $\frac{d}{b} > v$, then the ARI will be less than q.

For feasible values of the elements of the ARI, such as those given below:

$$q = 20\%$$
$$s = 25\%$$
$$d = 1$$
$$\mathbf{b} = 0.8$$
$$v = 1.3$$

ARI = 19 per cent. This is only slightly lower than the marginal productivity of capital, q.

Exercises

1. What will be the social rate of time preference in an economy where the expected growth rate of real per capita income is 3 per cent per annum, estimates of the average (and constant) elasticity of marginal utility with respect to per capita income is 0.9, and the rate of pure time preference is 2 per cent?

   If there are no distortions in the capital market, and the rate of growth is considered optimal, what will be the marginal productivity of capital in this economy?

2. A project is expected to draw 60 per cent of its capital requirements away from other investments, and 40 per cent from consumption by generating new saving. Of its net output over the life of the project, 20 per cent is expected to be available for re-investment, and 80 per cent will be consumed. Its investment costs will be $100 million spread over 4 years, and its net benefits of $12 million per annum will be enjoyed for 20 years after the project is completed.

   The real marginal productivity of capital in the economy is 28 per cent, the marginal propensity to save is 25 per cent, and the real rate of social time preference is 4 per cent. The consumption conversion factor is 0.8. Calculate the shadow price of investment if the consumption rate of interest in this economy is equal to the social rate of time preference. Then use the 'UNIDO Guidelines' approach to incorporating the investment premium and determine the NPV of the project.

3. If we assume that there are no savings in this economy and the consumption conversion factor is 0.8, calculate the accounting rate of interest. Use the LMST approach to incorporating the investment premium and estimate the NPV of the project.

4. Use the following data on the supply of and demand for capital in a country to determine its real social opportunity cost of capital. Use the methodology of the weighted cost of capital (see Section 13.6 for details of how to estimate the weighted SDR).

Suppliers of capital:

Group	Tax type	Marginal tax rate (%)	Elasticity of supply	Amount supplied ($L)
High income	Personal income	55.00	0.65	1850
Middle income	Personal income	40.00	0.45	985
Low income	Personal income	25.00	0.15	475
Foreign borrowers	Withholding tax	15.00	0.75	1250
Net govt saving	n.a.	0.00	0.00	450

Demanders of capital:

Sector	Tax or subsidy type	Marginal tax rate (%)	Elasticity of demand	Amount demanded ($L)
Manufacturing	Corporate tax	60.00	−0.85	1875
Mining	Business tax	35.00	−0.70	1186
Housing	Property tax	15.00	−0.40	879
	Subsidy on net of tax return	20.00	–	–
Fisheries	Subsidy on financial interest rate	30.00	0.60	1070

- The equilibrium nominal domestic market interest rate in the country is 18.00 per cent per annum.
- The average nominal cost foreign borrowings, AC_f, is 24 per cent per annum.
- The marginal cost of foreign borrowings,

$$MC_f = AC_f \times \left(1 + \frac{1}{\text{elasticity of supply of foreign borrowings}} \right).$$

- The expected rate of inflation in the country is 8.00 per cent over the next 20–30 years.
- The country's financial market is in equilibrium, so total savings = total investment.

References

Arrow, K.J., 1966. 'Discounting and public investment criteria' in Kneese and Smith (eds), *Water Research*, Resources for the Future, Baltimore.

Arrow, K.J. and Lind, R.C, 1970. 'Uncertainty and the evaluation of public investment decisions', *American Economic Review*, 60:364–78.

Chen, K.S et al., 1988. 'Productivity change in Chinese industry: 1953–1985', *Journal of Comparative Economics*, 12:570–91.

Dreze, J., 1974. 'Discount rates and public investment: a post scriptum', *Economica* **41**:52–61.

Eckstein, O., 1961. 'A survey of the theory of public investment criteria' in *Public Finances, Sources and Utilization*, NBER, Princeton University Press, Princeton, NJ.

Feldstein, M., 1964. 'The social time preference discount rate in cost benefit analysis', *Economic Journal*, Vol. 74, June, 360–79.

Harberger, A.C., 1972a. 'On discount rates for cost benefit analysis,' *Project Evaluation*, Macmillan, New York.

Harberger, A.C., 1972b. 'Professor Arrow on the social discount rate,' *Project Evaluation*, Macmillan, New York.

Hirschleifer, J., 1965. 'Investment decision under uncertainty: choice theoretic approaches', *Quarterly Journal of Economics*, 79 (4):509–36.

Hirschleifer, J., DeHaven, J.C. and Milliman, J.W., 1960. *Water Supply: Economics, Technology and Policy*, University of Chicago Press, Chicago.

Jenkins, G.P. and Harberger, A.C., 1991. *Manual — Cost Benefit Analysis of Investment Decisions*, Program on Investment Appraisal and Management, Harvard Institute for International Development, Cambridge, Mass.

Kay, J., 1972. 'Social discount rates', *Journal of Public Economics*, 1:359–78.

Krutilla, J.V. and Eckstein, O., 1958. *Multiple Purpose River Development*, Johns Hopkins University Press for Resources for the Future, Baltimore.

Lind, R.C, 1982. 'A primer on the major issues relating to the discount rate for evaluating energy options' in R.C. Lind (ed.), *Discounting for Time and Risk in Energy Policy*, Resources for the Future, Washington, DC.

Little, I.M.D. and Mirrlees, J.A., 1974. *Project Appraisal and Planning for Developing Countries*, Heinemann Educational Books, London.

Marglin, S., 1963a. 'The social rate of discount and the optimal rate of investment', *Quarterly Journal of Economics*, Feb, 95–111.

Marglin, S., 1963b. 'The opportunity cost of public funds', *Quarterly Journal of Economics*, May, 274–89.

Marglin, S., 1967. *Public Investment Criteria*, Allen and Unwin, London.

Mishan, E.J., 1971. *Cost Benefit Analysis*, Allen and Unwin, London.

Perkins, F.C., 1993. 'The impact of economic reform on productivity growth in Chinese industry: a comparative study of the Xiamen special economic zone', *Asian Economic Journal*, Vol. VII, 2:107–146.

Pigou, A.C., 1932. *The Economics of Welfare*, Macmillan, London.

Sandmo, A. and Dreze, J.H., 1971. 'Discount rates for public investments in closed and open economies', *Economica* Vol. 38, Nov, 396–412.

Scott, M.F.G., 1977. 'The test rate of discount and changes in base level income in the United Kingdom', *The Economic Journal*, 87:219–41.

Scott, M.F.G., MacArthur, J.D. and Newbery, D.M.G., 1976. *Project Appraisal in Practice; the Little and Mirrlees Method Applied in Kenya*, Heinemann Educational Books, London.

Sen, A.K., 1961. 'On optimising the rate of saving', *Economic Journal*, 71:479–496.

Sen, A.K., 1967. 'Isolation, assurance and the social discount rate', *Quarterly Journal of Economics*, 81:112–24.

Sjaastad, L.A. and Wisecarver, D.L., 1977. 'The social cost of public finance', in *Journal of Political Economy*, Vol. 85 June, 513–47.

Squire, L., Little, I.M.D. and Durdag, M., 1979. 'Shadow pricing and macroeconomic analysis: some illustrations from Pakistan', *The Pakistan Development Review*, Vol. XVIII, 90–112.

Squire, L., and van der Tak, H.G., 1975. *Economic Analysis of Projects*, Johns Hopkins University Press, Baltimore.

Stockfisch, J., 1969. 'The interest rate applicable to government investment projects' in H. Heinrichs and G. Taylor (eds), *Program Budgeting and Benefit-cost Analysis*, Pacific Palisades, California.

UNIDO, 1972. *Guidelines for Project Evaluation*, United Nations, New York.

Further reading

Dasgupta, A.K. and Pearce, D.W., 1972. *Cost-benefit Analysis — Theory and Practice*, Macmillan, London, Chapter 6.

Feldstein, M., 1964. 'The social time preference discount rate in cost benefit analysis', *Economic Journal*, Vol. 74, June, 260–79.

Jenkins, G.P. and Harberger, A.C., 1991. *Manual — Cost Benefit Analysis of Investment Decisions*, Program on Investment Appraisal and Management, Harvard Institute for International Development, Cambridge, Mass., Chapter 12.

Layard, R. (ed.), 1976. *Cost-benefit Analysis*, Penguin, Harmondsworth, Chapters 9–14.

Lind, R.C.,(ed.), 1982. *Discounting for Time and Risk in Energy Policy*, Resources for the Future, Washington DC, Chapters 1–3, 6,9.

Ray, A., 1984. *Cost Benefit Analysis - Issues and Methodologies*, Johns Hopkins Press for the World Bank, Baltimore, Chapter 5.

Squire, L., and van der Tak, H.G., 1975. *Economic Analysis of Projects*, Johns Hopkins University Press, Baltimore, Chapters 7 and 10, technical appendix.

Sugden, R. and Williams, A., 1978. *The Principles of Practical Cost Benefit Analyses*, Oxford University Press, Oxford, Chapter 15.

UNIDO, 1972. *Guidelines for Project Evaluation*, United Nations, New York, Chapters 13 and 14.

Endnotes

1   If a project developer has to pay high interest rates on loans to purchase capital equipment, this is also likely to discourage him from choosing capital intensive technologies.

2   They would therefore also have an internal rate of return greater than this SDR.

3   The total level of investment may not fall so much, however, if at least some government investment is financed out of the tax revenue collected.

4   They rejected the arguments of Arrow (1966) and Kay (1972) that the SDR should be merely the SRTP, as Dreze (1974) pointed out that this conclusion was based on the excessively simplistic and empirically unrealistic assumption that public investment was financed only from taxation, and that consumer savings decisions were only responsive to income levels, not to interest rates.

5   This approach is outlined in more detail in Jenkins and Harberger (1991), Chapter 12.

6   This example draws on Jenkins and Harberger (1991), Chapter 12.

7   Marglin's approach therefore entails valuing changes in current and future streams of investment and consumption caused by the project, in terms of a common numeraire. The numeraire used by the 'UNIDO Guidelines' is changes in consumption streams (valued in domestic prices); that is, all income changes caused by the project are valued as if they affect consumption. All project investment is valued as if it were financed by funds drawn away from consumption, and all project output is valued as if it were consumed. Any project inputs that are in fact drawn from investment, and any project output available for investment is identified and valued in terms of consumption flows, by multiplying them by the shadow price of investment.

8   LMST actually chose freely available foreign exchange in the public sector as their numeraire, but indicated that as this could be invested if the government chose, it was equivalent in value to investable funds.

9   The Squire and van der Tak shadow price of public funds, v, is basically equivalent to the 'UNIDO Guidelines' shadow price of investment, SPI, except that v is calculated in terms of the LMST numeraire — investment flows measured in terms of border prices.

10 Chen et al. indicated that the output elasticity of capital in Chinese industry was approximately 0.6, and the marginal productivity of capital was hence approximately 0.45. Perkins also estimated that the output elasticity of capital for China was approximately 0.6, and the marginal productivity of capital 0.42. These studies both found that constrained Cobb–Douglas production functions provided the best fit to China's industrial data.

11 Data on national income and consumption would be put in log form, so that the estimated coefficient on consumption would be the marginal propensity to consume $(1 - s)$. The marginal propensity to save, s, can then be simply estimated, $1 - (1 - s)$.

12 This is the case because if the net depreciation income available from the marginal project is all consumed, the marginal public sector project's return will be equivalent to an annuity, with the rate of return of q.

13 The issue of distributional weights is dealt with in Chapter 15.

CHAPTER 14
Social cost benefit analysis

14.1 The purpose of social cost benefit analysis

When undertaking financial or traditional economic project appraisals it is implicitly assumed that income distribution issues are beyond the concern of the project analyst or that the distribution of income in the country is considered appropriate. However, in many, if not most, developing and developed countries governments are not only interested in increasing efficiency but also in promoting greater equity. In most countries the existing distribution of income is clearly not considered to be ideal by the government or the population. Social cost benefit analysis or the social appraisal of projects has evolved to respond to this need. A simple example of a social appraisal of a project was given in Table 1.4 in Chapter 1.

A social appraisal of a project goes beyond an economic appraisal to determine which projects will increase welfare once their distributional impact is considered. The project analyst is not only concerned to determine the level of a projects' benefits and costs but also **who receives** the benefits and pays the costs. Social appraisal therefore tackles the moral and theoretical dilemma presented by the Hicks–Kaldor selection criterion — that a project is worth undertaking if it has the **potential** to produce a Pareto improvement in welfare.

In an economic analysis of a project it is implicitly assumed that a dollar received by any individual will increase the community's welfare by the same amount as a dollar received by any other individual. However, an extra dollar given to a very poor person, with an annual income of say only $US300, will usually increase that person's welfare by much more than would a dollar given to the same person if he or she became very rich, with an annual income of $US100 000. As a society we may be prepared to undertake a project, A, which increases the consumption of poor people by $100 per annum even if it reduces the consumption of rich people by $50. On the other hand, the community may not be prepared to undertake another project, B, which increases the consumption of the rich by $100 and reduces that of the poor by $50. The theoretical rationale in welfare economics for the social analysis of projects is therefore quite strong, as the marginal utility of income of a person who receives a low income is expected to be greater than the marginal utility of income of the same person if she or he receives a high income. An economic analysis of projects A and B would not capture these differences and would merely indicate that both had the same positive impact on community welfare.

14.2 Distributional weights

One of the most commonly used methods of undertaking a social cost benefit analysis is to introduce distributional weights into the cash flow. Distributional weights are attached to changes in income, costs and benefits, received by different income groups, ensuring that a project's impact on the income of low income groups receives a higher weight than the same dollar impact on the income of high income groups. The introduction of these distributional weights enables projects to be assessed on the basis of distributional as well as efficiency objectives.

14.2.1 The introduction of distributional weights into the cash flow

In an economic analysis, project generated changes in consumption enjoyed by all income groups are weighted at unity, $d = 1$. In a social analysis income accruing to (or being taken from) lower income groups would typically be given a distributional weight greater than one ($d > 1$). On the other hand, income accruing to (or being taken from) a high income group would be given a weight less than one ($d < 1$). A project that benefits a low income group would therefore have a higher **social** net present value than one that benefits a high income group, if all other, unweighted costs and benefits remain the same.

In the example shown in Table 14.1, the government of a country with a highly skewed income distribution is considering two mutually exclusive projects, A and B.

Table 14.1   The use of distributional weights in social analysis of projects ($L million)

	Project A		Project B	
	Poor	*Rich*	*Poor*	*Rich*
Cost paid by:	0	100	80	0
Benefits received by:	150	0	0	160
If distributional weights, *d*:	1	1	1	1
Economic NPV:	**+50**		**+80**	
Therefore do project B				
If distributional weights, *d*:	2	1	2	1
Cost paid by:	0	100	160	0
Benefits received by:	300	0	0	160
Social NPV:	**+200**		**0**	
Therefore do project A				

Project A's costs are borne by the rich and its benefits are received by the poor, while project B is the opposite. Its costs are borne by the poor and its benefits are received by the wealthy. Since the two projects are mutually exclusive the project with the highest NPV should be selected.

If an economic analysis were undertaken and distributional weights of unity were applied to the costs and benefits of the two projects, project B would have an NPV of $L80 and project A an NPV of $L50. Hence, project B should be selected. However, if the government decides that it values income going to the poor more highly than income going to the rich and applies a distributional weight of, for example, $d = 2$ to the low income group's income, project A would have a social NPV of $L200 and project B would have a social NPV of $L0. Project A would then be selected on the basis of a social cost benefit analysis.

14.2.2 Arguments for and against the use of distributional weights

There are several problems for analysts wishing to use this approach. The first is the difficulty of tracing the net income changes accruing to different income groups as a result of the project, even in the case of a relatively straightforward project. It may be very time consuming and expensive to identify who will bear the costs of a project, who will reap its benefits, and what the income levels of these different groups are. It has therefore been argued that the introduction of distributional issues into project appraisal will so increase the complexity of undertaking a cost benefit analysis that serious inaccuracies could become more common. This argument is very persuasive and may be conclusive for large projects with a diverse group of beneficiaries and whose income levels may be difficult to determine. The counter argument put by those supporting social analysis of projects is that, as distributional issues will be implicitly introduced into project analysis in any case, it is much better that they are treated in a consistent and rigorous way.

The second problem with the use of distributional weights relates to how the government or project analyst can objectively determine the appropriate set of weights to employ. Even if the distributional impacts of a large project can be traced, the marginal utility of income of these different groups may be very hard to determine. This determination of distributional weights is discussed in Sections 14.2.3 and 14.2.4.

Economists such as Harberger (1978) and Amin (1978) have opposed the formal inclusion of distributional objectives into cost benefit analysis. They claim that, by necessitating comparisons of the welfare that individuals receive from increasing their income by a fixed amount (say $1), social cost benefit analysis compromises the objectivity of project appraisal. Instead, Jenkins and Harberger (1991) recommend merely documenting which groups benefit and which lose from a project, leaving it to decision-makers to determine implicit, rather than explicit, distributional weights. This approach is discussed in Sections 14.4.1 and 14.4.2.

Supporters of social cost benefit analysis argue that failure to explicitly compare the utility received by different income groups within the framework of the project appraisal implies that the analyst gives equal weight to gains in consumption by all income groups, from the poorest and most destitute to the wealthiest groups in society. This would only be justified if it were assumed that the marginal utility of income, the change in utility experienced from a given increase in consumption, of all individuals was equal irrespective of their income levels.

Another argument advanced by those opposed to the introduction of distributional issues into cost benefit analysis is that projects should be selected in order to maximise national income and that the taxation and welfare systems should then be used to redistribute this income. This is a very reasonable and correct view in the case of the (mainly) developed, higher income countries, which have well developed fiscal and social welfare systems. In many developing countries, however, the fiscal system is weak and even regressive. Large proportions of the population, rich and poor, pay no tax at all and there are few social welfare payments. Corruption and the power of economic élites often ensure that the wealthy evade taxation and wield sufficient political power to prevent the emergence of governments committed to egalitarian fiscal policies. Marglin (1962) pointed out that in developed countries there may be political resistance to making direct transfers to target groups through the fiscal system. The only acceptable method of making transfers may be via public sector projects to provide social infrastructure, such as schools and hospitals or economic infrastructure, such as roads and irrigation facilities. If economy-wide mechanisms for promoting income redistribution are not available there may well be a justification for employing social appraisal of such projects.

In relation to distributional weights, Harberger (1978) points out that even if quite moderate distributional weights are employed, it would be possible to sanction acceptance of scandalously inefficient projects. For example, in Australia it may appear reasonable that changes in consumption enjoyed by families on an income of less than $A15 000 should be given an income distributional weight of 2, and consumption changes by those on an income of more than $A90 000 should be given a distributional weight of 0.5. However, this would imply that a project would be acceptable if it extracted $1 from the wealthy, which would then have a social value of $0.50 and gave only $0.25 to the poor, as the latter would then have a social value of $0.50 also. The use of such distributional weights could therefore result in projects being accepted that entail efficiency losses of 75 per cent of costs. Harberger argues that such inefficiency would be quite unacceptable to the electorate and he recommends that, if distributional weights are used, a caveat should be added limiting the extent of acceptable efficiency losses.

14.2.3 Methods of estimating appropriate distributional weights

Little and Mirrlees (1974) discussed consumption or distributional weights but it was left to Squire and van der Tak (1975) to fully work through a methodology for including distributional considerations into cost benefit analysis.

Their particular choice, among many possible alternatives, for the normalisation of the distributional weight, d, of a group in the society that receives a per capita consumption level of C, is:

$$d = \frac{\text{marginal utility of income at consumption level C}}{\text{marginal utility of income at the average consumption level}}$$

$$= \frac{MU_c}{MU_a} \qquad\qquad\qquad (14.1)$$

The marginal utility of income of a group in the society that receives a per capita consumption level of C, can be expressed as:

$$MU_c = C^{-n} \qquad\qquad\qquad (14.2)$$

This is the same parameter, n, used in the Squire and van der Tak consumption rate of interest formula in Chapter 13, equation (13.22). It can be thought of as a discretionary parameter, which is set according to the distributional objectives of the government and its bias towards egalitarianism. It represents the amount by which the government believes that an individual's marginal utility falls as his or her per capita income rises. The higher n is set, the more rapidly the marginal utility of income is assumed to decline as per capita consumption increases and therefore the greater is the apparent commitment of the government to egalitarianism. If n is set equal to zero the government has no commitment to egalitarianism.

Substituting (14.2) into (14.1), the distributional weight of the group with consumption level C can be defined as:

$$d = \frac{MU_c}{MU_a} = \left(\frac{C_a}{C}\right)^n \qquad\qquad\qquad (14.3)$$

where
> MU_c is the marginal utility of income of a group in the society that receives a per capita consumption level of C
> MU_a is the marginal utility of income of a group in the society that enjoys the average per capita consumption level
> C_a is the average per capita consumption
> C is the per capita consumption of the group concerned.

If $n = 0$, that is, all d are $= 1$, it implies that the government considers a one dollar addition to the consumption of one group in society will be equally valuable to a one dollar addition to the consumption of any other group.

If $n = 1$, $d = \dfrac{C_a}{C}$, then d equals the ratio of average per capita income in the economy to the per capita income of the group whose distributional weight is being assessed. If a target group has an income level that is only half the national average, the group's distributional weight would therefore be 2. Squire and van der Tak believe

$n = 1$ is possibly the right level for n, but levels of n between zero and 1 also imply a reasonable degree of commitment to egalitarianism.

If $n = 2$, it implies a very high commitment to egalitarianism by the government.

14.2.4 Determination of the level of n

The determination of the level of n, and therefore the set of distributional weights to use, will necessarily involve value judgements. Many methods have been attempted to increase the objectivity of the selection of distributional weights. One method is to ensure that value judgements involved are consistent with those embodied in other distributional policies, like the progressive tax schedule employed, or previous project selections when distributional issues have been important. If the tax schedule at the margin taxes high income earners 50 cents in the $1 and low income earners 25 cents in the $1, then the government is implying that it believes the sacrifice made by the two groups is equal. In this case, the ratio of these tax rates, 2:1, may be the appropriate ratio of the distributional weights of the two groups.

There are a number of problems with this approach, however. The income tax scale is not the only means by which income is redistributed. Indirect taxes on goods and services, like sales taxes and value added taxes, are in general much more regressive than direct taxation on income, and the direct taxation schedule may be used to correct for these regressive effects. The direct taxation schedule itself may not be the only means of doing this, because of the negative impact of a very progressive tax schedule on incentives. Transfer payments and social service provision are additional mechanisms for redistributing income and their impact on income redistribution must also be assessed when trying to form a consistent set of distributional weights.

It may be possible to determine average distributional weights that have been implicitly approved by the government by examining past project selection decisions where distributional issues were important. However, it would be necessary to examine a large sample of previous projects to obtain such information because it is doubtful whether distributional issues would have been treated in a consistent manner in such appraisals.

An alternative approach is to estimate the switching value of a particular distributional weight. This is the value of d that it would be necessary to place on income received by a target group, in order to make a project designed to assist them just worth doing. The government decision-maker can then decide whether he or she believes that this weight would be acceptable. The analyst should in any case always first undertake an economic analysis of alternative projects, without including any distributional weights, so that the decision-maker can clearly see what net benefits, if any, are being sacrificed in order to achieve a given redistribution of income.

The final possible approach is for the government decision-maker to merely formulate a set of distributional weights that he or she believes are in line with government policy. This approach is consistent with the decision-maker approach to the selection of a social discount rate. However, it is likely to lack rigour and may be highly subjective.

14.3 The Squire and van der Tak approach to social cost benefit analysis

The Squire and van der Tak definition of the net social benefits of a project integrates the efficiency and equity elements in cost benefit analysis (Squire and van der Tak, 1975). Assume that over its lifetime, a public sector project results in an increase in resources available to an economy of E. Of this total increase in resources C are consumed and $(E - C)$ are available for re-investment in the public sector. Total social net benefits of the project, S, will therefore be given by:

$$S = (E - C) + C \qquad (14.4)$$

To determine the cost to the economy of the increase in consumption in the first term, $(E - C)$ in terms of the Squire and van der Tak numeraire, freely investable funds held in foreign exchange, the consumption conversion factor **b** is used to revalue this consumption in border prices. To determine the **social** value of the increased resources generated by the project, the increase in public sector resources is weighted by W_g, the social welfare resulting from a marginal increase in public sector resources. The increase in private consumption is weighted by W_c, the social welfare resulting from a marginal increase in consumption (still denominated in domestic prices) by the group(s) benefiting from the project. Therefore, the total social net benefits of the project are given by:

$$S = (E - C\mathbf{b}) \times W_g + C \times W_c \qquad (14.5)$$

As W_g is the numeraire in the Squire and van der Tak approach, equation (14.5) is divided through by W_g, giving:

$$S = (E - C\mathbf{b}) + C \times \frac{W_c}{W_g} \qquad (14.6)$$

or $\qquad S = E - C\,(\mathbf{b} - \lambda) \qquad (14.7)$

where

$\qquad$ S are net social benefits
$\qquad$ C is the increase in consumption generated by the project
$\qquad$ E are net efficiency benefits
$\qquad$ $\lambda = \dfrac{W_c}{W_g} = \left(\dfrac{W_c}{W_{ca}}\right)\left(\dfrac{W_{ca}}{W_g}\right) = \dfrac{d}{v}$, the marginal social value of private sector
$\qquad$ consumption at income level C relative to the marginal social value of public investment
$\qquad$ **b** is the consumption conversion factor. That is:

Net social benefits	=	increase in real resources in the public sector	+	social welfare from increased private consumption

therefore:

Net social benefits = net efficiency   net social cost of
                         benefits   −   increased private
                                            consumption

To undertake a social cost benefit analysis, the analyst first calculates the project's net efficiency benefits, E, its net benefits before any distributional weights are attached. The net social costs of the project are then estimated as the cost to the economy of any increase in consumption accruing to different groups in the economy as a result of the project, bC, minus the social benefits derived from this consumption, $\frac{d}{v}C$. These net social costs (or benefits if the figure is negative) are then subtracted from (added to) the project's efficiency net benefits to determine the project's net social benefits.

The empirical estimation of v, the shadow price of investment, was discussed in the second appendix to Chapter 10. The analyst will also need to determine the distributional weights applicable to the target groups most affected by the project. In addition, it will be necessary to trace the project-induced changes in net income imposed on all groups with different distributional weights. Distributional as well as efficiency benefits of the project can then be estimated in a single framework to determine if the project is worth doing on equity, as well as efficiency grounds.

If $\frac{d}{v}$ > b, possibly because those benefitting from the project are in a low income target group with a high distributional weight, then the project's net social benefits will exceed its efficiency benefits. If $\frac{d}{v}$ < b then the project's social benefits will be less than its efficiency benefits.

14.3.1 Example of the Squire and van der Tak net social benefit approach

An irrigation project under consideration is expected to generate net efficiency benefits, or an economic NPV, E, of $L1 million. The project will increase consumption in the economy by $L600 000, half of which will go to low income farmers with a distributional weight of 2.5. The other half of the consumption generated will go to high income land owners, to whom the government has allocated a distributional weight of only 0.6. The consumption conversion factor for the economy, b, is 0.7, and the shadow price of investment, v, is 2.

Then the net social benefits of the project will be:

$$S = \$L1\,000\,000 - \$L600\,000 \left\{ 0.7 - \left[0.5 \times \left(\frac{2.5}{2} \right) + 0.5 \times \left(\frac{0.6}{2} \right) \right] \right\}$$

$$= \$L1\,000\,000 + \$L45\,000$$

$$= \$L1\,045\,000$$

The net social benefits of the project will therefore be slightly higher, by $L45 000, than its efficiency benefits in these circumstances. The social NPV of the project, $L1 045 000 will be slightly higher than its economic NPV, $L1 million, because at least half of the extra consumption it will generate is expected to be received by low income groups.

14.4 The Harberger and Jenkins approach to distributional issues in cost benefit analysis

As discussed previously, Harberger has argued strongly against the formal determination of distributional weights and the weighting of project-generated consumption flows. This is not only because of the ethical and empirical difficulties of estimating distributional weights but because of the inefficient project choices that this approach could sanction, Harberger (1968, 1974). As an alternative, Jenkins and Harberger (1991) recommend merely **tracing** the beneficiaries of the project, presenting details of the present value of their share of the project's net benefits and then leaving it to government decision-makers to decide if the project's re-distributive impact is appropriate or not.

In order to reveal the distributional impact of the project, once the project's economic NPV has been estimated using the appropriate social discount rate, SDR, it is decomposed into two parts:

$$NPV_{econ} = NPV_{fin(SDR)} + NPV_{ext(SDR)} \tag{14.8}$$

where $NPV_{fin(SDR)}$ represents the present value of the project's financial net benefits, discounted by the SDR, and $NPV_{ext(SDR)}$ represents the present value of the difference between the project's economic and financial NPV, if both were discounted using the SDR. This residual captures the **externalities** generated by a project. These include all of a project's indirect benefits (or costs) to an economy, which are therefore not accounted for by its direct financial net benefits.[1]

The first component of (14.8) can be further disaggregated by simply adding and subtracting $NPV_{fin(FDR)}$ to the right-hand side:

$$NPV_{econ} = NPV_{fin(FDR)} + (NPV_{fin(SDR)} - NPV_{fin(FDR)}) + NPV_{ext(SDR)} \tag{14.9}$$

where $NPV_{fin(FDR)}$ measures the present value of the project's financial net benefits discounted with the financial discount rate, FDR; that is, the financial NPV of the project.

The bracketed term $(NPV_{fin(SDR)} - NPV_{fin(FDR)})$ captures the difference between the present value of the project's financial net benefits, discounted by the SDR, and their present value discounted at the FDR. This is the project's effect on welfare if the financial rather than the economic discount rate is used in the economic analysis, that is, if the analyst fails to recognise the true cost of capital to the economy.

NPV$_{\text{ext(SDR)}}$ again represents the present value of the project's externalities, discounted at the social discount rate.

For example, if the real social discount rate is 6.4 per cent, and the real financial cost of funds to the implementing agency is 7.2 per cent, the NPV of the project's net benefits can be disaggregated:

$$NPV_{\text{econ}(6.4)} = NPV_{\text{fin}(6.4)} + NPV_{\text{ext}(6.4)}$$
$$= NPV_{\text{fin}(7.2)} + (NPV_{\text{fin}(6.4)} - NPV_{\text{fin}(7.2)}) + NPV_{\text{ext}(6.4)}$$

where

NPV$_{\text{fin}(7.2)}$ is the net financial benefit of the project to the implementing agency

$(NPV_{\text{fin}(6.4)} - NPV_{\text{fin}(7.2)})$ are the forgone externalities of investing capital in the rest of the economy rather than in the project (if too high a discount rate is used)

NPV$_{\text{ext}(6.4)}$ are the externalities generated by the project, or the net difference between the economic and financial prices of inputs and outputs.

The externalities represented by the last term on the right-hand side of the identity, NPV$_{\text{ext(SDR)}}$ can then be distributed across labour, government, consumers and other relevant groups, to show who gains and who loses from the project. This process will show the project's distributive impact. The types of externalities include the following major categories:

- Consumers obtain external benefits from the additional consumer surplus that the project generates. This is the difference between the financial benefits for which consumers actually pay and the total economic benefits that they receive.
- Labour receives external benefits in the form of gains in producer surplus as a result of the project. This may also include the difference between the wage paid by the project and the free market wage for the same category of labour.
- Governments derive external benefits from the project in the form of income tax, indirect taxes and tariff revenue and possibly other sources such as transfers from foreign donors.
- Finally, there is an external benefit or cost to the economy derived from the project's generation or expenditure of foreign exchange. If the local currency is overvalued, exporters will bear an external cost and importers will receive an external benefit.

The methodology for distributing the project's externalities is outlined in the following section.

14.4.1 An example of the Jenkins and Harberger approach to tracing distributional impacts

The Indonesian government is considering whether to undertake a project to install wells and sanitation facilities in rural villages and piped water in rural towns in one of its poorer regions. The major aim of the project is to improve access to clean water for drinking and household uses in order to raise living standards in the region. The government therefore needs to reassure itself that the major beneficiaries of the project will in fact be the village people using the wells, as well as establishing the project's economic NPV. The local water supply authority will charge households for piped water but the well water and sanitation facilities will be made available free of charge.

The distributional impact of the project is traced by first calculating the project's financial and economic cash flows. These are given in Tables 14.2 and 14.3. The financial cash flow of the project is then deduced from the economic cash flow, to create a third, residual table of the project's externalities, which is outlined in Table 14.4 .

Using the identity given in evaluation (14.9):

Economic NPV (@SDR) = financial NPV (@FDR) + [financial NPV (@SDR)
    – financial NPV (@FDR)] + NPV externalities (@SDR)
                                ($L million)

EcNPV (@ SDR)	FinNPV (@ SDR)	FinNPV (@ FDR)	Loss/gain SDR > FDR	NPV externalities (@ SDR)
(1)	(2)	(3)	(2) – (3)	(1) – (2)
46.251	(32.463)	(37.517)	5.054	78.714

The economic NPV of the project is $L46.25 million at the estimated real social discount rate of 11.3 per cent. The financial NPV of the project is minus $L37.52 million, at a real financial discount rate of 7.0 per cent. If the financial cash flow is discounted using the SDR, its present value is minus $L32.46 million. The net present value of the externality (in this case, welfare gain) as a result of the divergence between the financial and economic discount rate is given by:

$$(NPV_{fin(11.3)} - NPV_{fin(7)}) = \$L5.05 \text{ million}$$

The net present value of the externalities of the project were shown in equation (14.9) to be the difference between the project's economic NPV and the present value of the financial cash flow, discounted at the SDR:

$$NPV_{ext(11.3)} = NPV_{econ(11.3)} - NPV_{fin(7)} - (NPV_{fin(11.3)} + NPV_{fin(7)})$$
$$= NPV_{econ(11.3)} - NPV_{fin(11.3)}$$
$$= \$L78.71 \text{ million}$$

Each row in Table 14.4 represents a stream of externalities. The present value of each of these externalities is calculated by discounting them with the estimated real social discount rate, 11.3 per cent. These present values are given in the final column of Table 14.4. The project's positive and negative externalities can then be distributed between consumers of water in the villages, workers building the wells and the government, as shown in Table 14.5. This shows the project's distributive impact by indicating who gains and who loses from the project.

The present value of the time saving benefits received by villagers from the provision of well water over the life of the project was found to be $L32.5 million, while the benefits they enjoyed from the sanitation facilities were worth $L31.8

Table 14.2 Financial cash flow of water supply project ($L)

	Year				
	1	2	3	4	20
Capital costs					
Costs incurred in foreign exchange:					
Project management	682404	593282	566229	326638	0
Technical assistance	1357508	1205937	1257284	983961	0
Vehicles	304264	370233	178469	443242	0
Office accommodation	103806	148535	67777	73199	0
Materials for piped system	0	3547800	2554416	0	0
Other costs	4088	18606	20095	11035	0
Costs incurred in local currency ($L):					
Local staff, skilled	901880	1091597	1,649323	1955014	0
Local staff, unskilled	38640	69637	75960	82857	0
Materials for wells	0	189000	408240	514441	0
Materials for sanitation facilities	0	340502	1388016	1895867	0
Village labour for wells	0	95445	242871	301264	0
Village labour for sanitation facilities	0	287404	724615	1012997	0
Management and contracting for piped system	0	1769040	1273709	0	0
All other costs	231280	362578	571536	552359	0
Operating costs					
Costs incurred in local currency ($L):					
Maintenance piped systems	0	362103	857512	1492839	1492839
Maintenance — wells	0	10915	23576	38193	38193
TOTAL COSTS	3623870	10462612	11859626	9683907	1531032

	Year				
	1	2	3	4	20
Receipts ($L)					
Sanitation facilities	0	0	0	0	0
Value well water	0	0	0	0	0
Value piped water	0	303080	664571	850192	850192
TOTAL RECEIPTS	0	303080	664571	850192	850192
NET CASH FLOW	(3623870)	(10159533)	(11195055)	(8833715)	(680840)

Real financial discount rate: 7.0%
Real social discount rate: 11.3%

NPV (@FDR): $L(37516597)
NPV (@SDR): $L(32462639)

Figures in brackets indicate negative amounts
Source: author's calculations

Table 14.3   Economic cash flow of water supply project ($L)

			Year			
	CF*	1	2	3	4	20
Capital costs						
CF* Costs incurred in foreign exchange:						
Project management	1.05	716729	623124	594710	343068	0
Technical assistance	1.05	1425790	1266595	1320525	1033454	0
Vehicles	1.05	319477	388744	187392	465404	0
Office accommodation	1.05	108996	155961	71166	76859	0
Materials for piped systems	1.05	0	3725190	2682137	0	0
Other costs	1.05	4292	19537	21099	11587	0
Costs incurred in local currency ($L):						
Local staff, skilled	0.98	881838	1067340	1612671	1911569	0
Local staff, unskilled	0.68	26133	47097	51374	56038	0
Materials for wells	0.90	0	170100	367416	462997	0
Materials for sanitation facilities	0.90	0	306452	1249214	1706280	0
Village labour for wells	0.60	0	57267	145723	180759	0
Village labour for sanitation facilities	0.60	0	172443	434770	607799	0
Management and contracting	0.67	0	1179620	849326	0	0
All other costs	0.50	115640	181289	285768	276179	0
Operating costs						
Costs incurred in local currency ($L):						
Maintenance piped systems	0.67	0	241455	571801	995445	995445
Maintenance — wells	0.60	0	6549	14146	22916	22916
TOTAL COSTS		3598897	9608763	10459238	8150356	1018361

		Year			
	1	2	3	4	20
Benefits ($L)					
1.00 Sanitation facilities	0	1576800	3153600	5256000	5256000
1.00 Value well water	0	1469234	3205280	5387729	5387729
2.17 Value piped water	0	656275	1442119	2319634	2319634
TOTAL BENEFITS	0	3702309	7800999	12963362	12963362
NET CASH FLOW	(3598897)	(5906454)	(2658238)	4813006	11945001

Economic discount rate: 11.3%
Economic NPV: $L46250960

CF = Conversion factor
Figures in brackets indicate negative amounts
Source: author's calculations

Table 14.4   Residuals — externalities of water supply project ($L)

	Year				Present value
	1	2	3	4	
Externalities from project inputs					
Capital costs					
Costs incurred in foreign exchange:					
Project management	34325	29842	28481	16430	96400
Technical assistance	68282	60658	63241	49493	214425
Vehicles	15213	18512	8923	22162	57358
Office accommodation	5190	7427	3389	3660	17248
Materials for piped system	0	177390	127721	235857	235834
Other costs	204	930	1005	552	2205
Costs incurred in local currency ($L):					
Local staff, skilled	(20042)	(24258)	(36652)	(43445)	(111320)
Local staff, unskilled	(12507)	(22539)	(24586)	(26818)	(76839)
Materials for wells, cement	0	(18900)	(40824)	(51444)	(105719)
Materials for sanitation facilities	0	(34050)	(138802)	(189587)	(350,068)
Village labour for wells	0	(38178)	(97148)	(120505)	(240990)
Village labour for sanitation facilities	0	(114961)	(289845)	(405198)	(770360)
Management and contracting	0	(589420)	(424382)	0	(783613)
All other costs	(115640)	(181289)	(285768)	(276179)	(753390)
Operating costs					
Costs incurred in local currency ($L):					
Maintenance — piped systems	0	(120648)	(285711)	(497394)	(2979886)
Maintenance — wells	0	(4366)	(9430)	(15277)	(92533)
TOTAL EXTERNALITIES — from project costs	(24973)	(853850)	(1400389)	(1535551)	(5643050)

		Year			
	1	2	3	4	Present value
Externalities from project outputs — consumer surplus ($L)					
Value sanitation facilities	0	1576800	3153600	5256000	31829947
Value well water	0	1469234	3205280	5387729	32489108
Value water piped	0	353195	777548	1469242	8751494
TOTAL EXTERNALITIES — from project outputs	0	3399229	7136428	12112970	73070549
NET CASH FLOW	24973	4253079	8536817	13646721	78713600

NPV of externalities (@ SDR): $L78741673

Figures in brackets indicate negative amounts
Source: author's calculations

Table 14.5 Social analysis of water supply project ($L)

Distribution of externalities	Consumers	Labour	Government	Total
Piped water	8754707			
Well water	32500935			
Sanitation facilities	31841497			
Skilled labour		0		
Unskilled labour		76848		
Village		1011507		
Expatriate		0		
Income taxes (skilled labour)			111334	
Contract costs (piped systems)			3857234	
Tariffs — cement			455859	
Foreign exchange costs			(621734)	
All other costs			725412	
Total externalities	73097139	1088355	4528106	78713600

Figures in brackets indicate negative amounts
Source: author's estimations

million. Users of piped water also received external benefits of $L8.8 million, which represented the difference between the revenue they were expected to pay for the new water received and the estimated amount they would have been willing to pay, the listed tariff.

The unskilled and village labour on the project must be paid at the government fixed minimum wage, which is approximately double the unprotected sector wage for similar workers. As a result, together they received external benefits with a present value of $L1.09 million. The skilled labour and foreign technicians used on the project received salaries approximately equivalent to the unprotected labour market salaries for such categories of labour and therefore received no externalities from the project's operation.

The government received externalities with a net present value of $L0.11 million in income taxes on skilled labour and $L0.46 million from tariffs on imported items such as cement used in the project. In addition, externalities related to the financial value of the project's construction costs exceeding their economic costs resulted in a net transfer to the Indonesian government of $L3.86 million. All other externalities accruing to the government had a net present value of $L0.73 million.

The country also suffered a loss of welfare, negative externalities, of $L0.62 million due to the overvaluation of the domestic currency. This was due to the fact that the project used imported inputs to produce a non-traded good, water. The overvalued exchange rate resulted in the economic costs of these imported inputs being $L0.62 million greater than their financial costs.

14.5 Conclusions

In a situation where a project is only marginal from the point of view of an economic analysis but has strong positive distributional benefits, the analyst may consider undertaking either a Squire and van der Tak or a Jenkins and Harberger social analysis, in addition to the traditional economic analysis. The Jenkins and Harberger approach provides decision-makers with valuable information about the distribution of economic gains from a project. At the same time it avoids the need to make explicit judgements regarding the distributional weights that should attach to income flowing to different groups. The distributional weight approach results in a weighted NPV, which may make decision-making more straightforward. However, the extent to which the Squire and van der Tak approach is really of benefit to decision-makers will depend on the credibility attached to the distributional weights used. Furthermore, in all but the simplest of projects the empirical task of tracing the beneficiaries of a project and their income levels over its lifetime may prove very difficult. Consequently, the Jenkins and Harberger approach to determining the distributional impact of a project will usually not only be more empirically feasible but also a more credible guide to government decision-makers.

Exercises

1. The present value of the costs and benefits of two alternative projects under consideration will be borne by different income groups, as shown below:

| | Benefits received, costs borne by: | | |
($L million)	Rich	Poor	Total
Project			
Rural sanitation:			
Benefits	20	2000	2020
Costs	1500	50	1550
Airport:			
Benefits	2500	30	2530
Costs	1000	300	1300

The average income of the low income groups is half that of the high income groups. The government has a reasonably strong commitment to egalitarianism and it has been estimated from the taxation schedule and on the basis of past project selection decisions that the egalitarianism parameter, n, has a value of unity in this country. Calculate the distributional weights of the two income groups.

First compare the economic NPVs of two alternative projects and, using the distributional weights you have calculated, undertake a Squire and van der Tak social appraisal. The consumption conversion factor and shadow price of investment in the country are both equal to one.

2. A developed country is planning to build a new hospital. Eighty per cent of the patients will be low income people who will pay only $L5 to visit the doctor at the clinic. The benefit of providing each consultation is estimated to be $L50.

The remaining 20 per cent of patients have a higher income and will be required to pay an amount equal to the benefit of each consultation, $L50. The clinic will provide a total of 30 000 consultations per annum. The annual operating deficit of the clinic will be financed by a government grant.

The professional medical staff at the clinic are paid the market salary for such persons. The annual wage bill for skilled medical staff is $L150 000. However, the unskilled workers are paid at the government set minimum wage, which is 40 per cent higher than the unprotected market wage for such skill categories. The annual wage bill for unskilled workers is $L50 000 per annum.

The total investment in fixed assets to establish the clinic is $L1 million, spread over 3 years. Tariffs on imported medical equipment account for 20 per cent   of this total. Monopoly profits to the local construction contractor represent a further 10 per cent of the investment cost.

The clinic is expected to have a life of 25 years, and the real social discount rate in this country is 10 per cent.

Use a Harberger and Jenkins social distribution analysis to indicate which groups in the community the positive and negative externalities of this clinic project accrue to.

References

Amin, G.A., 1978. 'Project appraisal and income distributional weights in social cost benefit analysis', *World Development*, 6:139–52.

Harberger, A.C., 1978. 'On the use of distributional weights in social cost-benefit analysis', *Journal of Political Economy*, Vol. 86, Part 2, April, 87–120.

Harberger, A.C.,1984. 'Basic needs *versus* distributional weights in social cost benefit analysis', *Economic Development and Cultural Change*, Vol. 32, No. 3, April, 455–74.

Jenkins, G.P. and Harberger, A.C., 1991. 'Example of integrated, economic and distributive analysis', (Mimeo,) Harvard Institute of International Development, Harvard University, Cambridge Mass.

Little, I.M.D. and Mirrlees, J.A., 1974. *Project Appraisal and Planning for Developing Countries*, Heinemann Educational Books, London.

Marglin, S.A., 1962. 'Objectives of water resource development: a general statement' in A. Maase et al. (eds), *Design of Water Resource Systems*, Harvard University Press, Cambridge, Mass.

Squire, L. and van der Tak, H.G., 1975. *Economic Analysis of Projects*, Johns Hopkins University Press, Baltimore.

Further reading

Helmers, F., 1979. *Project Planning and Income Distribution*, Martinus Nijhoff Publishing, Amsterdam, Chapter 9.

Irvin, G., 1978. *Modern Cost-Benefit Methods*, Macmillan, London, Chapter 14.

Jenkins, G.P. and Harberger, A.C., 1991. *Manual — Cost Benefit Analysis of Investment Decisions*, Program on Investment Appraisal and Management, Harvard Institute for International Development, Cambridge, Mass.

Little, I.M.D. and Mirrlees, J.A., 1974. *Project Appraisal and Planning for Developing Countries*, Heinemann Educational Books, London, Chapter 13.

Ray, A., 1984. *Cost Benefit Analysis — Issues and Methodologies*, Johns Hopkins Press for the World Bank, Baltimore, Chapters 2–3, 6–7.

Squire, L. and van der Tak, H.G., 1975, *Economic Analysis of Projects*, Johns Hopkins University Press, Baltimore, Chapters 6–7, appendix.

Sugden, R. and Williams, A., 1978. *The Principles of Practical Cost Benefit Analyses*, Oxford University Press, Oxford, Chapter 14.

Endnote:

1   Jenkins, G.P. and Harberger, A.C. (1991). This is a broad definition of externalities including technological and pecuniary externalities such as consumer surplus.

CHAPTER 15

Handling risk and uncertainty in cost benefit analysis

15.1 Sources of uncertainty in project appraisal

Up to this point it has been assumed that project input and output prices and quantities are known with **certainty**, and can be included directly into the estimated cash flow of the project. In fact there may be considerable uncertainty regarding the estimated prices and quantities of major project inputs and outputs.

This uncertainty will have two major sources:

- Sources **internal** to the project, related to doubts regarding the technical or managerial capacity of the project to produce expected output levels using projected input levels.
- Sources **external** to the project, including movements in local and international price levels and the level of market demand for the project's output. These sources will be influenced by cyclical factors, changes in tastes and technological developments. Such influences are likely to be particularly important sources of uncertainty if the project's output will be exported or sold in an unprotected local market.

Uncertainty regarding the values of such crucial variables is likely to have a major impact on decision-makers' perceptions of the project's viability. The problem for the project analyst is how to handle such uncertainty within the rational framework provided by cost benefit analysis, so that it can be taken into account when selecting projects.

15.2 Handling quantifiable risk and uncertainty in project appraisal

In some projects it may be thought that the value of project variables are known with complete certainty. For example, the project's inputs and outputs may be bought and sold on the basis of long-term contracts or within a group of companies. In other situations, the project analyst may have little or no firm information about the future value of important variables, in which case she or he may operate under complete uncertainty.

Usually a project will fall somewhere in between these two extremes. There will be some knowledge on which to forecast future prices and quantities but these variables will not be known with certainty. When it is possible to assign numerical values to the probability that certain events will happen it is possible to handle the uncertainty associated with a project much more rigorously.

For example, the project analyst may be uncertain whether the sale price of aluminium produced by a project will be $1000, $2000 or $3000 a tonne. However, from historical time-series data on aluminium price movements, the analyst may be able to estimate that the probability of the price being at these levels is as outlined in Table 15.1.

Table 15.1   A simple probability distribution of aluminium prices

Price/tonne	Probability (%)
$L1000	20
$L2000	50
$L3000	30

If the analyst is able to assign values to the probability of various outcomes occurring, more rigorous methods of handling risk based on probability analysis can be used in project appraisal. These are considered first in Sections 15.3 to 15.5. If it is not possible to assign such probabilities, less satisfactory methods of dealing with uncertainty, such as sensitivity analysis and risk premiums must be employed. These are examined in Section 15.6.

15.3 Probability distributions

If values can be assigned to the probabilities of various outcomes, the project analyst can employ probability distributions in the cost benefit analysis. A probability distribution, $P(x)$, shows the various values, x_i, that a variable, x, may assume, accompanied by an indication of the probability that each value will occur, (p_i). A variable that has a probability distribution is defined as a variate.

The mean of the probability distribution, called the **expected value**, $E(x)$ of the variate is defined as:

$$E(x) = \sum p_i x_i \tag{15.1}$$

In the simple example given in Table 15.1, the expected value of aluminium prices, $E(x)$, is estimated in Table 15.2 to be $L2100 per tonne.

Once calculated, the expected value of the variate can be substituted into the project cash flow for the point values of project variables that have been used up to this point. A point value of a variable is one discrete value of a variable that is known

Table 15.2   The expected value of aluminium prices

Price/per tonne	Probability (%)	Price × probability
$L1000	20	200
$L2000	50	1000
$L3000	30	900
Total		2100

$\sum p_i x_i$ = expected value aluminium prices = $E(x)$ = $L2100 per tonne

with certainty, rather than a range of values that the variable may take, such as a probability distribution. The expected values of the project's inputs and outputs can be included in the project's cash flow to obtain the **expected value** of the NPV of the project.

There are various sources of data that can help the analyst to assign probabilities to the range of potential values of a variate. These include:

- extrapolation of historical trends
- experience with other similar projects in the same country or elsewhere
- game theory methods, including interviews of major players.

The other important parameter that should be estimated is a measure of the **dispersion** of the variate's values around their expected value. The variate's variance, standard deviation and coefficient of variation are all useful measures of dispersal of project parameters. Information on the dispersal of the NPV will show to the analyst how risky a project is, as it indicates the likelihood that the project will have a negative NPV.

The **variance** is defined as:

$$s^2 = \frac{\sum (X - X')^2}{(N - 1)} \qquad (15.2)$$

where

X' is the arithmetic mean of the sample of the variate, X; and
$N - 1$, the size of the population minus 1; $N - 1$ is used for small samples and N is used for large populations.

The **standard deviation**, s, is defined as the square root of s^2
The **coefficient of variation** is defined as:

$$\frac{s}{X'} = \frac{\text{standard deviation}}{\text{arithmetic mean of the sample population}} \qquad (15.3)$$

Projects will be perceived as being more risky the greater is the distribution of their input and output prices and quantities, and hence their NPV around their expected values. On the other hand, the closer the project's coefficient of variation is

Table 15.3 Probability distribution of the output levels of a plant ($L'000)

Output, Q_i	Probability of occurrence, P_i (%)	$Q_i \times P_i$
20	5	1
25	15	3.75
35	50	17.5
50	20	10
60	10	6
Sum = $E(Q_i)$ =		38.25

Expected value of output, $E(Q_i) = \sum Q_i \times P_i$

$\qquad\qquad\qquad = \$L38\ 250$

Variance, $s^2 = \sum \dfrac{(Q_i - Q')^2}{(N - 1)} = \$L282\ 580$

Standard error = s $\qquad = \$L16\ 810$

Coefficient of variation = $\dfrac{s}{Q'} = 0.44$

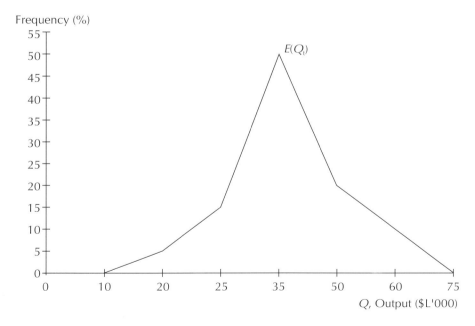

Figure 15.1 *Frequency distribution of the output level of a plant*

to zero the lower is the dispersal of the values of the variate around its expected value and the more likely it is that the expected value of the variate, $E(x)$, will be achieved.

For example, a project analyst may be uncertain about the exact nature of the output capacity of a plant planned for a project. However, after surveying the production levels of similar plants in operation in the country, she may find that the distribution of output levels is as given in Table 15.3.

The project analyst is then in a position to include the expected value of the output level into the project appraisal in the place of a point estimate of the output level. The probability distribution of the plant's output can also be mapped, as is shown in Figure 15.1.

15.4　Aggregation of probability distributions

15.4.1　Correlated variables

In any given project appraisal there may be several prices and quantities about which the analyst is uncertain. When estimating such a project's expected net present value and its probability distribution, it will be necessary to aggregate these probability distributions. In the case of correlated variables this is a relatively straightforward task.

For example, in the project illustrated in Table 15.4 the management of the enterprise is uncertain about the future demand for its clothing. In calculating the profits from the operation of the plant it will need to estimate the value of its inputs as well as the value of its output. However, input quantities will be dependent on the quantity of output demanded and hence total costs and total revenue will be correlated.

The managers of this project have found that even if output levels are $L100 000 or less, the value of inputs will remain at $L60 000 because of the level of fixed costs. As output values rise above $L100 000, input costs will rise proportionately. Consequently, the variates, revenue and costs, do not vary independently of each other. The joint probability distribution of these correlated variables is given in Table 15.4. The figures in brackets are the expected value of each variate.

Table 15.4　Joint distribution of correlated variables — garment factory ($L'000)

Frequency, F%	Input cost, TC_t	Output revenue, TR_t	Gross profit, π_t $(TR_t - TC_t)$
10	60 (6)	100 (10)	40 (4)
20	66 (13.2)	110 (22)	44 (8.8)
40	78 (31.2)	130 (52)	52 (20.8)
20	90 (18)	150 (30)	60 (12)
10	114 (11.4)	190 (19)	76 (7.6)
Expected value $\left(\sum F_t \times x_t\right)$	(79.8)	(133)	(53.2)

E (profits) = E (revenue) – E(costs) = $L53 200

The expected values of the project's total costs and total revenue can be found by multiplying the probability of occurrence of each value, F_t, by the values assumed by the respective variates, TC_t and TR_t. As these two variables are correlated the expected value of the firm's profit, π_t, can then be estimated as the difference between the expected value of output revenue, $L133\,000, and the expected value of operating costs, $L79\,800, that is, $L53\,200. The probability distribution of gross profit can also be graphed, as shown in Figure 15.2.

Frequency *(%)*

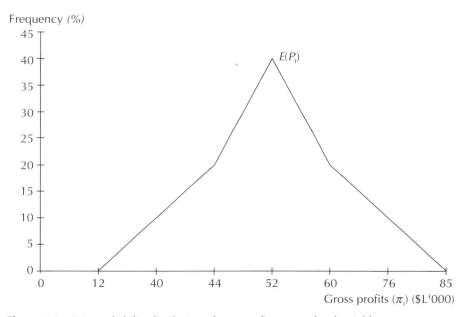

Gross profits (π_t) ($L'000)

Figure 15.2 *Joint probability distribution of gross profits — correlated variables*

15.4.2 Uncorrelated variables

Often it will be necessary to aggregate variates that have known probability distributions but are uncorrelated. This requires a more complex procedure. For example, the value of total revenue that would be earned by the steel plant could be disaggregated into the tonnage of steel produced and its average price per tonne.

$$TR_t = Q_t \times P_t$$

The price of steel is determined in the perfectly competitive world market and is independent of the quantity of steel produced by this plant. Similarly, we have been told that this enterprise will produce at its full production capacity given constraints due to power and raw material supplies irrespective of the price received for steel, over the expected range of prices considered. The probability distribution of the total revenue of this project is given in Table 15.5. The figures in brackets are the product of the value of the variate and its probability or frequency of occurrence. As

Table 15.5 Joint probability distribution of non-correlated variables — steel mill

Frequency, F_t (%) (1)	Output volume, Q_t ('000 tonnes) (2)	Price, P_t ($L'000) (3)	Frequency, F_t (%) (4)	Class intervals ($L m) (5)	Total revenue value, TR_t ($L m) (6)
10	10(1)	20 (2)	24	40–99 (70)	17
20	11(2.2)	15 (3)	44	100–159 (130)	57
40	13(5.2)	10 (4)	18	160–219 (190)	32
20	15(3.0)	7 (1.4)	8	220–279 (260)	26
10	19(1.9)	4 (4)	5	280–339 (310)	12
			1	340–400 (370)	4
Total	(13.3)	(14.4)	100		148

Expected value (total revenue) = $L149.4 million

the probabilities of obtaining different prices and producing various quantities of steel are quite independent, it implies that a price of $L20 000 per tonne of steel will only occur in 10 per cent of cases and in only 10 per cent of these cases will the output quantity be 10 000 tonnes.

The probability distribution of the steel mill's total revenue, TR_t, is established by multiplying all the values for P_t and Q_t pair-wise and regrouping them into the total revenue class intervals shown in the fifth column. The frequency with which total revenue falls within each class interval is determined by adding up the probabilities of all observations that fall in the particular interval. This is shown in the fourth column. The figures in the total revenue column (column six) are determined by multiplying the mid-point of each class interval (the bracketed figure in column five) by the estimated frequency with which total revenue falls within that class interval (column four). The expected value of total revenue, $E(TR_t)$, is determined by summing the expected total revenue figures in column six.[1]

As can be seen from Figure 15.3, the probability distribution of TR_t is almost normal. This is a characteristic of joint probability distributions of independent variables. This has implications for the distribution of the net present value of a project if we could assume that most variates entering the definition of net present value will be independent of each other. It implies that if a large number of independent variates enter into the estimation of the net present value, we could expect that the NPV's distribution would be normal, no matter what the shape of the distributions of the independent variates.

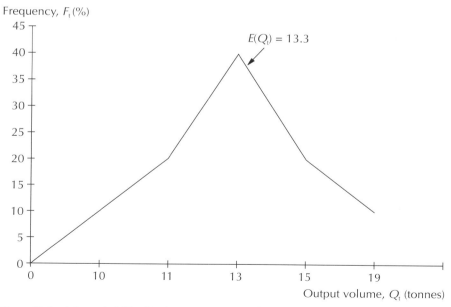

Figure 15.3 *Joint probability distribution — non-correlated variables*

15.5 Use of probability information in cost benefit analysis

The most satisfactory method of handling risk in cost benefit analysis is therefore to estimate the expected value and standard deviation of the project's net present value, $E(NPV)$, by aggregating distributional information about input and output variates that enter into the estimation of NPV. This is done using the techniques outlined above for correlated and non-correlated variables.

In the case of uncorrelated variables, this otherwise laborious process can now be handled by computer software packages like 'Riskmaster' (Savvides, 1989) and 'At Risk'. 'Riskmaster' is in fact just two large macros in Lotus 123. It enables probabilities, limits and relationships to be easily assigned to correlated and uncorrelated variates that enter the cash flow of the project. It then carries out a Monte Carlo simulation for a large number of random values of the variates that lie within the specified ranges and conform to the identified relationships between variables and the probability distributions of variates. Usually at least 200 simulation runs must be made, but higher numbers are preferable. The program then groups the values of the NPV estimated for each of these simulations into class intervals, much as was done mechanically in the example in Table 15.5. The resulting expected value of the project's NPV can then be estimated and its dispersal about this expected value determined and graphed in the form of a probability distribution.

15.6 The choice between risky projects — the gambler's indifference map

There may still be difficulty in handling risk systematically even when the expected values of projects' NPVs and their dispersals are known. This information does not always enable an analyst to choose between alternative projects, unless one is clearly superior to its alternative. A good example of this problem is given by the choice between two projects, A and B in Figure 15.4. The expected value of the NPV of project B, B', is higher than that of project A, A'. However, project B is also riskier than project A, as the projected distribution of its NPV about its expected value is greater than A's. There is even a risk that project B's NPV may be negative, which is not the case with project A.

Decision-makers cannot necessarily decide to choose the project with the highest expected value of net present value. This selection criterion ignores evidence about the different degrees of risk associated with projects, which is provided by the dispersal information. One method that has been developed to handle this problem is to estimate indifference curves for decision-makers, trading off risk as represented by the variance of the NPV, against the expected value of NPV. These indifference curves are called a 'gambler's' indifference map and are illustrated in Figure 15.5. They may provide a useful method of analysing information on both dispersion and expected values of NPV.

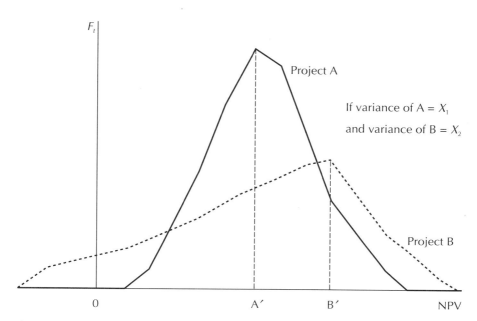

Figure 15.4 *The choice between two projects with different levels of risk and E(NPV)*

Information on the expected value of the NPV is given on the horizontal axis and the variance of various projects is given on the vertical axis. Any group of projects can then be represented on this map once the mean and variance of their NPV is known. Points on curve r_2 will be preferred to those on curve r_1. This is because on indifference curve r_2, for a given level of risk, X_1 (measured by the variance of NPV) the expected value of the NPV will be greater. Once the shape of the indifference curves r_0, r_1 and r_2 are known, it is possible to make a rational choice between projects of varying risk and expected net present value.

Using the example shown in Figure 15.4, a decision-maker with gambler's indifference maps as shown in figure 15.5, will prefer project A to project B. Project A's combination of risk and expected NPV falls on the more desirable indifference curve, r_2, because given the decision-maker's preferred trade-off between risk and expected NPV, the decision-maker would require project B's NPV to have an expected value of C to compensate for having to bear project B's higher risk, X_2.

Figure 15.6 shows that the more risk adverse the decision-maker, the flatter will be his or her indifference map curves. This is because for a small increase in the riskiness of the project, the risk adverse decision-maker will require a substantial increase in the project's expected NPV to feel equally well off. On the other hand, the indifference map curve of a risk lover, such as a gambler, will be quite steep. In this case, the decision-maker will require only a relatively small increase in the expected NPV of a project to compensate for a significant increase in the perceived riskiness of a project.

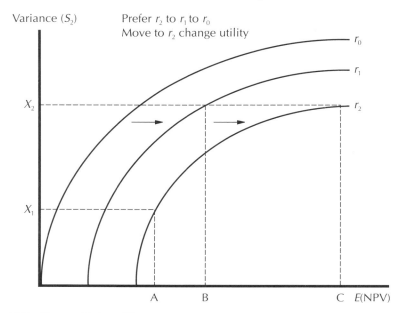

Figure 15.5   *The gambler's indifference map*

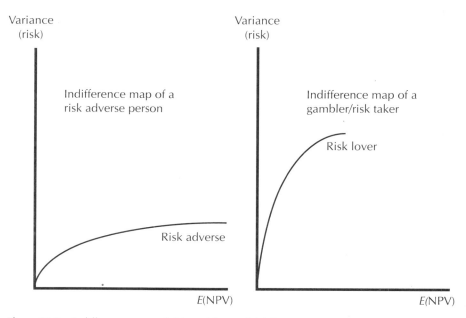

Figure 15.6   *Indifference maps of risk avoiders and risk lovers*

The main drawback of this method is that the formation of an indifference map of this nature is dependent on the decision-maker being able to conceptualise aversion to risk in this systematic form. The analyst may be able to assist in this process by devising games in which the decision-maker is helped to reveal preferences. In drawing up an indifference map of this nature, it would also be necessary to get a representative cross-section of views from all relevant government decision-makers to ensure that the constructed map reflected the true level of risk aversion of the government. Preferences regarding the trade-off between risk and expected NPV could also be judged ex-poste from past projects that have been accepted.

15.7 Handling pure uncertainty in cost benefit analysis

In some situations it may not be possible to ascribe numerical probabilities to various values of variables, such as input and output values. Many methods have been developed to handle such uncertainty in project appraisal, but none of them has been very satisfactory. Two common methods that will be examined here are the inclusion of a risk premium and sensitivity analysis.

15.7.1 Risk premia

This method of handling risk is used extensively in the private sector and merely entails adding a premium to the rate of return that must be earned by risky projects before they will be undertaken. Projects believed to be risky are therefore expected to achieve a higher rate of return than low risk projects. A higher discount rate is used to calculate the net present value of risky projects than is used to assess projects believed to be less risky. This has the effect of reducing the expected value of the riskier project's net present value.

One of the problems with this approach is that it will be very subjective unless empirical data is employed to determine how risky the project actually is and at what level the risk premium should be set. It is possible to obtain reasonably accurate data on the level of risk attached to investments in different industries from the average rates of return earned by firms in these industries, either in different countries or within the same country. Capital markets provide a good source of information on the level of risk premia.

One problem with risk premia is that their use implicitly assumes that risks increase the longer the project operates and therefore discriminates, probably unjustifiably, against long-gestating projects. In fact, most risk associated with projects is borne during the implementation and start-up phase due to cost and time over-runs.

15.7.2 Sensitivity analysis

A sensitivity analysis of a project simply entails varying key parameter values, singularly or in combination, to determine the impact of such manipulations on the project's net present value. This can be readily done using a program like Lotus 123 or Excel.

The variable that is most commonly varied in sensitivity analysis is the discount rate because of the considerable uncertainty that often attaches to the estimated rate. But total investment costs, implementation times, output levels and prices and operating costs are also commonly varied by amounts or percentages that seem reasonable on the basis of past experience. This is done in order to determine the sensitivity of the estimated NPV to changes in these variables. In some circumstances, a group of key variables may be varied together, to form a low case or high case scenario and the impact of these scenarios on the NPV may be measured to determine the robustness of the project under these circumstances.

The main problem with this approach is that variables are not usually varied by standard amounts, such as one standard deviation, because the probability distribution of the variable is frequently unknown. Rather variables are usually varied by randomly selected percentage values, such as 10 per cent or 20 per cent, etc. If the NPV of the project turns negative when relatively small and plausible changes are made in the values ascribed to such variables, it is an indication that the project may be rather marginal. If, despite testing quite large variations in the magnitude of various sensitive parameters, the project still has a positive NPV, it can be considered quite robust in the face of plausible risks.

An alternative approach that may be used is to calculate the level of a particular sensitive variable (or group of variables) that will just turn the project's NPV to zero — their **switching value**. The analyst will then have to decide whether this value (or set of values) could realistically occur. Figures can also be drawn showing the relationship between the project's NPV and various levels of sensitive project variables, to help decision-makers to understand the nature of risks confronted. This can also be handled by programs such as Riskmaster (Savvides, 1989).

The main use of sensitivity analysis is to identify which variables will have the greatest impact on explaining the level and dispersal of a project's net present value. Once these variables are identified, additional resources may then be devoted to determining more reliable point values or probability distributions for these sensitive variables so that a more thorough risk analysis can be carried out.

Exercises

1. Estimate the probability distribution and expected value of the NPV of a paper-making project if the correlated distribution of the present value of its costs and benefits are as given below:

	Probability				
	10%	*30%*	*40%*	*15%*	*5%*
PV costs	100	120	140	150	170
PV benefits	150	180	200	200	210

2. Calculate the probability distribution and expected value of the NPV of this project if the costs and benefits are **not** correlated. Group the estimated NPVs into class intervals and estimate their frequency.

3. Undertake a sensitivity analysis on the project described in exercise 4 at the end of Chapter 3, using discount rates of 7 per cent, 10 per cent 15 per cent. Graph the relationship between the discount rate chosen and the project's NPV.

Also estimate the project's NPV if:

- operating costs rise by 15 per cent
- investment costs rise by 20 per cent
- output prices fall by 25 per cent
- if all these events occur simultaneously.

References

Irvin, G., 1978. *Modern Cost-Benefit Methods*, Macmillan, London.

Savvides, S.C., 1989. *Riskmaster, version 1.1*, Nicosia.

Further reading

Arrow, K.J. and Lind, R.C., 1970. 'Uncertainty in the evaluation of public investment decisions', American *Economic Review*, 60:364-78, Reprinted in R. Layard (ed.), 1976, *Cost-Benefit Analysis*, Penguin, Harmondsworth.

Dasgupta, A.K. and Pearce, D.W., 1972. *Cost-Benefit Analysis-Theory and Practice*, Macmillan, London, Chapter 8.

Irvin, G., 1978. *Modern Cost-Benefit Methods*, Macmillan, London, Chapter 3.

Lind, R.C.,(ed.), 1982. 'Discounting for time and risk in energy policy', *Resources for the Future*, Chapter 6.

Overseas Development Administration, 1988. *Appraisal of Projects in Developing Countries*, HMSO, London, Chapter 6.

Pouliquen, L.Y., 1970. *Risk Analysis in Project Appraisal*, WB Staff Occasional Paper No.11.

Savvides, S.C., 1989. 'Risk analysis in investment appraisal', Harvard Institute for International Development, Development Discussion Paper, No. 276, Cambridge, Mass.

Sugden, R. and Williams, A., 1978. *The Principles of Practical Cost Benefit Analyses*, Oxford University Press, Oxford, Chapters 5, 12.

Endnote

1   This discussion draws on Irvin (1978).

Part Four

OVERVIEW AND CONCLUSIONS

CHAPTER 16

Overview and conclusions

16.1 Purpose of the text

This text is designed to provide professional practitioners and students with the tools to undertake financial and economic analyses of investment projects. Social cost benefit analysis was also examined briefly. These techniques can not only be used to determine the commercial viability and economic impact of alternative projects and programs but can also be employed to assess the impact on community welfare of other government policies and courses of action. Cost benefit analysis is likely to be particularly useful in assessing projects and policies where externalities and non-marketed goods are considered important. Examples of such policies may include programs to encourage the decentralisation of urban settlement, tariff liberalisation programs and the provision of job re-training schemes for unemployed people.

16.2 Financial analysis

Financial analysis was examined in the second part of the text, in particular in Chapters 2 and 3. Financial analysis is closely related to purely commercial project appraisals undertaken by private enterprises. When undertaking a financial appraisal the primary objective is to identify which projects will be financially viable to the implementing agency. These are projects for which the present value of benefits received by the implementing agency exceeds the present value of costs actually paid by them. All outputs and inputs including capital are therefore valued in terms of the market prices actually paid for them.

According to neoclassical theory, in a world of perfect competition, perfect information, no government and no public goods or externalities, the pursuit of private self interest and profit maximising behaviour would result in a Pareto optimal allocation of resources. Market prices would be set at market clearing levels and would equal the marginal utility that people gained from consuming these goods, their marginal social benefit, as well as the their marginal cost of production, their marginal social cost. Community welfare would therefore be optimised by the selection of projects on the basis of financial analysis alone.

The valuation of financial costs and benefits was considered, both in the absence and presence of distortions such as taxes and subsidies. Finally, the mechanics of constructing a cash flow, the project's stream of costs and benefits, were examined. This included the determination of project life and the setting out of fixed and working capital, operating costs, contingencies and revenue flows in a spreadsheet format.

16.3 Time preference and discounting

The concept of time preference was discussed in Chapter 4. The marginal rate of time preference is the rate of return on current income at which people will be just indifferent between receiving income now or in one period in the future. In a perfectly functioning capital market people will borrow and lend until they equate their marginal rate of time preference with the single market interest rate.

The concept of discounting is important for project appraisal because projects will usually produce a cash flow that stretches over several years. It will therefore be necessary to bring this cash flow into current value terms by discounting future income flows by some factor. As a first approximation, the marginal rate of time preference may provide a theoretically justifiable rate with which such discounting can be undertaken. In a financial analysis, the actual cost of capital to the implementors of a project should be used to discount the project's cash flow.

16.4 Choice of project selection criteria

The five major discounted measures of project worth were examined in Chapter 5; net present value, internal rate of return, domestic resource cost ratio, benefit cost ratio and net benefit investment ratio. All decision rules for the five measures collapsed to an identical relationship; if the present value of the project's benefits is greater than or equal to the present value of its costs then the project will be worth doing. In the case of mutually exclusive projects the project with the greatest net present value should be chosen. If there is a single-period budget constraint, those projects with the highest net benefit investment ratio should be undertaken until the budget is exhausted. Other measures cannot be used to rank independent projects.

16.5 Economic analysis of projects — cost benefit analysis

When they allocate resources, governments frequently wish to pursue broader objectives than merely the commercial profitability of their enterprises or investments. In general they will wish to promote community welfare in the broader sense.

Various possible government aims were considered within this broader objective, including:

- maximum growth in real per capita income or consumption for the current generation
- maximum rate of reinvestment so as to achieve more rapid rates of growth of consumption for future generations

- redistribution of income in a more egalitarian way between regions or different income or ethnic groups.

In a perfect, neoclassical world these objectives could be promoted merely by the free operation of markets and the allocation of resources on the basis of market-price signals. Projects could therefore be selected on the basis of financial appraisal criteria. However, this is made impossible by the widespread existence of goods and factor market imperfections, trade régime and domestic market intervention by government, imperfect knowledge, externalities and public goods, and the non-marginal nature of some large projects, resulting in changes in prices and hence consumer and producer surplus.

In the presence of these imperfections, the allocation of resources on the basis of market prices will not result in an optimisation of community welfare. This is because market prices will not necessarily reflect the marginal impact on consumers' welfare from consuming these goods nor the marginal social cost of their production.

In order to select projects that will optimise community welfare in these circumstances the first best solution will usually be to correct these market distortions. If this is not possible, it will be necessary to construct economic or shadow prices that do represent the marginal social benefits and costs of project outputs and inputs. An appraisal carried out using such economic prices will indicate the net impact of the project on community welfare. This is called a cost benefit analysis or an economic appraisal of a project.

16.6 Measurement of economic costs and benefits

Chapter 7 examined the method of measuring economic benefits and costs in markets in which there were no distortions and in ones in which there were distortions such as taxes, subsidies and price controls. It examined the concepts of consumer and producer surplus and transfers and their treatment in cost benefit analysis. The Harberger approach was employed to estimate the economic benefits and costs of projects in terms of the elasticity of demand and supply, market prices and any taxes or subsidies on project outputs and inputs.

16.7 Shadow pricing

The Harberger approach was also applied to the valuation of traded goods in Chapter 8. This examined the shadow pricing of traded goods on the basis of small and large country assumptions. Traded goods are valued at their marginal fob or cif price at the country's border, net of export taxes or import duties.

When a country is believed to have an overvalued exchange rate and the official exchange rate understates the true value put on foreign exchange, there is said to be a premium placed on foreign exchange. Thus, traded goods, when valued in border prices (net of tariffs) and converted into local currency at the official exchange rate, will be undervalued compared with non-traded goods, valued in domestic prices.

Chapter 9 dealt with the two alternative methods of incorporating a premium on foreign exchange. These were the approach developed by Little and Mirrlees (1974) and Squire and van der Tak (1975) called in this text the border price approach, and the approach developed in the 'UNIDO Guidelines' (UNIDO, 1972), called the domestic price approach. Traded goods are valued in border prices in both approaches, but in the border price approach these border prices are converted into local currency using the official exchange rate. Non-traded inputs and outputs are valued in their border price equivalents by using individual conversion factors. These are the ratio of the border price equivalent to the domestic price of the non-traded good concerned. Supply price conversion factors are derived by decomposing the non-traded good into its traded components, which are valued in border prices, and its residual non-produced, non-traded components such as labour, land and natural resources, which are valued in border price equivalents. If the domestic price approach is used to incorporate the foreign exchange premium, the value of traded goods is inflated by converting their border prices into local currency at the shadow exchange rate, which reflects the true value of foreign exchange to the country, and non-traded goods are valued in their domestic prices, adjusted for any distortions.

The shadow exchange rate, SER, can be approximated by the ratio of the value of trade in domestic prices, including the effect of tariffs and non-tariff barriers, to the value of trade in border prices, net of tariffs, etc. More sophisticated formulations of the shadow exchange rate were also examined, including that developed by Harberger (1972), Schydlowsky (1986) and Fontaine (1969). These attempted to capture the marginal nature of the estimation of the SER by including the elasticities of import and export supply and demand.

Chapter 10 discussed how labour is primarily shadow priced at its forgone marginal product — the loss of output elsewhere in the economy as a result of its use on the project. Adjustments may be made to capture the net social value of any increase in consumption made possible by the project and any decrease in leisure suffered. If there are freely operating labour markets, the wages paid in these unprotected labour markets should reflect the marginal social cost of employing labour.

Land and natural resources can also be valued at their market prices if the markets for these inputs are operating freely. If they are not, it may be necessary to calculate their marginal social value as the present value of the output produced using such land or natural resources, net of all other inputs used.

16.8 Externalities

The existence of externalities is another important reason why cost benefit analysis must be used to determine the true impact of a project on community welfare, and to help to allocate resources so as to maximise welfare.

Externalities are created when the operation or existence of a project results in a net gain or loss to society but not to those who implement the project. Consequently, this impact on welfare will not be reflected in the project's financial cash flow. If a project that creates externalities is evaluated using only a financial analysis, on the basis of the market price of its inputs and outputs, the analysis will fail to capture this external impact on community welfare. Various techniques for handling externalities were examined, including internalisation and direct valuation using methods such as direct valuation of the impact on private sector productivity and human capital and indirect measures such as hedonic pricing, travel time, replacement cost, and contingent valuation approaches.

16.9 Public goods

A comparable problem arises in the treatment of public goods, which are typically unmarketed and therefore priced at zero for efficiency reasons. A financial analysis of a project will not include the value of unmarketed public goods in the cash flow. However, the use of public goods does entail the use of an economy's resources and their production and consumption usually generates utility. It is therefore necessary to put a value on public goods that is as close as possible to their marginal social cost of production or their marginal social benefit in consumption. The method used to value them will depend on whether or not their supply can be readily expanded, in the case of project inputs, or they meet new demand, in the case of project outputs. Various methods of valuing public goods and social services were examined, several of which bore a close resemblance to methods used to value externalities.

16.10 The social discount rate

The social discount rate is the rate used to discount future project cash flows in the economic appraisal of a project. The choice of social discount rate is crucial in determining the overall size, average gestation period and capital intensity of a country's public works program.

In a perfect neoclassical world, with no government or capital market imperfections, there would be no difficulty in determining the social discount rate. It would be the equilibrium market interest rate at which the social rate of time preference, SRTP, equals the marginal productivity of capital, MPC, in the economy. However, in the presence of taxes on savers and investors, a premium will be placed on investment and growth will be sub-optimal. The market interest rate will no longer be the appropriate social discount rate and there will be no reason why the social discount rate should equal either the SRTP or the MPC, as these two rates will no longer be equal.

One solution to the problem of estimating the social discount rate in a distorted capital market was the approach adopted by Harberger (1972), Sandmo (1971) and Dreze — to estimate the weighted cost of capital. This was done using the same Harberger equation as was employed in relation to non-traded and traded commodities. The demand and supply price of investable funds, the MPC and SRTP respectively, were weighted with the elasticities of demand for and supply of investable funds. This approach is simpler to employ than the alternative one developed by Marglin and Feldstein.

Marglin and Feldstein's approach recognised that projects will typically produce changes in the net flow of both investable resources and consumption. The MPC will be the correct rate with which to discount future changes in the flows of investable resources, while the SRTP will be the correct discount rate with which to discount future changes in flows of consumption. Where these two flows are not valued equally by governments, it will be necessary to revalue them in terms of a common numeraire, either investment or consumption flows, so that they can then be aggregated. To do this a shadow price of investment is employed, which is equal in the simplest case to the ratio of the marginal productivity of capital to the SRTP.

In the 'UNIDO Guidelines' (Unido, 1972) consumption flows are chosen as the numeraire, so changes in the availability of investable resources caused by the project are inflated by multiplying them by the shadow price of investment. The resulting stream of consumption flows is then discounted by the consumption rate of interest, which is essentially the SRTP. Little and Mirrlees (1974) and Squire and van der Tak (1975) essentially adopt the Marglin and Feldstein approach, but investment flows are adopted as the numeraire. Changes in consumption streams caused by the project are deflated by the inverse of the shadow price of investment, $1/SPI = v$, to convert them into investment flow equivalents. They are then discounted by the accounting rate of interest, which is essentially the adjusted marginal productivity of capital. While theoretically correct the Marglin and Feldstein approach suffers from practical problems in implementation due to the difficulty of identifying the likely impact of a project on investment and consumption flows over its lifetime.

16.11 Social appraisal of projects

If the income distribution in a country is not considered optimal by the government it may wish to promote a more equitable distribution. Even if the highly restrictive assumptions of neoclassical theory are met, the allocation of resources or selection of projects either on the basis of market prices or shadow prices designed to correct for market imperfections will not help to achieve a more equitable distribution of income. One approach to overcoming this potential short-coming is to introduce income distribution weights into cost benefit analysis. These reflect the fact that the government values income transfers to certain disadvantaged groups more highly than transfers to average or high-income groups. Project appraisals that make use of such distributional weights are called social appraisals of projects, to distinguish them from project analysis based merely on efficiency criteria. The arguments for and against the introduction of distributional issues into cost benefit analysis and the use of distributional weights in particular were examined. The Squire and van der Tak formulation for calculating distributional weights and their definition of net social benefits of a project were also discussed.

An alternative approach to considering distributional issues, which was developed by Jenkins and Harberger, merely involves identifying how much particular groups benefit from a project. It is then left to the government decision-maker to determine if this distributional impact is appropriate.

16.12 Risk and uncertainty

Finally, ways in which risk and uncertainty can be handled in cost benefit analysis were considered. Quantifiable uncertainty can be handled by the estimation of probability distributions for the value of project outputs and inputs and the calculation of the expected value of the project's net present value and its variance, as a measure of project riskiness. Uncertainty can only be addressed by the less satisfactory methods of sensitivity analyses and risk premia.

16.13 Conclusions

The methodologies of financial and economic analyses can be applied to determine whether a wide range of public sector policies or projects, or private projects seeking government support, will make a positive contribution to community welfare. In undertaking an economic analysis the most serious distortions in an economy that are relevant to the project should be identified and corrected for first. More minor distortions can be corrected for if time and human resources permit. The approaches to shadow pricing presented in this text aim principally to be practical and readily applicable. Although some more complex approaches are also discussed, for example in relation to the estimation of the social discount rate and shadow exchange rate, it is recognised that the practitioner may often need to adopt simpler and approximate approaches. The recommended approaches to various issues in cost benefit analysis presented in this text try to strike a balance between accuracy and practical applicability.

Ultimately, the experienced practitioner will become a good judge of where this trade-off lies in her or his country.

References

Fontaine, E.R., 1969. 'El presio sombra de las divisions en la evaluacion social de projectos' (translation), Universad Catolica de Chile, Santiago.

Harberger, A.C., 1972. 'Professor Arrow on the discount rate', *Project Evaluation, Collected Papers*, Macmillan, N.Y., Chapter 5.

Little, I.M.D. and Mirrlees, J.A., 1974. *Project Appraisal and Planning for Developing Countries*, Heinemann Educational Books, London.

Sandmo, A. and Dreze J.H., 1971. 'Discount rates for public investments in closed and open economies', *Economica*, Vol. 38, Nov., 396–412.

Schydlowsky, D.M., 1968. 'On the choice of a shadow price for foreign exchange', *Economic Development Report*, No. 108, Development Advisory Service, Cambridge, Mass.

Squire, L. and van der Tak, H.G., 1975. *Economic Analysis of Projects*, Johns Hopkins University Press, Baltimore, Chapter 7.

UNIDO, 1972. *Guidelines for Project Evaluation*, United Nations, New York, Chapter 16.

Appendices

APPENDIX 1
Case study 1 — Rural water supply project

A low income developing economy has approached a donor country to provide rural areas of a backward province with clean water.

The donor first assessed the alternative technologies available for water supply and decided that wells were the most cost effective and sustainable method of supplying water to most villages, in terms of their average incremental cost.[1] Large piped systems had been installed in the past in this province, but had proved expensive to install, difficult to maintain and were subject to serious levels of illegal tapping, so that they frequently produced no water at all for many users for many hours of the day.

However, in a few towns, it was decided that small piped systems should be installed, tapping local water sources. In addition, the initial project design stage determined that investment in the rehabilitation of the existing large piped systems would yield a reasonable rate of return, so this was included as a component of the project. Finally, studies by health experts confirmed that the provision of rural water was unlikely have a significant impact in reducing gastric illnesses and skin diseases unless it was accompanied by the provision of sanitation facilities, such as public septic tank toilets and bathing facilities. Hence, these were included as a third component of the project. The project life is expected to be 20 years, including the implementation phase.

The project aims to install 5450 new wells in rural areas of the province. The new wells are expected to yield 30 litres of water per person per day, or 150 litres per household (average of 5 people). On average, each well will serve 24 households. Total per capita water consumption in the province is 22 litres per person per day, which is below the recommended daily minimum. Hence, it is expected that only 40 per cent of the water supply will be substituted for existing water sources, while the remaining 60 per cent will provide an increment in total supply.

The water from the rural wells will not be sold and therefore has zero financial value. The economic benefits obtained from the substituted water are the resources saved by villagers who no longer need to use less convenient, old wells, water holes or local streams. These resources are mainly the net time savings made by those responsible for collecting water, as water is not usually sold by water vendors in this province. Some of the resources saved from collecting water from the old sources must still be employed to collect it from the new ones. However, since there are no producers to be displaced when the supply 'price' (collection costs) of water falls as a result of the project, all of the gain in consumer surplus from this 'price' fall will represent an economic benefit of the project.

In relation to the newly available water, since the water from wells cannot be easily sold, people's willingness to pay for well water cannot be determined directly from market prices of the water. Hence, to determine the value placed on the newly available water, the time taken to collect this water is used as an indication of a minimum level of benefit received from water consumption.

To estimate the economic value of the newly available and substitute water, it is necessary to calculate the likely time savings and time spent (per cubic metre of water collected), and the opportunity cost of this time. Surveys of the likely savings from the location of new wells in the province were done. They found that, on average, households currently spend an hour a day collecting water and this would be cut by 30 minutes per day as a result of the project.

The value of this time can be deduced from data on the per capita income in the province, assuming there is no involuntary unemployment and people would either otherwise be working or voluntarily unemployed (resting) during this period. The average income of those collecting water (mainly adults) in the province is $L1712 per day, and it is assumed that people work on average an 8 hour day.

These time savings benefits do not include any measure of the improved water quality, which new and rehabilitated wells are expected to produce. Base line data is not available in the province against which to measure improvements in health as a result of previous water supply projects. However, in the past, rural communities in this province have been prepared to invest in rehabilitated wells, which produce no additional water, but do have better quality water. The cost of the water from these rehabilitated wells indicates that this minimum perceived health benefit may be at least $L70 per cubic metre of clean water, on top of the time savings benefits.

The project will involve rehabilitation of 10 piped networks in the province, and enable 3.1 million cubic metres of additional water to be sold per annum (1000 litres equal 1 cubic metre). It can be assumed that all of this water will meet new demand, and it is unlikely that this addition to the water supply will require a price fall to clear the market. The weighted average listed tariff of the local water supply authorities is $L594 per cubic metre ($m^3$). However, due to administrative problems of the water supply authorities (and possibly corruption), the actual revenue collected and declared by these authorities is only $L256 per m^3 of water supplied. This lower amount represents the financial benefit that the project could expect to generate per m^3 of water supplied. The economic benefit of the piped water may be considerably higher, as people may be willing to pay the listed tariffs for water. It is also possible that even the actual listed tariffs are unrealistically low and do not reflect people's true willingness to pay for piped water. However, in the absence of alternative information, it is assumed that the local water supply authorities have set tariffs close to people's willingness to pay for this water.

Some of the benefits from the supply of sanitation facilities will be hard to measure. There are many difficulties in the calculation of health benefits from sanitation supply projects. These problems are usually a result of the lack of reliable health statistics in many rural areas and the difficulty of isolating the health benefits generated by sanitation schemes. Despite the problems of estimating health benefits without baseline data, health benefits are very likely to be positive, and may be considerable. These are derived both from the increased quantity of water available for washing, reducing skin and eye diseases, and improved quality of drinking water reducing gastric and related diseases. Hence any measure of the benefits of water supply derived only from time savings will be the lower bound of the true measure of benefit obtained.

However, the sanitation facilities will also provide time saving benefits. Currently, people often walk long distances to rivers to wash, and into the surrounding forest to undertake toileting. The time savings from the convenient location of these facilities in the village are estimated by consultants to be at least 5 minutes per person per day. Approximately 800 000 people will be served by the sanitation facilities.

The main financial costs of the project are disaggregated into three parts, those incurred in:

- the installation of rural wells
- the provision of sanitation facilities (septic tank latrines and washing facilities)
- the rehabilitation of the large piped water networks.

This enables a separate analysis of each of the major components of the project. In each component, the costs should be listed separately depending on whether they are substantially:

- traded goods and services (costs incurred in foreign exchange), or
- non-traded goods and services (costs incurred in local currency).

The major traded goods and services are:

- the pipes and cement required to extend and rehabilitate the piped network
- cement for the wells and sanitation facilities
- the expatriate technical assistance (mainly engineers, but also project management, trainers and community and health experts)
- traded components of the contracting costs to rehabilitate piped systems, vehicles, office equipment and other minor costs including training material and water testing packs, which represent the remainder of the traded goods and services component of the project.

The major non-traded goods and services are:

- local skilled labour (employed as water technologists, community development officers and trainers)
- labour and materials supplied by the local contractors employed by the recipient government to rehabilitate the large piped networks
- unskilled labour used directly by the project
- unskilled labour provided by villagers to install wells and other facilities
- non-traded materials for wells and sanitation facilities, largely sand and gravel.

The financial costs of one rural well, rehabilitated piped system and sanitation facility (septic tank toilet and shower room) are given in Table A1.1. It is assumed that the operating costs related to each well, piped system and sanitation facility will begin from the year that each facility is completed.

Table A1.1   Unit costs of major project components ($L'000)

1. **Rural wells**	
Number of systems	5450
	Costs per system
Capital costs	
Costs incurred in foreign exchange:	
Project management	106
Technical assistance	183
Vehicles	70
Office accommodation and equipment	19
Other costs	1

Materials (cement)	256
Sub-total	635
Costs incurred in local currency ($L):	
Local staff — skilled	325
Local staff — unskilled	13
Materials (sand, gravel)	64
Village labour	193
All other costs	1609
Total	2839
Operating costs per annum	7

2. Piped system rehabilitation

Number of systems	10
	Costs per system
Capital costs	
Costs incurred in foreign exchange:	
Project management	22325
Technical assistance	179418
Vehicles	7999
Office accommodation and equipment	6979
Materials (pipes)	610222
Other costs	3764
Sub-total	830707
Costs incurred in local currency ($L):	
Local staff — skilled	31029
Local staff — unskilled	5892
Management and contracting	317315
All other costs	35057
Total	1220000
Operating costs per annum	45390

3. Sanitation facilities

Number of facilities	5450
	Costs per system
Capital costs	
Costs incurred in foreign exchange:	
Project management	314
Technical assistance	566
Vehicles	213
Office accommodation and equipment	54
Other costs	3
Materials (cement)	905
Sub-total	2055
Costs incurred in local currency:	
Local staff — skilled	1037
Local staff — unskilled	41
Materials	226

Village labour	623
All other costs	266
Total	4248
Operating costs per annum	20

The implementation schedule of the three components of the project is given in Table A1.2. As a simplifying assumption, all costs incurred are assumed to be strictly proportionate to these implementation schedules.

Table A1.2   Implementation schedule

	Number of facilities completed per annum					
	Year					
	1	*2*	*3*	*4*	*5*	*Total*
Rural wells	687	1028	1128	1236	1371	5450
Rehabilitation systems	0.7	5.1	3.7	0.3	0.2	10
Sanitation facilities	509	635	1187	1476	1643	5450

Of the total project costs, 70 per cent will be paid by the donor, 20 per cent by the recipient country government and 10 per cent by the community in the recipient country. Since this project is to be funded using grant aid there is no direct cost to the recipient government for the donor country's component. However, since such grant aid funds are limited and will usually be available for some other project in the same country if they are not spent on this project, they have a financial opportunity cost, which at the margin is equal to the recipient's long-term borrowing costs, domestically or abroad. Hence, the financial cost of funds to the recipient is the weighted sum of the long-term government bond rate of the recipient country and the cost of foreign borrowing to the recipient, where the weights equal the proportions of total recipient borrowing being raised from these sources. Virtually all of the recipient country's borrowing has been done overseas in the 1980s and early 1990s, and the World Bank projects that this trend will continue. The average real cost of these funds has been 6 per cent, but if the differential between recipient country and international inflation continues at approximately 4 per cent, the principal of this borrowing will also continue to rise by 4 per cent per annum in local currency.

To the recipient country community the cost of borrowing is equal to the average commercial lending rate in rural areas, which is approximately 30 per cent, in nominal terms. The inflation rate is expected to average 8.5 per cent a year over the life of the project.

There are several distortions in the recipient country's domestic goods and factor markets, the financial market and the trade régime, which create a divergence between the financial and economic prices of project inputs and outputs. Furthermore, many of the benefits of the project will be received only in the form of time savings, and not financial revenue. As a result, it will be necessary to undertake an economic appraisal of the project.

The donor costs include pipes and fittings supplied from the donor country, and consultancy and technical assistance costs. Checks on local recipient country and international pipe prices indicated that donor sourced pipe is priced at internationally competitive levels. Donor technical assistance consultancy rates are apparently also internationally competitive. Vehicles used by the project will be imported duty free, as will office equipment. However, accommodation rates are subject to some 'inflation', as they are fixed at the government's official contract rates. Hence, reflecting this domestic distortion, the conversion factor for accommodation and equipment is estimated to be 0.7. Approximately 50 per cent of this item consists of tradeables.

One major domestic cost item on which economic pricing is necessary is construction and installation costs. In the financial analysis, these are calculated on official recipient government contract rates. However, these are estimated by engineers on projects in the province to be double the free market rates for the work undertaken in these contracts. The contract rates incorporate official minimum wage rates for unskilled labour and government contract material costs (and some margin for payments to corrupt officials), and consequently are roughly double free market rates and prices. Hence, in the economic analysis, it is necessary to calculate a conversion factor to deflate these financial costs to their true economic value to the economy. The information to do this is included in Table A1.3.

Table A1.3 Economic value of local management and contracting costs $L('000)

	FV*	CF1**	Tariff rate (%)+
Skilled local labour	634630	0.98	0
Unskilled local labour	951945	0.68	0
Local materials	317315	0.50	0
Imported materials	475972	0.50	10
Hire of heavy equipment	793288	0.50	20

*FV is the financial cost of the input
**CF1 is the conversion factor to correct for local distortions in the market for skilled and unskilled labour, local and imported materials and heavy equipment employed directly by the project. The tariff rates must also be taken into account when estimating the border price equivalent of this non-traded good

In the local market for skilled workers there are apparently no major distortions. Hence the market wage costs of skilled workers (or 98 per cent of these) is also assumed to be their true economic cost to the country of the project's use of skilled labour. On the other hand, the presence of minimum wage legislation raises wages for unskilled workers in the formal sector so that the ratio of unprotected to formal sector wages for unskilled workers is 0.68. The conversion factor for all other local costs is assumed to be 0.5. Maintenance costs for the piped water systems are also likely to have the same components as the management and contracting component of the project. Hence the weighted conversion factor of this component of the project is used as the conversion factor for the piped systems' maintenance costs.

Cement is a major component of the materials cost of the project. It is a locally produced importable in the recipient country. The conversion factor for cement can be calculated from the information in Table A1.4.

The ratio of the market price of village labour to the official contract rates used in the financial analysis is 0.68. The conversion factor for other materials used in the construction

Table A1.4   Economic cost of cement (L'000)

	FV	CF1	Tariff (%)
CIF import price	166320	1.00	10
Freight saved	5000	0.80	0
Handling saved	2000	0.90	0
Trade margin saved	50	1.00	0
Freight	3000	0.7	0
Handling	1000	0.9	0

FV and CF1 are as defined for Table A1.3

of the village wells (sand, bamboo) is 1. The conversion factor correcting for local distortions in the maintenance costs of the village wells and sanitation facilities is 0.60.

The labour used in the project will spend its income in the manner outlined in Table A1.5. The tariffs applying to these goods are shown in the second column.

Table A1.5   Expenditure pattern of labour (per \$L1000)

	FV	Tariff (%)
Rice	300	20
Vegetables	100	10
Meat	100	20
Clothing	150	5
Housing	200	12
Other	150	5
Total	1000	

Simple estimates of the foreign exchange premium can be made from World Bank and GATT data on the border price value of imports, the value added component of exports, and the value of taxes on trade. The great bulk of these taxes are import duties as the level of export taxes and subsidies is not significant in the recipient country. Non-tariff barriers, NTBs, in the recipient country have approximately the same tariff equivalence as tariff barriers. Hence, the foreign exchange premium can be estimated as:

$$FEP = \frac{\text{value of taxes on trade} \quad + \text{tariff equivalent of NTBs}}{\text{value of imports} \quad + \text{exports at border prices}} \times 100\%$$

Import taxes gathered in the previous year were worth \$L968 billion, the tariff equivalent of non-tariff barriers is believed to be of a similar level, \$L1000 billion. The value of imports and exports in border prices are \$L16.4 billion and \$L21.8 billion, respectively.

The social opportunity cost of capital can be calculated using the Harberger formula. The weighted average elasticity of supply of savings in the recipient country is 1.12 and the weighted average real return on savings is 9.6 per cent. The weighted average elasticity of demand for investment funds is estimated to be −0.54 and the weighted average real marginal productivity of capital is 15.8 per cent. The ratio of investment to savings is 0.77.

The first of the major risks involved in this project is that it will not be possible to fully achieve the target of installing 5450 wells. There has been some slippage on the achievements of targets in the installation of wells in this province on previous projects. Similar under-achievements of water recovery targets is possible for the network piped system rehabilitation component of the project. Hence, in the sensitivity analysis the financial and economic viability of the project is determined if 20 per cent less water is produced from the well and the piped system rehabilitation components of the program.

The distributional analysis of the project breaks up the difference between the financial and economic NPV of the project into two components. These are the economic cost of using a financial rather than an economic (social) discount rate, and the value of externalities. The distribution of the externalities between villagers, the government and labour can also be shown.

Questions

1. Estimate the economic benefits of the well water, in terms of time savings and health benefits. Use Harberger-style diagrams to assist your estimation.
2. Estimate the financial and the economic benefits of the piped water.
3. Estimate the economic benefits of the sanitation facilities.
4. Set out the financial costs and benefits of the project over its 20 year life. Divide these into the project's three components (wells, piped system rehabilitation and sanitation facilities), as well as showing the total results for the project.
5. Estimate the financial discount rate appropriate for this project.
6. Estimate the financial NPV and IRR of the project. Estimate these for each of the project's three components as well as for the whole project.
7. Estimate the conversion factors of cement, and local management and contracting, using the border price approach.
8. Estimate the consumption conversion factor for labour used on the project, and indicate how this should be used in the analysis.
9. Estimate the shadow exchange rate of the recipient country.
10. Estimate the social discount rate of the recipient country.
11. Using the **border price approach**, undertake an economic analysis of the project, including all information given on conversion factors. Calculate the economic NPV and IRR. Estimate these for the project's three components as well as for the whole project.
12. Using the **domestic price approach**, undertake an economic analysis of the project. Calculate the economic NPV and IRR. Estimate these for the project's three components as well as for the whole project.
13. Undertake a sensitivity analysis, for the border price approach, taking account of the major risks identified.
14. Undertake a Harberger-style distributional analysis, for the border price approach results, first identifying the difference between the economic and financial NPV of the project, then splitting this into externalities and the effect of using the SDR, and finally, showing the distribution of the externalities.

Endnote

1   Wells of the type chosen for the project had been installed in an earlier project operated by the donor and proved to be quite cost effective. The method used to compare the cost efficiency of the different types of water supply technology was to calculate their average incremental cost, AIC. This is the ratio of the present value of the total costs of supplying water by each alternative technology, divided by the discounted volume of water supplied. For a fuller description of this methodology, see World Bank Staff Working Paper No. 259, 'Alternative concepts of marginal cost for public utility pricing: problems of application in the water supply sector', the World Bank, Washington, May 1977.

APPENDIX 2
Case study 2 — Waste treatment plant project

Project description

As a result of the introduction of new anti-pollution laws, industries in a developing country are required to treat their waste water so that it meets guidelines on acceptable biodegradable and non-biodegradable waste levels, before discharging it. As it would be technically difficult and expensive for industries, particularly the small ones, to comply with these regulations without assistance, the local government has decided to investigate the feasibility of establishing a waste water disposal plant to treat the effluent currently being discharged into a major local river. Industries would be charged for the service provided by the plant, which would enable them to meet their legal requirements under the new law.

The treatment plant project would have a 40 year life, including a 4 year construction

Table A2.1   Financial costs of water treatment plant project ($L '000)

Year	Project costs	Incremental operating costs	Incremental revenues	Net cash flow
1994	609			−609
1995	4847			−4847
1996	15757			−15757
1997	1001	862	2894	1031
1998		862	2894	2032
1999		862	2894	2032
2000		862	2894	2032
2001		862	2894	2032
2002		862	2894	2032
2003		862	2894	2032
2004		862	2894	2032
2005		862	2894	2032
2006		862	2894	2032
2007		862	2894	2032
2008		862	2894	2032
2009		862	2894	2032
2010	1275	862	2894	757
2011	5391	862	2894	−3359
2012		862	2894	2032
2013		862	2894	2032
2014		862	2894	2032
2015		862	2894	2032
2016		862	2894	2032
2017		862	2894	2032
2018		862	2894	2032

period starting in 1994. While civil works were expected to have a life of 40 years, electrical and mechanical equipment would have to be replaced in years 2010 and 2011.

A summary of the financial costs of the project are given in Table A2.1. Incremental operating costs and revenues for years 2019 to 2033 are the same as for year 2018. All costs are given in thousands of constant 1993 local dollars, $L.

Capital costs

Land for the plant will be provided by the local government authorities in the first year of the project, but is estimated to have a market value of $L200 000. The construction of the project will involve civil works costing $L250 000 in the first year and $L750 000 in both years 2 and 3 of the project. The pumping, settling and filtering equipment used will be imported at a financial cost of $L3 million in year 2 and $L10 million in year 3 of the project. This equipment is subject to a 20 per cent tariff, which is included in the financial costs quoted. Other equipment, including office equipment and vehicles, will have a financial cost of $L2 million in the 3rd year and $L200 000 in the 4th year of the project. These are also imported and subject to a 35 per cent tariff, which is included in the financial cost quoted.

Unskilled construction labour used on the project (apart from on civil works) will cost $L100 000 in year 2, $L400 000 in year 3 and $L100 000 in year 4 of the project. Skilled labour will cost $L50 000 in the first year, and $L200 000, $L400 000 and $L100 000 in years 2, 3 and 4 of the project, respectively. Working capital of $L50 000 will be accumulated in each of the second, third and fourth years of the project. The cost of foreign engineering consultants to advise on the installation of the pumping and filtration equipment will be $L500 000 in year 2 and $L1.5 million in year 3 of the project. The remainder of the capital costs of the project represent the management costs.

Of the total capital cost of installing new equipment, which will be required in 2010 and 2011, 10% will represent the cost of engineering consultants. It is expected that the same tariff rates, 20 per cent, will be imposed on the imported equipment, and these tariffs are therefore included in the quoted financial cost of the equipment.

In 2033, it is expected that the scrap value of the project's assets will be only 5 per cent of the cost of the equipment purchased in 2010 and 2011, and 10 per cent of the cost of the civil works. It is expected that the land's real value in 2033 will be double its 1994 value.

Operating costs

The project will be fully operational by year 4, 1997. Of the total annual incremental operating costs of $L862 000, unskilled labour will cost $L170 000, skilled labour $L230 000, fuel $L250 000, overheads $L80 000 and project management the remainder. The diesel fuel used is subject to a 30 per cent export tax.

Financial revenue

A charge of $L0.720/cubic metre of water treated will be levied on industries using the waste water treatment facility.

Cost of borrowing

The local government hopes to secure an Asian Development Bank loan for this project. If so, it will pay a concessional real interest rate of only 2 per cent per annum.

Economic analysis

There are a number of distortions in the factor, goods, foreign exchange and financial markets as well as in the trade regime of the country concerned. Furthermore, the project's economic benefits are expected to differ from its financial benefits. As a result, the government and the Asian Development Bank will require an economic analysis of the project to be undertaken.

Economic benefits

If the waste water plant were not established, the 70 local industries with access to the plant would be forced to install their own individual treatment facilities. The local authorities have estimated that the average capital cost of these individual facilities would be $L445 000. The break down of these capital costs (percentage spent on civil works, equipment, labour, etc.) would be the same as for the large treatment plant but the small plants would take only 1 year to install and there would be no need to replace equipment after 13 years. They would be constructed in 1996 and start operating in 1997. The scrap value of the small plants would be 5 per cent of their original investment cost. In addition, average operating costs would be $L16 000 per annum, with the components of operating costs being the same as those of the centralised plant. Since local industries would be willing to pay an amount up to the level that they will save by not having to provide their own treatment facilities, these savings will represent the direct economic benefit of the services of the centralised treatment facility.

Economic costs

Labour costs

Unskilled labour is in surplus supply in the region where the project will be located. This is due to the limited ability of agriculture to absorb more labour and the higher than equilibrium wages that must be paid in the formal sector as a result of government minimum wage regulations. Most of the project's labour will be drawn from agricultural employment, where wages in the unprotected rural labour market are 40 per cent lower than the project is required to pay. Most of these farmers would previously have produced grains. The sectoral conversion factor for grains has been estimated to be 0.75. However, it is estimated by demographers that every job offered in the formal sector results in 1.1 people immigrating from rural areas. Although it is not expected that the work on the project will be any harder than farming, the cost of living in the urban area is estimated to be 15 per cent higher than in rural areas. This will affect workers' valuation of the increased effort and presentation costs incurred in working on the project, λ, in the Squire and van der Tak SVT shadow wage rate formula.

Since the unskilled workers on the project are low income earners, the distributional weight attached by the government to changes in their income (d in the SVT shadow wage rate formula) is believed to be equal to the value it places on changes in investment expenditure in the country (v in the SVT shadow wage rate formula). The government's valuation of the increased effort and presentation costs incurred by workers, ϕ, relative to the workers' own valuation, λ, is equal to unity.

Skilled workers are 'in short supply' in the region, indicating that salaries offered by many employers, particularly in the public sector, may be below the level required to induce them to take up jobs in the region. The market salaries paid by the project are therefore set at a level expected to be near the equilibrium market clearing level for the skilled labour required, and a good measure (in domestic prices) of the output forgone by drawing skilled labour into the project. Most skilled workers will be drawn from the industrial and construction sector, which together have a weighted average sectoral conversion factor of 0.85.

The labour used in the project will spend its income in the manner outlined in Table A2.2. The tariffs (or export taxes) applying to these goods are shown in the second column.

Table A2.2   Expenditure pattern of labour (per $L1000)

	FV	Tariff (%)
Grains	420	(10)*
Other food	150	(16)*
Clothing	100	15
Consumer durables	50	30
Housing	220	4
Other	60	18
Total	1000	

* Figures in brackets represent export taxes. FV = financial value

The foreign engineering consultants and project's management are valued at the border price of employing these services in the country concerned. The conversion factor for overheads is the same as for skilled labour.

Civil works
The breakdown of the cost of the civil works on the project is as outlined in Table A2.3.

Table A2.3   Breakdown of civil works costs of project (%)

	Percentage of total costs	Percentage of tariff rate	CF*
Skilled labour	20	0	a**
Unskilled labour	10	0	b+
Local materials	25	0	0.85
Imported materials	15	10	
Hire of heavy equipment	30	20	

*CF = border price conversion factor
**a — employ estimate calculated in question 5
+b — employ estimate calculated in question 4

Foreign exchange premium

The exchange rate of the country is overvalued. There are high tariffs on imports, some export subsidies and a fixed exchange rate supported by exchange controls. The average tariff rate on imports is 17 per cent, while an average export subsidy of 3 per cent is paid on exports. Exports equal imports at $L20 billion per annum.

Land

If the land had not been used for the project it could have been used for a range of industrial, civic or residential uses. Since the land used is a rather small component of total project costs, and the potential output forgone by using it in the project is very heterogeneous, the standard conversion factor can be used to revalue the land in border prices.

Working capital

Since the working capital used by the project will be used to pay a proportion of operating costs, covering the project for the period between the payment of expenditures and the receipt of revenue, the weighted average conversion factor used to convert operating costs into border prices should also be used to revalue working capital in border prices.

Social discount rate

The economic cost of capital, the social discount rate in the country, can be estimated from the supply and demand elasticities of domestic and foreign lenders and domestic borrowers, each of which are subject to different tax and subsidy policies as outlined in Tables A2.4 and A2.5. In this country the market interest rate, MIR, is 22 per cent, and the inflation rate, f_e, is 8 per cent.

The estimated social discount rate can then be used to calculate the economic NPV and IRR of the project.

Questions

Answer all the following questions, show full workings for calculating conversion factors, and other shadow prices, as well as spread sheets used to calculate NPVs and IRRs. Use a parameters table to show all relevant information, and cell reference to the financial and economic spreadsheets.

1. Set out the financial cash flow of the project and estimate the financial internal rate of return, IRR, of the project.
2. Estimate the financial NPV of the project.
3. Estimate the financial cost savings of the local industries from not having to provide their own individual treatment facilities, and then convert these cost savings into border price equivalents (Hint: To convert the financial value of the cost savings into their border price equivalents, it is necessary to use the conversion factors estimated in questions 4–10. Show this calculation as an appendix at the bottom of the spreadsheet, referenced up to the parameters table, and then into the spreadsheets themselves.)
4. Estimate the consumption conversion factor for labour employed on the project and use it in the calculations of the shadow wage of labour.
5. Estimate the conversion factor for unskilled workers in border price equivalents, using the Squire and van der Tak formula.

Table A2.4 Suppliers of capital

Group	Type of tax	Marginal rate, t (%)	Elasticity of savings supply, λ_t	Savings supplied, S_t (SL billions)	Real net of tax SRTP, i'_i (formula)	i'_i	Share $\dfrac{S_i}{S_{total}}$	$i'_i \times \lambda_t \times \dfrac{S_i}{S_{total}}$	$\lambda i \times \dfrac{S_i}{S_{total}}$
High income	Personal income	40.00	0.65	700	$\dfrac{[MIR(1 - t_p) - f_e]}{1 + f_e}$				
Middle income	Personal income	22.00	0.20	200	$\dfrac{[MIR(1 - t_p) - f_e]}{1 + f_e}$				
Low income	Personal income	10.00	0.05	100	$\dfrac{[MIR(1 - t_p) - f_e]}{1 + f_e}$				
Foreign lenders	Withholding tax	25.00	5.00	6000	$\dfrac{\left[FIR(1 - t_w)\left(1 + \dfrac{1}{\lambda_f}\right) - f_e\right]}{(1 + f_e)}$				
Net govt saving	n.a.	0.00	0.00	1000					
Total				8000					

Notes:

MIR is the nominal market interest rate = 22%

FIR is the nominal foreign interest rate = 12%

λ_t is the elasticity of savings supply of lender i

t_p is personal tax

t_w is withholding tax

f_e is the rate of inflation = 8%

i'_i is the real net of tax SRTP

S_{total} is total savings

S_i is savings of lender i

For foreign borrowings, the marginal cost of funds is:

$$MC = AC \times \left(1 + \frac{1}{\lambda_i}\right), \text{ where:}$$

MC is marginal cost

AC is average cost

λ_i is elasticity of supply of foreign borrowings.

Table A2.5 Demanders of capital

Sector	Type of tax or subsidy demanded, I_i	Marginal tax rate (%)	Elasticity of demand, g_i	Investment ($L billion)	Real before tax return, on investment, q_i' (formula)	q_i'	Share $\dfrac{I_i}{I_{total}}$	$g_i \times q_i' \times \dfrac{I_i}{I_{total}}$	$g_i \times \dfrac{I_i}{I_{total}}$
Manufacturing	Corporate tax	29.00	−0.75	4000	$\dfrac{\left[\dfrac{MIR}{(1-t_c)} - f_e\right]}{(1+f_e)}$				
Mining	Business tax	35.00	−0.50	2500	$\dfrac{\left[\dfrac{MIR}{(1-t_c)} - f_e\right]}{(1+f_e)}$				
Housing	Property tax	25.00	−0.40	1000	$\dfrac{\left[\dfrac{MIR}{(1+s)} + R - f_e\right]}{(1+f_e)}$				
Fisheries	Subsidy on net of tax return	15.00	−0.70	500	$\dfrac{\left[\dfrac{MIR}{(1+s)} - f_e\right]}{(1+f_e)}$				
Total				8000					

Notes:

MIR is the market interest rate = 18%

g_i is elasticity of demand of investor j for investable funds

q_i' is the real marginal gross of tax return on investment

t_c is company tax

f_e is the rate of inflation = 8 per cent over the next 20–30 years

I_j is investment demand of the jth borrower

I_{total} is total investment

s is rate of subsidy

R is property tax, expressed as a proportion of total investment $= AC_r \times \left[1 + \left(\dfrac{1}{\text{elasticity of supply of foreign borrowings}}\right)\right]$

The country's financial market is in equilibrium.'

6. Estimate the conversion factor for skilled workers, in border price equivalents, using the Squire and van der Tak formula.
7. Estimate the border price conversion factor for civil works. Employ it in the economic analysis to revalue civil works in border price equivalents.
8. Use a simple 'UNIDO Guidelines' approach formula to calculate the foreign exchange premium, and standard conversion factor for the country.
9. Estimate the border price of land used in the project.
10. Calculate the weighted average border price conversion factor for operating costs.
11. Use the Sandmo and Dreze, and Harberger formula to estimate the weighted social discount rate in a distorted capital market for the country where the project is located.
12. Use all the calculated conversion factors and information about border prices provided to set out the economic cash flow of the project. Then estimate the economic NPV and IRR of the project, using the border price approach.
13. Undertake a sensitivity analysis of the economic analysis of the project:
    (a) using a social discount rate that is 20% below and 20% above the rate employed in the base case scenario
    (b) assuming that only 60 factories will use the water treatment plant rather than 70
    (c) assuming that the project's capital costs run over the estimated level by 15%.
    In each case calculate the economic NPV and IRR of the project under these assumptions.
14. Should the project be accepted by the government and the Asian Development Bank if the base case scenario is assumed to hold? State why or why not. If assumptions (a), (b) and (c) hold should the project be accepted or not? Again justify your answer in each situation.

Index

Page numbers in italic type refer to figures; page numbers followed by *t* refer to tables.